Runic Amulets and
Magic Objects

Runic Amulets and Magic Objects

MINDY MACLEOD and
BERNARD MEES

THE BOYDELL PRESS

First published 2006
The Boydell Press, Woodbridge

ISBN 978 1 84383 205 8

Transferred to digital printing

The Boydell Press is an imprint of Boydell & Brewer Ltd
PO Box 9, Woodbridge, Suffolk IP12 3DF, UK
and of Boydell & Brewer Inc.
668 Mt. Hope Avenue, Rochester NY 14620, USA
website: www.boydellandbrewer.com

A CIP catalogue record for this title is available
from the British Library

This book is printed on acid-free paper

Typeset by Pru Harrison, Hacheston, Suffolk

Contents

Illustrations

Acknowledgements

All illustrations are by Bernard Mees, except for figure 6 which is reproduced from L.F.A. Wimmer, *Die Runeninschrift* (1887), figure 13 from *Danmarks Runeindskrifter* (1941) and figure 14 from *Meddelelser om Grønland* 67 (1924). The runic fonts used are freeware by Odd Einar Haugen; see http://helmer.aksis. uib.no/Runefonter.

Preface

In 1997 the Uppsala professor, Dr Henrik Williams, was visiting Australia as a guest of the Department of Germanic Studies at the University of Melbourne. He had discovered, to his surprise, that there were two people in Melbourne writing independently on runic matters and decided to bring them together. The first products of our ensuing collaboration were two jointly written papers. We found that our differing backgrounds served to complement each other's weaknesses, if not always strengths, and we soon discovered we were often able to cover a lot more ground than a single writer could be expected to.

Our respective backgrounds as a Scandinavist on the one hand, and as a Germanist (who has also read in classics), on the other, are a good guide to the principal authorship of the different themes and geographies covered in this work. It grew from our second joint paper, which was inspired by an observation by the American linguist Dr Thomas L. Markey.

Research for this work was supported by two generous grants, from the Gladys Krieble Delmas Foundation of New York and the Greta Hort bequest to the University of Melbourne, which enabled research trips to Italy and Denmark respectively. Thanks are also due to the Departments of Medieval Archaeology and English at the University of Århus, Denmark. The University of Melbourne, and especially its Department of History, has also helped fund the study by means not just of the use of its facilities, but also in the form of publication subsidies.

Abbreviations

CIL *Corpus inscriptionum Latinarum*, ed. Theodor Mommsen et al., 17 vols (Berlin 1863–).

DR *Danmarks Runeindskrifter*, ed. Lis Jacobsen and Erik Moltke, 2 vols (Copenhagen 1941).

IK *Ikonographischer Katalog* of *Die Goldbrakteaten der Völkerwander-ungszeit*, ed. Karl Hauck et al., Münster Mittelalter-Schriften 24, 4 vols (Munich 1985–89)

N A Catalogue number from the runic archives in Oslo of an inscription from Norway (other than from Bergen) not yet published in *NIyR*, but listed in the downloadable University of Uppsala database 'Sam-nordisk runtextdatabas', http://www.nordiska.uu.se/forsk/samnord. html.

N B Catalogue number from the runic archives in Oslo of an inscription from Bergen not yet published in *NIyR*, but referenced in the Norwe-gian National Library on-line database 'Runeinnskrifter fra Bryggen i Bergen' http://www.nb.no/baser/runer/index.html.

NIyR *Norges innskrifter med de yngre runer*, ed. Magnus Olsen et al., 6 vols (Oslo 1941–); and cf. Jan Ragnar Hagland, 'Runer frå utgravingane i Trondheim bygrunn 1971–1994', which has been published on the internet (http:/www.hf.ntnu.no/ nor/Publik/RUNER/ runer-N774-N894.htm) as a preliminary version of *NIyR* vol. VII.

SR *Sveriges runinskrifter*, ed. Sven Söderberg et al., 15 vols (Stockholm 1900–).

U UR Catalogue number from Uppland Prehistorical Society's collections of an inscription from Sweden not yet published in *SR*, but listed in the downloadable University of Uppsala database 'Samnordisk runtextdatabas', http://www.nordiska.uu.se/forsk/samnord.html.

1

Introduction

MANY objects once thought of as having magical powers feature texts written in runes, providing sources that today shed light on the lives and experiences of the northern European peoples the ancient Romans first called Germans. These pre-Christian Germanic or Teutonic folk were not just early Germans or Scandinavians, though; they are the ancestors of several modern nations in Europe and beyond – from England and Holland to Austria and Germany and up to the Nordic countries, from North America to Australasia as well – and also include tribes who once ruled over other peoples such as the Franks, Lombards, Burgundians and Goths. The runic texts surveyed in this book are often previously misunderstood keys to comprehending the religious, cultural and social world of the early Germanic peoples prior to and during their conversions to Christianity, and the cultural and intellectual Latinising that followed the adoption of both the writing system and the official religion of the late Roman Empire.[1]

The study and interpretation of old Germanic inscriptions, though, can be a strange business. In fact it has been suggested that the first law of runic studies is that 'for every inscription there shall be as many interpretations as there are runologists studying it'. This may seem a bit too clever or even a little bewildering. But a lot of what passes for expert runic interpretation has too readily strayed into the fantastic in the past, and never more so than in considerations of the runic legends that appear on amulets and other similar items. This is at least part of the reason why no major contributions to the topic of this study have appeared before and why the subject of runic amulets has usually been treated so poorly when it has been assessed at all.[2]

---

[1] The general introductions to the study of runes in English are R.W.V. Elliott, *Runes*, 2nd ed. (Manchester 1989) and R.I. Page, *Runes* (London 1987). Studies of the traditions of individual countries include R.I. Page, *An Introduction to English Runes*, 2nd ed. (Woodbridge 1999), T. Spurkland, *Norwegian Runes and Runic Inscriptions*, trans B. van der Hoek (Woodbridge 2005), S.B.F. Jansson, *Runes in Sweden*, trans. P.G. Foote (Stockholm 1987), and E. Moltke, *Runes and their Origin, Denmark and Elsewhere*, trans. P.G. Foote (Copenhagen 1985). Other standard works include the still useful L. Musset, *Introduction à la runologie* (Paris 1965), W. Krause, *Runen* (Berlin 1970), and K. Düwel, *Runenkunde*, 3rd ed. (Stuttgart 2001).

[2] Cf., however, the recent sourcebook by J. McKinnell and R. Simek, *Runes, Magic and Religion* (Vienna 2004) and the useful surveys of later runic amulets: E. Moltke, 'Mediaeval rune-amulets in Denmark', *Acta Ethnologica* (1938), 116–47 and K. Düwel, 'Mitterlaltiche Amulette aus

This first apparent law of runic studies also masks the fact that many people who interest themselves in runic texts are often neither linguists nor experts in the study of inscriptions. Often what pass for expert interpretations of runic inscriptions turn out to be no more than educated guesses by specialists in medieval literature or archaeology. Our aim here is not to provide new readings or linguistic interpretations of the runic texts we assess, though on occasion it has become obvious to us that some commonly accepted interpretations have proven implausible when the amulet inscriptions are taken in their proper context. Our main approach is epigraphic: we have arranged the inscriptions according to type, and then assessed them in terms of what they have in common, an approach that has often enabled us to sort plausible interpretations from the improbable even before considering other issues.

The usual interpretative approach in runic studies is basically etymological. We have mostly refrained from etymological argument here, though. Etymological analysis is essential when assessing fragments of only partially understood languages. Nonetheless it is often done in the absence of other considerations – later or etymologically reconstructed meanings are often blithely read onto early forms without due attention being paid to matters such as immediate context and broader meaning relationships, or what linguists call collocation and semantic fields.[3]

The traditional approach has also often proven too restricted in its horizon – few runologists seem to be interested in comparing runic texts with similar expressions from other epigraphic traditions. We have been open to comparing runic amulet texts with those appearing on Greek and Roman amulets especially in light of the progress made in the last few decades in the understanding of Graeco-Roman magical practice. We have also been influenced by some of the methods developed in Etruscan studies, where given the difficult nature of the language, a stress on isolating and comparing formulaic elements is considered essential. The impressive recent developments in the understanding of Celtic and other areas of early European epigraphy have also proved significant to our assessments.

The texts surveyed in this book appear on a wide range of media commonly dubbed amulets by runic scholars, including pieces of jewellery, pendants or plates of copper, bronze or iron, worked pieces of bone and sticks or crosses of wood. Experts in medieval studies, though, often call an inscribed object carried or worn for magical reasons a *talisman*; a similar item is only an *amulet* for these

---

Holz und Blei mit lateinischen und runischen Inschriften', in V. Vogel (ed.), *Ausgrabungen in Schleswig* 15 (Neumünster 2001), pp. 227–302. The only comprehensive attempt to survey runic magic is the often speculative S.E. Flowers, *Runes and Magic* (Frankfurt a.M. 1986). Cf. also from an archaeological perspective A.L. Meaney, *Anglo-Saxon Amulets and Curing Stones* (Oxford 1981) and M.K. Zeiten, 'Amulets and amulet use in Viking Age Denmark', *Acta Archaeologica* 68 (1997), 1–74.

3   The best analysis of early runic grammar is the often-idiosyncratic E.H. Antonsen, *A Concise Grammar of the Older Runic Inscriptions* (Tübingen 1975), which is indebted to the 1965 Russian original of È.A. Makaev, *The Language of the Oldest Runic Inscriptions*, trans. J. Meredig (Uppsala 1996), and Nordicists still tend to rely on A. Noreen, *Altisländische und altnorwegische Grammatik*, 4th ed. (Halle a.S. 1923), or later works substantially dependent on it.

scholars if it is inscriptionless.[4] Those who study the classical and early Near Eastern world, however, maintain a different view and instead call both types of objects *amulets*. In fact more modern items of a similar ilk – for instance lucky rabbit's feet and four-leaf clovers – are better known in normal speech merely as *charms*. But the distinctions often made between amulets, talismans and charms are usually artificial. The word *talisman* comes from an Arabic description for magical stones, rings or other objects that were known to the ancient Romans as *amuleta* – so it does not make much sense to call any sort of ancient charm a talisman. On the other hand, the word *charm* can be a confusing description as the same term can equally apply to a spoken or chanted spell, or even merely a more mundane effect, such as charisma – personal charm. *Talisman* and *amulet* are actually synonyms, then, though *amulet* is the usual description used in runic and classical studies for what medievalists often distinguish as talismans.

Other words for amulets or charms in English include *periapt* (cf. Greek *periapton* 'pendant') and *phylactery* (cf. Greek *phylaktêrion* 'amulet'). In normal use, however, the description *phylactery* is usually restricted to amulets with clear religious associations, most commonly the small cases with sacred writings folded up in them (*tefillin*) traditionally used in Judaism. Similar items in Christian environments are usually just called amulets, though, as they normally have no official standing as religious items. The distinction between amulet and phylactery or periapt is, again, somewhat artificial, and not one an ancient Greek would have made.

Some distinction has to be maintained, though, between a charm that can be worn or carried in any circumstance and one that is only meant to be used in a religious rite or sacred setting. An object that is dedicated and then dropped into a sacred spring, for example, is often styled an *ex voto* or *votive* – its characteristic function is that it has been offered to the sacred; it is the material equivalent of a prayer. Of course it can be difficult to establish a clear boundary between magic and religion in some circumstances. Prayers, for example, are often used in magical spells. In fact some people hold that magic is merely loosely organised or somehow devolved religion. An *ex voto*, however, has a restricted religious function. Votive items can be reused as amulets given the right circumstance – votives taken out of religious sanctuaries, even if by improper means, have sometimes subsequently come to be used as amulets. So it is often the use, rather than the type of object, or even the inscription it may bear, that distinguishes amulets and phylacteries from votives.

Amulets have been used by many different societies at many different times – they are perhaps as much a part of the modern world, in the form of lucky socks, caps or medallions, as they are of earlier societies. There has been a noted reluctance among many scholars, however, since the 1950s especially, to think of objects like amulets in a pan-Germanic or long historical perspective. This modern approach, although clearly influenced by French literary theory, first

---

4 R. Kieckhefer, *Magic in the Middle Ages* (Cambridge 1989), p. 77, which is probably still the best general survey of its type for medieval times as a whole, notwithstanding its typically inaccurate section on runes.

emerged as a reaction to German scholars who claimed Old Norse and Anglo-Saxon literature was part of their own 'Teutonic' cultural inheritance. In the nineteenth century the old Germanic past seemed especially important to many scholars and commentators seeking to explain their own worlds. Taken to ridiculous extremes under the Nazis, this type of historical understanding spawned a backlash, especially in Britain, and a less sweeping and romantic approach to history soon became the norm. A hostility to a wider and deeper perspective has permeated Anglo-Saxon and more recently Old Norse studies since that time. But this seems particularly limiting in a runic studies context. Both the runic alphabet and the amuletic tradition betrayed in the earliest inscriptions show a striking similarity in each of the attested Germanic traditions. Although mindful of the potential pitfalls of the comparativist or Germanic-continuity approach, we do not think it appropriate to limit the scope of our work by remaining too faithful to methodologies and approaches born out of reactions to past academic trends, rather than close analyses of the subject matter itself.[5]

There were several native words for 'amulet' in the old Germanic languages, then, though none of them retain this meaning today. The Old English noun *þweng* 'band, amulet', for instance, is related to Modern English *thong* and obviously originally signified something tied or worn (it may be based on *ligatura*, a Latin term for 'amulet' with a similar meaning). Another word, Old High German *zoupargiscrîp*, which literally means 'magical writing', is similarly a physical description, this time, presumably, of a phylactery containing folded-up religious writings – the term after all is only known from clerical contexts. A second type, instead, is obviously formed from descriptions of the powers of amulets, most commonly being based upon words indicating health or good fortune (which in old Germanic tradition were often considered to be the same thing), such as Old Norse *heill* and Old English *lybesn*, both of which are derived from words originally signifying 'health' but which had come to refer to 'magic'. A similar further term for 'amulet', Old English *healsbōc*, which literally means 'health-book', is also reminiscent of medieval German *zoupargiscrîp*, but may at first have referred to a book upon which people swore oaths before it came to refer to amulets more generally. Yet magical powers can be ascribed to all manner of objects, so we will not limit ourselves merely to rune-inscribed pendants, rings or the like in this survey.[6]

Some distinctions have to be observed in the use of the word *rune*, however, a term that has developed several meanings in contemporary English. In this study it is used with the meaning it had when it was reintroduced to English by antiquarians in the seventeenth century after having fallen out of use in the late Middle Ages. Nonetheless, the term *rune* originally had two meanings: in Old English it could mean both 'runic letter' and 'secret' or 'knowledge' – the modern literary employment of *rune* as a word for 'poem' was originally adopted from Finnish usage. Some have argued that there were in origin two different terms, then, one

---

5   Cf. R.D. Fulk and C.M. Cain, *A History of Old English Literature* (London 2003), pp. 195–96, 203–4 and 230–31.

6   Flowers, pp. 143–44.

related to *row* and indicating a sense of carving, the other to *rumour* and originally referring to communicating. The original meaning for *rune* equally may just
have been '(hushed) message' (cf. German *raunen* 'to whisper' and Early
Modern English *round*) and the same word came to be used equally for secrets,
whispers, wisdom and writing, the last as written characters conveying meaning
without actually making a sound. There does not seem to have been anything
particularly secret or magical (or poetic) about the letters of the runic alphabet
originally, despite the development of one of the forms of the word to signify
secrecy or knowledge.[7]

It is certain that the use of the word *rune* as 'secret' or 'knowledge' had come
to be associated with magic at an early period, though. The ancient Goths, for
instance, used an expression *haliurunnae*, literally meaning 'Hell-runer' to refer
to sorceresses, and in Old English the etymologically identical compound
heller^ne translates 'pythoness' (i.e. seeress or witch). Old High German even
had the equivalent compounds *hellirûna* (literally 'Hell-runes') for 'necromancy', *hellirûnâri* for 'necromancer' and *tôtrûna* (literally 'death-runer') for the
feminine 'necromancess'. The magical plant, the mandrake, is still called *Alraun*
(i.e. 'great-rune') in German today, the fates and furies were called *burgr^nan*
'guarantee-runers' in Old English and one Old High German text even records a
compound *leodrûna*, literally 'song-runer', with the meaning 'sorceress'.[8]

A similar connection between *runes* and *lioða* or magical 'songs' is evident in
Old Norse literary sources, a linkage seen also in medieval Norse words such as
roner for magic spells in Danish folk songs and *rúnokarl* 'magician' (literally
'rune-man'). When we consider that the English word *spell* can refer both to
writing (as a verb) and magic (as a noun), and the description *glamour* (which
originally meant magical charm) is a corruption of *grammar*, the homophony
between *rune* 'secret' or 'knowledge' and *rune* 'runic character' seems almost
destined to have eventually led to semantic interference and even confusion
between these two terms. In fact magical applications of runes are frequently
alluded to in the collection of Old Norse mythological and heroic poetry known as
the *Poetic Edda*, and medieval Icelandic family sagas are also forthcoming with
details of runic sorcery. Runic 'songs' (and it is with this meaning that the term
rune was first loaned into Finnish) consequently fell foul of the writ of the Christian church, and even though *rune* had been considered innocent enough to gloss
'divine mystery' in the Gothic and medieval English translations of the Bible, in
the Scandinavian languages the term eventually seems to have become restricted
to runic letters and witchcraft. One Anglo-Saxon charm claims to be effective
'against every evil song-rune (*leodr^nan*), and one full of elfish tricks', and
post-medieval Norse books of magic often use magic sigils called 'runes' in the
spells they contain. In fact a Norwegian archbishop felt compelled three times in

---

[7] R.L. Morris, 'Northwest-Germanic r^n- ›rune‹', *Beiträge zur Geschichte der deutschen Sprache und Literatur* 107 (1985), 344–58, C.E. Fell, 'Runes and semantics', in A. Bammesberger (ed.), *Old English Runes and their Continental Background* (Heidelberg 1991), pp. 195–229 and cf. M. Pierce, 'Zur Etymologie von Germ. *runa*', *Amsterdamer Beiträge zur älteren Germanistik* 58 (2003), 29–37.
[8] Flowers, p. 152.

the mid-fourteenth century to issue proclamations against those who engaged in 'medications, runes, black magic and superstition', while around 25 Icelandic men lost their lives following accusations of practising witchcraft (which typically included claims of employing runic magic) long after runes had ceased to be used as a living writing system on the island.[9]

The runic alphabet or *futhark* is so-named for the first six letters of the standard runic-letter ordering, the runic ABC, or *rune* or *futhark row*. The first form of writing used by the Germanic peoples, the earliest possibly runic inscription dates from the first half of the first century, though the runic tradition does not seem to have begun to flourish until about a hundred years or more after that date. Yet from that time it remained in continuous use in some parts of the Germanic world for well over a thousand years. In fact, originally employed by most of the Germanic tribes, runic inscriptions have been found all over Europe, from Ireland to Russia, from Greenland to Greece – just about wherever early Germanic folk and later the Vikings wandered. Runes did not fare well in face of the growing use of paper and parchment, though, and when runes are found in medieval manuscripts they are usually only employed in a playful manner, merely as monkish curiosities. Runic writing died out earliest in mainland Europe, and then England with the Norman Conquest, but remained a living tradition in the Nordic countries until the close of the Middle Ages. Indeed in some remote areas of Scandinavia a hybrid runic-Roman form of writing even lingered on as long as the late nineteenth century.

The origin of the runes also remains a matter of some controversy, though they are generally linked to one of the major ancient European alphabetic traditions, much recent scholarship focussing especially on Latin or the northern (Alpine) outcrop of the Etruscan tradition. What is certain, however, is that runes eventually became the everyday writing system of Viking-Age Scandinavia, and continued in use well into the Christian Middle Ages, often alongside the Roman alphabet introduced by the Latin-speaking Church.[10]

It is misleading to speak of one runic alphabet, however, as there were several different runic systems employed by different Germanic peoples at different times. Oldest is the runic alphabet usually known as the *older futhark*, which was once used throughout Germanic Europe. The continental form of the older runes seems to have died out by the eighth century, though, apart from in Frisia in the northern Netherlands. This older runic alphabet instead was extended by the Frisians, and across the English Channel also by the Anglo-Saxons, whose standard runic alphabet or futhark row contained some modified runic letterforms as well as incorporating several new ones: runes equivalent to digraphs such as æ and æ were added, while some old runes such as that originally for *z* were given new values. The opposite development occurred in Scandinavia, however, where letters which had become redundant or were otherwise judged unnecessary first

---

9   The last execution took place in 1685, although prosecutions continued until 1720; see Ó. Davíðsson, 'Isländische Zauberzeichen und Zauberbücher', *Zeitschrift des Vereins für Volkskunde* 13 (1903), 150–51.

10 The various theories are surveyed in B. Mees, 'The North Etruscan thesis of the origin of the runes', *Arkiv för nordisk filologi* 115 (2000), 33–82.

began to drop out of use. A major reduction subsequently occurred, with runes like *t* now assuming the ability to represent two sounds (in this case both *t* and *d*). The older *e*-rune and *o*-rune were both lost in this way, runic *i* and *u* being used in their places. By the ninth century a *younger futhark* had emerged to become the runes of Viking-Age Scandinavia, although even they appear in two related variants, usually descriptively referred to as the *long-branch* and *short-twig* runes. A more extreme variant, the *staveless* alphabet, even continued this streamlining further and dispensed with the main stems or *staves* of each younger runic letterform altogether. Later on still the younger runic alphabets were modified again, with *dotted* variants of some runes introduced to distinguish between similar sounds, while some entirely novel runes were also adopted. These forms of the runic alphabet are often called the *medieval futharks*, following the insistence of Scandinavian scholars that only the latter part of the *Medium Ævum* that renaissance writers first declared separated their own age from ancient times is to be called medieval. Yet even within the standardised runic alphabets provided in the table given on p. 13, it must be remembered that the runes enjoyed considerable graphic variation: they can have more rounded or angular features; they can face in different directions or be written lying on their sides or even appear in inscriptions fully upside down. In fact in some cases, even completely different individual and local variants of many of the standard runes are attested.[11]

The older futhark contained a runic letter for every sound needed to represent early Germanic speech, including the runes *þ* for the sound represented in English by *th* and *ŋ* for English *ng*. It also had a character for what seems originally to have been a slightly differently articulated *i*, often distinguished in transcriptions by a diaeresis (*ï*), and a letter for *z* which later came to signify an *r*-like sound (which is usually represented as *R* when early Norse inscriptions are transcribed into Roman type), different from the standard *r*. Interpreting younger texts can often be difficult, though, as the reduction in letters meant that the same spelling could render *bit*, *bet* or *bid* or *pet*. In this book we have endeavoured as much as possible to render younger inscriptions in forms as similar as is reasonable to those of literary Norse even when the spelling of the inscriptions might suggest a different transcription. We have also taken the opportunity availed by computer text-editing to use normalised runic type to represent actual texts, rather than the bold san-serif Roman type traditionally employed by runic scholars.

The complications of runic writing were exacerbated by the development of many of what seem to modern eyes whimsical practices and inventions. First, like many early Greek and Etruscan texts, runic inscriptions are often only haphazardly punctuated and they rarely separate individual words out with spaces. Often

---

[11] Studies of some of the peculiarities of runic writing include: I. Sanness Johnsen, *Stuttruner i vikingtidens innskrifter* (Oslo 1968), K.-E. Westergaard, *Skrifttegn og symboler* (Oslo 1981), K.F. Seim, 'Grafematisk analyse av en del runeinnskrifter fra Bryggen i Bergen' (Unpublished thesis, Bergen 1982), R.L. Morris, *Runic and Mediterranean Epigraphy* (Odense 1988), B. Odenstedt, *On the Origin and Early History of the Runic Script* (Uppsala 1990), T. Spurkland, 'En fonografematisk analyse av runematerialet fra Bryggen i Bergen' (Unpublished dissertation, Oslo 1991), M. MacLeod, *Bind-runes* (Uppsala 2002) and eadem, 'Ligatures in early runic and Roman inscriptions', in G. Fellows-Jensen et al. (eds), *Jelling Runes* (Copenhagen 2006).

early runic inscriptions have no punctuation at all, though some punctuate words rather than sentences. On occasion it is even word elements that are marked out by dotted or crossed *interpuncts* (·, :, ⁝, × etc.), where other times runic writers only marked out phrases with these symbols. Runic inscriptions can be written from left-to-right (dextroverse), from right-to-left (sinistroverse) or even vary between the two (a practice called *boustrophedon*). A runic inscription may even begin at the bottom of an object and scroll its way up, or read in another irregular manner.

Runic writers also liked to ligature pairs or more of runic letters together, forming *bind-runes* sharing a stem or branch, e.g. ᚴ for ᚠ + ᚼ (which in this book will otherwise be represented for typographical reasons as ᚠᚼ). Similar modifications, especially in early inscriptions, could be made to individual runic shapes, creating enhanced or *decorative* runic letterforms such as ᚨ for the usual ᚠ. Runic letters could also be repeated as a mark of emphasis in early texts, or even repeated and ligatured, a rare type of decorative letterform usually referred to as a *mirror-rune*; for instance ᛂ for a mirrored ᚱ. Other features such as facing the wrong way around also seem to be used on occasion in order to emphasise particular words or phrases. But in the main such practices seem to have been haphazard, ephemeral or even playful, and the appearance of a reversed rune or ligature in an inscription is not a guarantee that highlighting or punctuation was the intention of the carver.

The early runic spelling system, again much like that of early Greek or Etruscan practice, also failed to distinguish between short and long consonants (like the long *n* in English *unnecessary*) or vowels, even if these crossed word-boundaries. An English expression like *big gorilla* could be rendered *bigorilla* in a runic text that did not use interpuncts. Another spelling oddity is the frequent omission of *n* and *m* before other consonants, probably because inscribers thought it was not strictly necessary to indicate them, a practice which again is also characteristic of archaic Italian inscriptions. Some inscribers, on occasion, also hyper-corrected their spellings, including what seem to be parasitic vowels (like the extra vowel heard in Irish pronunciations such as *filum* for *film*). In general our normalisations represent the forms thought by linguists to underlie the runic spellings, including the (tacit) correction of spelling errors or anomalies whenever these can be detected.

From a reasonably early time, or perhaps even from the instance of their inception, each rune also had a meaningful name, a noun linked to its sound value; for example the *f*-rune, ᚠ, was called *fé* 'cattle, wealth' and runic *u*, ᚢ, was *úr* 'aurochs (wild ox)'. We know most of these names from the runic poems and other grammatical tracts written down in Norway, Iceland, England and on the Continent during the Middle Ages. Moreover, sometimes it seems that a rune could stand as a logographic representation of the word denoted by its name, much as an *m*-rune, ᛗ, was used as a *runic ideograph* for its name *mon* 'man (person)' in some Old English manuscripts. Some inscriptions make sporadic use of such runic shorthand, although this is a fairly rare occurrence, and some modern interpreters have clearly made too much of this kind of abbreviation in recent times.

Also from a reasonably early stage, the runes of the futhark row were divided into three groups or *families*. Some of the early futhark-row inscriptions indicate this division into groups of eight runes each; in the reduced, younger-futhark row of Viking-Age Scandinavia, the first group contained six runes and the following two five each. The families are designated in Norse literary sources by the name of the first rune in each group, i.e. 'Cattle's group', 'Hail's group' and 'Tyr's group'. Moreover, simple numerical codes were based around this division of the various futhark rows, so that instead of simply writing the appropriate rune, it could instead be designated by its place in the group (e.g. 1:1, the first rune in the first family = an *f*-rune etc.). Such codes, often quite varied in their expression, were represented by special sequences of runes, modified runic letterforms or even completely new symbols. These and other forms of runic cryptography or *cryptic runes*, however, are comparatively rare in runic amulet inscriptions.

Cryptographic writing, along with similar word or letter games, is widely attested in the medieval Scandinavian runic tradition (including even that of outposts such as Northern Britain) and usually seems to have no purpose other than a demonstration of cleverness (or emphasis). Yet romantic speculation, which has even been accompanied by a fair degree of pseudo-scholarship, has imbued many such runic inscriptions with an aura of magic and mystery of which they are largely undeserving. Certainly the bulk of the rune-stone texts of Viking times are disappointingly formulaic, stating simply that one person raised the stone concerned in memory of another. The more diverse texts from later in the medieval period cover a much wider range of topics, ranging from simple owner inscriptions, to memorial texts, obscene graffiti to business letters and even proposals of marriage. Like any other alphabet, then, the runic one was employed for a variety of uses, including, seemingly inevitably given the period, magical purposes.

In fact surprisingly few of the practices associated with runic writing seem to be inherently magical. One that undoubtedly is, though, is the appearance of certain magical symbols in connection with runic texts. But these symbols – swastikas (which are called *sólarhvél* 'sun-wheels' in Old Norse), triskelia (↻) and others including various tree-like shapes (↑, ↟, ↟) – are not restricted to runic contexts, and despite their often rune-like quality it is obvious they were equally thought to be of magical portent whether appearing in runic inscriptions, as part of pictorial decorations, or even standing by themselves. The magical symbols often found associated with runic writing are reminiscent of magical signs from the classical magical tradition called *charaktêres* or *sigils*. The closest parallel to the runic use of similar signs comes, however, from North Etruscan tradition, where various asterisk-like (✳), arrow-like (∨, ⩚) and 'herring-bone' (>>>>>>) signs were used as supplements to religious dedications. Crosses and other symbols accepted as suitably Christian later supplant these symbols in younger Scandinavian texts. In fact later inscriptions also witness the development of a new series of apparently magical forms (↟, ↟ etc.) which look as if they may originally have derived from certain kinds of decorative or cryptic runes. But there are several other parallels between classical amulet texts and magical spells and the early runic amuletic tradition, which leads to the suspicion that the entire Germanic amuletic tradition is ultimately dependent on Mediterranean models, much as the runic alphabet certainly was.[12]

---

[12] M. MacLeod and B. Mees, 'On the **t**-like symbols, rune-rows and other amuletic features of early

Classical sources describe many magical practices, such as the gathering of medicinal herbs accompanied by rituals and incantations, the performance of rites at particular times of year, the carrying of certain parts of animals, plants or stones about the body or their application to wounds, and some fragmentary finds on loose sheafs of papyrus even preserve the remains of complex magical spells. There is no doubt that early Germanic folk also practised magic of these types, some of which represent shared or similar prehistorical European (or Indo-European) inheritances, others that are later inventions or adoptions. In fact several books of spells are known from the Germanic-speaking countries that stem from the late medieval and early modern periods, and the spells in these books clearly are often mixtures of continuations of the magic of classical times as well as Christian mysticism, and, sometimes, local Germanic beliefs. But it is often difficult to sort out the indigenous from the imported in these works, and despite the claims of some modern mystics, the spells of these books at best only dimly accord with the magic described in medieval literature. Instead, the evidence from medieval literary sources indicates that much Germanic magic was expressed, as in classical tradition, by stylised, or actually sung language. A magical act is literally called a song or the like among many of the early European peoples, e.g. Latin *carmen, incantatio*, Greek *epôdê* (cf. English *ode*), Old Irish *bricht* (which is also a type of poem), Anglo-Saxon *leoð*, *sang* or *gealdor* (the latter from *gealan* 'sing') and cf. Modern English en*chant*ment. Moreover, the Old Norse term *galdr* 'incantation, magical charm', the Scandinavian equivalent of Anglo-Saxon *gealdor* (as well as the medieval German word *galster* 'charm', which is also literally something 'sung') clearly describes the type of magic that was expressed in runic inscriptions.

Norse sources differentiate between two main forms of magic, *galdr* and *seiðr*, the latter of which, that originally meant 'binding', is often disparagingly referred to in Old Icelandic literature as womanly and evil. It is tempting to think of these two as 'white' and 'black' magic respectively, although it is far from clear that *galdr* was always used for good or that *seiðr* was always employed maliciously. A parallel to the Norse tradition of *seiðr* is known only from marginal English and German sources, however, and the later Scandinavian spell books are described only as containing *galdrar*. *Seiðr*, which does not appear to have any relationship with classical 'fixing' or 'binding' magic, seems to have been judged as being unworthy of recording in these later works. Yet though described at length in Old Norse literature, perhaps it was just the case that *seiðr* had never developed into a tradition amenable to being written down.[13]

runic inscriptions', *Interdisciplinary Journal for Germanic Linguistics and Semiotic Analysis* 9 (2004), 249–99.

13 D. Strömbäck, 'Sejd', in J. Brøndsted et al. (eds), *Kulturhistorisk leksikon for nordisk middelalder*, 22 vols (Copenhagen 1956–78), XV, pp. 76–79. Old English *ælfsidan* ('elf-*sidan*') and *sidsa* appear only as descriptions for ailments in medical works; see A. Hall, 'The meanings of *elf* and elves in medieval England' (Unpublished dissertation, Glasgow 2004), pp. 117ff. Goddesses with the related epithet *Sait(c)hamia* are attested in Roman-era inscriptions from the Rhineland and there is an Old Saxon cognate *siso* 'magical incantation' which also seems to feature the expected zero-grade form of the root *sai-* 'tie, bind' also represented in English

The word *seiðr*, though, is closely related to words for 'magic' witnessed in the neighbouring Celtic and Baltic traditions, which suggests that it is a very old word.[14] The notion of *galdr*, a term which, in contrast, is only broadly paralleled in other European languages, may well represent a newer tradition, one growing in popularity and seemingly also closer in nature to the formulaic incantations known from the ancient Middle Eastern and Graeco-Roman worlds. But though beliefs popular in the antique cultures of the south and east coloured many of the magical practices popular in Continental Europe during the Middle Ages, it is not clear that the magical songs of Germanic tradition any more than weakly reflect the often highly complex and structured traditions used in classical times.

Yet what constituted this sort of magic? The usual definitions of magic in Greek and Roman tradition focus on the fact that classical spells usually aimed to compel certain results whereas religious practices proper were not so overtly coercive. It is clear that the ancients were not overly credulous though – often a spell was merely one of several acts resorted to in order to bring about a desired result. The use of a spell against rats, for example, seems typically to have been complemented by poison and traps. Magic was just one of the modes, albeit a supernatural one, that could be employed to see a certain result achieved.[15]

Classical spells also had several typical features that are paralleled in some runic texts apart from the use of magical sigils or what the magical papyri describe as *charaktêres* (some of which were clearly merely regular letters of the alphabet with loops or other modifications attached). Ancient spells often also included a range of *logoi* or sequences of vowels which were thought to be of astrological significance. There was an extensive range, too, of *voces magicae* or 'mystical words', which included creations that seem to have been based on alphabetic terminology (like *abracadabra*, probably a development of *abece-darium* 'ABC'), religious terms rearranged as palindromes (like *ablanath-analba*, often thought to be based on Hebrew *ab lanath* 'Thou art our Father') and various holy names, mostly of Hebrew or Christian origin.[16] These mystical words and other magical creations are often linked with Gnosticism, an ancient form of religious faith influenced by Pythagorean numerology that was declared by early churchmen like St Irenaeus to be a Christian heresy. Ancient amulets that contain *voces magicae, charaktêres* and the like, though, are often described as Gnostic, even if their owners were not Gnosts at all, but still believed in the powers of amulets whose inscriptions were partly based upon the numerology, naming magic and astrological beliefs that were so strongly a

---

sinew; see *CIL* XIII, nos 7915–16 and cf. R. Much, 'Germanische Matronennamen', *Zeitschrift für deutsches Altertum und deutsche Litteratur* 35 (1891), 321–23.

[14] It is clearly related etymologically to Lithuanian *saitas* and Welsh *hud* 'magic'.

[15] H.S. Versnal, 'Magic', in S. Hornblower and A. Spawforth (eds), *The Oxford Classical Dictionary*, 3rd ed. (Oxford 1999), pp. 908–10.

[16] On the various types of classical magic see T. Hopfner, 'Mageia', in G. Wissowa et al. (eds), *Paulys Real-Encyclopädie der Altertumswissenschaft*, 2nd ed., 59 vols (Stuttgart etc. 1894–1980), XIV.1 (27. Hbd.), pp. 301–93 and C.A. Faraone and D. Obbink (eds), *Magika Hiera* (New York 1991).

part of Gnostic practice and also had their parallels in the Jewish tradition of the Cabbala.[17]

As in the magic spells described in ancient sources, curative charms are particularly prevalent in recorded Germanic magic, whether these be spoken or written (healing with words) or herbal (healing with plants) or both in nature. The classical traditions of *defixiones* or binding spells and *agôgai* or leading charms are also paralleled in some Germanic written sources, as are some of the magical techniques known from Graeco-Roman sorcery: transference of some property from one thing or person to another, the invocation of divine and infernal powers, and various forms of analogical ('sympathetic') or protective ('apotropaic') magic. Yet in general the texts on runic amulets are quite unlike those which typically feature in the classical tradition.

Like any other alphabet, the futhark was employed for a variety of uses; not intrinsically at first magical in itself, it was used to record names and short communications, for memorial formulations, for religious expressions, for games and coded messages, as well as for texts of a magical nature. Evidently, then, runes could come to be thought to have taken on some the magical power that they were often used to impart. In the past, however, too many scholars have embraced fantastic notions of runic magic, which has led many recent investigators, in turn, to embrace a largely sceptical approach to such issues. In fact some specialists in runic studies today evince a tendency to seek to deny any magical element whatsoever in runic inscriptions, an extreme and unnecessarily reactive approach to the failings of earlier investigators. It is not always easy to separate simple wishes, admittedly, for instance for love or health, from ritual invocations designed to ensure these things. But this is part of what we have tried to do in this book, which we hope will lead to a greater understanding of the early Germanic intellectual world and runic expressions of northern European magic.

---

[17] G.W. Macrae, 'Gnosticism', in B.L. Marthaler et al. (eds), *The New Catholic Encyclopedia*, 2nd ed. (Detroit 2002), VI, pp. 255–61.

The Principal Runic Alphabets

1. *Early inscriptions (c. 50–750)*

ᚠ ᚢ ᚦ ᚨ ᚱ ᚲ ᚷ ᚹ : ᚺ ᚾ ᛁ ᛃ ᛇ ᛈ ᛉ ᛊ : ᛏ ᛒ ᛖ ᛗ ᛚ ᛜ ᛞ ᛟ

f u þ a r k g w   h n i j ï p z s   t b e m l ŋ d o

2. *Anglo-Saxon and Frisian inscriptions (c. 500–1000)*

ᚠ ᚢ ᚦ ᚩ ᚱ ᚳ ᚷ ᚹ ᚻ ᚾ ᛁ ᛡ ᛄ ᛣ ᛤ ᛋ ᛏ ᛒ ᛖ ᛗ ᛚ ᛝ ᛞ ᚪ ᚫ (ᚣ ᛠ)

f u þ o r c g w h n i j ȝ p x s t b e m l ŋ d œ a æ (y ea)

3. *Viking-Age Norse inscriptions (c. 750–1100)*

A. Long-branch

ᚠ ᚢ ᚦ ᚬ ᚱ ᚴ : ᚼ ᚾ ᛁ ᛆ ᛋ : ᛏ ᛒ ᛘ ᛚ ᛦ (ᚤ ᛁ ᚷ)

f u þ ǫ r k   h n i a s   t b m l R (y e g)

B. Short-twig

ᚠ ᚢ ᚦ ᚭ ᚱ ᚴ : ᚽ ᚿ ᛁ ᛅ ᛌ : ᛐ ᛓ ᛘ ᛚ ᛧ (ᚤ ᚷ)

f u þ ǫ r k   h n i a s   t b m l R (y g)

C. Staveless

ᛚ ᛚ ᛚ ᛚ ᛚ ᛚ : ᛚ ᛚ ᛚ ᛚ ᛚ : ᛚ ᛚ ᛚ ᛚ :

f u þ ǫ r k   h n i a s   t b m l R

4. *Later medieval Nordic inscriptions (c. 1100–1500)*

A. Sweden and Denmark

ᚠ ᚢ ᚦ ᚮ ᚱ ᚴ : ᚼ ᚽ ᛁ ᛂ ᛁ : ᛐ ᛒ ᛘ ᛚ ᛦ ᚡ ᛩ ᚯ ᚵ ᛂ ᛍ ᛑ ᛈ

f u þ o r k   h n i a s   t b m l R v y ø g e æ c d p

B. Norway

ᚠ ᚢ ᚦ ᚮ ᚱ ᚴ : ᚼ ᚽ ᛁ ᛂ ᛁ : ᛐ ᛒ ᛘ ᛚ ᛩ ᚯ (ᚯᚯᚯᚯ) ᚡ ᚵ ᛁ ᛂ ᛑ ᛣ

f u þ o r k   h n i a s   t b m l y ø (ǫ)   g c æ e d p

The Names of the Runes

RUNE	ATTESTED LETTER-NAMES		
	Old English	Nordic	Gothic
ᚠ	*feoh* ‘wealth, cattle’	*fé* ‘wealth, cattle’	*fe* ‘wealth, cattle’
ᚢ	*ˆr* ‘aurochs’	*úr* ‘drizzle, aurochs’	*uraz* ‘aurochs’
ᚦ	*þorn* ‘thorn’	*þurs* ‘giant, ogre’	*thyth* ‘goodness’
ᚨ ᚩ ᚭ	*ōs* ‘mouth’	*óss* ‘river-mouth, As, god’	*aza* ‘?’
ᚱ	*ræd* ‘ride’	*reið* ‘ride’	*reda* ‘ride’
ᚲ ᚳ ᚴ	*cēn* ‘torch’	*kaun* ‘ulcer, sore’	*chozma* ‘boil’ (?)
ᚷ	*gyfu* ‘gift’		*geuua* ‘gift’
ᚹ	*wynn, wen* ‘joy’		*uuinne* ‘joy’
ᚺ ᚻ ᚼ	*hægl* ‘hail’	*hagall* ‘hail’	*haal* ‘hail’
ᚾ	*nȳd* ‘need’	*nauð* ‘constraint’	*noicz* ‘?’
ᛁ	*s* ‘ice’	*ís* ‘ice’	*iiz* ‘ice’
ᛃ ᛄ ᛅ	*gēr* ‘year’, *iar* ‘?’	*ár* ‘year’	*gaar* ‘year’
ᛇ	*ēoh, h* ‘yew’		*uuaer* ‘cauldron’
ᛈ	*peorð* ‘?’		*pertra* ‘?’
ᛉ ᛦ	*eolhx, ilcs* ‘elk’ (?)	*ýr* ‘yew, bow’	*ezec* ‘coin, bronze bit’
ᛊ ᛋ	*sigel* ‘sun’	*sól* ‘sun’	*sugil* ‘sun’
ᛏ	*T , t r* ‘Tyr, glory’	*Týr* ‘Tyr, god’	*tyz* ‘god’
ᛒ	*beorc* ‘birch’	*bjarkan* ‘birch twig’	*bercna* ‘birch twig’
ᛖ	*eh* ‘horse’		*eyz* ‘horse’
ᛗ ᛘ	*man* ‘man (person)’	*maðr* ‘man (person)’	*manna* ‘man (person)’
ᛚ	*lagu* ‘liquid’	*l gr* ‘liquid’ (*laucr* ‘leek’, *lin* ‘linen’)	*laaz* ‘liquid’
ᛜ ᛝ	*Ing* ‘Ing’		*enguz* ‘Ing’
ᛞ	*dæg* ‘day’		*daaz* ‘day’
ᛟ	*æðil, ēþel* ‘land, ancestral home, landed property’		*utal* ‘inheritance’ (?)
ᚪ	*æc* ‘oak’		
ᚫ	*æsc* ‘ash’		
ᚣ	*ȳr* ‘bow’ (?)		
ᛠ	*ēar* ‘grave’ (?)		

2

Gods and Heroes

THE Norse gods are described in the *Saga of the Ynglings* as *galdra smiðir*, 'smiths of incantations', so it is not too surprising to find invocations to them on early runic amulets.[1] The most obvious way of calling on the divine to fill an object with magic powers, then, might seem to be to inscribe a message requesting that the gods (or a particular god) bless the item concerned. In fact we do have a clear example of such an inscription in runes, on a buckle, perhaps once part of a saddle strap, found at a site known as Vimose (literally the 'holy bog' or 'moor') in Denmark. Quite a number of items, holy and mundane, were deliberately thrown into the moor in Roman times and more than one of the items recovered later by archaeologists from Vimose turned out to be rune-inscribed. The buckle dates to the third century and is clearly engraved with a religious message. The inscription is often thought to be Gothic in language, just like several other stray finds from about the Baltic seaways are, indicating that a few Gothic-speaking peoples remained behind in this area some centuries after the great Gothic migrations firstly to modern-day Poland and from there eventually into Southern Europe. The inscription is etched onto the back of the buckle and reads:

ᚠᚱᛗᚠᚷᚠᛁᚾᛏ
ᚠᚠᛁᚠᚾᛈᛁᚷᚠ

Aandaga ansula Ansau wīja.

'End ring to the As I dedicate.'

There has been some controversy in the past concerning the correct reading of this inscription partly because the first term (which seems to be related to our word *end*) begins with a double *a*-rune-spelling, a strategy that has only recently been shown to be occasionally used in runic inscriptions to highlight a word, much as is done with capital letters today. *Andaga ansula*, which looks to mean 'end ring', then, may be a way to describe a buckle, perhaps a deliberately poetic one. More clearly, though, the term *As* appears here, and is, of course, the singular of *Æsir*, the name of the principal group of gods in Norse mythology; it probably refers in the present context to Odin, who under his byname Gapt or Gaut the Gothic

---

[1] *The Saga of the Ynglings* is part of *Heimskringla*, the Icelander Snorri Sturluson's chronicle of the kings of Norway.

historian Jordanes recounts was the chief god of his people. As has long been recognised, the inscription is also clearly poetic in its form: the first three terms alliterate and taken together the four words even seem to form similar types of rhythmic measures or feet. Consequently, it seems to be a line of poetry, much like a motto or an epigram. Both religious and magical sayings are often metrical in form and frequently seem to have been sung rather than spoken. But then any speech directed toward the gods might have been likely to be expressed in a song-like or poetic manner as a way of showing respect to the divine.[2]

Inscriptions similar to the Vimose text, however, are quite rare for runic, especially among the earliest finds. More commonly, other, less direct ways were relied upon to invoke divine help. One is the use of what, when they appear in Greek and Roman tradition, are usually called *historiolae* or narrative charms, which were clearly used in order to attempt to invoke a form of sympathetic magic.

Ancient narrative charms were generally inscribed on amulets in order to imbue them with beneficial medicinal properties. One such ancient medicinal *historiola*, found on a rolled-up sheet of silver, invokes the tale of a mermaid, Antaura, and her encounter with the Greek goddess Artemis. Dating from the third century AD, the amulet was found in the ruins of the Roman city of Carnuntum, in modern-day Austria. The text inscribed on the amulet is incomplete, but it begins:

> For migraines. Antaura came out of the ocean; she cried like a deer; she moaned like a cow. Artemis Ephesia met her: "Antaura, where are you bringing the headache? Not to the . . .?"

This is a fairly uncontroversial amulet inscription, mainly because it is well preserved and is an example of a fairly easily recognisable type. But amulet texts can also be highly abbreviated or otherwise more difficult to explain – the Carnuntum text is remarkably easy to interpret even though only the opening section of it is preserved. In less well preserved, briefer or less straightforwardly expressed examples we usually need to bring in more context to be able to analyse such an amulet text properly.[3]

For instance, the Greek geographer Strabo informs us that the peoples of north-western Italy venerated Artemis most among all the gods and the

---

2   W. Krause with H. Jankuhn, *Die Runeninschriften im älteren Futhark*, 2 vols, 2nd ed. (Göttingen 1966), no. 24. Much of the controversy over the correct meaning of the text revolves around the interpretation of *Andaga ansula* and whether the text is Gothic or not rather than its basic votive meaning, although a one-time Gothic presence in the area seems clear enough from classical testimony; see J. Czarnecki, *The Goths in Ancient Poland* (Coral Gables 1975), pp. 15 and 67–100, H.F. Nielsen, *The Early Runic Language of Scandinavia* (Heidelberg 2001), pp. 49–50 and 159–60 and cf. also E. Seebold, 'Die sprachliche Deutung und Einordnung der archaischen Runeninschriften', in K. Düwel (ed.), *Runische Schriftkultur in kontinental-skandinavischer und -angelsächsischer Wechselbeziehung* (Berlin 1994), pp. 56–94, B. Mees, 'Runic **erilaR**', *NOWELE* 42 (2003), p. 51 and MacLeod and Mees, 'On the **t**-like symbols', n. 18 for other details.

3   R. Kotansky, 'Incantations and prayers for salvation on inscribed Greek amulets', in C.A. Faraone and D. Obbink (eds), *Magika Hiera* (New York 1991), pp. 112–13.

inscriptions left behind there seem to corroborate his report. Among them is an inscription on an oddly, apparently fish-shaped, figurine cast in bronze with a hole in it for hanging, found by archaeologists among the remains of a religious sanctuary near the Alpine town of Sanzeno, near Trent. Probably an amulet rather than a votive, it features the names of four ancient mythological figures: Diana, Esia, Liber and Vesuna.

Diana is of course the ancient Italian name for Artemis and the grouping on the amulet appears to be similar to that found on two ancient Italian mirrors where the mythological figures Minerva, Fufluns, Artemis and Esia are depicted in a scene together. The mirrors depict Esia as a shade brought by Artemis to Fufluns in the company of the goddess Minerva. Liber and Fufluns are both archaic Italian names for the Greek god Dionysus and Esia is the Etruscan name for Ariadne, the daughter of Minos of Theseus and the Minotaur fame. Greek mythology also tells us that Artemis killed Ariadne, but that Dionysus (Artemis' brother) later married her; so the Sanzeno sequence of names appears to be an attempt to represent this scene (or perhaps rather this relationship) in a highly abbreviated manner. It too, then, appears to represent some sort of divine narrative charm concerning Artemis, albeit a highly abbreviated one, used to make an item holy or powerful. Given space is usually in short supply with the loose items typically used as amulets, the inscriptions that they carry are often abbreviated; so the possibility that any listing of divine figures on a runic amulet is part of a divine charm of some sort should not be dismissed lightly.[4]

Several runic inscriptions appearing on early brooches and other items of jewellery do bear inscriptions similar to that on the Sanzeno find. The best known is one which appears on a brooch from Nordendorf, Germany, discovered in the nineteenth century and which, as has long been recognised, features the names of two, or more probably three, figures from pagan Germanic mythology.

The Nordendorf brooch is of the safety-pin variety, the technical, Latin term for which is *fibula*. Safety-pin brooches were quite common in early medieval times and, favoured by most of the Germanic peoples, they were worn by both sexes. The bow-shaped brooch dates to about the sixth century, the roughly scratched text is written on the back of the decorated part of the fibula and its runes read:

ᛚᛟᚷᚨᚦᛟᚱᛖ
ᚹᛟᛞᚨᚾ
ᚹᛁᚷᛁᚦᛟᚾᚨᚱ
ᚨᚹᚨᛚᛖᚢᛒᚹᛁᚾᛁᛇ

Logaþore,
Wōdan,
wīgi-Þonar.
Awa Leubwiniï.

4 The Sanzeno find is the subject of a forthcoming study by T.L. Markey, 'An *interpretatio Italica* among the Casalini (Sanzeno) votives and another Helbig hoax', part of which is adumbrated in idem, 'A tale of two helmets', *Journal of Indo-European Studies* 29 (2001), 139. Cf. also A. Morandi, *Il cippo di Castelciès nell'epigrafia retica* (Rome 1999), where it is no. 22, and B. Mees, 'The gods of the Rhaetii', forthcoming.

This text clearly contains the names of at least two well-known Germanic gods, Odin and Thor, or for the latter rather *wīgi*-Thor 'blessing-Thor'. These are two of the four major Germanic deities whose names are preserved in those of the days of the week, and which take slightly different forms in each of the different Germanic traditions.

Day of the week	Modern English	Old English	Old Norse	Runic German	Modern German
Tuesday	Tyr	Tiw	Týr		Ziu
Wednesday	Odin	Woden	Óðinn	Wodan	Wotan
Thursday	Thor	Þunor	Þórr	Þonar	Donar
Friday	Frigg	Frig	Frigg		Fricka

A third figure is also mentioned in this inscription, *Logathore*, who seems to be the Old German counterpart of Lodur, a figure cited as a friend of Odin's by the Icelandic skald Eyvind, and who accompanies Odin in a scene in the Norse mythological poem the *Seeress's Prophecy* (*Vǫluspá*).[5] Lodur, Odin and blessing-Thor would thus form a triad, the usual number in which pagan gods appear in both ancient and early medieval German and Norse sources. As Logathore literally means 'trickster' or 'sorcerer' it is often thought that this is a byname for Loki, the Norse trickster-god, or perhaps even a negative reference to Odin, and hence further that this inscription therefore records a convert to Christianity denouncing the pagan gods. One well-known German mention of Odin is, after all, in a renunciation of a triad of Germanic gods, in the baptismal vow of the Saxons and Thuringians used during their conversion under St Boniface, the apostle of Germany:

> *Do you forsake the devil?*
> I forsake the devil.
> *And all devilish sacrifices?*
> And I forsake all devilish sacrifices.
> *And all devilish works?*
> And I forsake all devil's work and words, and Thunaer and Woden and Saxnote, and all the monsters who are their companions.

The Christian renouncing interpretation, though, is based substantially on debatable semantic interpretations and would be more believable if the brooch bore any Christian symbols or a verb such as 'forsake' – the key term that would be expected to appear if this interpretation were correct.[6]

Yet it is not immediately obvious which myth or tradition the Nordendorf

---

5 The god's name Lodur has been tentatively identified on a wooden gaming-piece from Tønsberg; see K. Gosling, 'The runic material from Tønsberg', *Universitetets Oldsaksamling Årbok* 1986–88, pp. 175–85. The name **lutiʀ**, Lóðurr (?), also appears on an early tenth-century coin, as does (several times) the name Thor, while the word *guð* 'god' appears on over a thousand coins: see I. Hammarberg and G. Rispling, 'Graffiter på vikingatida mynt', *Hikuin* 11 (1985), 63–78.

6 W. Braune, *Althochdeutsches Lesebuch*, 14th ed., ed. E.A. Ebbinghaus (Tübingen 1962), no. XVI.2.I.

divine names might refer to specifically either. The names which follow those of the gods, however, do suggest what the context may have been. The first, Awa, is a woman's pet name, like Katie to Katherine, and Leubwini is either a man's name or a description of a man (perhaps a pet or nickname) that means 'love-friend'. The final rune, *ï*, is of unclear function, but it may be no more than a decorative punctuation mark. It is a marginal rune, and is usually employed just as a variant form of the standard *i*-rune; so it may serve only as a way of highlighting the finality of the last *i* of Leubwini. Alternatively, it may even be an attempt to mark out the grammatical case of Leubwini more clearly, i.e. as an oblique form indicating something happening to or concerning Leubwini. Awa and Leubwini seem to be a couple, then, which suggests the brooch may be some sort of love amulet. In fact the burlesque *Thrym's Lay* (*Þrymskviða*) in the *Poetic Edda* relates how Loki gets Thor to dress up as a bride as part of a ridiculous, though successful, scheme to recover his hammer from the giant Thrym. In the poem, the thunder god retrieves his hammer when it is brought out in order to bless his marriage – and the association of Thor's hammer with the blessing of a marriage in this source seems to be reflected in some instances of early German poetry. Thus, with its invocation of 'blessing-Thor', the Nordendorf brooch appears to record a divine triad as part of an otherwise mostly laconic love amulet.[7]

A clearer example of an abbreviated runic narrative charm first came to light in the mid-1990s. It is an inscription on a silver belt-buckle found near Pforzen, in the foothills of the Bavarian Alps, and it also dates to the sixth century. It reads:

ᚠᛁᚷᛁᛚ·ᚨᚾᛞᛁ·ᚨᛁᛚᚱᚢᚾ
ᛖᛚᚨᚺᚺᚢ·ᚷᚨᛋᛟᚲᚲᚢᚾ

Aigil andi Ailrūn
elahhu gasōkkun.

'Aigil and Ailrun search for an elk.'

Like the Vimose text, this inscription is a complete sentence and, much again as at Vimose, it appears to show some metrical or stylistic features. Each line appears to have six syllables, rhymes, and *Aigil*, *Ailrūn* and *elahhu* both alliterate and show a form of assonance centred on the sound *l*. Moreover, each of the lines is metrically the same, rhythmically and in length. The text appears, then, to be a short poem; it may even be a line taken from a longer work.

More surprising for the first experts who interpreted the inscription, however, was the identity of Aigil and Ailrun. They are quite clearly the German equivalents of two figures, Egil and Olrun, who appear as minor characters in the Norse *Lay of Volund* (*Vǫlundarkviða*). Although much of the tradition about them is

---

7 Krause with Jankuhn, no. 151. The Christian reading of the Nordendorf names is due to K. Düwel, 'Runen und interpretatio Christiana', in N. Kamp and J. Wollasch (eds), *Tradition als historische Kraft* (Berlin 1982), pp. 78–86 and again (with more arguments) idem, 'Runeninschriften als Quellen der germanischen Religionsgeschichte', in H. Beck et al. (eds), *Germanische Religionsgeschichte* (Berlin 1992), pp. 356–59; and cf. E. Marold, 'Die drei Götter auf dem Schädelfragment von Ribe', in W. Heizmann and A. van Nahl (eds), *Runica, Germanica, Mediaevalia* (Berlin 2003), pp. 403–17.

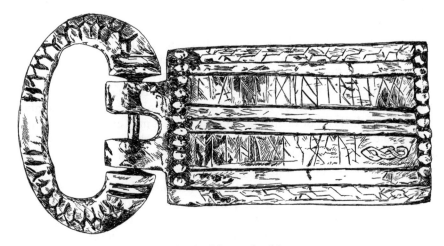

Fig. 1. Pforzen buckle

lost, Aigil and Ailrun seem once to have been much better known figures in Germanic myth. Today, we can only piece together fragments of their story.

Egil was the brother of Volund the smith, a 'prince of elves' who is also mentioned in Anglo-Saxon sources such as *Beowulf* by his English name Wayland. Norse sources also recount that Egil was famed for his skills as an archer. In fact in *Thidrek's Saga* Egil features in a William Tell-like scene where he is required to shoot an arrow at an apple sitting on the head of his three-year-old son. Moreover, according to the Norse version of the story of Wayland, Egil's wife, Olrun, was a valkyrie, i.e. she, too, had a supernatural background.

Egil is also named (as *Ægili*) and is pictured in a scene on the rune-inscribed Franks casket, an early Anglo-Saxon treasure now in the British Museum. One side of the casket shows Egil with bow and arrow defending a tower from attack, inside which is a woman, presumably his wife Olrun, who is supplying him with more arrows. Germanic heroic figures are often mentioned in alliterative pairs, e.g. Hengist and Horsa the first Anglo-Saxons to come to Britain, or Ibor and Ibiw the ancient Lombard heroes. So it does not seem necessary to regard Aigil and Ailrun as gods, but rather like Ariadne they were possibly semi-divine – they belonged to the magical world of elves, trolls, swan-maidens and dwarfs. The mention of Aigil and Ailrun searching for an elk suggests a hunting scene, so presumably the Pforzen charm was thought to make the wearer of the buckle a better hunter. It truly is an outstanding text and a clear indication of how close culturally the Germans still were to their English and Scandinavian cousins in the years just before the Christian conversion.[8]

---

8   The Egil and Olrun legend is further assessed in E. Marold, 'Egill und Ǫlrún – ein vergessenes Paar der Heldendichtung', *Skandinavistik* 29 (1996), 1–19, though cf. the scepticism of Page, *Introduction*, p. 177. McKinnell and Simek, pp. 57–59, survey the main interpretations of the second line of this inscription to have appeared to date, none of which accepts the straightforward derivation of the verb from *sōkjan* 'seek' or offers a more convincing reading for the oddly written noun other than *elahhu* 'elk'.

The text of the Pforzen amulet also clarifies somewhat a legend on a pendant found in the mid-nineteenth century at Skodborg, Denmark. The pendant is a common type of jewellery that goes back to large Roman coins known as 'medallions' which were typically worn as belt-hangings in the fifth and sixth centuries throughout Germanic Europe. These objects are usually made of gold, typically bear stylised pictures of Roman emperors' heads in their centre, and are technically termed *bracteates*. The Skodborg legend, which runs anticlockwise around the rim of the bracteate, reads:

ᚠᚾᛋᚠᚠᚠᚠᛈᛁᛏᚠᚾᛋᚠᚠᚠᚠᛈᛁᛏᚠᚾᛋᚠᚠᚠᚠᛈᛁᛏᛋᚠᚠᚠᛈᛁᛉ

Auja Alawin auja Alawin auja Alawin-ja Alawīd!

'Be lucky Alawin, be lucky Alawin, be lucky Alawin and Alawid!'

If the Pforzen buckle is any guide, Alawin and Alawid again appear to be the names of semi-divine heroes, although on this occasion they are figures who are otherwise unknown. Their names, which are masculine and mean 'great friend' and 'great width' respectively, appear in addressing forms (vocatives) which is in keeping with the command (or wish) 'be lucky!' The wishing of luck is well attested among Greek and Latin as well as later Norse amulet inscriptions, for instance in the common legend 'good luck to the user'. Moreover, names in *Al-* 'great, all', although relatively commonly used of men and women in later medieval times, often referred to divine figures in antiquity: for example many of the Germanic mother goddesses attested in the Rhineland in Roman times have epithets of a similar form, including *Alateivia* 'greatly divine', *Alagabia* 'great giver' and *Alaferhwia* 'greatly fertile'.[9] In fact another runic inscription that contains such an *Al-* name that is also inflected in an addressing form seems to refer to a divinity. Found near Værløse, also in Denmark, it is a safety-pin brooch that dates to about the year 200. The runes read in clearly cut characters:

ᚠᛚᚨᚷᛟᛞᛋ

Alugod!ᛋ

As it was found in the grave of a woman who died in her twenties or early thirties, *Alugod*, despite appearing in an addressing (vocative) form, has often been interpreted as a woman's name. This short text is rounded off with a swastika, a divine symbol which in Germanic tradition seems to have made the object that bore it holier or luckier – the Skodborg amulet, for example, has one in its inner section. The form Alugod, literally 'great god', seems an unlikely name for a woman and may refer instead to Odin, but it is hard to be sure. Clearly, an address to the 'great god' would have made the brooch appear blessed or lucky, even if this somewhat more direct approach seems a little prosaic when compared with the texts on the Nordendorf or Pforzen amulets. Yet Alugod is probably a divine byname, called a

---

[9] Krause with Jankuhn, no. 105. Krause's quibble that enclitic *-ja* 'and' is not found later in Norse neglects the fact that it is an inheritance from Indo-European and so must have been part of the proto-language. On the Rhenish *Ala-* names see B. Mees, 'Early Rhineland Germanic', *NOWELE* forthcoming 2006.

heiti in Norse, a poetic way of referring to a god or goddess – i.e. by function, rather than by actual name. Odin is known by bynames such as Alfǫður 'All-father', Sigfǫður 'Victory-father', Fimbultýr 'Awesome-god' and Sigtýr 'Victory-god' in the Old Norse Eddas after all. So once again we seem to be dealing with an indirect way of calling on divine help.[10]

Moreover, there are two other texts which may represent similar addresses to Odin, the interpretation of each of which, however, has been a matter of some controversy. The first comes from England and dates to the late sixth or seventh century. It is also a safety-pin brooch, disc-like in shape, and it was found in the early 1990s near the village of Boarley, Kent. Its in parts irregular legend seems to read:

ꛁꚠꛏꛉ
ꛗ

Liot! ꛘꛗ

Although slightly oddly spelled with its reversed *l*-rune and an even stranger-looking *o*-rune, the most straightforward reading is as *Liot*, a name primarily meaning 'wild' or 'free', but which could also mean 'warrior'. It also seems to be inflected as an addressing form, however, and could well represent another byname of Odin, who also has Old Norse bynames such as Herian 'Warrior', Ygg 'Terrible' and Glapsvið 'Maddener'. The apparent name is also accompanied by two magical symbols: one an arrow-head-and-tail-like shape found in several other runic amulet inscriptions, the other a character, also found on a Scandinavian amulet of similar date, that later crops up as a (pseudo-)rune in the literary tradition of Anglo-Saxon monks. The Boarley legend appears to be similar to the inscription on the Værløse brooch, both grammatically and in its use of magical symbols, even more so if both are to be accepted as containing divine names. And there is a third, albeit much earlier and more controversial legend, this time from Northern Germany, that may also belong to this formulaic type.[11]

In 1979 an ancient safety-pin brooch was discovered languishing in a box in a German archaeological museum, the object having been recovered some years earlier from a site near a village called Meldorf. It also bore an inscribed legend, but unlike the other inscribed Germanic brooches, the fibula was very much earlier than it was thought could be possible for a rune-inscribed object by many experts at the time. Although some senior scholars accepted it as runic, others thought its very brief legend might equally be written in Roman letters. The proper interpretation of its text has also been much disputed, partly because it is so early a find – dating from the first half of the first century – as well as because of its brevity. No inscriptions in Roman letters have been found on Germanic brooches (or even comparable pieces) to date from this region, however, and reading the inscription as if it is in Roman letters is also problematic gram-

---

10 Krause with Jankuhn, no. 11. Although originally a grammatical neuter, Germanic *god* had become masculine by this stage.

11 D. Parsons, *Recasting the Runes* (Uppsala 1999), pp. 46–47; MacLeod and Mees, 'On the t-like symbols', p. 262.

matically. The inscription on the early German brooch and a likely reading if it is runic are:

ᛁᚦᛁᚾ

Iþīh!

Although the letters are inscribed in a zigzagging decorative style known as tremolo, they are not very well formed, and the most straightforward reading is to start from the *i* and read either runic *Iþih* or Roman *Idin* (though there have been some who have even preferred to read the inscription in reverse). Yet if it is runic and is to be read in the most obvious way, the Meldorf text appears, much like *Alugod* and *Liot*, to represent an addressing form. *Iþīh* would be a name meaning 'traveller' or 'itinerant', and it would also, unlike the interpretations often suggested, be perfectly grammatically regular. The root *iþ-*, after all, is clearly found in Germanic words like Old Saxon *frithi* 'rebel, fugitive' (where the prefix *fr-* produces a negative meaning), and names suffixed with *-īg* or *-īh* were quite common in early Germanic times, especially among the bynames of the mother goddesses from the Rhineland. So again, then, this description may well be a byname, perhaps of Odin who is renowned for his wandering ways in Norse sources (hence his Eddic *heiti* such as Vegtam 'Way-tame' and Gangleri 'Wanderer') and is often thought to have been called upon by early Germanic merchants for protection during their travels. Although there are no accompanying magical signs such as would make this inscription formulaically just the same as the Værløse text, the use of an addressing form, possibly of a god's byname, probably marks this out as a religious inscription, indicating that the brooch was thought to be divinely blessed. Addressing forms typically only appear in religious inscriptions in Greek and Roman tradition after all. The Meldorf inscription appears to be the earliest example of runic writing recovered to date, and if it is to be accepted as genuinely runic, it would indicate how ancient and how important a sacred or talismanic use of writing was to the early Germanic peoples.[12]

Another, later example of an amulet that may belong to this broad type is a rune-inscribed comb found along with some other items in a refuse heap in Setre, Norway in 1932. The goods the comb was unearthed with date the find to the late sixth or seventh century, and its inscription, which features a mixture of older and younger runes, reads:

ᚺᚨᛁ ᛗᚨᛉ
ᛗᚨᚢᚾᚨ
ᚨᛚᚢᚾᚨᚨᛚᚢᚾᚨᚾᚨ

Hail maʀ mauna! Alu Nanna! Alu Nanna!

'Hail maid of maids! Dedication Nanna! Dedication Nanna!'

[12] Cf. B. Mees, 'A new interpretation of the Meldorf fibula inscription', *Zeitschrift für deutsches Altertum and deutsche Literatur* 126 (1997), 131–39 and idem, 'Early Rhineland Germanic' for Rhenish *-īg*.

This, again, is a controversial inscription, although the transcription given here is the most commonly accepted one. The reading *Nanna* on the third line of the inscription, for instance, at first appears odd, but can be justified on orthographic grounds as the two *a*-runes of the younger futhark are being used here, and the younger *ą* usually indicates that an *n* or *m* was (once?) pronounced after it. *Nanna* is also the name of a goddess, the wife of the god Balder from Norse mythology. Moreover, the first two lines may be part of a prayer, and the expression 'maid of maids' is well known from later Norse sources. Some queries have been raised about this interpretation, however, as both 'hail' and 'of maids' appear in slightly irregular forms. The alternative readings proposed, though, for instance that we identify two names, *HalmaR* and *Mauna* in these lines, do not alter the amuletic nature of the item. In fact reading them as names would give the comb a clearer purpose: Halm and Mauna would be a man and a woman, respectively, suggesting that the Setre comb is a love amulet. Despite some of the more fanciful proposals to appear to date, most experts accept the twofold reading *Alu Nanna*, although not all are as sure that this is a reference to the goddess of this name.

The term *alu* employed here appears quite commonly in early runic amulet legends and, like *auja*, belongs to a special category of words that are typical of Germanic amulets, but which only rarely appear as part of full sentences. Functionally, they seem to be the Germanic counterparts of the *voces magicae* of Gnostic amulets, but unlike the charm words of the classical tradition, they clearly are not divine or sacred names. The precise meaning of *alu* has been a matter of some dispute, though it is usually thought either to refer to amulet magic (and is sometimes simply translated by runic scholars as 'magic') or be a metaphor (or metonym) for it. Most recently *alu* has been shown also to appear in North Etruscan votive use, however, where the term clearly means 'dedication'. The ramifications of this discovery will be investigated more fully in chapter 4, but it is clear that runic amulet charm words functioned much like non-alphabetic symbols such as swastikas and the tree-like shape encountered on the Boarley brooch, i.e. they were thought to make the amulet more powerful.[13]

It is one of the peculiarities of the early Germanic languages, however, that vocative or addressing forms of words are not spelt differently from standard dictionary (nominative) forms if they are feminine. Given this, *Nanna* (repeated twice) may well be an addressing form, and an expression *alu Nanna!* would probably have had much the same function as *auja Alaw d!* or *Alugod!* ᛉ: the phrase appears likely to have been a plea to (the goddess) Nanna to bring benefit upon the wearer of the comb. Unlike the earlier inscriptions, however, the Setre text is not as laconic, but may include part of a ritual address to the goddess as well as a two-fold invocation of her name.[14]

13 Krause with Jankuhn, no. 40. Runic *alu* is explained as a loanword in T.L. Markey, 'Studies in runic origins 1', *American Journal of Germanic Linguistics and Literatures* 10 (1998), 188–89 and see MacLeod and Mees, 'On the **t**-like symbols' for its status as a charm word. The interpretations of the Setre comb presented here are those of M. Olsen and H. Schetelig, *Runekammen fra Setre* (Bergen 1933) and Antonsen, no. 115. T. Birkmann, *Von Ågedal bis Malt* (Berlin 1995), pp. 92–97 surveys other treatments of the inscription.

14 Another older inscription often thought to feature a reference to a pagan god is the Thorsberg

The chief god Odin also features in an apparent triad, comparable to that on the Nordendorf brooch, occurring on a piece of a human skull found at Ribe, an important old Viking settlement in Denmark. It is generally assumed that the skull piece, measuring 6 × 8.5cm and taken from the top of a cranium, was not that of a recently killed victim specially decapitated for the purpose, but had been exposed for some time before the runes were engraved on it. Also, despite the presence of a small circular hole allowing the skull piece to be worn as an amulet, it should not be regarded as an early example of Scandinavian trepanation, i.e. medical perforation of the skull, as the hole is carved from the inside, although some interpretations of the text have been based on this idea or at least have taken the inscription as a symbolic representation of it.

The Ribe text is a 'transitional' inscription which predates the Viking period. It was probably executed in around the year 725, some three-quarters of a century before the famous raid on Lindisfarne, and it features a mixture of older and younger runes. Two lines of inscription occur, the first following the outline of the skull piece, and the second curling around underneath and interrupted by the piercing. Although imperfectly understood, the text might be read as follows:

ᚢᛚᚠᛆᚼᛆᚢᚴᛆᚦᛁᛏᚼᛆᚢᚴᚼᛆᛏᛁᛆᛆᛁᚼᛁᚼᛏᛒᛒᛆᚱᛁᛁᚼᛆᛁᚦᛆ
ᚦᚼᛁᛘᚼᛆᛁᚼᚱᚠᛁᚼᛆᚠᛏᛆᛁᚱᚠᛆᛏᛁᛏ ᛒᛆᛆᚱ

Ulfʀ auk Ōðinn
auk Hōtȳʀ
hialp Buri es
viðr þæima: værki auk dværgynni.
Bur.

'Ulf and Odin
and High-Tyr
is help for Bur
against these: pain and dwarf-stroke.
Bur (carved).'

This versified translation (and even the transliteration of some few runes) is not unproblematic and several others have been proposed, some of which translate *bur* as a noun meaning 'hole' or 'borer', referring to the 4–5mm perforation of the object, rather than a proper name. The final name can also be framed in a mythological context: Odin and his brothers were the sons of Bur (or Bor in the works of Snorri), himself son of the mythological figure Buri.[15] In the translation provided here, however, the charm appears simple enough and fits into a readily understandable amulet type: an enumeration of a divine triad (marked out by the

---

chape find from about the year 200 (Krause with Jankuhn, no. 31). Its legend only seems to feature a bipartite man's name, however, *Wolþuþewaʀ Niwajemariʀ*, i.e. (literally) 'Glory-servant Not-poorly-famed'. Given the existence of regular names like Gothic *Wulþuwulfs* 'Glory-wolf' and Old German *Wuldberht* 'Glory-bright', the later Norse god Ull (earlier *Wulþ- and literally meaning 'Glorious-one') is unlikely to have had anything to do with *Wolþuþewaʀ*.

15 McKinnell and Simek, p. 50, point out that the names Búri and Burinn also belong to dwarfs, and some scholars read the last section as referring to the conquering of the dwarf rather than to dwarf-stroke.

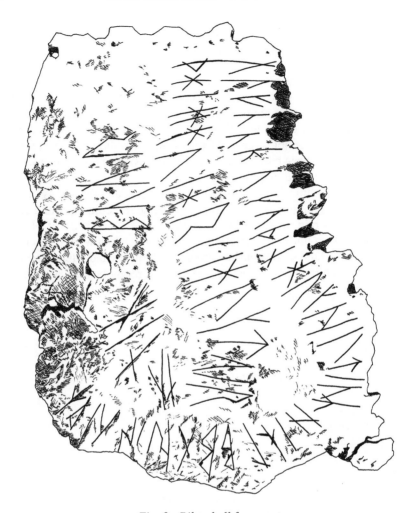

Fig. 2. Ribe skull fragment

punctuation and the apparent use of a singular 'is' rather than plural 'are'), an assurance of its power and finally a carver signature with the *u*-rune written twice, perhaps as a decorative flourish. Odin's proficiency as a healer is attested in the Eddic poem the *Sayings of the High One (Hávamál)*, where he is said to know the spells 'which the sons of men need, those who want to live as leeches (i.e. physicians)'. The role of the dwarf as an agent of disease is also well attested in Germanic folklore, although we have no sure guide as to exactly what form of 'dwarf-stroke' the Ribe charm was supposed to ward against.[16]

16 N.Å. Nielsen, *Danske runeindskrifter* (Copenhagen 1983), pp. 53–58, Moltke, *Runes and their Origin*, pp. 151–53 and 346–49 and M. Stoklund, 'The Ribe cranium inscription and the Scandinavian transition to the younger reduced futhark', *Amsterdamer Beiträge zur älteren Germanistik* 45 (1996), 199–209. The importance of the 'borer' is stressed in an interpretation based on the notion of sympathetic trepanation by A. Kabell, 'Die Inschrift auf dem

This interesting artefact clearly mentions the chief god, Odin, in company with two other names, which as Odin's name is never borne by ordinary mortals indicates that some kind of divine trinity is involved. After all, Odin is commonly mentioned in triads of Norse gods, although the divine constituents often vary. In the *Seeress's Prophecy*, for instance, he appears at the dawn of creation in company with the gods Hoenir and Lodur, the latter of whom also seems to appear with Odin and 'blessing-Thor' on the Nordendorf brooch. Odin also appears at the world's creation in Snorri's *Prose Edda* with his brothers Vili and Ve. Moreover, as in the Ribe and Nordendorf inscriptions, his name often appears second in divine triads as if it were deliberately being flanked by the accompanying figures. For instance, in the baptismal vow of the Saxons and Thuringians, the swearer had to forsake 'Thunar and Woden and Saxnote'. Similarly, a rhyming charm in a spell from a sixteenth and seventeenth-century Icelandic collection has him appear in the company of two other figures whose names mean 'All-holy' and 'Evil' respectively: 'Ølvir, Odin, Ille / you will bewitch everything!'[17]

The first of the names on the Ribe skull piece, Ulf, literally 'wolf', may be a poetic reference to another divinity or perhaps Odin himself who, after all, was associated with wolves. He was the owner of the wolves Geri and Freki, and he faced his adversary the Fenris Wolf at Ragnarok – in fact we may even be dealing with the apocalyptic Fenris Wolf itself.[18] The second name, High-Tyr might also have either of two meanings. Tyr is the name of an Old Norse warrior god, although his name is also a general Norse word meaning 'god', so it is not absolutely clear whether the warrior-god Tyr or some other divinity is intended here. Alternatively, as Odin is often described by such compounds, e.g. Sigtýr 'Victory-god', Fimbultýr 'Mighty-god' (and compare his appearance as the eponymous speaker Hárr, the 'High One', in the *Sayings of the High One*), we may equally be dealing with three mythological names referring to Odin (much as Ølvir and Ille may well be in the Icelandic spell mentioned previously). The Norse god Tyr is often associated with the Fenris Wolf, however, who bit off the war god's hand. In fact the Old Icelandic runic poem bluntly calls Tyr the 'one-handed god' and 'wolf's leftovers'.[19] Evidently some kind of divine triad is involved here, although its exact significance or relationship to disease remains somewhat unclear.

Another inscription, this time referring to the exploits of the popular Norse god Thor, is found on a small copper plate from South Kvinneby on the Swedish island of Öland. This eleventh-century square amulet, measuring around 5cm², is covered on both sides by several lines of runic text winding backward and

Schädelfragment aus Ribe', *Arkiv för nordisk filologi* 93 (1978), 38–47; cf. also P.E. Mørup, 'Lægelig runemagi i 700-tallets Ribe', *Fra Ribe Amt* 24 (1989), 408–14.

[17] *Galdrabók*, no. 41.

[18] Some scholars, however, read the first name as *Ulfúrr*, showing the ending -úrr common to so many figures of Norse mythology.

[19] R.I. Page, 'The Icelandic rune poem', *Nottingham Medieval Studies* 42 (1998), 29 and 36. A recent treatment by O. Grønvik, 'Runeinnskriften fra Ribe', *Arkiv för nordisk filologi* 114 (1999), 103–27 even identifies a concise narrative charm referring to the gods' binding of the evil wolf.

forward, along with the rough outline of a fish. Stemming from a much later period than the amulets considered to date, it also has a hole bored through it as well as signs of wear, so it was probably worn as a pendant. This is not merely a protective invocation, however; rather, the inscription refers to an episode from a myth featuring Thor, which suggests we are dealing with a narrative charm. The pre-Christian belief in assistance from the divine pantheon led, in the Norse pagan world as elsewhere, to the development of such expressions. Typically these recounted mythological episodes in which a god overcame some adversity, the idea being that a similar adversity would thus be overcome by the owner of the charm.

The runic text, whose first line employs some decorative runic letterforms, reads:

×ᚼᛁᚱᛁᛋᛏᛁᚴᚦᛁᚱᛒᛁᚱᚴ
ᛒᚢᚠᛁᛘᛅᛦᚠᚢᛚᛏᛁᚼᚢ
ᚦᛁᛋᚦᛅᛦᚢᛁᛋᛁᚾᛒᚱᛅᛚ
ᛏᛁᛚᚢᚠᚱᛅᚾᛒᚢᚠᛅᚦᚮᚱᚴᛅᛏᛁᚼ
ᛅᚾᛋᛘᛁᛦᚦᛅᛘᚼᛅᛘᚱᛁᛋᛅᛘᚼᚢᛦ
ᚼᛅᚠᛁᚴᛅᛘᚠᛚᚤᚠᚱᛅᚾᛁᛚᚢᛁᛏ
ᚠᛅᛦᛅᚴᛁᛅᚠᛒᚢᚠᛅᚴᚢᚦᛁᛦᚢ
ᚢᚾᛏᛁᛦᚼᛅᚾᚢᛘᛅᚢᚴᚤᚠᛁᛦᚼᛅᚾ
ᚢᛘ

Hǣr rīsti ek þǣʀ berg, Bōfi.
Mǣʀ fullty! Īhūð (?) es þǣʀ vīss.
En brā haldi illu frān Bōfa.
Þōrr gǣti hans með þēm hamri sem uʀ hafi kam.
Flȳ frān illvētt! Fǣr ekki af Bōfa.
Guð eru undiʀ hānum auk yfiʀ hānum.

'Here I carved for you (runes of) help, Bofi.
Help me! Knowledge (?) is certain for you.
And may the lightning hold all evil away from Bofi.
May Thor protect him with that hammer which came from out of the sea.
Flee from evil! It (?) gets nothing from Bofi.
The gods are under him and over him.'

The text here is obviously poetic, employing instances of assonance and alliteration, although it does not seem to follow a standard Norse metre. It also seems to make an allusion to the famous tale of Thor's great fishing expedition known from several pictorial and literary sources. The *Poetic Edda* recounts in *Hymir's Poem* (*Hymiskviða*) how Thor sailed out with the giant Hymir to fish for the monstrous Midgard Serpent. Baiting his line with the head of an ox, Thor managed to hook the evil serpent, but when he struck at its head with his hammer, it sank back into the sea. An alternative version of the story is also given in the recounting of the tale in Snorri's *Edda*. In his retelling, Snorri describes how the enraged Thor threw his hammer at the serpent after the frightened giant cut it free from his line: 'people say that this struck its head off in the waves; but I think the truth is that the Midgard Serpent is still alive and is lying in the ocean'. As the hammer was renowned for always returning to the hand of its owner, this seems to fit the reference on the amulet, which, with its depiction of a fish, is presumably meant to ensure safety at sea, or perhaps luck in fishing.[20]

Just as Odin was known as 'lord of the spear', the hammer was the weapon closely associated with the thunder-god Thor. His most prized possession, his hammer Mjollnir was the greatest treasure possessed by the gods, as with it Thor was able to keep their home Asgard safe from its enemies. Several stories recount his prowess in throwing it and slaying giants, and he was clearly thought to offer protection from hostile elemental forces. In particular, the story of Thor on the famed fishing expedition is depicted on a number of stone monuments found throughout Scandinavia and the British Isles.

Thor was also responsible for thunder, lightning and rain, and his weapon was a symbol of the destructive power of stormy weather. The carver of the amulet seems to be appealing to the thunder god for security, presumably at sea, where sudden storms posed a very real danger without protective deities hovering over-head and below. Several spells against drowning are known from Scandinavian spell books of a much later date, after all. In fact the Eddic *Lay of Sigrdrifa* (*Sigrdrífumál*) mentions magical runes that could ensure safety at sea and one of the versions of the Faeroese ballad *King Alvur* tells of a rune-inscribed staff that was used to calm dangerous waves.[21] The image of the fish on the amulet has previously been interpreted as a Christian symbol, but, taken in conjunction with the reference to Thor's fishing trip, it may merely be acting here as a pictorial symbol further representing the mythological episode or be indicative of a concrete desire for a good catch. After all, depictions of fish are also found on a sixth-century rune-inscribed fishing weight from Førde, Norway and, more contemporaneously, as runic cryptograms from the old wharf at Bergen, Norway.[22]

The thunder-god Thor was very popular during the Viking Age and it is worth remembering that he is the only pagan god invoked on rune-stones from Scandinavia. Depictions of his hammer are found on runic memorials throughout Sweden and Denmark, and at least five such inscriptions end with a direct appeal to the god to bless the funerary monuments which bear them using a formulation comparable to the description 'blessing-Thor' on the German Nordendorf amulet.

---

[20] The most credible interpretation of the Kvinneby amulet (based on a new reading of the opening runes) is found in B. Westlund, 'Kvinneby – en runinskrift med hittills okända gudanamn?', *Studia anthroponymica Scandinavica* 7 (1989), 25–52. It had previously been investigated at length (with a largely discredited transcription and interpretation as a poem invoking protection against the shingle-causing demon Amr) by I. Lindquist, *Religiösa runtexter* 3 (Lund 1987), although we have accepted his controversial reading of conjectured *hūð*, based on a comparison with OE *ingehȳð*, 'thought, mind, knowledge'. Cf. recent interpretations, however, which ignore the multi-staved runes proposed by Westlund and also identify charms against skin diseases; e.g. O. Grønvik, 'En hedensk bønn', in F. Hødnebø et al. (eds), *Eyvindarbók* (Oslo 1992), pp. 71–85 and J. Louis-Jensen, ' "Halt illu frān Būfa!" – Til tolkningen af Kvinneby-amuletten fra Öland', in S. Ó Catháin et al. (eds), *Northern Lights* (Dublin 2001), pp. 111–26.

[21] T.L. Markey, 'Studies in runic origins 2: From gods to men', *American Journal of Germanic Linguistics and Literatures* 11 (1999), 192.

[22] Louis-Jensen, ' "Halt illu frān Būfa!" ', tentatively identifies the 'fish-of-life' of Celtic and Scandinavian folklore here.

Small amulets in the form of his hammer, usually designed to be worn as pendants, are also found throughout Northern Europe and beyond, perhaps in some cases as a reaction to the crucifixes borne by Christians. Thor is also named in an eleventh-century runic charm against blood-poison from Canterbury (described in chapter 6) where he is called upon to bless the wound-causer.

Further reference to the two principal Norse gods, Thor and Odin, is found on a rune-inscribed stick from Bergen that has been dated to about the year 1185. Since the 1950s, excavation of the former medieval port at Bergen has brought to light hundreds of rune-inscribed objects, most of whose inscriptions are profane. Some of these clearly are not, however, although an invocation of pagan deities is surprising at this date as Norway was supposedly fully Christian by the twelfth century. Although the first Christian king of Norway, Haken the Good, died around the year 960, the conversion of Norway to Christianity was actually achieved by the two king Olafs: Olaf Tryggvason (regnant 995–1000) and St Olaf (1014–30). The stick, therefore, may have no supernatural function, but rather simply represent the recording of a traditional literary quotation or blessing. After all, fragments of identifiable Norse poetry recur on several other Norwegian rune-inscribed sticks. This particular text is otherwise unparalleled, however, and it is written in an unusual poetic metre known as *galdralag*, literally 'incantation-metre'. Possibly, then, it originated as some form of charm, although whether it was still regarded as magical in the late twelfth century is open to question. The rune-stick is broken, so the text might be incomplete. The remaining runes, however, read:

ᚼᚫᛁᛚ:ᛋᛂᚦᚿ:ᛆᚠ:ᛁᛈᚿᛈᚿᛦ:ᚠᛆᚦᛆᛦ
ᚦᛆᚱ:ᚦᛁᚠ:ᚦᛁᚠ:ᚠᛁ:ᛆᚦᛁᚼ:ᚦᛁᚠ:ᛏᛁᛞᛁ:

Heill sé þú	*ok í hugum góðum!*
Þórr þik þiggi,	
Óðinn þik eigi.	

'Hail to you	and (be) in good spirits!
May Thor receive you,	
may Odin own you.'	

The sentiments expressed here are somewhat obscure and the exact purpose of the stick difficult to ascertain. The idea of Odin's ownership of his fallen warriors recurs throughout Old Norse literature and is made explicit in the prose *Tale of Styrbjorn* (*Styrbjarnar þáttr svíakappa*) in the Icelandic collection of tales known as *Flateyjarbók*. This tale records that, prior to the Battle of Fyrisvellir in the year 960, the Swedish king Erik, after sacrificing to Odin, cast a stick over the opposing army while making the traditional battle cry: 'Odin owns all of you!' A close parallel to this practice is also described in *Eyrbyggja Saga* where the Icelander Steinthor hurls a spear (the weapon associated with Odin) over the heads of his enemies before a fight, 'according to ancient custom, to bring them good luck', echoing Odin's own action remembered in the *Seeress's Prophecy* of casting a spear over a war-host to begin the first war. We are similarly reminded of the social hierarchy of the Norse afterlife in the Eddic poem *Harbard's Song* (*Hárbarðsljóð*), where Odin, disguised as a ferryman, reminds Thor in a boastful exchange: 'Odin owns the earls who fall in battle and Thor owns the race of serfs.'[23]

It has therefore been supposed that this inscription from Bergen is a funerary charm appealing to the gods to receive the corpse, although the opening line willing good health and spirits does not seem to accord too well with this view. It may alternatively represent a traditional pagan greeting; similar sentiments can be found in a number of Old Germanic texts, including the Eddic verse *Hymir's Poem* where a servant-girl greets the giant Hymir with the words *Ver þú heill, Hymir, í hugum góðum!*, 'Hail to you, Hymir, in such good spirits!' The final line, depending upon the receiver's view of the heathen gods as welcoming deities or agents of evil, might be alternatively regarded as a blessing or a curse. Whether this inscription, postdating the conversion by more than a century, represents active paganism then, or is merely a record (or perhaps even a parody of) an only dimly remembered pagan past, remains unclear.

A single deity, the chief god Odin, is invoked on yet another rune-stick from Bergen, and again the reference at first seems surprising in view of the late date of the object (probably between 1375 and 1400, the end of the runic period) and the contemporary Christianity referred to in the text. The inscription runs as follows:

ᛂᚴ᛫ᚯᚱᚯᚦᛁᚴᛅᚦᛂᚬᛘᛆᚦᚼᛁᚦᚢᛐᛅᛘᛆ᛫ᛐᚱᚠᛁᛅᛐᛅ-
ᛅᛐᛅᚦᚢᛆᛁᛋᛆᚼᛘᛆᚱᚬᛅᛘᚬᚦᛆ᛫ᛘᛅ᛫ᛆᛁᚱᛋᛐᛅᛚ
ᚠᛁᚱᚴᛁᚱᛁᚺᛐᛁᚬᛁᛁᚼᛘᛂᚱᚬᚢᚦᛆᛁᚬᛅᛐᛅᚦ
ᛆᛁᛐᚬᛁᚦᛁᚴᛅᚦᛅᛚᚱᚱᚬᛁᚦᛁᚴᛁᛂᚼᚼᛘᛆᚱᛅᚦᛂᚬ
ᚬᚢᛂᚱ᛫ᚯᚱᚦᛅᛚᚴᚴᛅᚱᛅᚠᛅᚱᛘᛅᚦᚯᛚᚢᚼᛁᚦᚢᛘ
ᛐᚢᚦᚢᚬᚢᚯᚦᛁᛚᚺᚴᛘᛆᚱᚬᛅᛘᚬᚦᛂᛋᛆᚱᛋᛐᛅᛚᛅ

Ek særi þik, Óðinn, með heiðindómi, mestr fjánda;
játa því; seg mér nafn þess manns er stal;
fyr kristni; seg mér nú þína ódáð.
Eitt níðik, annat (?) níðik; seg mér, Óðinn!
Nú ér særð ok árafár (?) með ǫllu heiðindómi.
Þú nú ǫðlisk mér nafn þess er stal. A(men).

'I exhort you, Odin, with heathendom, greatest of fiends;
assent to this: tell me the name of the man who stole;
for Christendom; tell me now your misdeed.
One I revile, the second I revile; tell me, Odin!
Now is conjured up and lots of devilish messengers (?) with all heathendom.
Now you shall get for me the name of he who stole. A(men).'

This is a supplication to Odin to reveal the name of a thief, and similar charms and prayers entreating that thieves and other malefactors be revealed are known from all over the Scandinavian and broader European world. In fact the Greeks and Romans had developed elaborate forms of curses which could be used in cases of

23 The nearest literary parallels of this text are discussed in A. Liestøl, *Runer frå Bryggen* (Bergen 1964), pp. 37–38 and idem, 'Rúnavísur frá Björgvin', *Skírnir* 139 (1965), 29–30; cf. also E. Marold, 'Runeninschriften als Quelle zur Geschichte der Skaldendichtung', in K. Düwel (ed.), *Runeninschriften als Quellen interdisziplinäre Forschungen* (Berlin 1998), p. 380 and McKinnell and Simek, p. 128.

thievery, including what is often called a 'judicial prayer' where the stolen item, though absent, was dedicated to a god who was then exhorted to pursue the wrongdoer in order to retrieve the item and then punish the thief. This example addresses Odin directly, much as a prayer would, although the Bergen charm seems otherwise quite different from a typical Greek or Roman thievery curse.[24]

Although a capricious and untrustworthy god, Odin was renowned for giving wise counsel to his champions. He was also a practitioner of the mysterious form of sorcery known as *seiðr*, an apparently shamanistic form of magic often used to reveal hidden truths. The Eddic poem *Balder's Dreams* (*Baldrs Draumar*) calls him *galdrsfaðir* 'father of incantations' and several references to magical practices are found in the *Sayings of the High One* which supposedly represent the words of Odin himself. Odin (as Woden) is also the only Germanic god to be named in an Anglo-Saxon charm; in the so-called *Nine Herbs Charm*, from an eleventh-century collection, Woden 'then smote that adder so that she flew apart in nine bits' with nine 'glory-twigs' (often identified as rune-sticks) which were effective against poison.[25] Odin (Wodan) is also named in an Old High German healing charm from Merseburg (for more on which see chapter 6), there, as so often, in the company of several other gods. Along with Loki, his memory also may have survived into the late nineteenth century in a Lincolnshire sickness charm, usually thought to be of Nordic origin:

> Father, Son and Holy Ghost,
> Nail the devil to this post –
> With this mell (i.e. hammer) I thrice do knock
> One for God and one for Wod and one for Lok.[26]

In fact Odin also heads a list of the Norse gods that is to be recited in an Icelandic spell to reveal the name of a thief found in the sixteenth and seventeenth-century book of black magic mentioned previously. Known simply as the *Galdrabók* (i.e. 'book of incantations'), the Icelandic collection features some spells calling on pagan gods and Christian devils – it seems that the old Norse gods were thought by this date simply to be local equivalents of Satan and Beelzebub. Another spell against theft from the *Galdrabók*, for example, lists Thor, Frigg, Beelzebub and Odin. Most of the spells with titles like *To Find Out a Thief* from late sources of this type employ mixtures of magical herbs or blood (as does this one) in connection with sigils, rather than make use of magical names, although several of the gods from the first *Galdrabók* list are also found, their names encoded into elaborate runic monograms, in another traditional Icelandic spell to compel a thief to return stolen goods.[27]

No specific gods are invoked on another runic amulet, the Schleswig rune-stick, which does however allude to the Æsir, the chief group of Norse

---

24 This stick is briefly discussed by J.E. Knirk, 'Tor og Odin i runer på Bryggen i Bergen', *Arkeo* 1 (1995), 29–30. On classical thievery curses see H.S. Versnal, 'Beyond cursing', in C.A. Faraone and D. Obbink (eds), *Magika Hiera* (New York 1991), pp. 60–106.

25 G. Storms, *Anglo-Saxon Magic* (The Hague 1948), no. 9.

26 E.A. Philippson, *Germanisches Heidentum bei den Angelsachsen* (Leipzig 1929), p. 153.

27 *Galdrabók* nos 33 and 45; J. Árnason, *Íslenzkar þjóðsögur og æfintýri* 1 (Leipzig 1862), p. 450.

divinities. Fifteen centimetres long and carved on four sides of a wooden stick, dated on archaeological grounds to the eleventh century, the runic text can be read as follows:

> ᚱᚢᚾᛅᛦ.ᛁᛅᚵ.ᚱᛁᛋᛏᛁ.ᛅ.ᚱᛁᚴᛁᛅᛏᛅ.ᛏᚱᛂ.ᛋᚢᛅ
> ᚱᛂᚦ.ᛋᛅᛦ.ᚱᛁᚴᛁ.ᛘᚬᚵᛦ.ᛅᛋᛁᛦ.ᛅ.ᛅᚱᛏᛅᚵᚢᛘ
> ᚼᚢᛚᛅᛦ.ᛅᚢᚴ.ᛒᚢᛚᛅᛦ.ᛘᛂᛚᛁ.ᚦᛂᛦ
> ᛅᚱᛋ.ᛋᚢᛘ.ᛘᛅᚵᛁ

Rūnaʀ iak risti	*ā rīkianda trē.*
Svā rēð sāʀ rīki mogʀ:	
Āsiʀ ā ārdagum!	*Hullaʀ auk bullaʀ;*
mæli þæʀ ars sem magi.	

'Runes I carved	on the ruling stick.
Thus spoke the powerful youth:	
Æsir in days of yore!	Hurlys and burlys;
may they say for you (your) arse is like (your) stomach.'	

It is not particularly easy to discern the motivation for carving this stick and it might at first be thought simply to represent a rather coarse verse (and not a particularly well-written one at that) deriding gluttony rather than any real appeal to the Norse gods. The reference to the Æsir might then simply be explained in view of the ancient *ljóðaháttr* ('song-arrangement') metre in which the verse is composed as *Æsir* is elsewhere collocated with the expression *árdagum* 'days of yore' in Eddic verse. Old Germanic poetry is typically formulaic, full of standard phrases that were memorised by poets so that they could readily be employed to satisfy the often-complex stylistic dictates of alliteration and metre. This runic text may, then, be supposed to represent the crude musings of a rather unskilled poet using familiar, though somewhat vacuous, alliterative pairs in a poem which is essentially about someone whose belly is full to bursting. The sentiments of this text have even been compared with the Jutlandic maxim 'Poor people do have a limit – but not until the first mouthful is coming out the other end.' The Æsir god Thor also had rather a reputation for greed (at his mock wedding to Thrym described in *Thrym's Poem* he is recorded as devouring an entire ox, eight salmon, all the dainties intended for the women and three casks of mead) as did the trickster-god Loki (whom Snorri describes as taking part in an eating contest against the personification of fire). Thus in poking poetic fun at a greedy companion, the composer's mind might be thought to have fallen naturally to the tales told of the gluttonous gods in days of yore. The text has also been considered a form of *níð*, a kind of ritual scorning or humiliation of an enemy which was often expressed in verse, but these are usually sexual in nature (see further chapter 9).[28]

More credibly, however, the stick may represent a genuine charm against

28 The Schleswig rune-stick is discussed in Moltke, *Runes and their Origin*, pp. 387–89 and Nielsen, *Danske runeindskrifter*, pp. 214–15; cf. F.-H. Aag, 'Slesvig runepinne', *Maal og minne* (1987), 17–23. The troublesome participle defining the 'tree' has been variously interpreted as based on Old Norse *rikja* 'drive', *ríkja* 'rule', *rekja* 'reach out, extend, explain' or more recently (and less convincingly) *reka/rækja* 'drive away' (hence 'driftwood') or *hrekja* 'mock'.

diarrhoea or vomiting, the 'hurlys and burlys' (the expression is presumably related to Old Danish *hulder-bulder* or English *hurly-burly* 'commotion, tumult') here referring to a rumbling stomach, heartburn or perhaps flatulence.[29] In fact the opening lines are rather formal in tone and the appeal to the Æsir may be a genuine plea for help against indigestion, perhaps even an emetic, with the last line an indirect reference to vomiting induced by the gods. Equally, of course, it may represent a curse, perhaps on the unnamed powerful youth, to afflict him with stomach troubles. A curse entitled *Fart Runes* in the *Galdrabók* employs 'eight As-runes, nine need-runes and thirteen ogre-runes' to plague its victim's belly with 'crapulence and wind' and 'great flatulence' so that 'farting may never stop, neither by day nor by night'.[30] Indeed fart runes also occur on a rune-stick, probably from 1250–1300, from Bergen reading:

ᛍᚼᛍᛏ:ᚿᛁᚦᚼᚱ:ᛆᚴ.ᚱᛆᛏ:ᚱᚢᚿᛆᚱ:ᚱᛁᛍ:ᚢᚴ.ᛆᚴ.ᚠᛁᛍ:ᚢᛁᛏ:

Sezt niðr ok ráð rúnar;
rís úpp ok fís við!

'Sit down and interpret the runes;
rise up and fart!'[31]

Given the kinds of texts found on rune-sticks in general, we seem justified in regarding the Schleswig stick, too, as another case of a runic charm, much as is more clearly the circumstance with a further rune-inscribed stick, one of the latest of the Norwegian finds.

Yet another reference to Norse mythic beings is found on a further rune-stick from Bergen. This late charm dates from about the year 1335 and invokes elves, trolls, ogres and valkyries, all familiar figures from Norse myth and folklore. Unfortunately broken off at one end and thus lacking the completion of each of the four lines, it reads:

ᚱᛁᛌᛏᛂᚴ:ᛒᚮᛏ:ᚱᚢᚿᛆᚱ:ᚱᛁᛌᛏ:ᛂᚴᛒᛁᛆᚱᚴ:ᚱᚢᚿᛆᚱ:ᛂᛁᚿ:ᚠᛆᛚᛏᚢᛁᚦ:ᛆᛚᚠᚢᛘ:ᛏᚢᛁᚠᛆᛚᛏᚢᛁᚦ:ᛏᚱᛆᛚᛆᛘ:ᚦᚱᛁ
ᚠᛆᛚᛏ:ᚢᛁᚦ:ᚦᚢ. . .
ᚢᛁᚦᛂᚿᚿᛁ:ᛌᚴᚦᛆ:ᛌᚴᛆᚼ:ᚢᛆᛚᚴᛦᚱᚱᛁᚢ:ᛌᚢᛆ:ᛆᛏ:ᛂᛁᚴᛂᚼᛁ:ᚦᛆ:ᛆᛏᚾᚢᛁᛚᛁ:ᛚᛂᚢᛁᛌ:ᚴᛆᚾᛆ:ᛚᛁᚢᛁ:ᚦᛁᚾᚢᚠ
. . .
ᛂᚴᛌᛂᚾᛏᛆᚱ:ᚦᛂᚱ:ᛂᚴᛌᛂᚾᛆᚦᛂᚱ:ᛦᛚᚼᛁᛆᚱ:ᚦᛂᚱᚼᛁ:ᛆᚴᛆᚦᛆᛚᛆ:ᛆᚦᛂᚱ:ᚱᛁᚾᛁ:ᚢᚦᛆᛚᛂ:ᛆᚢᚴ:ᛁᛆᛚᛆᚢᚾ:ᛘᛆᚦ:ᛌᛁᛏᛏᚢ
:ᛆᛚᛆᚱᛁ:ᛌᛆᚴᚦᚢ:ᛆᛚᛆᚱᛁ. . .
ᛆᚾᛏ:ᛘᛂᚱ:ᛌᛂᛘ:ᛌᛁᛆᛚᚴᚱᛂ:ᚦᛂᚱ:ᛒᛂᛁᚱᛁᛌᛏ:ᚱᚢᛒᚢᛌ:ᚱᛆᛒᚢᛌ:ᛂᚦ:ᛆᚱᛆᚾᛏᛆᛒᚢᛌ:ᛚᛆᚢᛌ:ᛆᛒᚢᛌ:ᚱᛆᛌᛆ:ᚠᛆᚢᛆ
. . .

Ríst ek bótrúnar; *ríst ek bjargrúnar;*
einfalt við álfum,
tvífalt við trollum,
þrífalt við þu[rsum]. . .
Við inni skœðu *skag-valkyrju,*

29 Aag takes them as the dative object of the verb, i.e. 'Your arse and stomach will announce noise and trouble for you.'

30 *Galdrabók* no. 46.

31 N B584.

svát ei megi,   *þótt æ vili –*
lævís kona! –   *lífi þínu g[randa]*

Ek sendi þér,   *ek sé á þér,*
ylgjar ergi   *ok úþola.*
Á þér hríni úþoli   *ok jǫluns (?) móð.*
Sittu aldri,   *sof þú aldri . . .*

ant mér sem sjalfri þér.
Beirist (?) rubus rabus et arantabus laus abus rosa gaua. . .

'I cut cure-runes;   I cut help-runes;
once against the elves,
twice against the trolls,
thrice against the ogres . . .

'Against the harmful   *skag*-valkyrie,
so that she never shall,   though she ever would –
evil woman! –   injure (?) your life.

'I send you,   I look at you,
wolfish perversion   and unbearable desire.
May distress descend on you and *jǫluns* wrath.
Never shall you sit,   never shall you sleep . . .

'(that you) love me as yourself.'
Beirist (?) rubus rabus et arantabus laus abus rosa gaua . . .

Although obviously malicious in intent, the purpose of the charm, as well as its intended recipient, is not immediately clear. The text seems to begin as a benevolent formulation before abruptly switching to the infliction of distress and misery, presumably upon the recipient of the charm rather than the baleful valkyrie. The pronoun *sjalfri* 'yourself' in the last intelligible line is a feminine form and the lines appear to constitute a rather spiteful kind of charm aimed at securing the love of a woman. In fact it seems to fit well into a Norse tradition of *kvenngaldrar* 'women-incantations' (or *kvennrúnar* 'women-runes', as they are referred to in a spell for bewitching a woman and winning her love in the *Galdrabók*).[32]

The bulk of the text is composed in a mixture of the Norse metrical forms *fornyrðislag* ('old-story-metre') and *ljóðaháttr* ('song-arrangement'), and the opening half-stanza is in the incantatory metre of *galdralag*, as is the 'Hail to you' rune-stick from Bergen described above. These opening lines also correspond closely to a famous passage from the *Lay of Sigrdrifa* where a wakened valkyrie recounts several stanzas of runic lore to the hero Sigurd, explaining: 'These are book-runes, these are help-runes, and all the ale-runes and valuable runes of power . . .'

It seems likely that the form *bócrúnar* 'book-runes' of the old Norse Lay is in fact a misspelling for *bótrúnar* 'cure-runes' as in the runic amulet. The *bjargrúnar* 'help-runes' (directed to be used on amulets in the *Lay of Sigrdrifa*) recur not only on the Norwegian amulet, but also in the elliptical expression on the Kvinneby amulet with its carved *berg* '(runes of) help', as well as on a fragmentary silver

---

[32] The valkyrie stick is discussed by Liestøl, *Runer frå Bryggen*, pp. 41–50 and revised in idem, 'Rúnavísur frá Björgvin', pp. 33–39. The spell is *Galdrabók* no. 34.

amulet recently found in Østermarie on the Danish island of Bornholm.[33] The amulet fragment, which probably dates from the late eleventh century, was pierced to be worn as a pendant. The now sadly disconnected text, written in boustrophedon style, is clearly intended to invoke protection, but has only the following runes remaining:

ᚴᛁᛈᚤᛅᛒᛆᛁ . . . ᛒᛁᛆᛋᛁ . . . ᛏᚱᛏᛋᚤᛅ
ᛋᚿᛏᚱᛁᛋᛏᛏᛆ . . . ᚱᚿᛏᛏᛆᛏᚿᚤ . . . ᛏᛆᛒᛁᚿ . . . ᛏᚤᛁᚱᛁᛋᛋᛏᛒᛁ-ᚱᚤ

Sigmōðʀ . . . þēʀ si. . .(?) arnsmo (?)
Svā ristiʀ . . . rūnaʀ auk . . . hæil i . . . Āki ræist bi[a]rg.

'Sigmod . . . for you (?) . . .
So I carve . . . runes and . . . amulet (?) in (?) . . . Aki carved (runes of) help.'

The runes on the Norwegian stick are carved against creatures of increasing malevolence, i.e. elves, trolls and ogres, although these clearly were chosen to follow the alliteration of 'once, twice, thrice'. A similarly threefold injunction against supernatural beings, although in a descending hierarchical order, is also found in the compilation of Old English medical charms known as *Lacnunga*. The Anglo-Saxons attributed disease to many supernatural causes, in particular to elves, who were believed to cause pain (elf-shot).[34] In a metrical charm against a sudden puncture or stinging pain (*færstice*), with a rare reference to the (hostile) pagan pantheon, the incantation assures:

> Were it Æsir shot, or elves' shot
> Or hag's shot, now I will help thee.

Perhaps more crucially, the Norwegian charm also seeks to counter the influence of a '*skag*-valkyrie', though what *skag* precisely signifies is linguistically unclear. Valkyries were the handmaidens of the war-god Odin, the 'choosers of the slain', who cleared the battlefield of corpses and sometimes even decided the course of battle. We have already noted that the runic charm has analogies with the literary runic counsels of the valkyrie encountered by the hero Sigurd and a further parallel with Eddic poetry is found in the *First Lay of Helgi Hundingsbani* (*Helgakviða Hundingsbana I*) where the hero Sinfiotli accuses his enemy Gudmund of having been a '*skass*-valkyrie', an expression remarkably similar to '*skag*-valkyrie'. Accusations of femininity and sexual perversion are a common enough form of abuse in Norse literature (especially in the tradition of *níð*). Furthermore, it has been suggested that the manuscript which records the Hundingsbani poem evidences a copying error here: *skass* for *skag*, much as the *Lay of Sigrdrifa*'s *bókrúnar* is often corrected to *bótrúnar*.[35] The spelling *skag* is probably the correct form, then, and is comparable to the verb *skaga* 'stick out' and the name *Skǫgul* (or *Geirskǫgul*) borne by one of the evil valkyries of Norse

---

33 M. Stoklund, 'Bornholmske Runeamuletter', in W. Heizmann and A. van Nahl (eds), *Runica, Germanica, Mediaevalia* (Berlin 2003), pp. 854–70.

34 Hall, pp. 106–31 and 168–71.

35 On the amendment to *skass*-valkyrie (and further amendments) see Liestøl, *Runer frå Bryggen*, pp. 44–46 and idem, 'Rúnavísur frá Björgvin', pp. 37–38.

myth. In fact there is a similar Gothic term *skōhsl* 'evil spirit, demon' (comparable to German *schicken* 'send') which also derives from an original meaning 'stick out' that later came to signify 'supernatural sending'. The Norse description *skag* might, then, refer to the same kind of magical sending found in an almost contemporary valkyrie spell recorded from a witchcraft trial in Bergen in the year 1324, which the witch Ragnhild Tregagás used to dissolve the marriage of her former lover, Bárd:

> I send out from me the spirits of (the valkyrie) Gondul.
> May the first bite you in the back.
> May the second bite you in the breast.
> May the third turn hate and envy upon you.

Clearly, although the precise meaning is unclear, the fiendish nature of the *skag*-valkyrie is paramount in the Bergen charm. Bloodthirsty valkyries such as Thrud and Gunn are also mentioned in the poetry of the Karlevi and Rök rune-stones from Sweden, and amulets in the shape of valkyries have been identified in Viking-Age Scandinavian graves where they were placed presumably because they were thought to have protective powers.[36]

Despite beginning with what seems to be a healing formulation, the essence of the malediction seems instead to be contained in the third verse where the runic carver transmits all kinds of dire consequences to his intended victim. The phrase 'I look at you' is often thought to refer to casting the 'evil eye' upon the victim and indeed the idea of evil emanating from a person's glance is widespread in many societies, not least early Norse ones where sagas often refer to placing a bag over the head or otherwise disempowering the evil eye of a suspected witch. But in fact this runic verse closely corresponds to a love spell in the Icelandic *Galdrabók*, the curse formulation of which contains the words:

> I look at you, and you lay on me
> love and affection of your whole mind.
> Nowhere may you sit, nowhere may you be at rest
> unless you love me.[37]

The threatened *ylgjar ergi* and *úpola* in the runic verse, while defying precise interpretation, may be compared with a similar formulation in the Eddic poem *Skirnir's Lay* (*Skírnismál*). In the poem, Skirnir, an emissary of the god Frey, threatens the non-compliant giantess Gerd, who has dismissed Frey's proposal of marriage, with the words *þurs ríst ek þér ok þría stafi, ergi ok œði ok ópola*, 'I carve for you an ogre (*þurs*, presumably the þ-rune which bore this name) and three staves: perversion and madness and unbearable desire'.[38] The *Galdrabók* spell also makes threats similar to those in the Eddic poem, calling on Odin to afflict the victim with a range of ill-affects, from burning to rotting to freezing, to

---

[36] Liestøl, *Runer frå Bryggen*, p. 47; Zeiten, pp. 10–11.
[37] *Galdrabók*, no. 34. Similar love spells are recorded in J. Árnason and Ó. Davíðsson (eds), *Íslenzkar Gátur, Skemtarnir, Vivivakar og Þulur* 4 (Copenhagen 1896–1903), p. 104.
[38] See K. von See et al., *Kommentar zu den Liedern der Edda* 2 (Heidelberg 1997), pp. 134–37, who stress the sexual nature of *opola* and provide literary parallels to the expressions found here.

having torn clothes, 'until you love me with all your heart', or even more perversely at the end: 'unless you will have me of your own free will'. Presumably, then, the dire consequences of the Bergen charm were predicated on the victim's failure to reciprocate a sexual advance. It seems we are dealing with a sinister form of love charm, which, like Skirnir's and that of the *Galdrabók*, or similar Icelandic spells threatening the recipient 'unless you love me as yourself' or 'unless you love and desire me with all your mind and heart', are intended to compel the acquiescence of the victim through the threat of all sorts of evil affects. Classical love spells also often contain similarly threatening language, but perhaps the closest parallel to the runic charm is found in an early-fifteenth-century amatory spell from Switzerland known as *The Stammering Woman* which also features tripartite supernatural sendings:

> I look for you
> and send after you
> nine valiant wolves.
> Three that will bite you to pieces,
> three that will tear you to pieces,
> three that will lap and suck up your precious blood,
> and so lay on you this burning desire,
> your heart and also your mind,
> your sleeping and your waking,
> your eating and drinking;
> until in your heart my goodness you may nevermore forget.
> You must become a wondrous joy for me
> like wax by the fire.
> May Lucifer in Hell help me
> and all his companions.[39]

Despite its obviously malevolent intent, much of the Norwegian inscription remains unclear. The precise meaning of *jǫlun* is uncertain, although the word is known elsewhere from an inscription treated in the next chapter. It is reminiscent of the Old Norse element *jǫlr* 'yellowy-brown' and is perhaps comparable to the similarly unexplained *jǫll* of obviously unpleasant significance brought amongst the gods by the spiteful Loki in the Eddic *Loki's Quarrel* (*Lokasenna*). In contrast, the concluding words, *rubus, rabus et arantabus* etc., appear mostly to be nonsensical, Latin-like abracadabra words, although *rubus* means 'bramble' or 'blackberry' in Latin and *rabus* is similar to Latin *rabio* 'to rave' (hence *rabid* and *rabies*). This expression seems generally of a form commonly attested among ancient and medieval herbal charms and appears here probably only in order to increase the potency of the charm.[40]

Here, then, we have an incantation which in part closely resembles a valkyrie's

---

[39] E. Hoffmann-Krayer, 'Zum Eingang des Weingartner Reisesegens', *Schweizerisches Archiv für Volkskunde* 8 (1912), p. 65; cf. Liestøl, 'Rúnavísur frá Björgvin', p. 36.

[40] The concluding magical words may perhaps represent a botched rendition of unfamiliar Latin, however; H. Dyvik, 'Addenda runica latina', in A. Herteig et al. (eds), *The Bryggen Papers, Supplementary Series* 2 (Bergen 1988), pp. 1–9, suggests perhaps the *pax portantibus, salus habentibus* formula found on several medieval runic amulets. The interpretation of *jǫlun* is

curative wisdom poem recorded in the *Poetic Edda*, but which was apparently employed to blight the life of an unwilling woman unless she submitted to the will of her suitor. Yet the charm was apparently also intended to counteract various evil influences, in particular that of an evil valkyrie. The role of the corpse-choosing valkyries became increasingly confused in later Norse mythology with that of the Norns, the supernatural females responsible for determining human destiny, so we should probably understand the reference to a *skag*-valkyrie in these terms. After all, two further medieval Norwegian inscriptions refer directly to these Norse figures of fate. Another rune-stick from Bergen uses a poetic paraphrase involving Norns to refer to love or desire, calling it 'the former dwelling of the Crag-Norns'. The role of the Norns as determiners of destiny seems to be affirmed in a wooden inscription carved into the walls of Borgund stave church, Norway, part of which reads 'the Norns did both good and evil, great toil they created for me', a notion reinforced in the words of Gudrun in the Eddic *Short Poem of Sigurd* (*Sigurðarkviða in skamma*) and the *Lay of Regin* (*Reginsmál*) when she complains that 'the hateful Norns created long torment for us'.[41]

The amulets considered in this chapter, then, seem to share a broad commonality. When considered chronologically they even seem to develop from simple invocations of help, through narrative charms, to the stage in which, as the Christian period begins, they appear to have taken on forms somewhat more like those found in Norse literary sources as well as in folk sayings, later spell books and charms. Although the material is somewhat sparse, it is nevertheless interesting to note the continuous appearance of gods familiar from Nordic sources over a wide geographical area and a lengthy temporal period, which is even clearly continued in the lore of later magical sources like the post-medieval Northern books of spells. Moreover, invocations are found not only to the chief gods, Thor and Odin, alone, in pairs or in triads, but also to a myriad of other early deities and heroic figures, some of whom are otherwise only poorly or even not attested at all. We even find references to the other fantastic creatures – elves, trolls, ogres, dwarfs and valkyries – which populated the Germanic mythological world, their appearance testifying to the enduring legacy of the pagan tradition. They are called upon for a variety of purposes: to guard and protect, to win love, to curse, even to discover the name of a thief. Later these figures seem to have been mixed up with Christian devils, much as was the case with many pagan figures in other parts of Europe. But there were other ways to achieve all manner of effects with runic amulets without calling specifically upon personifications of supernatural powers – the standard recourse in Graeco-Roman magic – as shall be seen in the following chapters.

---

discussed by B. Söderberg, 'En runstrof från Bryggen', in *Ingemar Olsson 25 augusti 1988* (Stockholm 1988), pp. 361–67, who regards the four sides of the stick as independent and unlinked texts. She compares the word with later dialectal *jolla* 'to babble, talk rubbish' and translates 'the temper of a mad person'. On a proposed etymology of *joll* see eadem, 'Till tolkningen av några dunkla passager i Lokasenna', *Scripta Islandica* 35 (1984), 43–86. An amendment to *jǫtuns* 'giant's' is championed by L. Lozzi Gallo, 'On the interpretation of **ialuns** in the Norwegian runic text B257', *Arkiv för nordisk filologi* 116 (2001), 135–51.

[41] *NIyR* no. 351. See Hall, pp. 171–79, for a discussion of other dangerous female supernatural figures of Germanic experience.

3

Love, Fidelity and Desire

R ATHER than invoke the gods or other supernatural or semi-divine figures, a significant number of the inscriptions found on rings from Greek and Roman times simply bear short amatory messages such as 'love me'. In fact this practice lives on today in what traditionally have been called 'posy rings' – rings inscribed with short romantic dedications like 'forever yours'. It is clear that there often is a not entirely rational side to 'posy' inscriptions; in a way modern posy rings (and similarly inscribed lockets etc.) can be thought of as amulets of a sort. Yet the ancient Greeks and Romans did not share the concept of romantic love that is so much a part of life today, so such inscriptions should not be understood merely as early amorous engravings of a recognisably modern type and meaning. They can be amatory or erotic – they concern love, marriage, faithfulness, lust and sex – but they are not necessarily romantic; romantic love is usually thought to be a development of twelfth-century troubadour culture, i.e. of the old French tradition of knights and ladies and fine amour, of medieval *cortesie*. Love and sex were thought of in different terms in ancient and early medieval times.[1]

Ancient examples of posy-like inscriptions are merely one expression of a whole range of magical texts imploring or demanding love, sex or fidelity from or for either the owner of the item or another person named in the inscription. Ancient erotic inscriptions might be as much a form of amuletic chastity belt or bawdy aphrodisiac as a testament of devotion. We should not let modern notions of love and desire cloud our understanding of amatory charms that predate the development of the courtly tradition and the modern notion of romantic love.

A common form of ancient amatory text is the *agôgê* or leading charm. This Greek term is used by classicists to describe all sorts of ancient charms and spells, often rather freely, but the description does seem to account fairly well for the central feature of many Greek and Roman magical amatory writings. An extreme form of a leading charm was found over a century ago in Maar, a German village

---

1   The classic introduction to the medieval tradition of courtly love is C.S. Lewis, *The Allegory of Love* (Oxford 1936), though for more recent commentary see R. Boase and D. Bornstein, 'Courtly love', in J. Strayer et al. (eds), *Dictionary of the Middle Ages*, 13 vols (New York 1982–89), III, pp. 667–74. On ancient love charms see J.J. Winckler, 'The constraints of Eros', in C.A. Faraone and D. Obbink (eds), *Magika Hiera* (New York 1991), pp. 214–43 and cf. idem, *The Constraints of Desire* (New York 1990), esp. pp. 71–98.

near the modern city of Trier, the town which in the early centuries AD was the capital of the Roman-occupied parts of Germany.

The Maar inscription, on a broken piece of pottery, consists of a slightly imperfect enumeration of the letters of the Roman alphabet, a magical E-like symbol (an example of what is known as a Gnostic 'ring-letter') and an accompanying line of Latin text:

ABCDEFGHIKLMNOPRRSTVXV ⋿
I bind Artus, son of Dercomognus, the fucker, Artus Aprilis Celsius the fucker.

The verb 'bind' used here indicates an extreme case of a spell better represented in a less laconic text. An example from Mautern, Austria, this time inscribed on a lead spell-tablet, makes somewhat clearer what the 'binding' is supposed to signify:

> Pluto, or we should call him Jupiter of the Underworld, and Eracura, the Juno of the Underworld, have already hastily summoned the one named below and surrendered the shade of snɐıɹǝsǝↃ snuɐıuuıS snıןǝɹn∀
> Thus, O Silvia, you will see your husband returned, much as his name is written here.

This spell is composed in a style known as *similia similibus* – a 'just as . . . so too . . .' composition, one typical of, and especially suited to, cases of sympathetic magic. Clearly, the intention of the charm is for Silvia to get her husband Aurelius Sinnianus Ceserianus returned to her just as she had got him back a previous time when the underworld gods had tried to take him away before his time in the land of the living was truly up – the 'getting back' nature of the text is even emphasised by the writing of the name of Silvia's husband upside down (i.e. so it is, in effect, written back-to-front). The 'binding' of Artus in the Maar text, then, refers to forcing him to desist from his wandering ways – after all, coarse descriptions like 'fucker' are rather common in classical amatory charms. Artus' cognomen (his formal name) Celsius is also spelled in a strange manner (with a K, a letter usually avoided in Latin, and no E), presumably all the better to indicate he is the object of the curse, much as the upside-down Aurelius Sinnianus Ceserianus is in the spell text from Mautern.[2]

Yet not all spells or amuletic texts classed as leading charms, i.e. those which seek to lead the victim into some sort of sexual or amatory behaviour, are written by aggrieved lovers. A very clear runic example, remarkably similar otherwise to the Maar find, occurs on a silver bow brooch discovered in the 1830s at Charnay, a village in Burgundy, France. The inscription on the bow of the Charnay brooch seems to be Burgundian in language – one of only a handful of recordings of this poorly understood Germanic tongue. The brooch dates to the sixth century, i.e. the period of the supremacy of the old Burgundian kings whose downfall is the subject of the *Song of the Nibelungs*. Its runes read:

---

[2] The Maar find is *CIL* XIII, no. 10008.7, while the Mautern spell is discussed in R. Egger, *Römische Antike und frühes Christentum* 2 (Klagenfurt 1963), pp. 24–33.

ᚠᚢᚦᚨᚱᚲᚷᚺᚾᛁᛃᛈᛉᛊᛏᛒᛖᛗ
ᚢᚦᚠᛁᚾᚦᚨᛁᛗ
ᛗᚨᛏᛁᚠᛏᚷ
ᚠᚱ
ᛊᛁᚠ

fuþarkhnijïpzstbem
Unþfinþai Iddan Liano.
Kr(istus?)
Ïia(ō?)

'May Liano discover Idda.
Christ (?), Iaô (?)'.

The part of the text marked out with interpuncts, although slightly misspelled (a reversed *n* has incorrectly been written for an *i*) is a leading charm: 'May Liano discover (i.e. be led to) Idda', with *finþai* a term related to English *find*. Instead of being a charm to win back a spouse, then, the Charnay amulet seems to be one which aims to help its owner win a lover in the first place. The runic ABC or futhark row functions much like the Latin example does at Maar, to reinforce the charm, a technique investigated more fully in the next chapter. The final runes, which unlike the main text are carved on the foot of the brooch, seem to be attempts to represent abbreviated holy words that often appear on Christian amulets from the late Roman world, i.e. presumably *Christ* (cf. the chi-rho monogram, ✗, which is made out of the first two letters which spell *Christ* in Greek) and the common Gnostic sacred name *Iaô*, an originally Hebrew description for 'God (the Father)'.[3]

Another early runic leading charm was found in the late 1920s near Bülach, in the canton of Zürich. It is the only runic inscription to have been found in Switzerland to date but also belongs to the same 'leading' type as the amulet from Charnay. The silver disc-shaped brooch it was found on dates to the late sixth century and its slightly naively scratched legend reads:

ᛉᚱᛁᚠᚱᛁᛗᛁᛚ
ᛗᚢ
ᛉᛏ
ᛗᛁᚲ
1 1

Frifridil duft mik.
L(auk), l(auk).

'Dear beloved desire me! Leek, leek.'

Frifridil is a familiar or pet form of old German *fridil*, a word which can mean 'beloved' or 'husband'. In fact the two *f*-runes face in opposite directions here, as if to make the doubling of the first syllable stand out. The term is clearly masculine and the syllable repetition has a familiarising force similar to that in French *Mimi* (the pet form of *Marie*) or *Lulu* (familiar for *Louise*). The two reversed

---

3 Krause with Jankuhn, no. 6.

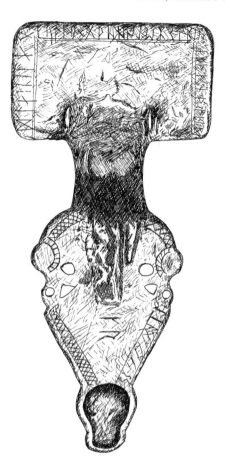

Fig. 3. Charnay brooch

l-runes are probably abbreviations of the old German word for 'leek', a vegetable associated with penises, lust and fertility in Germanic tradition, the name of which often appears on early runic amulets; the abbreviated terms seem to function similarly to the apparently abbreviated Christian holy names on the Charnay brooch, i.e. as magic words that made the amulet more powerful. It seems that the owner had some reason to doubt her husband's fidelity, then, though the brevity of the text does not rule out the possibility that this was merely a matter of 'just in case', rather than the more dramatic circumstances that evidently led to the execution of the Maar charm.[4]

---

[4] Krause with Jankuhn, no. 165. The explanation of the verb *duft* on the Bülach fibula as 'desire' (or rather a causative/perfective 'Erwerbung durch Gewalt oder Anstrengung') was first proposed by J.M.N. Kapteyn, 'Eine altalemannische Runeninschrift', *Anzeiger für schweizerische Altertumskunde* new series 37 (1935), 210–12, though Krause's (vowel-less) interpretation (as 'you take me') does not affect our overall explanation. Krause's expansion of the single *l*-runes, although it has been criticised, must be seen in the context of our discussion of runic charm words in the next two chapters, and the frequent reduction of this term to three or even fewer letters.

It is with these clear examples of runic leading charms in mind, then, that we should approach a number of briefer, though still clearly amatory runic finds, all of which come from Germany and date from the sixth and seventh centuries, i.e. the Merovingian period. All of these texts are marked by the appearance of the old German term *leub* 'love' or its variants *leubo, leuba* or *leubi*, often with little further explanation. In fact a bow brooch found in a woman's grave near Engers in Rhineland-Palatinate in 1885 (but which was stolen by thieves and melted down in the 1920s) had only one word inscribed upon it:

ᚠᛗᚢᛒ

Leub.

'Love.'[5]

Usually when a single word signifying a wish, a herb or an action is found on a rune-inscribed object, the term is classed as an amuletic or charm word, much as 'leek' is in the Bülach inscription – here the intention, if this interpretation is correct, is to win (or retain) the wearer love. Other similar inscriptions, such as another brooch, this time from Schretzheim in Bavarian Swabia, however, show *leub* or one of its variants in combination with other descriptions or names, usually declined in oblique forms (i.e. signalling 'of', 'from', 'for' or 'to'), and are suggestive, rather, of simple posy-ring inscriptions. Given that Southern Germany had been converted by this time, texts like this are sometimes represented as signifying Christian rather than amorous love. The Charnay and Bülach amulet brooches are both from this period too, however, and are both of the leading type, and although the similarly amatory-appearing Nordendorf brooch with its divine triad, Lodur, Odin and Thor, evidently belongs to a different type, the *leub* inscriptions mostly seem to be abbreviated love charms; they aim to win (lead to?) or keep (lead back?) a lover or love for their owner.

These always brief texts often indicate a relationship between a man or a woman and 'love'. In fact most of the runic texts from Germany were written by women – it seems that the Latin alphabet was the preferred written form for men at the time and that the amatory texts from Merovingian Germany are mostly expressions of women's beliefs. A straightforward example is the late-sixth-century Schretzheim brooch inscription which reads:

ᛋᛁᚦᚹᚨᚷᚨᚾᛞᛁᚾ
ᚠᛗᚢᛒᛟ

Siþwagandin leubo.

'For the wayfarer, love.'

It is not absolutely clear how *leub, leubo, leuba* and *leubi* are to be interpreted each time they appear: whether as special amuletic charm words, descriptions, forms of address or the like. Linguistic analysis suggests that *leub* is a noun or adjective ('love, lief'), that *leubi* must be an adjective ('loving, affectionate') and

---

5   Krause with Jankuhn, no. 142.

that *leubo* and *leuba* are adjectives, names or familiar forms ('beloved', 'dear' or 'darling'), masculine and feminine respectively. The 'love' term that accompanies the form *Siþwagandin* is masculine, however, which probably indicates it applies to 'the wayfarer' rather than the owner of the brooch (it was found in a woman's grave). All the *leub* words signify 'love' of some form or another, but many of these texts are too brief for us to be sure what they mean.[6]

Some of the *leub* (etc.) inscriptions are somewhat less laconic; a few even feature verbs. Yet when verbs do appear among the *leub* texts, typically it is still not completely obvious what relationship the 'love' or 'beloved' has to do with the action specified: is it leading to or from, or are these inscriptions closer in nature to the text on the amatory-seeming Nordendorf amulet (discussed in the previous chapter)? For example a bronze bulla, i.e. a capsule or locket used by women for holding perfume – in this case still containing the shrivelled remains of a fragrant plant – also excavated from a woman's grave at Schretzheim, bears the almost pidgin-like runic legend:

ᚠᚱᛟᚷᛁᛊᛞ
ᚠᛚᚠᚷᚢᛏᚦ:ᛚᛗᚢᛒᚠ:ᛞᛖᛞᚢᛏ

Arogis d(eda?).
Alagunþ leuba dedun.

'Arogis did (?). Alagunth love (they) did.'

As in the other Schretzheim find, the 'love' description agrees in gender with the name that precedes it, although the verb which follows, a plural, seemingly does not. It appears it must refer to both names, then, though it is not absolutely clear which line of text (the first is on the lid, the second on the bottom of the bulla) was supposed to be read first.[7]

The Germanic verb *did* is also usually thought to have already developed its 'causative' nature by this time, i.e. it usually indicated merely that something had been done, but not specifically what. Its original meaning was closer to 'create' or 'set up' (it is distantly related to Latin *fecit* 'made'), but it seems that either we are dealing with an abbreviated, elliptical expression here – i.e. the couple did something but the text does not make clear what – or 'love' is what Alagunth and Arogis both did. At any rate they can scarcely both have 'created' the bulla.

There is another Southern German runic example where 'love' and 'did' are found in conjunction, although this time in an inscription that is worn and in parts difficult to read today. It was found on a silver strap-end, part of a bejewelled girdle, in a man's grave from Niederstotzingen in 1963. Dating to the first half of the seventh century, the strap-end was made from a band of silver that was originally part of a sheath mount which was inscribed before it was reused. Clearly created in a masculine context, the difficult runic text reads:

---

6   Krause with Jankuhn, no. 156. Previous interpretations of the *leub* inscriptions have mostly foundered on the preconception that *leubo* and *leuba* must be personal names. Cf., however, the use of the femine adjective *liubu* 'dear' along with an obliquely inflected man's name (*swestar mīnu liubu mez Wage*, 'my sister dear to me, to Wag') on the Norwegian Opedal stone; Krause with Jankuhn, no. 76.

7   Krause with Jankuhn, no. 157.

ᛒᛁᚷ-ᛂ:ᛚᛚᚢᛒ
ᚢᛗᛊᛒ ᚹᛚᚹᛁ-

Big[a]ns leub
uer B(iga?) dedu[n].

The only features of this text which seem to be generally agreed on are the appearance of the term *leub* (either *lliub* with an emphasised *l* or a slightly irregular *leub*) and a somewhat clumsily ligatured form of the verb *dedun*. The other parts of the inscription are more difficult to make out, but it seems likely that we are dealing with a name beginning with *B* here (presumably *Biga*) and perhaps the expression *wer* 'man, husband' (if not another name, *Breu* or the like read in reverse). If so this suggests we are essentially dealing with the same sort of inscription as appears on the Schretzheim bulla: it indicates a couple (Biga and her man) who 'did love (each other)'.[8]

A longer *leub* inscription was discovered in the early 1980s on an item unearthed near the southern German village of Neudingen. It was found on a distaff, an implement used for spinning thread and one typically associated with women; in fact so much so that they were often described as carried by creatures such as Norns and became associated with witches from late medieval times. Its, again, almost pidgin-like legend reads:

ᛚᛒᛁ:ᛁᛗᚾᛒᚠ:ᚾᚠᛗᚠᛚᛗ:
ᛒᛚᛁᚦᚷᚾᚦ:ᛈᛦᚠᛁᛏᛦᚾᛏᚠ

L(eu)bi Imuba Hamale.
Bliþgunþ wrait rūna.

'Love, Imuba, for Hamal.
Blithgunth wrote (these) runes.'

It is not uncommon to find frequently used terms such as 'rune' or even charm words (like 'leek') abbreviated in early runic inscriptions, so the Neudingen text with its abbreviation *lbi* makes it seem as if *leubi* is more than merely an affectionate form with little more consequence than finding the word *dear* on a posy ring. The text appears to have been written by a certain Blithgunth hoping that it would have some effect on Imuba, someone who perhaps could not write herself. The style Imuba is clearly a pet form to a name like Irmenburg and Hamal is a well-attested early German man's name. Like 'the wayfarer' at Schretzheim, though, Hamal appears inflected in an oblique form ('to Hamal, for Hamal'), whereas in the leading charms from Charnay and Bülach it is the woman's name or pronoun that appears in the objective case ('lead to Ida', 'lead to me'). The laconic German *leub* texts seem stylistically more like the legend on the Nordendorf brooch, then, with its woman's name Awa and what seems to be an obliquely inflected masculine form, Leubwini. Consequently, if the various forms of *leub* are acting as charm words, they seem to be replacing Nordendorf's divine triad, i.e. taking on the amuletic function of a heavily abbreviated narrative

8   T. Looijenga, *Texts and Contexts of the Oldest Runic Inscriptions* (Leiden 2003), pp. 248–49.

charm. So the Nordendorf triad and the charm word *leub* seem to have the same effect formulaically as do the terms *alu*, *auja* or the tree-like symbol or the swastika on the pendants, combs and brooches considered in chapter 2.[9]

In fact late in 2001 a disc brooch was uncovered near Bad Krozingen which bears an early German runic inscription that is exactly of this basic *leub* type: a woman's name plus *leub* plus a man's name inflected in an oblique form. It was unearthed from a woman's grave dating to about the year 600, and the other grave goods, including a garnet-inlaid gilt disc brooch, indicate that the dead woman was of high social status. The brooch's inscription reads:

ᛒᛟᛒᚠ:ᛚᛗᛑᛒ
ᚠᚷᛁᚱᛁ᠅ᛗ

Boba, leub, Agirīke.

'Boba, love, for Agirik.'

Boba and Agirik are both names attested in Merovingian written sources and appear here in an expression that probably represents the elliptical formula or basic style underlying several of the other German amatory texts.[10]

This interpretation of the *leub* inscriptions is also underscored by one of the runic finds from Weimar, that on a bow brooch of Merovingian date. Excavated from a woman's grave, its inscription reads:

ᚻᚠᚱᛁᛒᚱᛁᚷ
ᚻᛁᛒᚠ:ᛚᛁᛒᛁ:ᛚᛗᛟᛒ

Haribrig.
Hiba liubi leob.

The name Hiba is a pet form of a woman's name, almost certainly of the full form Haribrig that is written on the foot of the brooch. The slightly variant spellings *liubi* (for *leubi*) and *leob* (for *leub*) are merely indications this text is written in the old Thuringian dialect of German, and their juxtaposition clearly shows that *leubi* and *leub* have slightly different meanings and uses, though what these were precisely remains unclear. Moreover, the other rune-inscribed brooch found at Weimar bears Hiba's name again:

ᚺᛁᚷ
ᛒᛑᛒᛟ:
ᚻᛁᛒᚠ:

---

9   Looijenga, p. 248.

10   G. Fingerlin et al., 'Eine Runeninschrift aus Bad Krozingen (Kreis Breisgau-Hochschwarzwald)', in H.-P. Naumann (ed.), *Alemannien und der Norden* (Berlin 2003), pp. 224–65. A further example of a *leub* inscription was found in a cave at Kleines Schulerloch, Bavaria during the Nazi period. But though it fits the formulism argued for here perfectly (a woman's name + *leub* + an oblique man's name), it is often considered a modern creation given the unexpected site and date of its discovery; see R. Nedoma, 'Die Runeninschrift auf dem Stein von Rubring', in W. Heizmann and A. van Nahl (eds), *Runica, Germanica, Mediaevalia* (Berlin 2003), pp. 489–92.

Sig[ibaþ].
Bubo.
Hiba.

The letters *Sig-* suggest an abbreviated or incomplete name here and more runes discerned by one recent investigator wrapped around the foot of the brooch may complete the name as *Sigibaþ*. Clearly a man's name, the familiar style Bubo would appear, then, to be its pet form. We are seemingly dealing with a couple, Bubo (Sigibath) and Hiba (Haribrig) then here; the inscriptions are evidently affirmations of the love Hiba feels for Bubo. Unlike the Schretzheim, Niederstotzingen and Neudingen texts, however, there is no hint of the past or need for the amulet to work upon the man in order to win or maintain love. The first of the two inscriptions with its use of the *leub* charm words is, nevertheless, obviously meant as an amuletic text, whereas the second is certainly at least a form of amatory expression, though there is no clear written indication that it was any more than a recording of love, i.e. of the type which is found on posy rings today.

Another *leub* find from Weimar, inscribed this time on an amber bead, appears to have belonged to another woman, another Ida:[11]

ᛁᛈᚨ:ᛒᛁᚷᛁᛏᚨ:ᚺᚨᚺᚹᚨᚱ:
:ᚠᛈᛁᛗᚢᛏᛗ:ᛁᛋᛗ:ᛚᛗᚢᛒ   ᛁᛈᚢᛏ:

Ida Bigina Hahwar.
Awimund isd leob Idun.

'Ida Little-purchase. Hahwar.
Awimund is (the) love of Ida.'

Bigina is usually interpreted as a separate woman's name, but it is related linguistically to the English verb *buy* – it appears to mean 'little purchase' and is probably a nickname of Ida if not a reference to the bead. The Hahwar of the first line is a man whose name also appears on another Weimar find in connection with Ida, this time in an inscription on a belt-buckle:

ᚦᛁᚢᚦ:ᛁᛈᚨ:ᛚᛗᛟᛒᛁᛈᚨ:ᚺᚨᚺᚹᚨᚱ:

Þiuþ Ida leob Ida. Hahwar.

'Good Ida, love Ida. Hahwar.'

On this occasion we appear to be dealing with two texts on items belonging to a woman, Ida, inscribed by the same man. Moreover, the sentiments of the buckle text are reminiscent of some of the inscriptions found on ancient Gaulish spindle-whorls which were obviously given to their female owners by men, presumably their suitors. They can range from innocent declarations such as 'I am a young girl, good and pretty', to the coarser 'May I mount your motherhood?'[12] These

---

11 The Weimar finds are Krause with Jankuhn, nos 147–49.
12 The Gaulish posy inscriptions are surveyed in P.-Y. Lambert, *La langue gauloise* (Paris 1991), pp. 122–25 and are mirrored in numerous Latin finds.

sorts of amatory texts do not seem to be amulets in the sense of a leading charm, then – i.e. a talisman which has a specific, spell-like purpose – but belong to a less formal world of amorous messages and bawdy posy. Hahwar may well have been Ida's father or brother, and appears to have the same role as Blithgunth does at Neudingen here. The use of a form of the charm word *leub* in each case probably still makes them amuletic inscriptions. A different purpose might explain the inscription on another brooch, from German Freilaubersheim, though:

ᛒᛟᛋᛟ:ᛈᚱᚨᛗᛏ:ᚱᚢᚾᚨ
ᚦ<:ᛗᚨᚦᛁᚾᚨ:ᚷᛟᛚᛁᛗᚨ:

Bōso wraet rūna.
Þ(i)k Daþina gōlida.

'Boso wrote (these) runes.
Dathina sang of you.'

Found in a woman's grave, the brooch inscription seems to have been written by a man called Boso for the female owner Dathina. Boso literally means 'magician', although it was a fairly common name in Merovingian times so we should probably not read too much into this. Still, it is not entirely clear what the verb *gōlida* means here. It is usually compared to a similar verb from Gothic meaning 'greeted' though the closest Old High German forms are the verb *galan* 'to sing' (past tense *gôl*, a form also found in compounds) which forms the base of *galstar* 'charm', the early German equivalent of Old Norse *galdr* 'incantation'. So *gōlida* could easily have meant 'enchanted' or the like, with 'you', a singular pronoun, referring to her lover. It could equally as easily just have meant 'praised you' (if not 'serenaded you'), though. It is not clear if this is an amulet inscription following a recognisable formula, then, or whether it is, rather, an expression closer to a posy-ring inscription than to a more developed type of magical writing such as a leading charm.[13]

A similar difficulty arises with other runic inscriptions that do no more than mention the names of a couple or otherwise hint at being amatory texts. The following Southern German inscription, for example, was found in 1996 in an ancient graveyard at Pforzen, just as was the belt-buckle described in chapter 2. The inscription appears on the inside and outside of an ivory ring-support from an ornamental bronze disc that was almost certainly an amulet. Dating to about the year 600, the ring's worn text can still partly be read as:

------ᚷᛁᛋᚨᛚᛁ-
-ᛖ:ᚨᛟᛞᛚᛁᚾᚦ:ᚢᚱᚨᛁᛏ:ᚱᚢᚾᚨ:

. . . Gīsali
. . .e Aodlinþ wrait rūna.

---

13 Krause with Jankuhn, no. 144. C.J.S. Marstrander, review of H. Arntz and H. Zeiss, *Die einheimische Runendenkmäler des Festlandes* (Leipzig 1939), *Norsk tidsskrift for sprogvidenskap* 11 (1939), 298ff., notes that Freilaubersheim's *gōlida* could mean 'enchanted'; the interpretation 'greeted' seems to have caught on mainly due to the erroneous notion that Gothic (because it is attested earliest) always preserves older meanings.

'. . . Gisali
. . . Aodlinth wrote (these) runes.'

It seems quite possible that a word like *leub* has been lost from this inscription and the remaining -*e* suggests that an obliquely inflected name may once have begun the inside line of the ring's text. What remains of the first six runes on the outside of the ring has been read as *?lu?ul*, however, which is also suggestive of the common runic charm word *alu*, perhaps written twice. So, much as is the case with the many even briefer inscriptions on personal items, we cannot be sure that this was an amatory text. In fact only the item it was written on suggests this is an amuletic inscription. Still, as the *leub* texts and runic leading charms attest, the recording of amatory expressions seems to have been one of the commonest reasons for inscribing runic legends on women's possessions in Germany in early medieval times.[14]

Given the *leub* formula and the distaff from Neudingen, it also becomes tempting to include a well-known Frisian example in the category of amatory amulet texts. It appears on a piece of yew wood, probably a weaving-slay, from Westeremden in the Netherlands, that was discovered in 1928. It has only loosely been dated to between the years 550 and 750, and its runes are thinly carved and not as legible as they once were. From what remains today, and what was seen by earlier runologists, though, it seems to read:

ᚠᛗᚾᛥᛁᚺᛁᛏᚾᛁᛗᛅ-ᛥᛁᚺᚾᚨᚠᛗᚾ

Ādugīslu me[þ] Gīsuh(i)ldu.

Two names clearly appear here, most probably a masculine and a feminine, linked by a word usually read as *með* 'with'. *The later Frisian descendants of this word such as mithi* usually retain the final vowel of the original form *medi*, however, and it is not absolutely clear that the second name is feminine. We might translate 'Adugisl with Gisuhild' and, given the Neudingen distaff, interpret this as an amatory amulet text. But without a clearer indication than just 'with' linking the apparent couple here, i.e. such as the appearance of a formulaic term like *leub*, we cannot be absolutely sure this message was intended to be any more than a posy-like inscription, despite the magical associations often imputed to weaving implements of this nature.[15]

Runic amatory texts are far from being restricted to the Continent, though. In fact inscriptions of the amatory 'posy' type are also common among medieval Scandinavian finds. Yet in contrast, remarkably few amatory runic texts have been found so far in England. Indeed even when they do occur, these early English instances are often treated guardedly by Anglo-Saxonists. A relatively clear case seems to appear on a disc, almost certainly a spindle-whorl, from Whitby, North Yorkshire, however, which, much like the Gallo-Roman spindle-

---

14 K. Düwel, 'Pforzen, § 2', in J. Hoops, *Reallexikon der germanischen Altertumskunde*, 2nd ed. (Berlin 1976–), XXIII, pp. 116–18.
15 Looijenga, pp. 311–12.

whorl finds, was probably inscribed by a man who gave it as a present to his beloved. Made of jet, the legend on this undated Anglo-Saxon piece reads:

ᚢᛖᚱ

Uēr.

'Token of friendship.'

The inscription on the Whitby disc is very short, though, and only the inscribed spindle-whorls from a much earlier period if not the legends on the Neudingen distaff and Westeremden slay give us any guide to its context. The most likely reading seems to be as a dialectal form of the Old English word *wǣr* 'token of friendship', a term originally meaning 'vow' which is related to *Vár*, the name of the Norse goddess of marriage. Otherwise, we might be entitled to read a short name *Wer* here, though this would be masculine, a form which on an item so strongly associated with women's work would appear more than a little strange. The sequence might also just stand for *wer* 'man, husband', much as seems to appear at Niederstotzingen, although we would expect the word to appear in an oblique form if the inscription were intended to signify 'from your husband' or a similar sentiment.[16]

With texts like these, then, it is often only context that tells us whether an amatory legend is an everyday expression, a posy ring-like inscription or even an outright formulaic magical charm. There are many examples of runic texts from Scandinavia, however, that seem a lot like the messages found today on lavatory doors or declarations of the type which young lovers feel compelled to write on trees, light-poles and park benches.

Several texts are found on rune-sticks excavated from medieval Bergen, for instance, a town which was already a thriving seaport at the time. The inscription found on a rune-stick there, *Ingibjǫrg unni mér þá er ek var i Stafangri*, 'Ingibjorg loved me when I was in Stavanger' might well have been thought to be a posy inscription if it had been found in Stavanger; but coming from Bergen it seems to be little more than a bawdy boast. Coarser still is another Bergen rune-stick: *Smiðr sarð Vigdísi af Snældubeinum*, 'Smith fucked Vigdis of the Snelde-legs (folk).' These mundane texts can clearly be separated from posy-like or outright amuletic finds.

Happily enough, other comparable Scandinavian inscriptions of an everyday amatory nature seem to express more tender emotions. A text inscribed on a wheel found in Oslo, for example, reads: *Nikulás ann konu þeirri vel er Gýríðr heitir, stjúpdóttir Pitas-Rǫgnu*, 'Nikulas loves well the woman called Gyrid, step-daughter of Petr-Ragnar.' Another inscription on a bone from the same site states *Ása ann St, ek veit*, 'Asa loves St. I know' – whether this message was recorded by those involved or someone else happy to be in on the affair we may never know. Further north, from Trondheim, simpler runic declarations of love are known; a wooden needle, for example, has an inscription reading *Unna ek*

---

[16] Page, *Introduction*, p. 170 and see T.L. Markey, 'Icelandic *sími* and soul contracting', *Scripta Islandica* 51 (2000), 133–39 for the semantics of *Vár*.

meyju enn betr, enn betr, 'I love the maiden even better, even better', while a tenth- or eleventh-century stray piece of bone simply states *Ek ann ekkju v(el)*, 'I love the widow well.'[17]

These gently amorous messages occur alongside cruder expressions of erotica similarly scratched into a variety of runic objects and deposited in the remains of the ports, markets and other parts of medieval Scandinavian towns. It is no easy matter to weed out the amuletic love charms, designed to secure or maintain the affection of the beloved, from the multitude of wishful or boastful runic expressions of amatory desire, although a number of them suggest that they are more than merely idle boasts or dreams of sexual conquest.

In medieval Scandinavia the first three letters of the runic alphabet, ᚠᚢᚦ, *fuþ* spelt out the term for female genitalia, *fuð*. Consequently, to inscribers used to adding rune rows to amulet inscriptions like that on the Charnay brooch, the term *fuð* 'vagina', like the futhark row itself, may have been regarded as something of a lucky sequence. The remarkable orthographic coincidence may explain the relatively frequent appearance of *fuð* in contexts which may suggest it could be used as an amulet charm word much like *lauk* 'leek', the phallic herb, is on the brooch from Bülach.

While the word *fuð* does not seem to have become taboo or otherwise limited to magical use, neither need all the examples of *fuð*-inscribed objects be restricted to bawdy masculine contexts. Perhaps acting as a carpenter's ABC or abridged demonstration of runic proficiency, *fuþ* is carved into the walls and roofs of a number of medieval Danish and Norwegian churches as well as the rocky outcrop of Storhedder in Norway. Various motivations might underlie the scratching of isolated *fuð* into bones from Sigtuna and Lund, Sweden, and as far afield as Poland, on several Norwegian rune-sticks and on various Scandinavian wooden, stone and tin implements such as knives, bowls, lids, skewers, handles and even a wooden cross. An example from Bergen occurs under the base of a wooden cup, a place otherwise typical for Christian protective phrases (like *Ave Maria*, 'Hail Mary') and signs. The term occurs alongside 24 *m*-runes on a bone from Lund and between two names on a zoomorphic bronze buckle from Gotland: *Þorkell/ Þorhildr, fuð, Ulfkell(?)*. *Fuð*, which perhaps could also mean 'anus', is paired with the Norse word *ars* 'arse' on a further rib-bone from Sigtuna and the same pairing can be seen on a piece of bone from Danish Schleswig that bears a short irregular, but suggestively crude text, *b fuikþ* as well. On a longer message on a fragmentary stick from Viðey, Iceland we can identify the words *ást* 'love' and what might be read as *fuð*, and, in cruder compounding, vulgar Norwegian wits amused themselves by affixing the word to each of their names in the following message on a stick from Bergen: *Jón silkifuð á mik, en Guðormr fuðsleikir reist mik, en Jón fuðkula rœðr mik*, 'Jon Silky-vagina owns me, and Guthorm Vagina-licker carved me, and Jon Vagina-swelling reads me.'[18]

---

17 The Oslo wheel is N A7, the bone N A199. The Trondheim needle is N A258 and the 'widow' bone-piece is *NIyR* no. 840.

18 Some of the *fuð* texts are mentioned in Moltke, *Runes and their Origin*, pp. 356, 459, 463–64, 478–79 and 533; cf. also H. Gustavson, 'Verksamheten vid Runverket i Stockholm', *Nytt om runer* 12 (1997), 29–30. Much of the Norwegian material can be found in K.F. Seim, *De*

Another common name for the female organ, *fitta*, is found on a rib-bone from Uppsala together with the woman's name Thora. It is not entirely clear that this is a case of extension of any amuletic use of 'vagina', although another obscure type of bawdy inscription is perhaps more suggestive of some sort of female magic. These are represented by a piece of bone from Lund, Sweden which seems to read *fuðtramʀ hagi B. . .*, 'May the vagina-demon arrange B. . .' and two rather obscure rune-sticks from Bergen. The first of these alliteratively states *Felleg er fuð, sin byrli. Fuðǫrg*, perhaps 'Foul is the drink-bearer to the vagina. Vagina-mad (i.e. perverse)'; the second perhaps *Fuðrǫg lín-smyl. Fuð*, 'Vagina-mad (i.e. perverse) linen-troll (i.e. woman). Vagina.' Like *fuð-ars*, *fuðǫrg* (and perhaps *fuðrǫg*) looks like it might have originally been a play on *fuþork*. It is possible, then, that these inscriptions represent an elaboration of the fortuitous connection between an Old Norse word for 'vagina' and the first few letters of the futhark row rather than merely a coarse compliment or an expression like the unsavoury descriptions of women which appear on the Bergen love amulet considered in the previous chapter. Another Schleswig bone reading *fuð-buk[kr]* 'vagina-buck (i.e. he-goat)' (or perhaps 'goat-arse'), however, suggests that we might sometimes be dealing with crude epithets for men rather than women here, describing their sexual successes in a vivid, condensed manner. After all, a coarsely alliterative Norse text is found on a cattle rib-bone from Starigard, northern Germany, one side of which appears to read: *kūkr kyss kuntu, kyss!*, 'Cock (i.e. penis), kiss the cunt, kiss!'[19]

A further inscription on a piece of wood from Bergen is similarly blunt, with a text that states: *Rannveig rauðu skaltu serða. Þat sé meira enn mannsreðr ok minna enn hestreðr*, 'You will fuck Rannveig the red. It will be bigger than a man's prick and smaller than a horse's prick.' In order to judge the function of the inscription correctly, we would need to know more about the context, such as whether Rannveig owned the bone or had given it to a lover. But the mention of horse's pricks does not seem too far removed from the world of vaginas, fuþ(ark rows), leeks or even Germanic fertility charms here. On the other hand, a cattle rib-bone from Oslo describing a sexual act appears to represent, instead, a case of insulting an enemy (*níð*). In view of the prevailing Norse censure of passive homosexuality, it seems unlikely that the text is making a positive reference to sodomy when it tells us that *Óli er óskeyndr ok stroðinn í rassinn . . . vel fór þat*, 'Oli is unwiped and fucked in the anus . . . that sounded good.'[20]

vestnordiske futhark-innskriftene fra vikingtid og middelalder (Trondheim 1998), pp. 265–74. The finds from Schleswig are in M. Stoklund and K. Düwel, 'Die Runeninschriften aus Schleswiger Grabungen', in V. Vogel (ed.), *Ausgrabungen in Schleswig* 15 (Neumünster 2001), pp. 141–68; those from Schleswig and Oldenburg in M.L. Nielsen et al., 'Neue Runenfunde aus Schleswig und Starigard/Oldenburg', in K. Düwel et al. (eds), *Von Thorsberg nach Schleswig* (Berlin 2001), pp. 201–80.

[19] On the Uppsala rib-bone see E. Svärdström and H. Gustavson, 'Runfynd 1974', *Fornvännen* 70 (1975), 166–77. The Lund bone is discussed in Moltke, *Runes and their Origin*, pp. 463–64 and the Bergen rune-sticks by Seim, *De vestnordiske futhark-innskriftene*, pp. 267–69.

[20] The rude Bergen wood-piece is N B628. On the Oslo bone see J.E. Knirk, 'Arbeidet ved Runearkivet, Oslo', *Nytt om runer* 6 (1991), 13–16. The standard investigation of Norse homosexuality is P.M. Sørensen, *Unmanly Man*, trans. J. Turville-Petre (Odense 1983).

Interesting as these may be for social or sexual historians, such obscene runic expressions are peripheral to any examination of amuletic runes where carvers use runes to try to effect their desires rather than simply spell them out for private or public amusement. A further series of amatory Scandinavian inscriptions are those addressed directly to a lover, although whether they were actually intended for the lover to read remains unclear. Several runic inscriptions say simply 'kiss me!', e.g. a vertebra from Oslo (*kyss mik!*) and a coopered wooden bowl from Bergen (*kyss þú mik!*). The same demand is apparently also found on a fragmented timber building stock from Trondheim which seems to contain the runes . . . *kyss mik!, mér er . . .*, 'kiss me!, . . . is . . . to me' (and a flat rune-stick from Trondheim with an unclear text nevertheless seems to read *þá ann ek*, 'Then I loved' or perhaps 'I loved you'). A graffito carved into Gol stave church in Oslo also bears a longer message of this type: *Kyss á mik, þvíat ek erfiða!*, 'Kiss me, because I am troubled!' Sometimes the wish is intensified by the addition of a futhark row, much as at Charnay; e.g. a rune-stick from Bergen contains a complete futhark row plus the words *Ást mín, kyss mik!*, 'My beloved, kiss me!' The Skara bone from Sweden also seems to indicate that the rune row had some connection with love as one side of it contains the first seven letters of the futhark while on the second only the words *ást sín Ot. . .*, 'his/her love Ot. . .' can be discerned. A rounded stick from Bergen also contains an incomplete futhark row as well as the words *Ólafr kysti D. . .*, 'Olaf kissed/may kiss D. . .'. There seems to have been a connection between the rune row and amatory texts in Scandinavia, then, perhaps triggered by the suggestive likeness of *fuð* and *fuþark*.[21]

Many of the direct appeals for love even demand some kind of reciprocity. Somewhat reminiscent of the texts on Roman amulets or Gallo-Roman spindle-whorls as well as of early German love lyrics of the *Dû bist mîn, ich bin dîn*, 'thou art mine, I am thine' kind are those found on two rune-sticks from Bergen from the fourteenth and thirteenth centuries respectively: . . . *þú mik man ek þik!*, '(Think) of me, I think of you!' and, cut in decorative triple-outline runic forms, *Mun þú mik, man ek þik! Unn þú mér, ann ek þér!*, 'Think of me, I think of you! Love me, I love you!' A counting-staff from Bergen even addresses a certain Gunnhild with the words *Unn þú mér, ann ek þér, Gunnhildr! Kyss mik, kann ek þik!*, 'Love me, I love you, Gunnhild! Kiss me, I know you (well)!' An early-twelfth-century wooden weaving-knife from Lödöse, Sweden, with a hole at one end, similarly pleads *Mun þū mik, man þik! Un þū mēr, an þēr! Barmi mik!*, 'Think of me, I think of you! Love me, I love you! Have mercy on me!' All of these were presumably inscribed by enamoured carvers and presented to the objects of their affection. They are probably, then, examples of amorous posy-like texts, even if they are not amuletic inscriptions of a clearly formulaic kind.[22]

How many of these examples were regarded by their carvers as more than posy

---

21 The 'kiss me' inscriptions include N A41, N B540, *NIyR* nos 566, 843 and 866. The Bergen sticks are N B17 and N B371. On the Skara bone see H. Gustavson et al., 'Runfynd 1989 and 1990', *Fornvännen* 87 (1992), 153–74.

22 The Bergen rune-sticks are N B118, N B465 and N B556; for Lödöse see E. Svärdström, *Runfynden i Gamla Lödöse* (Stockholm 1982), pp. 15–21.

texts, i.e. as magical expressions manipulating fate or the emotions of their loved ones, we shall probably never know for sure. Those not using terms like *fuð* or futhark rows may well have represented only wishful thinking or even a bashful formal request. Later Norse literature describes the throwing of rune-sticks into the laps of women to gain favour and Scandinavian amatory texts seem also to explain an instance in Anglo-Saxon poetry where a rune-stick bears a message of hope from a lord to his estranged lady. The passage comes from the *Husband's Message*, a poem from the *Exeter Book* immediately following a riddle (*Riddle 60*) whose answer seems to be 'rune-stick'. The rune-stick's counsel from the *Husband's Message* is as follows:

See here! The man bade me tell you,	he who engraved this slip of wood,
bejewelled lady,	to keep close
within your heart	the words of promise
that the two of you in days gone by	repeated so often,
when you could live together	in festive halls,
the very same	land to walk,
and let friendship flower . . .	
Make your way to the sea,	to the gull's home,
board your ship,	sail south along
the sea-lanes	to meet your man,
to the land where	your prince awaits you.

Then follow five runes, ᚻ *s*, ᚱ *r*, ᛇ $\widehat{ea}$, ᚹ *w*, ᛗ *m*, supposedly signifying that:

as long as he lived	he would fulfil the pledge,
the faith given	between friends,
that the two of you in days gone by	repeated so often.

The runes here appear merely to constitute a code, using the names of the runes ideographically to indicate that heaven (*sigel-rad* 'sun-road'), earth ($\widehat{ear}$-*wyn* 'corn-joy') and the man (**m**on) would witness and declare the oath together. The rune-stick in the *Husband's Message* thus appears to be more than simply a runic love-letter. But does it and its runic lore represent no more than a literary flourish or is the description of the stick and the cryptic use of the six runes based on a recognition that some amatory rune-sticks could act as magical charms?[23]

The English description of a runic 'posy-stick' cannot fail but to remind us of further Scandinavian examples, such as that from Bergen with the following partly encoded message: *Byrli minn, unn mér! Ann ek þér af ástum ok af ǫllum huga*, 'My cupbearer, love me! I love you with all of my heart and desire.' More straightforward expressions of this type are found on further rune-sticks from Bergen, e.g. *Slíka vilda ek mína sem þú est*, 'Just as you are is how I wanted mine',

---

23 On love magic in Norse literary sources see A. Holtsmark, 'Kjærlighetsmagi', in J. Brøndsted et al. (eds), *Kulturhistorisk leksikon for nordisk middelalder*, 22 vols (Copenhagen 1956–78), VIII, pp. 444–47; cf. also A. Bæksted, *Målruner og troldruner* (Copenhagen 1952), pp. 82 and 98. For the rune-stick and ideographs in the *Husband's Message* see the comments in B.J. Muir (ed.), *The Exeter Anthology of Old English Poetry* 2, 2nd ed. (Exeter 2000), pp. 697–98.

or as part of a longer message on a wood-piece from Lödöse, Sweden, *Ver þū vinr min, Arnfinnr!*, 'Be my friend, Arnfinn!' A last such text, carved on a rib-bone from Oslo, is the following, somewhat cocky message: *Ann sá þér, er risti rúnar þessar, Þordís!*, 'He who carved these runes loves you, Thordis!' The reverse continues: *Þóra! Ek kan gilja*, 'Thora! I can seduce.'[24]

But should any of these amatory inscriptions be thought of as amuletic or are they all to be understood merely as runic love-letters? The text on the rune-stick from Bergen described in the last chapter, with its invocation of elves, trolls, ogres and valkyries, could confidently be considered an amatory enchantment and such a spell-inscribed object was probably used as an amulet. Odin, the lecherous god well versed in rune-craft, boasts of his conquests in the Norse *Song of Harbard*, gleefully recounting how he used *miklar manvélar* 'mighty love-spells' on witches to seduce them from their men. Two verses in the *Sayings of the High One* deal with arousing the affections of women (see chapter 10) and the dark magical practices of *seiðr*, allusions to which are sprinkled liberally throughout Old Norse literature, seem particularly associated with erotic magic. Various kinds of amatory spells and charms are described in the Eddas and the sagas, and the use of magic writings to win love is a recurring theme in Norse literature.

This writing often took the form of runes. We have already discussed the curse of the god Frey's emissary Skirnir on the unwilling giantess in *Skirnir's Journey*, which climaxes with a somewhat obscure threat invoking physical misery, mental anguish, sterility, an appeal to supernatural powers and finally runes. With the production of the runic trump card, the giantess Gerd yields to Skirnir's entreaties and curses, agreeing to surrender her love to Frey. Runic love magic is also described in the Icelandic tale *Egil's Saga* where botched runes carved by a local youth to win the love of a Swedish maiden instead cause her to become ill. A humorous example of runic love magic is also described in some early Icelandic Sigmund poems: Ingrid is given a drink containing runes but instead gives it to a sow, which then becomes infatuated with the carver of the message.

In fact what appears to be an amorous charm with some kind of astrological aspect is carved on a twelfth-century rune-stick from Trondheim. This inscription opens with a futhark row, then mentions the zodiacal sign Leo, apparently as an indication of when the text was carved:

ᚷᚠᚦᚢᚯᚱᚴᚼᚾᛁᛆᛋᛏᛒᛘᛚᚤᛚᛅᛟᛚᛆᚧ
ᚦᛆᛏᛁᚱᚤᚦᚽᚦᚱᚿᛆᚱᚤᚦᚽᚦᚱᛁᛁ
ᚴᛁᚽ:ᚱᛏᛁᛌᚱᚿᛑᚼᚱᚦᛌᚼᚱ:ᚠᚱᛁᚼᚴᚧᛏᛘ

fþuorkhniastbmly. Leo lá.
Þat er mánaðr, vár mánaðrti(ð).
Kina (?) reist rúnar þessar frjákveld.

'*fþuorkhniastbmly*. (The sign of) Leo lay.
It is (the) month, our time of the month.
Kina (?) carved runes this eve of Friday (i.e. Thursday).'

---

[24] The Bergen sticks are N B192 and N B493; on the Swedish stick see Svärdström, *Runfynden i Gamla Lödöse*, pp. 21–22. The Oslo bone is N A36.

The text appears to have been carved by a woman, Kina or Kinna (perhaps a pet form of Kristina) while the sun was in Leo. The inscription was executed one Thursday night, the night which, in popular Scandinavian tradition, was considered favourable for occult practices and rites of divination. Although our understanding of Scandinavian astrology at this early time is somewhat sketchy, it appears not unlikely that the carver was using runes at an astrologically propitious time to win the favour of the man she loved.[25]

The runic finds from Bergen and the Anglo-Saxon poem also remind us of another possible indication that a text might be considered a magical charm: its poetic form. Verse, as well as being a mnemonic device, is often thought capable of increasing the potency of spells which, as the terms usually employed to describe magic indicate, were often chanted or sung. The writing of love poetry was forbidden in medieval Iceland, indicating the power such writing could be thought to have.[26]

In fact many of the medieval Scandinavian inscriptions that are amatory in nature were composed in recognisable poetic metres, or at least in stylised, verse-like language. The following twelfth-century rhyming text on a rune-stick from Bergen, shaped like a small paddle, also contains a direct appeal to a lover:

. . . ᚴᛅᚿᚴ:ᛁᛏᛣᛁᛁ:ᚦᛁᚱ:ᛋᛁᛣᚦᚢᛘᛅᚿᛏ:ᚱᚠᛣᛘ:ᛁᚠ:ᛣᛁᚱ:ᛁᛏᚼᚠ:ᛋᛣᛁᛣ:ᚿᛘ:ᚦᛁᚱ:ᚠᛣᚠᚿ:ᚿᛏᚱᛁᛣᛣᛁᚱ:ᚿ
. . .

. . . Kann ek segja þér, sem þú mant reyna af mér,
at ek skal unna þér engu verr enn mér. . .

'. . . I can say to you, as you will experience with me,
that I will love you no less than myself. . .'

Dating to about the year 1170, this inscription appears to be more than a simple love-letter or even a posy text. Poetic and clearly reciprocal, it may have been considered a magical inscription – it is even rhetorically comparable with the charm on the Bergen stick considered in the previous chapter which towards the end also commanded 'love me as you love yourself'. Not all poetic texts on rune-sticks have a similar claim to being considered magical though.[27]

A verse in the Eddic metre of *ljóðaháttr*, referring to the delights of love, is found on a four-sided stick from Bergen that has been dated to the late thirteenth century. Once containing up to 300 runes, this literary fragment is now sadly deficient and largely illegible, although part of one line provides a description of what appears to be a cosily intimate relationship:

. . .ᛁᛁᛣᛏᛁᚦᛁᛅᚦᚱᛁ:ᛁᛁᚿᚠᛁᚨᚱᛁ:ᛁᛏ.ᛁᚠᚦᛅᚦᛅᛁᛏᛅᚠᚠ.ᛏᚱᚿᛁᛏᛁᛅᛏᛅᚠᚠ.ᛁᛣᛁᛁ.ᚨᚠᚠᛅᚤᛁᛏᚨᛦᚠᛅᚱ:
ᛣ.ᛁᚤᛏᚦᛅᛁ.ᛁᚿᛁᚱᛣ.ᚿᚼᛁᚱ:ᛋᚠᚨᚦᛁᛁᛏᚦᛅ.ᚿᚤᚨᚠᛁᛁ

. . . *til fjǫrs.*

---

25 *NIyR* no. 815.
26 A. Holtsmark, 'Kjærlighetsdiktning', in J. Brøndsted et al. (eds), *Kulturhistorisk leksikon for nordisk middelalder*, 22 vols (Copenhagen 1956–78), VIII, pp. 438–43.
27 N B535.

Sæll ek þá þóttumk *er vit sátumk í hjá,*
ok komat okkar m(aðr) á meðal.
Yfir né undir *sakaðatk um okkart* [*ráð*?]

'. . . to life.

'Blessed I thought myself, when we sat together,
and no person came between us.
Neither above nor below (i.e. nowhere) did I say
about our (relationship) that . . .'

Despite being a piece of runic love poetry, this inscription betrays no clearly magical features. On the contrary, the text contains at least two lines strongly reminiscent of other pieces of verse known from Old Icelandic literary sources. The beginning of the first fully preserved half-line calls to mind the Eddic *Lay of Hamdir* (*Hamðismál*), where the fiendish Iormunrekk anticipates the death of two heroic brothers in the same terms: *Sæll ek þá þættumk / ef ek sjá knætta / Hamði ok Sǫrla / í hǫllu minni*, 'Blessed I would think myself / if I were to see / Hamdir and Sorli / in my hall.' The phrasing of the next part of the runic text is somewhat suggestive of a poem supposedly composed by Gisli Sursson at the burial mound of his slain friend Vestein: *Betr hugðak þá . . . Vésteini / þas vit í sal sátum / Sigrhadds við mjǫð gladdir, / komska maðr á miðli / mín né hans, at víni*, 'Better I thought it was . . . for Vestein / when we sat in the hall / of Sigerhadd, mead-happy, / and no man came between / me and him over the wine.' Unlike the preceding Bergen inscription, then, there is no real indication that we are dealing with a charm here other than that which any piece of love poetry may be thought to produce.[28]

Further fragments of what appear to be merely instances of Norse love poetry recur in runic texts. A fragmentary mid-thirteenth-century stick from Bergen originally bore three lines of runic verse in the elaborate skaldic metre *dróttkvætt*. Today, we can only read parts of it, with some difficulty:

'ᚽᛋᛏᚠᛋᛏ:ᛚᛋᚢ''ᛋᚽᛚᛋᛏᛋᛚᛁᚽᚠᚢᚽᛁᚱᚠᛦᚱᛁᚱᚢᚱ
---ᛋᛘ:ᚿ---ᚱᛯᛋ-ᛘᚿᚱᚠᛦᚱᛁᚱᛘᛋᚽᚽᛋᛘ. . .

Snót gat lausan láta,
Lín-Gunnr, fyrir ver [sín]um,
e[nn e]r hó[n]
mær fyrir mǫnnum . . .

'A wise one may let loose,
Battle-goddess, for her husband,
still she is
a maid for men . . .'

This text at first appears strange and riddling, but this is a feature characteristic of Norse poetry. *Lín-Gunnr* 'battle-goddess', for example, is a fairly unremarkable kenning or poetic paraphrase for 'woman' and the runic fragment appears merely to refer to the deceptive nature of women, not to any magical effect. Women's

28 Liestøl, 'Rúnavísur frá Björgvin', pp. 30–32; cf. idem, *Runer frå Bryggen*, pp. 35–37.

duplicity was a common theme in Norse wisdom texts, with the *Sayings of the High One* itself warning:

> The words of a girl no one should trust,
> nor what a woman says;
> for on a whirling wheel their hearts were made,
> deceit lodged in their breast.

A rough translation of the runic text might be, then: 'A clever woman may deceive her husband, yet still be regarded as a maid.'[29]

Despite the vast collection of verse warning of the treachery of the female sex, the *Sayings of the High One* nevertheless reveals that 'no sickness is worse for the wise man than to have no one to love him'. Unsurprisingly, unrequited desire, or unhappy love affairs, are also features of Norse inscriptions, surely as a reflection of the travails of medieval Nordic life. In one inscription, on a stick from Bergen dating to about the year 1300, after recording a routine mercantile transaction, the unhappy runic scribe complains in verse:

> ᚡᛆᚱ ᚴᛂᚿᚿᛁᚱ ᚢᛁᚱᛆ ᚢᛁᛏᚱ ᚢᚵᛚᛚᛆᚦᛆᚿ ˈᛁᛏᛁᛏᛆ
> ᛆᛁᚱ ᚿᛂᛘᚱ ᛆᚴᛏᛆᚴ ˈᛏᛆᚱᛆᛘ ᛆᛚᚢᚿᚿˈ ᚵᚱᚢᚿᚿᛏᛆᚱ ᛘᛁᚴ ᛒᛚᚢᚿᚿᛏᛁ

Vár kennir (mér) víra	*vitr úglaðan sitja.*
Eir nemr opt ok stórum	*ǫluns grundar mik blundi.*
'Wise Var of wire	makes (me) sit unhappy.
Eir of mackerels' ground	takes often and much sleep from me.'

Although a very difficult text full of poetic riddles, this nevertheless does not seem to constitute any kind of spell. Var was the Norse goddess of marriage and the kenning 'wise goddess of wire (i.e. filigree)' means simply 'wise (bejewelled) woman', so this line means 'women make me miserable', or perhaps 'marriage makes me miserable'. The other figure, Eir, is the goddess of healing and 'fish-ground' is probably a further kenning for gold. Thus 'goddess of the gold' appears to be another kenning for 'bejewelled woman', i.e. presumably women in general. The whole line is probably to be understood, then, as 'women often take a lot of sleep from me'. After all the ability of women, or tribulations in general, to deprive men of sleep is well attested in Germanic literature. There is even a runic puzzle cut into Bø church in Norway obviously based on this theme. It features lines based on the kennings for runic letter names which, when resolved, provide the answer to the puzzle's clue *svefn bannar mér*, 'prevents me sleeping': the woman's name Gudrun. Despite the complex word play and layered meanings, then, neither of these pieces of runic poetry complaining about women appears to be magical in nature.[30]

29 Liestøl, *Runer frå Bryggen*, pp. 32–33 and idem, 'Rúnavísur frá Björgvin', pp. 49–50.

30 This text and a number of literary analogies are discussed by J. Louis-Jensen, 'To halvstrofer fra Bryggen i Bergen', in J.R. Hagland et al. (eds), *Festskrift til Alfred Jakobsen* (Trondheim 1987), pp. 106–9, eadem 'Norrøne navnegåder', *Nordica Bergensia* 4 (1994), 35–52 and cf. Liestøl, *Runer frå Bryggen*, pp. 29–32, idem, 'Rúnavísur frá Björgvin', pp. 44–45 and Page, 'Icelandic rune-poem', pp. 31–32.

Obviously women caused hardship and aroused heartache for Scandinavian men, and indeed, even blatantly adulterous love is referred to in some metrical runic texts, although not in the manner of the leading charms from Bülach and Mautern. A late-twelfth-century rune-stick from Bergen describes the traditional lover's dilemma in the following manner:

ᛆ͡ᚿᚽᚴ'ᚢᛆ ᚴᛆᚿᛆᛘᛆᚿ'ᛆᛏᛘᚽᚱ:ᚦᛦᚴᛁᚴᛆᛚᛏᚱᚽᛚᛏᚱ⁝ᚽᚿᚽᚴᚽᛘᚢᛁᚿᚱ:ᚢᛁᚠ'ᚦᚽ'ᚢ͡ᛆ
ᛆ'ᛆ. . .

Ann ek svá konu manns,
at mér þykkir kaltr eltr.
En ek em vinr vífs þessa.
Ása . . .

'So do I love a man's wife
that even fire seems cold to me.
And I am a friend of this woman.
Asa . . .'

Similarly, an early-fourteenth-century rune-stick from Bergen reads:

✢ᛆᚿᚽᚴ:'ᚢᛆ: ᚴᛆ͡ᚿᛆ:ᛘᛆ͡ᚿᛋ:
ᚴᛁᚦᛆ:ᛏᛆᚴᛆ:ᚠᛁᛆᛚᛚ:ᚢᛁᚦ:ᛚᚽᚵᛁᚢᛘᚴ:'ᚢᛆ:ᚼᚢᚵᛁᛆ:ᚱᛁᚿᚵᚽᛁᚦᚱ:ᛆᛏ:
ᛁᛆ͡ᚱᚦ:'ᛒᚱᛁᚿᚵᚱ::ᚱᛆᛘᚽᚿ'ᛋᚴᛆᛚᛆᚦᚱᚽᚿᚽᚴᚼᛆ'ᚴᚵᚽᚼᛆᛘᚿᛆᚼᚢᛁᛏᚽᚱ'ᚢᛘᛁᛆᛚᛚᚽᚱᛚᛁᚵᚵᚱ

Ann ek svá konu manns
víða taka fjǫll við.
Leggjumk svá hugi á,
hring-reið, at jǫrð springr.
Hrafn skal áðr en ek
horskri hamna hvítr
er sú mjǫll er liggr.

'So much do I love a man's wife,
the wide mountains begin to sway.
We hold such a love for each other,
Ring-wagon (i.e. noble lady), that the world is rent asunder.
The raven shall become
white as the snow which lies
before I give up the wise (woman).'[31]

Although we can only guess at the physical or even reciprocal nature of the relationships alluded to here, these two texts are immediately reminiscent of the continental tradition of fine amour: an adulterous, although strictly unconsummated relationship between a knight and his lady. This central feature of the romantic tradition does not emerge in continental literature until the twelfth century, however; before that time women only appear as minor figures, as wives and daughters, in, for example, the eleventh-century *Chansons de geste* – they are never central characters, the heroes' objects of desire, until the appearance of the

31 The Bergen sticks are N B496 and N B644. Another apparently adulterous liaison is referred to in a rune-stick from Tønsberg, Norway, discussed in chapter 6.

court lyrics of the old French troubadours. These runic texts are quite unlike the almost woman-free world of Charlemagne's paladins or even the adulterous Sir Tristan of Beroul. Women are generally stronger characters in early Germanic tradition, but remarkably few episodes in Norse poetry fit so well into the world of Andreas Capellanus and Chrétien de Troyes as these runic love texts do.

Another love-triangle is apparent in the rather heart-rending proposal of marriage that appears on a rune-stick found under the floor of Lom stave church, Norway, with some of the runes scraped off, perhaps by the already affianced but presumably bewildered addressee Gudny. It reads:

-ᚼᚾᛅᚱᚦᛅᚱ:ᚼᛁᛋᛏᛁᚱ:ᚠᚤ------:ᚠ-ᚦᛅᚱᛁ:ᚠᚾᛁᚦᛁᚾ:ᛅᚱᛁᛁᚼᛏᚾᛁᚠᛅᚼ
ᛅᚠᚼᚾᛁᚱᚤᛁᛁᚠᚾᛁᚼᚱᚾᛁᚠᛁ:ᛁᛏ:ᛒᛁᚦᛁᛅᚦᛁᚼ:ᛁᚠᚦᚾᚾᛁᚱᛏ:ᛏᛁᛉᛁᚤᛁᚦ
. . .ᛒᛅᛁᛁᛁ:ᚾᛁᚱ-:----ᛁ:ᚦᛁᛁᚱᛅᚦ:ᛅᚠᛅᛅᛏᛁᛉᛁᛁᚤᛁᚱ
ᚦᛁᚼᚾᛁᚠᛁ

Hávarðr sendir Gu[ðnýiu] Guðs kveðju ok sína vingan.
Ok nú er minn fullr vili at biðja þín, ef þu vilt eigi með
[Kol]beini ver[a. Hug]a þitt ráð, ok lát segja mér þinn vilja.

'Havard sends Gudny God's greeting and his friendship. And now it is my full desire to ask for your hand, if you do not want to be with Kolbein. Think over your intentions, and have me told of your desire.'

Inscriptions such as these testify to the everyday nature of so much runic communication coexisting alongside the enduring use of runic writing in the magical sphere.[32]

A further inscription that is probably also to be grouped with amatory runic texts, this time both magical and malevolent, appears on a bone weaving-tablet from Lund, Sweden. An expression more reminiscent of the unrelenting tone of *Skirnir's Journey* and the obstreperous desire of the Bergen *skag*-valkyrie stick is this much-discussed curse from the Viking period which reads:

ᛋᛁᚵᚢᛅᚱᛅᛦ:ᛁᚱᛁ
ᛅᛁᚱ:ᛁᛘᛅ:
-ᛘᛁ:ᛘᛁ.ᚠᚱᛅᛏ.
ᛅᛅᛚᛚᛅᛏᛏᛁ:

Sigvaraʀ Ingimārr hafa [m]un minn grāt; aallatti.

'Sigvor's Ingimar shall have my weeping, *aallatti*.'[33]

The combination of runic curse and an object typically associated with women's work makes it clear that this is no posy text. But unlike the binding spells considered earlier, the intent of the curse is clearly not to hold or lead back a lover, or even to arouse desire, but instead to seek revenge – perhaps on another woman's lover if we read Sigvor's Ingimar as a genitive rather than a matronymic, i.e. 'Sigvor's (son) Ingimar'. We are reminded again of the *skag*-valkyrie and other

---

[32] A. Liestøl ' "Will you marry me?" under a church-floor', *Mediaeval Scandinavia* 10 (1977), 35–40.

[33] Or perhaps 'shall have my misery' (*mín grand*).

dangerous feminine magic that the man who created the Bergen text believed that women could effect against his charm or the malevolent valkyrie spell of the jealous Bergen witch. Old Norse literature is full of strong female characters whose powers enable them to render men impotent if spurned: much of the drama of the Icelandic classic *Njal's Saga*, for example, is initiated by Queen Gunnhild of Norway who famously sabotages her lover Hrut's marriage by rendering him unable to penetrate his exasperated wife.

The Lund text ends in an untranslatable sequence of runes, *aallatti*, seemingly a magic word or cry designed to unlock the magic of the spell, the transference of the sign of misery from the inscriber to her victim. It is possible that *aallatti* is a coded abracadabra-like charm word, the nature and origin of which will be dealt with more fully in the next chapter.[34]

A further expression of apparently jealous spite seems to be carved on a wooden beater from Bergen, the author here presumably a male:

ᛁᛚᛆᚼᛂᚠᛂᚱ᛫ᛆᛘᛆᚦᚱᛂᚱ-ᛂ-ᛂᚱ᛫ᛚᛁᚠᛆ ᚠᛆᚽᛆ᛫ᛂᛁᚽᛁᚢᛂᚱ. . .

Illa hefir sá maðr er hefir slíka konu . . .

'Evil take the man who has such a woman . . .'[35]

Similarly malicious sentiments may be expressed on a famous bone from Trondheim, previously translated as *Unn-ak mæyju, ek vilat rea Erlends fúla víf, ekkja hagaði*, 'I loved the maiden; I don't want to plague Erlend's hideous wife; as a widow she will be suitable for me' and indicating jealous ill-will towards the married Erlend. The reading, although widely cited, is perhaps somewhat fanciful in view of the sorry state of the object in question, from which few firm conclusions can now be drawn. A similarly questionable reading applies to a small rounded silver amulet belonging to the base of a button-shaped ornamental container from one of the graves at Birka, Sweden. Probably dating to the ninth century, it has the following mixture of long-branch and short-twig runes in boustrophedon text:

ᛆᚽᚼᚽᚴᚢᚴᛘᚢᛦᛆᛐ
ᚱᛁᚴ
ᚦᛆᛏᛁᚴᚢᚴᛘᚽᚼᚽᛆ
ᛋᚽᚴᛆᚱᚽᛐᚼᛁᛏᚦᚽ

A somewhat speculative interpretation of the Birka inscription, making use of ideographic readings, is: *Annomk ungm(enni) ūʀ atrek[i]. Þat ek ungm(enni) nāna sakaʀ at hitt þā.* This can loosely be translated as 'I drive the young man from his undertaking. This I magically pronounce (?) over the young man, because he has already achieved this (a part of his undertaking)', which is suggestive of an erotic context. The runes, placed on the top of the base and thus

34 Moltke, *Runes and their Origin*, pp. 358–60; older literature is cited under *DR* no. 311. This inscription, as well as the Trondheim bone (*NIyR* no. 461) discussed below were promoted by M. Olsen, 'Om troldruner', *Edda* 5 (1916), 225–45 in his (at the time) celebrated and influential exploration of rune magic.

35 N B552.

concealed from view were apparently not intended to be seen on this object, which may have been given as a gift. Pierced with three holes, it was perhaps intended to be worn riveted to a belt, a scabbard or some other daily item of apparel, its invisible runes working the effect desired by the inscriber, perhaps a woman hoping to turn the affection of a young man from a rival, or even a spurned male hoping his beloved will be unsuccessful with her new paramour.[36]

More clearly an amatory find, a rather perplexing verse replete with poetic paraphrase appears on a shaped mid-thirteenth-century rune-stick again from Bergen. Although its text, conforming to the strict *dróttkvætt* rules of rhythm and alliteration, is not fully understood and requires some degree of emendation, it was obviously written by a man in honour of the object of his desire, who in the inscription is alluded to as a 'beautiful, dangerous woman'. The runic poem can be read as follows:

ᚠᛂᛚᛚ᛫ᛏᛁᛚ᛫ᚠᚱᛁᚦᚱᛆᚱ᛫ᚦᛂᛚᛚᚢ᛫ᚠᛆᚱᛚᛂᚠᚼᚱᛆᚱ᛫ᛘᛂᚱ᛫ᛆᚱᛚᛆ᛫ᚠᛁ'ᚴᛆᛚᛚ᛫ᚠᛂ'ᛏᛁᛒᛆᛚᛆ᛫ᚠᛆᚱᚿ᛫ᛒᛦᚱᚼᛆᛘᛆᚱ
ᚿᛆᚱᚿᛆ᛫ᚦᛂᛁᛘᚢᛁᚼᛏᛁ᛫ᚼᛂᚢᛁᚱᚦᚢᚿᛏᛆᚱ᛫ᚦᛆᚱᚿᛚᚢᚦᚱ'᛫ᛂᛆᛚᚢᚿ᛫ᛒᚢᚦᛆᚱ᛫ᚵᛚᛆᚢᛘᛆᚱ᛫ᚠᛦᚵᚼᛁᛆᚱᛏᛆᚢᛘᛆ
ᚠᛆᛚᛏᚱ'ᚠᛆ'ᛚᛂᚵᚼᛆ᛫ᚼᛆᛚᛏᛂᛏ᛬ᛆᛘᚿᛁᛆ᛫ᚢᛁᚿᛋᛁᚦ᛫ᛆᛘᛆᚱ᛫ᛂᚦ᛫ᚿᛆ'᛫ᛋᛂᛏᛆᛘᚢ'᛫ᛆᛘᛆᚱᛁ᛫
ᚠᛆᛚᛏᚱ'ᚠᛆᛚᚠᚼᛆ᛫ᚼᛆᛚᛏᛂᛏ᛬ᛆᛘᚿᛁᛆ᛬ᚢᛁᚿ'ᛋᛁᚦ᛫ᛆᛘᛆᚱ᛫ᛂᚦᚿᛆ'᛫ᛋᛁᛏᛆᛘᚢ'᛫ᛆᛘᛆᚱᛁ᛫

Fell til fríðrar þellu
fárligrar mér árla
fiskáls festibála
forn byrr hamarnorna.

Þeim vigdi hefir Þundar
þornlúðrs jǫlunbúðar
glauma gýgjar tauma
galdrs fastliga haldit.

Omnia vincit amor, et nos cedamus amori.
(*galdrs fastliga haldit. Omnia vincit amor, et nos cedamus amori.*)

'The old wind of the Crag-Norns
turned early for me
to the beautiful, dangerous fir-tree
of the feast-bales of the fish-depths.

'To this blest (place) has Thund's
thorn-trumpets' *jǫlun*-booths (?)
bustle, of ogress reins
of incantation, tightly held (?).

'Love conquers all, and let us yield to love.
(of incantation, tightly held. Love conquers all, and let us yield to love.)'

Unlike the previous two texts filled with riddling phrases, this inscription specifically mentions magic; in fact it is somewhat reminiscent of the more clearly spell-like Bergen *skag*-valkyrie text. The paraphrase 'fish-depths' in the first verse means 'sea' and 'fir-tree of the feast-bales (of the fish-depths)' is an elaborate kenning for a woman (like the 'goddess of mackerels' ground' in the 'Wise Var' Bergen text discussed earlier). Thus the 'feast-bales (of the fish-depths)' represent '(sea) gold' and a 'fir-tree of gold' is a '(bejewelled) woman'. This

36 A. Nordén, 'Magiska runinskrifter', *Arkiv för nordisk filologi* 53 (1937), 147–87.

dangerous woman is also clearly an object of desire, which here is metaphorically described as the 'old wind of the Crag-Norns', a supernatural phenomenon beyond human control. This is reminiscent of Snorri's description in *Poetic Diction (Skaldskaparmál)*, the second part of his Eddic treatise: 'passion should be periphrased by calling it troll-women's wind'; or the poetry of Hauk Valdisarson from the end of the twelfth century, where desire is described as the 'dwelling of the crag-women'.

The second, even more complex verse has not yet been satisfactorily interpreted and the diversity of plausible kennings and textual emendations renders it difficult to arrive at a definite understanding of even the main idea of the verse. Thund is a byname of Odin (also attested in the *Sayings of the High One*) that probably means 'mighty', so we can speculatively assume that Thund's thorn could be a kenning for a spear or sword. Consequently we might interpret Thund's thorn-trumpet as a shield, if this is a reference to the sound spears or swords make when clashing against shields in combat (perhaps the incantation or magic song of the shield). This expression might be thought to evoke battle in general, then, and the blest place (or grove) of battle could feasibly be a warrior, perhaps a reference to the author of the text.[37]

Little can be taken for granted here, although the image of the ogress riding with serpent reins is familiar from depictions on rune-stones as well as the description of Balder's funeral in Snorri's *Prose Edda*. But what magic is holding tightly remains somewhat unclear. The *gýgjar glauma* could conceivably be the mount of the ogress (i.e. a wolf), her *tauma* 'reins' snakes. The 'booths', if they are interpreted as the dwelling-places of snakes (i.e. dragons), might then be thought to represent gold; so it has been suggested that the reference is to a gold-adorned *jǫlun* who has a tight hold over the warrior. Some scholars, in desperation, have sought to explain the word *jǫlun* away as a spelling mistake for *jǫtun* 'giant' or have compared it with *ǫlun* 'mackerel', making the *jǫlun*-booths, dwelling places of the *jǫlun*, a reference to the depths of the sea (cf. *ǫlun-grund*, *ǫlun-jǫrð*, 'the sea'). Together with an interpretation of thorn-trumpets as ships (the thorn representing the mast) and Thund of the ship as a kenning for a seaman, the image is consequently mooted in this interpretation as that of a sailor rather than a warrior held fast by love.

Most of this is speculation, however, and bottoms out in our ignorance of what *jǫlun* refers to. The word is attested only twice, once in this runic text and once in the erotic *skag*-valkyrie amulet considered in the previous chapter (there in reference to *jǫlun*'s misery). A *jǫlun* is clearly something that causes or experiences *jǫl-* or *jǫll*, and the unwelcome *jǫll* brought by Loki in the mythological tale *Loki's Quarrel* is usually interpreted as some sort of strife or unease. It seems

37 We have chosen to trust the text and not emend ᚢᛁᚼᛐᛁ to *lundi* (although expected internal rhyme with *Þundar* may indicate this was the term in the original composition), but accept that it is a derived form of *vígja* 'to bless' which might have been a homonym to *lundr* '(sacred) grove' at any rate. The Crag-Norn text is discussed in Liestøl, *Runer frå Bryggen*, pp. 27–29, idem, 'Rúnavísur frá Björgvin', pp. 40–43 and, with differing interpretations, in A. Liestøl et al., 'Dróttkvætt-vers fra Bryggen i Bergen', *Maal og minne* (1962), 98–108; cf. also Marold, 'Runeninschriften als Quelle', pp. 688–90.

plausible, then, given the amatory context, that *jǫlun búðar* refer to hearts. But it is not only the mention of the inexplicable *jǫlun* which is reminiscent of the women's magic of the Bergen inscription; where Bergen had valkyries, ogres, elves and trolls, here we have Crag-Norns, a dangerous woman and an ogress's serpent reins. If we interpret the woman more literally as a dangerous sea-woman (rather than a woman with sea-gold, i.e. jewellery), she is also vaguely reminiscent of the sea-maid referred to in a Greenlandic charm discussed at the end of the chapter.

The verse does not seem to be a narrative charm based on identifiable mythic figures, but rather to centre on the hold the love of the dangerous woman had over the author of the text – the widespread medieval motif of love for an otherworldly woman has also been identified here. A loose interpretation of the poem might be, then: 'the valiant author's heart is spellbound by his love of a beautiful, dangerous woman'.

The text concludes with the Latin phrase 'love conquers all, and let us yield to love', a line which is repeated underneath, probably in a different, less practised hand. This phrase is a well-known quotation from Virgil's *Eclogues*, the first part of which is found in a further two runic inscriptions. The incomplete citation appears on a thirteenth-century perforated rune-stick and in decorative double-outline runes on an embroidered shoe, both from Bergen.[38] The phrase was popular in medieval love poetry and Virgilian verse often appeared on ancient love-amulets. Presumably, then, the Crag-Norn text constitutes a complex poem meant as some sort of love charm, a suggestion perhaps supported by the switch to Latin, a foreign and hence exotic language. After all, Virgil was admired during the Middle Ages not only for his poetry but also for his perceived magical prowess. The intrusion of a Latin phrase, however, must be viewed in the light of some other runic inscriptions which feature selections of Latin love poetry.[39]

A fragmentary but nevertheless more familiar poem, entirely in Latin this time, is found on another rune-stick from Bergen. The runes are clear and well formed, and cover three sides:

. . . ᚵᚱᛂ: ᚵᛁᛂ:ᛁᚵᚿᛁ:ᛒᚢᛌ:ᚴᛆ͡ᛚᛂᛌᚴᚮ:ᛂᛁᚢᛌ: ᚴᚮᛏᛁ:ᛏᛁᛂ:ᛁᚿᛆᛘ͡ᚮᚱᛂ:ᚵᚱᛂᛌ:ᚴᚮ. . .
. . .ᛌ:ᛆᚵᛆᛘ:ᛏᛂᚿᛂᚱᛁ:ᚢᛁᚱᚵᚮ:ᛌᛁᚴ.ᛆᚵᛆᛘᚢᛌ:ᛆᛘᛒᚮᛌ:ᛌᚢᛘᚢᛌ. . .
. . .ᛐ--ᛆ:ᛚᚢᛌᛁᛌ:ᛆᚵᚮᚿᛂ:ᚤᛁᛚᚢᛘ.ᛂᛘᛆ:ᚴᚢᛂᚱᚢᛚᛁ:ᛏᛂᚱᛁᛆᚱ. . .

[Virginis e]gregie	*ignibus calesco*
(et) eius cotidie	*in amore cresco . . .*
	. . .s agam teneri
virgo sic agamus	*ambos sumus . . .*

[38] The rune-stick is *NIyR* no. 605, the shoe N B605. The text is also found in Roman letters on an oaken reliquary box, *NIyR* no. 303, where it follows a Latin ABC, a sign that the quotation may be being used in an amuletic manner, as well as on two small buckles from Old Lödöse, Sweden; see P.H. Rosenström, 'Nya medeltidsundersökningar i gamla Lödöse', *Västergötlands fornminnes-förenings tidskrift* (1963), 259–85.

[39] D. Comparetti, *Vergil in the Middle Ages*, trans. E.F.M. Benecke, 2nd ed. (London 1908) and J. Wood, 'Virgil and Taliesin', *Folklore* 94 (1983), 91–104. See also C.A. Faraone, 'Taking the "Nestor's cup inscription" seriously', *Classical Antiquity* 15 (1996), 83ff., on the ancient use of poetry in magical charms.

| . . .n--a | lusis agone. |
| Philomena querule | Terea r[etractat] . . . |

'For the beautiful girl	I burn with love.
And every day	my love for her grows . . .
	. . . I may drive tenderly
My love, let us do it so	we are both . . .
	. . . in jest, with agony.
Philomena lamenting	struggles with Tereus . . .'

Despite the mention of the classical mythological characters Philomena (usually Philomela) and Tereus, this inscription is clearly no narrative charm. Instead, the incomplete text obviously represents a love poem comprising elements from at least two different known poems. Two sections are paralleled in the famous poetic anthology known as the *Carmina Burana*, a thirteenth-century codex stemming from a Benedictine monastery in Bavaria, although versions of many of the poems found in it are also known from other medieval continental collections, and are probably the work of the wandering scholars and clerics of the twelfth and thirteenth centuries.

Fragments of the *Carmina Burana* poem *Amor habet superos* (*Love Holds the Living*) recur in the first and second lines of the inscription, although the runic text is closer (though still slightly different) to a variant version of the poem found in a Florentine manuscript. Fragments from two stanzas of *Axe Phebus aureo (Phoebus from the Golden Sky)*, another poem from the *Burana* codex, can also be recognised in the final line.

Phoebus from the Golden Sky, a lament over the tribulations of love, alludes to the classical myth of Philomela, whose tongue was cut out after she was raped by Tereus, but who revenged herself on her ravisher by weaving her story into a tapestry and was subsequently changed into a sweet-singing nightingale. The runic version was carved in around 1300, and, although deficient in parts, does not appear to be amuletic at all, but is instead a proud testimony to the remarkable exchange of language and literature between Bergen and the rest of Europe at this time.[40]

It is in this context, then, that another poetic fragment in Latin, this time without known parallels, found on a thirteenth-century stick from Bergen, should be seen. The text begins in Norse:

ᚻᛁᚠᚿᛁᚼᚿᛆᚱᛁᚠ. . .
ᚿᛁᚴᛆᚱ:ᛁᛘᛁᚼᛁᛏᚼ :ᚠᛏᛆᛁ:ᛁᛘᛆᚱᛁᛁ

Alinn var ek . . .
Decor amenitas, flos amoris.

'I was born . . .
A charm of delightfulness, a flower of love.'

The presumably unfinished opening line is reminiscent of the beginning of one of King Harald Hardradi's poems from *Songs for Pleasure* (*Gamanvísur*), variants

---

40 The runic Latin stick is *NIyR* no. 603; the poems are *Carmina Burana*, nos 88 and 71.

of which are found in three Icelandic manuscripts, as well as of a nearby four-teenth-century Bergen rune-stick (*Alinn var ek þar er alma Upplendingar bendu*, 'I was born where the men of the Uplands bent their bows'). The language of the present inscription then switches to Latin, apparently beginning a love lyric of some kind. What we seem to have here, then, is a poetry-loving bilingual at work, who was probably influenced by continental literature (although the poetic imagery could also conceivably be a reference to the Virgin).[41]

On the other hand we have at least one example of a runic Latin love amulet, one that was found at the old monastery and hospital of Æbelholt, Denmark. Made of bone and broken in three places, it dates to about the first half of the thir-teenth century and bears the following fragmentary, at least substantially Latin text:

ᛏᛦᛆᚱᚠᛦᛦ:ᛁᚱ...ᚦᚴᛁᚱᛦᛆ:ᚼᛏᛏᚱ:ᛏ-...
ᛏᚦᛆᛁᚿᚱᛆ:ᚿᛆᚼ:...ᚱ:ᚼᛏᚱᛆᚱᛆᚠ.ᚠᛏᚼᛏᛏᛁᚱᛏᚠᚱ...

Amorem el. . . þhækko staar t. . .
ago auro vos. . .l sanroron gasdaer ang. . .

'Love . . . with gold I drive you . . . ang(el?) . . .'

It is difficult to say precisely what this inscription means in its present state. The text probably represents a love charm of some kind, presumably rendered (at least partly) in Latin to increase its potency. Another amuletic text, this time on a piece of lead, was also found at the same site, but it only seems to contain nonsense words such as *hilch. . . hlþoh. . . . horþl*, which seem a lot like those often found in medieval healing charms. Perhaps some of the sequences on the first text, then, may also represent similar abracadabra-like gibberish. There is nothing surprising about finding love charms in monasteries: we might recall papal complaints from the time about the clergy preparing love potions and practising wizardry, or the partly cryptic text carved into a small rune-stick found in Urnes stave church in Norway, apparently informing us that *Arni prestr vill hafa Ingu*, 'Arni the priest wants to have Inga.' The amuletic nature of the first Æbelholt text could suggest, however, that some of the other fragments of Latin love poetry carved in runic letters may also represent love charms; after all the context of the Æbelholt inscription is all that clearly indicates it is an amulet today, not neces-sarily its content. At any rate it seems safe to contend that the use of the Latin quote from Virgil also added some mystery to the Crag-Norns love text described above, strengthening the impression that this mostly otherwise quite unparalleled inscription was intended to be some sort of enchantment.[42]

A curious text that seems to have a more clearly magical content is what is apparently a Norse spell which recurs in various forms on runic sticks found in Bergen and even as far afield as Greenland. Three rune-sticks seem to contain corruptions of a text, with an alliterative pattern based on the sound *s*, that refers

---

[41] *NIyR* no. 606 and cf. N B88. See also K.F. Seim, 'Runic inscriptions in Latin', in A. Herteig et al. (eds), *The Bryggen Papers, Supplementary Series 2* (Bergen 1988), pp. 24–65.

[42] For the Æbelholt amulet see Moltke, *Runes and their Origin*, pp. 490–91. The Urnes stick is *NIyR* no. 337.

to a seated *snót úljóta*, 'lovely lady' or *konu vena*, 'beautiful woman'. Nonetheless, these inscriptions have been compared with nonsense lines similar to the English nursery rhyme about the sailor 'who went to sea, and what did he see? He saw the sea.' Runic tongue twisters such as this occur, for instance, on two rune-sticks from Bergen and one from Trondheim:

ᛉᚦᛆᛐᛁᛑᛁᛐᚼᛁᚱᛁᛁᛑᛁᛐᛁᛁᚴᛁᛐᛁᚼᛁᚱᛁᛁᛑᛁ ᛁᛁᛚ . .

Hvat sá sá, er í sá sá? Sik sá sá, er í sá sá . . .

'What did he see, who saw in the tub? Himself he saw, who saw in the tub!'[43]

The following examples refer to women, however, and seem to represent some sort of amatory rather than semantically empty expression of word play. The earliest and most complete version of the charm is found in Narsaq (close to Erik the Red's Brattahlíð), Greenland, along with a complete futhark row and several unidentifiable cryptic runes or repeated runic characters. Carved on a lumpy long stick of pine whose knotted surface gives it a rather dragon-like appearance, its four sides are covered in runes or rune-like scratches, the main part of which may be read:

ᛓᛆᛁᛁᛆᛁᛁ ᛁᛐ ᛁᛁᛆᛁᛆᛁᛁᛐᛐᛒᚼᚴᚱᛐᚿ ᛉᛁᛐᛁᚱᛁᛦᛐᚱᛁᛁᚿᛁᛁᛁ ᛁᛁᚱᛁᛆᛁᚼᛐᚼᛁ . . .
ᚠᚿᚦᛆᚱᚴᛉᚼᛁᛐᛁᛦᚤᛐ
ᛐᛐᛐᚠᚷᚷᚷ.ᚷᚷᚷᚷᚷᚷ.ᚷᚷᚷ.ᚷᚷ.ᛐᚷᚷᚷᚷᚷᛐᛐᛐᛐᛐᚷᚷᚷ.ᚷᚷᚷ.ᚷᚷᚷ.ᚷᚷᚷ.ᚷᚷᚷ.ᚷᚷᚷᚷ

Á sœ, sœ, sœ,
es Ása sat.
Bibrau (?) heitir mær sú
es sitr á bláni
fuþorkhniœstbmlʀ aaal. . . aaaaa. . .

'On the sea, sea, sea,
where Asa sits.
Bibrau (?) is the name of the maid who
is sitting on the blue . . .'

The stick can be confidently dated to the late tenth or early eleventh century. The text is rather mystifying, although as translated here it is vaguely reminiscent of the verse in *Vafthrudnir's Sayings* (*Vafþrúðnismál*): 'Corpse-swallow is his name, who sits at the end of the heavens, a giant in eagle's shape.' Obviously based on assonant word play of some kind, the text has a range of possible meanings and seems to constitute a rather primitive kind of verse, perhaps a play on the words *á sœ* 'on the sea' and *Ása*, which, although translated above as the woman's name Asa, could instead be read as a reference to the gods (another plausible translation runs *es Ása sát*, 'the watch-seat of the Æsir').[44]

---

43 N B566, N B617 and *NIyR* no. 825; cf. J.E. Knirk, 'Learning to write with runes in medieval Norway', in I. Lindell (ed.), *Medeltida skrift- och språkkultur* (Stockholm 1994), pp. 196–97.

44 The Narsaq stick was first published by E. Moltke, 'En grønlandsk runeindskrift fra Eirik den rødes tid', *Tidsskriftet Grønland* (1961), 401–10, who tentatively identified a magic formula in epic form against sea- and weather-demons. It is further discussed (including jocular 'tongue-twister' interpretations) by M. Stoklund, 'Objects with runic inscriptions from Ø 17a',

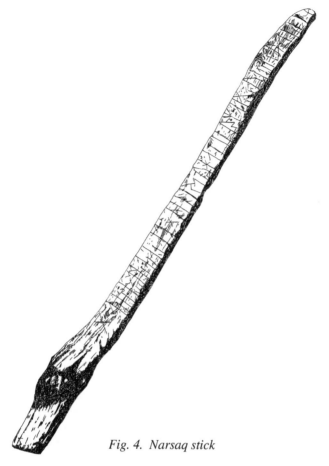

Fig. 4. Narsaq stick

A rune-stick from Bergen contains a longer, similar inscription, only the last part of which is relevant here (the rest, which includes a narrative concerning the apostle Andrew, is discussed in the chapter on Christian amulets). In an apparent juxtaposition of pagan and Christian elements, the text concludes with the runes:

ᛁᛏᛁᛏᛨᛁᛏᛁᛏᛈᛄᛖᚾᛁᛖ:ᛁᚦᚾ:ᚼᚾᛄᛦ:ᛁᛁᛏᛁᛦ:

Sé, sé, Sessi. Sé konu væna. Sé þú hvar sittir.

'See, see, Sessi. See the beautiful woman. See where she sits.'

Comparable with these is yet another stick from Bergen, of which only the following runes can be made out:

Meddelelser om Grønland 18 (1993), 47–52. Moltke, comparing it with the Norse rainbow bridge Bifrost, reads the name as Bifrau (Bifrey, Bifró) and the final word as the name (in the dative) of the giant Bláinn, whose skull formed the vault of heaven. The ambiguity of the main runic message is demonstrated by H. Guðmundsson, 'Rúnaristan frá Narssaq', *Gripla* 1 (1975), 188–94.

ᛋᛅᛋᛁ.ᛋᛁ.ᛋᛅᛋᛋᛁ.ᛋᚾᚮᛏ ᚢᛚᛁᚮᛏᛅ

Sessi. Sé, Sessi, snót úljóta.

'Sessi. See, Sessi, the lovely lady.'

The variance between the three attestations of this expression suggest that this is not a round or saying, much as does the appearance of the futhark row, the rune-like symbols and even a Christian narrative in conjunction with these texts. In fact, without the references to beautiful women, these might even be compared with a further Bergen rune-stick discussed in more detail in chapter 8 which also has a Christian reference and a magical symbol. It reads: *sisesisisesil sisiþaniralat. Dixit Dominus Domino, sede a dextris meis, 'sisesisisesil sisiþaniralat.* The Lord said unto (my) Lord, sittest thou at my right hand.'

The see-see sequence seems, then, to be a charm, although what exactly it was supposed to achieve is unclear. It is somewhat reminiscent of a narrative charm, though the figure Bibrau is otherwise unknown. There are magical manuscript parallels to the repeated use of the *s*-sound, and the combination of *sé, sé,* etc., the futhark row and references to a beautiful woman still remain strongly suggestive of love magic at work.[45]

Love magic of all kinds, designed to attract or secure affection, or doom despised lovers, thus appears to have been practised by Scandinavian rune-carvers. The range extends from simple appeals for affection to curse formulations, often augmented by poetry, foreign language or even magic words and sounds. There is nothing so formal as the runic leading charms from the Continent among the Scandinavian finds – these formulaic texts instead seem to be products of contact with the magical tradition of the Graeco-Roman world. The Merovingian *leub* amulets also appear to represent a local development not paralleled in the North, though their context – on items such as women's jewellery and a distaff – is reminiscent of those of the Whitby spindle-whorl, the Lödöse weaving-knife and the weaving-tablet from Lund. In contrast, Scandinavian men and perhaps Anglo-Saxons, too, seem to have preferred objects more typically associated with writing, i.e. rune-sticks, to record their charms of love, whereas amatory finds of clearly masculine context seem absent altogether from the Continent. The Scandinavian finds seem much more varied and even sometimes rather more sophisticated, too, however, and probably represent a different magical approach to affairs of the heart.

---

45 The Bergen rune-sticks are *NIyR* no. 628, N B404 and N B524. The last reads perhaps instead *Sé, sé, sé, Sessi, snót úljóta,* 'See, see, see, Sessi, the lovely lady' or *Sessi! Sé Sissi (Cecelia), snót úljóta* etc., and is briefly discussed in Liestøl, 'Rúnavísur frá Björgvin', pp. 46–47. For manuscript parallels (e.g. *sisisill bivivill; sa sa sa sa sa salutem in domino sa*) see Guðmundsson, p. 190, n. 4 and compare a piece of bone from Trondheim, *NIyR* no. 824, with the following runes: *isisa isisa.*

4

Protective and Enabling Charms

Victory-runes you shall know if you want to have victory,
and carve them on the sword hilt,
some on the mid-ridges, some on the battle-marks,
and name Tyr twice.

THIS is one of the rune-lore stanzas from the Eddic tale the *Lay of Sigrdrifa*. It describes the use of 'victory-runes' in what seems a clear description of an amuletic employment of runes, i.e. using them to create a magic sword. In fact 'victory-runes' (*sigrúnar*), or at least 'battle-runes' (*valrúnar*, *wælrūn*), are mentioned several times in both Old Norse and Old English literary sources, although not in circumstances that make it clear what they actually are. A similar description is also known from the Old English poem *Solomon and Saturn*, however, where we are told 'On his weapon he inscribes a host of battle-marks (*wælnota*), baleful book-staves, (and) bewitches the blade in sword-fame.' The Eddic *Skirnir's Journey* also at one point describes a sword as *málfár* 'counsel-adorned' and another seemingly related practice is described in *Beowulf*, where an owner's name is found inlaid in golden runes on the crosspiece of a sword reputedly forged by giants (i.e. one with a supernatural connection). Moreover, the practice of inscribing runes, especially names, on a sword's pommel, hilt or blade presumably in order to make it a better weapon is attested in several early English inscriptions.[1]

The best known inscription of this sort is probably the one that appears on a short sword, a scramasax, found over a century ago in the River Thames. Now in the British Museum, the ninth-century scramasax is roughly contemporary with both *Solomon and Saturn* and the Old Norse *Lay*, and the inscription on its blade reads:

ᚠᚢᚦᚩᚱᚳᚷᚹᚻᚾᛁᛄᛇᛈᛉᛋᛏᛒᛖᛗᛚᛝᛞᚪᚫᚣᛠ ᛒᛖᚪᚷᚾᚦ

---

[1] Cf. Markey, 'Studies in runic origins 2', pp. 141ff. It has also been suggested that the golden runes of *Beowulf* may not be of this type, but rather continue a tradition also found in the Old French *Roman de Brut* where Charlemagne's sword Joyeuse is similarly described as 'marked with golden letters'; see T. Snædal Brink and J.P. Strid, 'Runfynd 1981', *Fornvännen* 77 (1982), 239. K. Düwel, 'Runes, weapons and jewellery,' *The Mankind Quarterly* 22 (1981), 69–91, would extend this scepticism to the 'victory runes' of the *Lay of Sigrdrifa* too, although ignoring the clear English evidence from a similar date.

Fig. 5. Lindholmen amulet

fuþorcgwhnij3pxstbŋdlmœœayea Be͡agnoþ.

The name Beagnoth is the only part of this text that is linguistically meaningful – the rest of the inscription is a futhark row, much as appears on the Charnay brooch and several of the Norse amatory inscriptions. As in the leading charms and other amatory finds, the scramasax's runic equivalent to an ABC clearly has an amuletic or magical function and it seems fairly obvious what effect an amuletic inscription on a sword-blade might have been thought to have. But what was the significance of futhark rows? Texts of this type, of course, are not restricted to weapons. Similar early runic inscriptions occur on other items, but often the kind of magical effect they were supposed to have is not as obvious as appears to be the case here or in an amatory find.[2]

Another example of a text like this was found in a place known as Lindholmen, in Denmark, in the middle of the nineteenth century. It is a piece of bone worked more-or-less into the form of a crescent-shaped serpent or fish and it can obviously only be an amulet. It carries a similar inscription to that on the Thames sword-blade, except that the runes do not form a proper futhark row, but given their length and grouping, rather only suggest one. The fifth-century amulet's inscription, whose runes are written with tripled staves and strokes, reads:

ᛖᚲᛖᚱᛁᛚᚨᚷᛊᚨᚹᛁᛚᚨᚷᚨᚺᚨᛏᛖᚲᚨ᛬
ᚠᚠᚠᚠᚠᚠᚠᚨᚨᚨᚨᛉᛉᛉ᛬ᛒᛗᚢᛏᛏᛏ᛬ᚨᛚᚢ᛬

Ek Erilaz Sawilagaz ha(i)teka.
aaaaaaaazzznnn[n]bmuttt alu.

'I am called Earl Sunny, . . . dedication.'

Once again, then, this amulet inscription is essentially a name (expanded into a full naming sentence), with an assortment of 21 runic letters arranged into some sort of pattern or code, one often compared with the Lund weaving-tablet's more pronounceable-looking final sequence *aallatti*. The Lindholmen inscription also includes a further element, however, a term *alu*, which is also found in combination with the pagan goddess Nanna's name on the Setre comb, though which, just like *lauk* 'leek' (or its early Germanic form *laukaz*), is commonly found on early runic amulets. But what was the purpose of the Lindholmen amulet? The Thames scramasax inscription was clearly engraved in order to make the sword it is on

2 Page, *Introduction*, pp. 80 and 113.

more powerful; so was the Lindholmen amulet supposed to be a lucky charm? Or did it, like the copper amulet from South Kvinneby, perhaps have something to do with fishing or sailing instead? It is impossible to tell now, without any more context, if the Lindholmen amulet was supposed to help its bearer to avoid some misfortune or whether it was supposed to make it easier for its owner to achieve something such as a better catch. Both the Thames scramasax inscription and that on the Lindholmen amulet do, however, belong to an amulet type whose essential features can be analysed, even if the precise purpose of the text, whether it is to protect the owner from something, or to enable the user to do a thing (or do it better), is not always immediately clear.[3]

There are several rune-inscribed items of a similar type where a non-amatory purpose is expressed, however, some of which are clearly intended to enable the user of the item to do something better, others which instead are protective. Many of the clearest carry only short texts, are found on Germanic brooches and come from the European Continent. Despite their brevity and the variation in items upon which they are found, they all seem to represent a formulism comparable to that of the Thames and Lindholmen finds, and they are also reminiscent in some aspects of the repeated last line of the Setre comb inscription described in chapter 2. A system can be discerned behind this formulism, and uncovering and explaining it will be the main focus of this chapter.

In 1885 two long silver bow brooches were excavated from a find site in Hungary near a small village called Bezenye. The find location indicates that the rune-inscribed items are probably of Lombard manufacture – the Lombards were still living on the Pannonian plains at the time these fine mid-sixth-century brooches were made; they did not invade Italy until the year 568. The inscriptions on the brooches are inscribed on the back of their bows; their contents are somewhat similar and read, respectively:

ᚷᛟᛞᚨᚺᛁᛞ
ᚢᚾᛃᚨ

Godahi(l)d (w)unja.

'Godahild, joy.'

ᚨᚱᛊᛁᛒᛟᛞᚨ
ᛊᛖᚷᚢᚾ

Arsiboda segun.

'Arsiboda, blessing.'

Like the German *leub* inscriptions, these are laconic amulet texts wishing their owners, both Lombard women, joy and blessing respectively. Their essential form is a name plus a special or magical word, and though the wishes these words indicate appear to be Christian in sentiment, they are found here in texts that are

3 Krause with Jankuhn, no. 29. On Lindholmen *Sawiligaz* (not *sā Wīligaz*) and *erilaz* 'earl' (and not 'Herulian' or 'rune-master' as is often supposed), see Mees, 'Runic **erilaR**'.

nothing like those usual for amulets of the Gnostic tradition or any other known early Christian type.[4]

Some similar inscriptions are also known from Germany and may also represent finds from early Germanic Christian contexts. One such example was found on a brooch unearthed in the late nineteenth century near Bad Ems, on the River Lahn. It is a late-sixth-century find, it probably belonged to a Frank, and its legend, obviously scratched into the back of its 'bow' some time before its owner died, reads:

ᛗᚨᛞᚨᛚᛁ
ᚢᛒᚨᛞᚨ

Madali um(bi)bada.

'Madali, protection.'

We do not know whether the Bad Ems brooch came from a man's or woman's grave, but Madali is a man's name, and given the usual practice evidenced in these and the *leub* inscriptions is being followed here, he was probably the owner of the amulet. At first the amulet text seems quite sinister, however, as *umbada*, the most obvious reading, would be the negative of *bada* 'comfort' (a term related to English *bed*), i.e. 'discomfort'. Another German runic find, unearthed in the 1960s, bears a similar message, however, pointing to a spelling error (haplography) in the inscription, i.e. *umbada* for *um(bi)bada* 'safety, protection'.[5]

The other *bada* inscription, also found on a bow brooch, dates to the mid-sixth century and was discovered in the early 1970s in a woman's grave near the German town of Kirchheim unter Teck. After the term *bada*, the inscription is quite difficult to read, but it does contain a decorative, triple-branched *a*-rune, a form which is generally only used to highlight names, so presumably we are dealing with a woman's name beginning with *H* here. What can clearly be read is the following:

✕
ᛒᚨᛞᚨᚺᛁᚱᛁ
ᛉᛗᛁᛚ

✕ *Bada H. . .*

'Comfort, H.'

The name might have been Hlaidmiu, but the inscription is very worn so it is hard to be sure. A cross-like shape can also be made out above the inscription, though rather than an inclined Maltese cross it may once have been a swastika or other pre-Christian symbol of some sort.[6]

There is clearly a tendency, then, for short, early runic texts to exhibit the terse, on first acquaintance presumably elliptical (or insufficiently explicit), type also

---

4   Krause with Jankuhn, no. 166.
5   Ibid., no. 142.
6   Looijenga, p. 247.

seen in several of the *leub* inscriptions. In fact the names and amulet function words can also on occasion appear as part of slightly more loquacious expressions much as the Lindholmen amulet contains a fuller naming phrase. These longer texts usually remain laconic in some manner or another, however, suggesting that they are expansions, not fuller forms which the terser instances are based upon. For instance one way such a text can appear less brief, but still retain its terseness, is when it features another linguistically intelligible element, as in the following example.

A Norse inscription similar to the German *bada* texts is also known from medieval Dublin. Found during an excavation at Fishamble Street, it is written on a piece of deer antler and is carved in younger long-branch runes. It probably dates to the early eleventh century and reads:

ᚼᚢᚱᛏ:ᚼᛁᛏᚱᛏᛅ:ᛚᛏ:ᛏᚢᛋᛏᛅ

Hurn hiartaʀ, lá, Aussaʀ.

'Hart's horn, protection, Aussaʀ.'

The term *lá* (earlier *hlé*) used here is related to English *lee*, a word originally meaning 'shelter, protection' although now it is usually restricted only to a nautical sense (lee side, lee shore). The Dublin text also introduces an element not found in the continental brooch inscriptions considered so far, however, a description of the item upon which it is found, a feature which crops up fairly regularly in other runic amulet finds.[7]

Another Norse protection inscription, this time from Strand, Norway, also makes reference to the item upon which it is carved. A clearly pre-Christian text, it features another apparent extension of the usual laconic type though – the inclusion of an abbreviated 'is' (a copular verb), linking the item description and the amulet-function word. A bit less terse, then, than the continental or Dublin finds, it appears on a brooch dating to about the year 700 and its legend runs:

ᚾᛁᚠᛚᛁᚾᛏᚼᚼᛁ

Sigli (i)s ná-hlé.

'Brooch (i)s corpse-protection (i.e. against the walking dead).'[8]

Another simple way in which a laconic amulet text of this type could appear more like a normal sentence is by the inclusion of a demonstrative 'this'. Such an expansion is probably to be seen in the text found on a now-corroded lead ring unearthed in the nineteenth century from a grave at Coquet Island, Northumberland. Featuring a Maltese cross, it is only known today through drawings and is undated, but it seems formerly to have read:

✠ᚦᛁᚼᛁᚼᚼᛁᛗᚠ--ᚱ-ᚷᚷ

---

[7] Moltke, *Runes and their Origin*, pp. 363–65; M. Barnes et al. (eds), *The Runic Inscriptions of Viking Age Dublin* (Dublin 1997), no. 12.
[8] Krause with Jankuhn, no. 18.

✢*Þisi sciel[d?]. . .*

'This shield (?). . .'

The full Anglo-Saxon text may never be recoverable, but after the cross we are clearly dealing with a demonstrative 'this'. The following text is fragmentary but the sequence *sciel. . .* may once have stood for Old English *sciell* 'shell' or *scield* 'shield' (or perhaps even *scielan* 'shall' or the like), and thus appears to have been either a metaphorical description of the ring as a protective item, or a charm function word signifying the same.[9]

These texts also appear to be paralleled by a further, significantly wordier pre-Christian runic amulet legend. This time, however, two of the basic elements seem to have been linked and expanded upon in a much more eloquent manner. The longest early runic inscription that is often thought to mention protection appears on a wood-plane, i.e. a wooden weapon-sharpener, that was found over a century ago in the Vimose bog. Made of ash and broken in three, the originally 30.5cm-long Vimose plane is a little earlier than the apparently Gothic brooch described in chapter 2 that was also found there. Its archaeological context indicates that the weapon-sharpener dates to about the year 200, though its runes, unfortunately, are not all as clearly legible:

ᛏᚨᛚᚷᛁᛃᛟ
ᚷᛁᛋᚨᛁᛟᛃ᛬ᛈᛁᚱᛁᛃᚺᛚᚨᛟ---
ᛏᛁᛒᛁᛋᚺᛏᛗᚨᛏᛟ᛬ᚻᛏ-᛬ᚱᛗᚷᚢ

Talgijō. Gisaiōj wiliz hlao. . . (?) tibins.
Hleunō an[a]regu.

'Plane. Spearman, you may want . . . offerings.
Protection (?), I counsel.'

This inscription is reminiscent of a narrative charm, but there are several problems that make it difficult to interpret, both in terms of meaning and reading. It clearly begins with a laconic description of the item it appears on, much as in the Dublin find. And though the spelling of the second term has been scrambled slightly, it appears to read *gaisijō* 'spearman' – presumably a designation for the owner of the wood-plane if not his nickname. The words immediately following the verb *wiliz* 'you may want' are also difficult to read as this part of the plane is only poorly preserved, but *tibins* 'offerings' on the next line seems to be what is wanted (i.e. the verb's object). It is obvious that this part of the text is some sort of narration, one perhaps even being 'told' by the wood-plane. It may be that the plane is suggesting 'though you may want booty O warrior, I only give protection'. At the very least we seem to have a second element typical of runic amulet inscriptions, a name, expanded and linked with a word describing the function of the item.

A further difficulty that arises, though, is that much like modern English *lee*, early Germanic *hleunō* had more than one meaning; apart from 'protection',

9   Page, *Introduction*, pp. 158–60.

hleunō could also mean 'fame'. Moreover, fame is obviously something that a spear-sharpener could metaphorically 'counsel' by helping the spearman to win his battles. The use of the verb *anaregu* 'I counsel' would also make better sense with a meaning 'fame' as this form of *hleunō* is related to words like English *loud* (earlier *hlūd*), and a reference to the plane 'counselling' fame would have parallels in other enabling amulet texts. The element beginning as *hlao-* is probably to be restored as *hlaoisai* 'for renown', then, and the plane appears to be counselling the warrior who wants 'spoils for renown' that he can only win fame by first using the sharpener's magic to enhance his spear. So although the item description *tal(g)ijō* 'plane' remains unconnected to the rest of the text, i.e. it betrays the pidgin-like quality typical of other amulet inscriptions of this general type, the name *Gaisijō* 'Spearman', and the words *hleunō* 'fame' and its grammatically related variant *hlaois* 'renown' appear to have been built up or expanded into a short narrative charm.[10]

The Vimose wood-plane inscription, however, is one of several early runic texts that feature a short narrative linked to the function of the items which they appear on. Reminiscent of mythological or divine narrative charms, these inscriptions all seem to be amuletic in nature and as such all appear to have been intended as enabling magic.

Such an inscription appears on another implement used for sharpening: an early whetstone of Germanic manufacture. The perhaps sixth- or seventh-century whetstone comes from Strøm, Norway, and its runic legend is:

ᛈᚠᛏᛗᚼᚠᛏᛁᚺᛁᛏᛟᚺᛟᚱᚠᚠ
ᚼᚠᚼᚠᛋᛁᚠᛈᛁᚼᚠᚦᚾᚷᛁᚷᛁ

Wate halli hino horna!
Haha skaþi! Haþu liggi!

'Wet this stone, horn!
Scathe, scythe! The fallen lie!'

The text here clearly alliterates (**h**alli **h**ino **h**orna etc.), displays a regular metre and appears to be a poetic encouragement or charm. Evidently the Strøm text was supposed to ensure that the whetstone would be particularly effective on implements sharpened on it. Spells to be used on whetstones are known from post-medieval sources, but nothing quite like this metrical narrative, based around the description 'stone' and the whetstone's sharpening function, is recorded among them. It probably confirms the suspicion, though, that the Vimose plane text is also an enabling charm – a partly more laconic, formulaic text, and partly a full narrative charm (as at Strøm) then – as does, presumably, the next example too.[11]

A similar, but more complex legend is found on a spear-shaft that was

[10] Krause with Jankuhn, no. 25; Seebold, 'Sprachliche Deutung', pp. 66–68. *Anaregu* is clearly a form of the strong 'reckon' verb preserved in Gothic *garehsns* (< **ga-reg-sni-*) 'definite time, plan, determination', and cf. Gothic *rahnjan* 'reckon' and Old English *regnian* 'decide, arrange'.

[11] Krause with Jankuhn, no. 50.

excavated in 1877 from the Kragehul bog, near Flemløse, Denmark. Carved with runes decorated much as those on the Lindholmen amulet are, it reads:

ᛗᛉᚱᛁᛁᚠᛉᚠᛊᚾᚷᛁᛊᚠᚠᛊᛗᚾᚺᚠᚺᚠᛁᛏᛗᚷᚠᚷᚠᚷᚠᚷᛁᛏᚾᚷᚠᚺᛗ
ᚱᛁᚺᚠ
ᚺᚠᚷᚠᚠᚠᛈᛁᚺᚾᛒᛁᚷ . . .

Ek Erilaz Ansugīsalas Mūha haite.
Gagaga gīnu gahellija,
hagala wīju bi g[aize].

'I am called Earl Muha, Ansugisal's (son).
I cry a roar resoundingly,
I invoke hail in the spear.'

Although it has been broken into several pieces, this fifth-century text obviously begins, much as at Lindholmen, with a naming sentence, but it then continues with what appears to be a chant or a charm. Like the inscription on the Strøm whetstone and as in several of the runic myth-narrative texts, this part of the inscription alliterates and is metrical. It seems to be a charm to make the spear strike with the fury of hailstones, and as we shall see, both the terms *gagaga* 'roar' and *hagala* 'hail' have their reflections in other amuletic inscriptions as charm words. The Kragehul inscription is clearly an elaborate amulet text, with an extended naming expression, as well as what seems to be a poetic expansion on an item description and some typical charm-function words, much as is found also at Vimose and probably also at Strøm. Yet most runic texts that are found on weapons are less loquacious; rather, they are generally more strictly formulaic, much like the Thames scramasax legend is. And it is in this context that several other, rather briefer early inscriptions on weapons and armour, reminiscent of the simple amulet texts like the *bada* charms, should also probably be understood.[12]

Several early Germanic spearheads have names inscribed upon them that on first inspection appear to refer to the spear, much like the Norse gods Thor and Odin or heroes like Beowulf and Sigurd own weapons with names of their own. A striking example is a spearhead from a place called Mos on the Swedish island of Gotland, which bears an inscription that seems to be Gothic in language. Its inscription is:

ᚷᚠᚱᛁᛉ

Gaois.

'Howler.'

This name is etymologically related to the term *gagaga* (which is in turn similar to imitative English words like *cackle* and *gargle*) on the Kragehul spear-shaft, and the amuletic nature of the Mos find seems to be guaranteed by the appearance of magical symbols known as tamgas, inlaid, as is the inscription, in silver into the metal of the spearhead. Tamgas – complicated magical symbols usually featuring

---

12 M. MacLeod and B. Mees, 'The triple binds of Kragehul and Undley', *NOWELE* 38 (2001), 17–35.

*Fig. 6. Dahmsdorf and Kovel
spearheads*

crescent-shaped and cursive script-like elements – were adopted by the Goths
from peoples they encountered when they first arrived at the shores of the Black
Sea; so this spear seems to have belonged to a Goth who wandered back to
Gotland after his people had begun their centuries-long migrations south.[13]

A similar example was found in 1865 during railway-works at Dahmsdorf,
some distance south of Berlin. Like the Mos spearhead, the Dahmsdorf find is
decorated with silver tamgas on the side that bears the inscription, and a swastika
and a triskelion are inlaid on the reverse side. The spearhead probably dates to the
third century and where it was found suggests it may have been made by
Burgundians, as classical writers attest that the region about Dahmsdorf was
under Burgundian control at that date. Its text reads:

ᚾᚨᚾᛃᚨ

Ranja.

'Router.'

_____

[13] Krause with Jankuhn, no. 34.

The spear may seem, then, to have been thought to invoke fear in whoever faced its bearer in battle. But a nickname 'Router', literally 'causes to run (away)', could, of course, equally have applied to its owner.[14]

Tamgas also occur on a third early Germanic spearhead, from Suszyczno, Ukraine, although it is usually referred to by the name of the local district it was found in, Kovel, which before 1945 had been part of Poland. Looted by Nazi archaeologists during the German occupation, it has not been seen in public since the end of the war. Another apparently Gothic inscription from about the third century, its silver-inlaid text runs:

TIᚠᚱIᛟ$

Tilarīds.

'Thither-rider.'

Again, it is not absolutely clear, though, at first whether the name Tilarid referred to the spear or to its Gothic owner.[15]

A similar find from the Merovingian period is also known from Germany. Excavated from an Alemannic graveyard in Wurmlingen, Southern Germany, the spear is decorated with symbols reminiscent of tamgas and some even of runes. Its silver-inlaid legend reads:

ᛁᛗᛟᚱIᚺ

Idorīh.

This time the name on the spear cannot refer to the weapon, but is instead clearly one of a series of Germanic men's names featuring the same ending, *-rīk* or *-rīh*, that is preserved today in modern forms like Henry (Henrik, Heinrich). The initial character is a rare variant of the *i*-rune (also used on the Vimose plane) whose employment here probably represents another instance of name highlighting. But most importantly of all, the Wurmlingen find seems to put paid to the notion that names which are found on similarly decorated spearheads inevitably refer to the spears themselves rather than their owners.[16]

Several other rune-inscribed weapons and pieces of armour carry names like those on the silver-inlaid finds from Eastern Europe but without the accompanying magical symbols. In fact there are three spearheads, one from Vimose and two from Illerup, Denmark, that bear the same name, *Wagnijō* 'Wayfarer'. One is even stamped into the metal of the spearhead suggesting it is the name (or nickname) of the spearhead's maker, not necessarily its owner or even the spear itself. The silver-inlaid names on the spearheads from Mos, Dahmsdorf and Suszyczno, however, seem quite different from those typically found on weapons and other early rune-inscribed items. There are no cases where symbols like tamgas

---

[14] Ibid., no. 32.

[15] Ibid., no. 33.

[16] Ibid., no. 162. Another example of a rune-inscribed spear-head with tamgas is the early Gothic inscription from Rozwadów, Poland (ibid., no. 35), but it is not clear how its fragmentary text . . .*krlas* should be interpreted.

accompany rune-inscribed objects that have names which can only refer to the weapons (or brooches etc.) themselves, though. On the contrary, there are many cases where such an interpretation can clearly be ruled out. So despite the suggestive nature of names like 'Router' or 'Howler', formulaic comparison suggests these are only nicknames or epithets of the spears' owners, not names of the spears themselves. These are amuletic inscriptions, then, of another minimal type: a name plus magical symbol(s).

The tamgas seem to function, much as is the case with the magical symbols encountered in chapter 2, as functional equivalents of charm words or futhark rows. In fact there is a certain repetitiveness in many of the inscriptions on items that are obviously amulets. The Thames scramasax and Lindholmen amulet texts are alike as they both contain letter sequences and names or naming expressions. Similarly, the inscriptions on the brooches from Hungary and the German *bada* texts are much the same with their recording of names and single words indicating what effect the amulet was supposed to bring about. Even the longer texts are analytically mostly the same; though much expanded, they seem to accord to the same general pattern. The silver-inlaid spearheads are also similar in what seems to be a formulaic sense with their owners' names and magical symbols. There are many other rune-inscribed items which seem to mix these basic elements together in other combinations – some even without names or longer naming expressions – though also, evidently, in order to achieve an amuletic effect. Consider the following early-fifth-century example on a spear-shaft recently excavated from another Danish bog called Nydam:

ᚠᛗᚱᛗᚾᚦᚠᛗᚠᛗᚱᚻᛏᛦᚾᚱᚠᛗᚱᚱᚨᚠᚦᚻᚱᚨ

*adleuþleaelnt*ᚱ*uladllaanhl* ᚨ

This inscription seems completely uninterpretable linguistically, but if we take the use of letter sequences and magical symbols elsewhere as a guide, the Nydam shaft must have been an amulet.[17] Similarly, a brooch found in the ruins of the Roman town of Aquincum, near Budapest, Hungary, reads:

ᚠᚢᚦᚠᚱᚲᚷᚠ
ᛋᚱᚠᛁᚼ᛬ᚲᚩᛁᚠ

Fuþarkgw
jlain k(i)ngia.

'. . . Brooch.'

Only the term *k(i)ngia* 'brooch' is clearly interpretable in the text on this fifth-century find which is probably of Lombard make. The letter sequence, beginning as a futhark row, however, suggests that it, too, is an amulet. (Indeed it may also be that *jlain* is a scrambled form, perhaps a name like *Linja*.)[18] In fact if we consider the early rune-inscribed items with letter sequences, charm words

---

[17] M. Stoklund, 'Arbejdet ved Runologisk Laboratorium, København', *Nytt om runer* 12 (1997), 4–5.

[18] Krause with Jankuhn, no. 7.

and amuletic symbols as a whole, a clear five-part formula or type (or typology) emerges – all of these items feature a selection of up to five basic amulet text-forming elements:

1. LETTER SEQUENCES, either futhark rows or apparently coded assortments of runes.
2. NAMING EXPRESSIONS, often just a single name, but sometimes a more complex construction, typically in the first person: 'I am called NN.'
3. The terms often called formula or CHARM WORDS, including *alu* and *laukaz*.
4. SYMBOLS, such as tree-like shapes, tamgas, swastikas and triskelia.
5. ITEM DESCRIPTIONS, such as 'brooch', 'pendant', 'horn' or the like.[19]

This general scheme makes interpreting some of the otherwise most difficult amulet inscriptions a much simpler task. The Thames scramasax is clearly a LETTER SEQUENCE + NAMING EXPRESSION, the Lindholmen amulet can be analysed as a NAMING EXPRESSION + LETTER SEQUENCE + CHARM WORD and the otherwise impenetrable Nydam shaft text is a LETTER SEQUENCE + a SYMBOL. Many of the complex texts found on the rune-inscribed golden pendants from the fifth and sixth centuries can also be explained just as simply. Consider this otherwise mystifying example from Overhornbæk, northern Denmark:

ᛃᚾᚦᚠᚦᛁᛁᚾᛁᚺᚢᛁᚠᚠᛗᚪᛣᚢᛁᚢᚢᛊᚪᛈᛇ

ǂuþaþit?ih uilald ᛏïuiuujᛏwᛇ

'. . . Pendant . . .'

Although there are several inverted and otherwise irregular characters on the pendant, the five-part amulet typology suggests that we can interpret the pendant legend as a (futhark row-like) LETTER SEQUENCE + ITEM DESCRIPTION + SYMBOLS. Moreover, the sequence *ïuiuujw* suggests another feature common to runic amulet inscriptions, i.e. the jumbling or coding of a word much as we have already seen at Vimose, in this case probably of the verb *wīju* 'I consecrate'. The backward- and forward-facing E-like characters also clearly act to flank or frame the text. In fact these additional two features, coding and framing, can be seen in some English runic amulet inscriptions.[20]

Another example of this kind of amulet text appears on a silver mounting for a sword also retrieved from the Thames. It dates slightly earlier than the Thames scramasax, to the eighth century, and its odd-looking inscription reads:

ᚻᛒᛗᚱᚠᛟᚾᛏᛁᛒᛦᚠᛁᛗᚱᚾᚠᛟᚠᛒᚻ

sberædht ïbcai erhadæbs

At first the only thing that seems very clear about this inscription is the runic ABC (or rather BCA) at the centre flanked by the two *i*-runes, ᛁ and ᛁ. If we interpret

---

[19] The five-part typology and its origin are more fully discussed in MacLeod and Mees, 'On the t-like symbols', along with a comprehensive bibliography.
[20] Krause with Jankuhn, no. 4; *IK* no. 140.

this as a letter sequence, however, we should expect the nearly identical texts that flank it to be names, item descriptions or charm words. In fact they can both be read as the same deliberately coded man's name, with the first two letters, SB, indicating the elements that make up the syllables of the name, i.e. SB/er/æd/ht → S[æd]-B[er][ht], *Sædberht*. This text is analytically the same, then, as that on the Thames scramasax, albeit much more cunningly coded.[21]

Another early English magic sword inscription occurs on a silver-gilt pommel uncovered by chance over a century ago in the parish of Ash, Kent. Of a style that dates the sword to the mid-sixth century and with the inscription rather poorly executed, the Ash legend also features flanking text (even the *c*-runes point in opposing directions) some of which is illegible unfortunately. Although treated with suspicion by some scholars, and admittedly its runic *r* is malformed and its three *e*-runes are also rather odd, the following legend seems clear enough:

--ᚻᛁᛃᛁᚷᛁᛗᛖᚱᚣᚱᛁᚻ---

Eic Sigimēr ᛉ *cie.*

'Edge, Sigimer, edge.'

Given that 'edge' is a poetic way to refer to a sword in Old English, this amulet text should probably be analysed as (flanking) ITEM DESCRIPTIONS + NAMING EXPRESSION, perhaps even + SYMBOL, too, if the strange sign after Sigimer's name is not merely a carver's mistake.

Five-element analysis probably also explains an inscription that appears on a mounting for a scabbard of early Anglo-Saxon make. Found at Chessel Down on the Isle of Wight, its text reads:

ᚠᛉᚠ:ᚴᚲᚱᛁ

Æcco særi.

'Æcco, I invoke.'

There have been many different interpretations proffered for this inscription in the past, most attempting to link *særi* to Old English *sār* 'wound, sore'. But this linkage is linguistically implausible, and *særi* just seems to be derived instead from the early English form of the verb that appears twice on the Bergen rune-stick described in chapter 2 where Odin is invoked in order to find out the name of a thief. Rather than an address to Æcco, which is unknown as a supernatural name (or even Tyr as the rune-lore cited at the beginning of this chapter might suggest), though, the five-part amulet formula suggests that *særi* is functioning as a CHARM WORD here and Æcco is just a personal NAME. It seems that scabbards, the holders of swords, were also considered worthy of carrying amulet inscriptions in the early Anglo-Saxon world.[22]

The most common charm word in these laconic inscriptions, however, is *alu*, a

---

[21] Page, *Introduction*, p. 182. In fact the right-hand sequence may have been meant to be read *Sædbearh* (or the like) rather than be an erroneous rendition of *Sædberht*.

[22] Page, *Introduction*, pp. 10–11 and 181.

linguistically controversial term that probably means 'dedication'. A relatively clear example with this word is found on a wooden axe-haft excavated from the Nydam bog. Dating to the first half of the fourth century, its runes read:

ᛈᚠᚷᚠᚷᚨᛏᛁᛇ
ᚠᛏᚾᚦᛈᛁᚺᚷᚾᛉᛁᚲᛁᚨᚠᛇᚦᛁᚦᚠᛏᛏᛏᚠᛇ

Wāgagastiz
alu wīgu sīkijaz Aiþalātaz.

'Wagagast, dedication, I consecrate, Aithalat from the sike.'

The style Aithalat 'Oath-sayer' has been interpreted as an epithet or nickname, so we are presumably dealing with a NAMING EXPRESSION 'Wagagast Oath-sayer from the sike (i.e. a sluggish stream)' and two CHARM WORDS, albeit with the variant form *wīgu* appearing for the more regular *wīju*. The Nydam axe-handle inscription is analytically the same, then, as that on the scabbard from Chessel Down, although extended by having two charm words and a fuller naming expression.[23]

A similar description to that found on the Ash pommel may also appear on one of the items recovered from the Kragehul bog. Perhaps a bit later than the inscribed spear-shaft, i.e. probably from the early sixth century, and carved with the same decorative runic letterforms as appear on the Lindholmen and Kragehul amulets, the following text can be read on the fragmentary remains of a knife-haft:

ᚢᛗᚠ·ᛒᛗᚱᚠ
ᚠᚠᚾ

Uma Bera aau.

'Haft, Bera, dedication.'

The text *aau* appears to stand here for *alu* 'dedication', and in fact several other weapons excavated from Danish bogs are inscribed with similar variations on this word. Several are known on arrow-shafts from Nydam, and the short sequences like *lua, la* and the like on these finds seem to have little other possible explanation than as similarly scrambled forms of the charm word *alu*. Consequently, it seems safe to interpret the Kragehul knife inscription as an ITEM DESCRIPTION + NAME + CHARM WORD.[24]

Most runic amulets of the five-part type are relatively straightforward, though, and do not feature flanking or any form of letter permutation. There also seems to be no essential difference between most of the English, Scandinavian and continental European texts of this type. In fact the parallelism is quite precise and rather longer-lived than even many comparatists might expect. One fairly simple example, for instance, is found on a ring that was excavated at the Thames Exchange in the late 1980s. It cannot be dated accurately, but its inscription clearly reads:

23 McKinnell and Simek, pp. 94–95.
24 Krause with Jankuhn, nos 19 and 28.

ᚨᚠᚢᚦᚾᛁᛁᛏᛗ

ᚨ *fuþni Ine.*

'. . . Ine.'

This text can be analysed as SYMBOL + LETTER SEQUENCE + NAME, but its purpose, whether protective or enabling, remains as unclear as it is for the Lindholmen amulet. The name Ine was borne by a king of Kent who reigned for over 40 years, from 685 to 726, and who is famous for promulgating a law-code. Ine is a common enough Anglo-Saxon name, though, so it seems unlikely that the ring has anything to do with the like-named Kentish king.[25]

It is in the context of the Thames Exchange ring, then, that the golden rune-inscribed ring named (spuriously) for the great twelfth-century Danish archbishop Absalon should be understood. First recorded by sixteenth-century Scandinavian antiquarians, it dates to the thirteenth century and its text, carved on an extended rim surrounding its stone, reads:

ᚦᛁᚱᚴᛏᛁᚱᚨᚨᚨᚨᚨᚨ

Þorgæir yyyyy.

'Thorgeir . . .'

This ring inscription also clearly fits into the five-part typology: it bears a NAME + a LETTER SEQUENCE, the latter even of the same length – five characters – as that which appears on the Thames Exchange ring. The Danish ring seems to have had little to do with the archbishop it was later named for, but it must surely also have been an amulet ring. The similarities shared by inscriptions such as the rings of Ine and Thorgeir seem unlikely to have been the result of cultural contact or trade, but rather appear to attest to the longevity and importance of the five-part amulet text-forming formula.[26]

The most common and varied of all runic amulet texts, however, are those which appear on golden medallion-like pendants called bracteates. Usually worn hung from the belt and generally only about 3cm in diameter, these pendants were especially popular during the migration period – they date from about the years 360–600 – and examples have been found from all over Scandinavia, Central Europe, the Low Countries and England. Their runic texts were evidently, at first, employed as replacements for the legends typically found on large Roman gold coins known as 'medallions' that were often presented to third and fourth-century Germanic chieftains, evidently in the hope of ensuring their allegiance to Rome (or rather of buying them off). But the runic examples are never suggestive of the form or contexts of their Latin predecessors. The few early Germanic pendants that have legends in Latin letters do seem to be based in the names or styles of emperors – usually the only written adornment found on Roman medallions. One found at Haram, Norway, for instance, clearly contains an imperial style: D(ominus) N(oster) CONSTANTIVS P(ius) F(elix) AVG(ustus), i.e. 'Our

---

[25] K. Gosling, 'Runic finds from London', *Nytt om runer* 4 (1989), 12.
[26] Moltke, *Runes and their Origin*, p. 486.

Emperor Constantius, dutiful, auspicious, august'. Others tend to have more corrupt legends, however; the most extreme, found in Mauland, Norway, bears only hints of such a form in its mixture of Roman letters, rune-like characters and symbols: ⊲IↃSOII⚡ⱂS⅃⅃ᴳⳒC⊗ⱀⱀSISS⊥OC∈. One, from Kälder, Sweden, even seems to feature a palindrome *siususuis* (twice) in its otherwise nonsensical legends SIΛSΛSΛISSIVSVSΛIS (on one side) and TTSVSΛISI VSVSΛSI (on the other). Much as the appearance of the swastika at Mauland suggests, then, the Germanic pendant legends often seem already to have had quite a different purpose to those of Roman medallions; i.e. the pendants had come to be seen as potentially magical even before the five-part runic amulet formulism was first applied to them.[27]

Like the legends often found on modern coins, though, the amuletic pendant texts remained subsidiary to the main decorations of the bracteates; typically the runic texts circle around the pendants' iconography, although rarely they may be found within it. Four general types of these pendants are also usually distinguished by specialists today: early ones whose iconography closely follows that of Roman medallions; those which depict a stylised man's head in profile; ones which show a fuller figure of a man often accompanied by animals such as birds; and lastly those which feature only animals – the pendants most removed from their Roman predecessors.

Sometimes these pictures suggest mythological scenes, e.g. a pendant from Scania which shows a man whose hand is being bitten by a wolf, much as the Norse war-god Tyr lost his hand to the Fenris Wolf. Usually, however, they are merely Germanic stylistic variations on typical Roman medallion and coin decorations, such as the she-wolf symbol representing the foundation-story of Rome or victorious emperors mounted on horses. The motifs found, especially on the later examples, have occasioned much speculation in recent times – some investigators suggest all sorts of Germanic mythological figures and scenes can be discerned in bracteate decoration. Yet it must be acknowledged that the runic texts do not seem to refer to what is depicted on the bracteates. Despite the suggestive nature of the more complex later examples, we have little idea what the decorations were supposed to mean – assuming, that is, that modern experts are correct in assuming they were intended to impart discernible messages – unlike many of the runic legends that were more obviously included because runes are supposed to be read.[28]

The proliferation of amulet pendants during the period of the Germanic migrations can be ascribed in part to the amount of gold flooding the North in light of

---

[27] The standard edition of the bracteates is *IK*. In general, see also S. Nowak, 'Schrift auf den Goldbrakteaten der Völkerwanderungszeit' (Dissertation, Göttingen 2003). The cited bracteates are *IK* nos 124, 268 and 286.

[28] The mythological interpretations of bracteate iconography proposed remain unconvincing in many respects, despite the attempts to find connections between the intriguing conjectures often proffered and what the runic texts say; *pace* K. Hauck, 'Brakteatenikonologie', in J. Hoops, *Reallexikon der germanischen Altertumskunde*, 2nd ed. (Berlin 1976–), III, pp. 361–401 and idem, 'Die runenkundlichen Erfinder von den Bildchiffren der Goldbrakteaten (Zur Ikonologie der Goldbrakteaten, LVII)', *Frühmittelalterliche Studien* 32 (1998), 28–56, etc.

the buying-off policy being followed by Rome at the time. But this recent opulence alone cannot explain the popularity of these items which are obviously also magico-religious expressions. In fact the amuletic nature of the rune-inscribed examples is reminiscent of the similar upsurge in the use of amulets during the La Tène Celtic migrations a thousand years earlier. The employment of the pendants in what was a time of great social upheaval seems comparable to the upsurge of religious feeling often seen today when crisis strikes modern societies.

Almost one-third of the over 900 exemplars of Germanic pendants found to date carry runic inscriptions, making the pendants by far the most common rune-bearing items from the fourth and especially fifth and sixth centuries. The five-part pattern also reaches its most expressive with the pendants and, in fact, appears to undergo some expansion on them. The decoration on these pendants similarly becomes freer and more intriguing over time. There are even some runic shapes that are peculiar to pendant legends, all of which are struck from dies or moulds rather than actually being inscribed. Some of the legends are merely maker's signatures or seem to have been composed or copied from other pendants by illiterate craftsmen. They are highly varied and imaginative, though, much as, increasingly, is the accompanying decoration, in contrast to the drab assortment of Latin names, motifs and imperial styles that are found on the Roman proto-types the Germanic pendants are based upon.

Many of the pendant legends are typical five-part amulet texts. A golden pendant found at Vadstena, Sweden, in the late eighteenth century for instance (of which another example, struck from the same mould or die, was later found nearby at Motala) has the following runic legend:

ᛏᚢᚹᚨᛏᚢᚹᚨ·ᚠᚢᚦᚨᚱᚲᚷᚹ:ᚺᚾᛁᛪᛁᛒᛦᛉ:ᛏᛒᛖᛗᛚᛜᛟᛞ:

Tuwa, tuwa, fuþarkgw:hnijïbʀs:tbemlŋod.

'Offering, offering . . .'

The Vadstena text clearly consists of a futhark row separated into its traditional three families and two (repeated) charm words, forms which the Germanic verb *taujan* 'offer, make', often used in dedicatory inscriptions, is etymologically based on. In terms of the amuletic formula the only exceptional feature here is the repetition of the charm word. But it is quite common for amulet pendants to have two or more charm words feature in their texts.[29]

Much as with the Vadstena pendant, many runic amulets have charm words on them that appear to be ritualistic in origin. Witness, for example, the following legend found on a gold pendant from Darum, Denmark featuring *alu*, the etymo-logically controversial charm word *par excellence*:

---

[29] Krause with Jankuhn, no. 2; *IK* no. 377. *Tuwa* is clearly a zero-grade form of the root of *taujan* equivalent to Sanskrit *dúvas* (collective) 'offerings', and cf. Old Saxon *twithon* 'grant, give', Lithuanian *duoti* 'to give' etc.; see O. Grønvik, 'Runeinnskriften på gullhornet fra Gallehus', *Maal og Minne* 1 (1999), 1–18 or more formally T.L. Markey, 'The dedicatory formula and runic *tawide*', forthcoming.

ᚻᛁᚾᛋᛁᛚ ᚠᛚᚢ

Niujila alu.

'Niujila, dedication.'[30]

Sometimes the charm words appear in abbreviated forms too, presumably because they were so well known. Compare these two Danish pendant legends, the first also from Darum, the second from Skonager, near Ribe:

ᚠᚱᛟᚺᛁᛚᚠ ᛚᚠᚦᚢ

Frōhila laþu.

'Frohila, invocation.'

ᚻᛁᚾᚹᛁᛚᚠ ᛚᚦᚢ

Niuwila l(a)þu.

'Niuwila, invocation.'[31]

In fact some of the pendants bear words which are so abbreviated that it is not always clear how to read them. For example, an early golden pendant, a late-fourth-century medallion imitation from Svarteborg, Sweden, clearly contains an abbreviated charm word, but it is not immediately obvious which one:

ᛋᛋᛁᚷᚠᚾᚢᛉ ᛚ

Ssiganduz l(aukaz).

'Sigand, leek.'

It is usually assumed that an isolated *l*-rune in an amulet text represents the charm word *laukaz* rather than *laþu* because 'leek' is thought by some authors to have been the original name for the *l*-rune. Interestingly enough, the element Sigand here also literally means 'magician', but the double-*s* spelling is clearly a highlighting feature, suggesting Sigand must be the pendant owner's name, perhaps his nickname, rather than a description of his occupation.[32]

Much as at Lindholmen, in each of the examples from Darum and Skonager we have a name and a charm word, but they give us little idea of what each amulet was supposed to be used for except to indicate that it had some sort of connection with the supernatural or the divine. It may seem that amulet pendants with legends like these were religious items like Christian scapulars or St Christopher's medals. Yet pendant texts exist that bear several different charm words, e.g. the following example on a golden pendant that we only know was found somewhere in Scania, southern Sweden:

---

30   Krause with Jankuhn, no. 104; *IK* no. 43.
31   Krause with Jankuhn, nos 117 and 118; *IK* nos 42 and 163. The *-h-* in *Frōhila* (< **Fraujila*) seems to represent a case of the irregular glide 'sharpening' first noted by S. Bugge, 'Zur altgermanischen Sprachgeschichte', *Beiträge zur Geschichte der deutschen Sprache und Literatur* 13 (1888), 504–15.
32   Krause with Jankuhn, no. 47; *IK* no. 181.

ᚱᚦᚾᛏᚠᚾᛇᚠᛃ·ᚷᚠᛃᚠᛃᚾᚱᚾ

Laþu, laukaz, gakaz, alu.

'Invocation, leek, cackle, dedication.'

The term *gakaz* is an imitative word like Kragehul's *gagaga* and the Mos spear-head's legend *Gaois*. It is often connected with a word for the cuckoo derived from an imitation of the noise that bird makes, but it seems more likely given the other imitative parallels that it also refers to a battle roar or the like. The term 'leek' here might be supposed to indicate that the pendant is a fertility or amatory amulet, though, and that the votive terms *laþu* and *alu* are just generic charm words. But then 'leek' could also indicate (sexual) potency here, making the amulet a powerful warrior charm.[33]

A slightly less obvious case appears on a pendant found at Ølst, Denmark. Its legend is:

ᚺᚠᚷ ᚠᚾᚾ

Hag(ala), alu.

'Hail, dedication.'

The pendant also has two swastikas on it, but it is not clear if either was supposed to complement the runic legend. The term *hagala* is, though, usually thought to be found here (perhaps abbreviated only due to haplography), the same word as is used at Kragehul in the expression 'I invoke hail in the spear.' It seems fairly obvious how hail might be invoked in a charm on a spear – i.e. to make the spear strike like hailstones. Yet surely hail could only be cited on a pendant in a meta-phorical (or, rather, metonymic) manner: hail is a powerful (and dangerous) form of weather, so imprinting the word 'hail' on the pendant was presumably an attempt to signify 'power', i.e. it is an indirect, 'just as . . . so too . . .' or sympathetic form of amuletic charm word.[34]

Two further possible examples of the use of the charm word *hagala* 'hail' are often thought to appear abbreviated only as *h* on a stone amulet and a metal armament find. The first appears on a small soapstone tablet from Kinneve, Sweden, which, though it cannot be dated with much accuracy, clearly reads:

-ᛉᛁᚤᚠᚾᚾᚺ

-siz alu h.

'-s, dedication, hail (?)'

The first element, of which the first letter (or perhaps two) has been lost on a chip that has broken off, probably once spelled a short name like As or Aus. The final *h* rather more clearly appears to be an abbreviation, however, and given the name of

---

[33] Krause with Jankuhn, no. 120; *IK* no. 149.
[34] Krause with Jankuhn, no. 123; *IK* no. 135.

the runic letter *h* is always given as 'hail' in later sources it seems likely that we are dealing here with an abbreviated charm word.[35]

The other example of this type is probably much earlier than the Kinneve find; in fact it appears on a shield boss deposited along with other weaponry in the bog near Thorsberg hill, just south of the German-Danish border, and reads, somewhat more obviously:

ᚠᛁᛊᚷᛉᚺ

Aisgz h.

'Challenger, hail (?)'

It is hard to see how else to interpret this find from the end of the second century other than as a personal name (perhaps the nickname of the shield's owner) plus an abbreviated charm word *hagala*.[36]

Another assortment of charm words of a suggestively military kind was found in the 1980s on a pendant unearthed at Undley, Suffolk, which shows further parallels with the text on the Kragehul spear. The Undley bracteate's legend reads:

ᚷᚠᚷᛖᚷᚠ:ᛗᚠᚷᚠ:ᛗᛗᛞᚢ

Gagoga, maga, mēdu.

'Roar, strong, reward.'

The third term here could have either of two meanings as early English ᛗᛗᛞᚢ could equally spell *mēdu* 'reward' or *medu* 'mead'. Yet this selection of terms, apparently mostly or even all (if we accept the 'reward' translation for ᛗᛗᛞᚢ) referring to the military sphere, again seems to indicate that the amulet was supposed to make the wearer strong or successful. The early English equivalent of Kragehul's *gagaga* is accompanied by otherwise new, but obviously complementary terms here. But can most of the pendant legends be linked to magic of a military kind?[37]

It seems that all sorts of charm words can appear bundled together on amulets, although *alu*, *laþu* and *laukaz* are the clear favourites. There are also many examples in which the charm words (much as in the Nydam arrow-shaft finds) appear to have been coded or scrambled into otherwise uninterpretable letter sequences. A relatively clear example was first discovered at Allesø, Denmark, but other copies, all with the same legend, have since been found nearby at Bolbro and Vedby:

ᛁᛚᚾᚤᛋᛉᛈᚠ ᚤᛁᚾᛏ:ᛗᚠᛈᛁ

Lau(ka)z ᛋ owa z(a)lut e(u)aþl

---

35 Krause with Jankuhn, no. 52.
36 Krause with Jankuhn, no. 21; Antonsen, no. 1.
37 MacLeod and Mees, 'Triple binds'.

Fig. 7. Undley, Lelling and Tjurkö pendants

This pendant legend appears to use abbreviation and coding to distort the charm words which appear on it: *laukaz, tawōz* (cf. *tuwa, taujan*), *alu*, and finally (a scrambled and reversed or framing) *laþu*. In fact the Allesø text is paralleled by other pendant legends ranging from a highly abbreviated ᛚᚢᛉᚠ (i.e. *l(a)u(ka)z (u)þa(l)?*) from Hesselager, Denmark, to the following two at first mostly perplexing sequences from Darum, Denmark, and Nebenstedt, Northern Germany, respectively:

ᛚᛚᛖᛏᛋᛜᛉᛦ·ᚱᛌᛁᛚᛌ·ᚠᛒᛦᛗᛏᛚ
ᛚᚠᛗ:ᛏᛋᛜᛉᛦᚱᛌᛏᛌᛌᚠᛒᛦᛗᛏ

llet ᛋ oz.rüli.aþzmtl
lae:t ᛋ ozrilliaþzet

We can readily make out some features that distinguish these two texts from the one on the Allesø bracteate, e.g. a *t*-rune (ᛏ) appears here where Allesø has a (similarly shaped) *z*-rune (ᛦ) and a completely new sequence (separated out by interpuncts on the Darum pendant) that reads *rüli*. The variations between the Darum and Nebenstedt texts, e.g. where an *a*-rune (ᚠ) has become an *l* (ᛚ) or an *e*-rune (ᛗ) has become an *m* (ᛗ), appear to be just die or mould-maker's errors. On the other hand, the new sequence of the Darum and Nebenstedt pendants seems to be a transposed form of *irilaz*, however, a variation of the title *erilaz* 'earl' known from other Scandinavian runic texts – *rüli* (or rather *zrülia → üirilaz*), with its two decorative *i*-runes is presumably to be understood as indicating an amuletic naming expression here. The other main difference between these two legends and the one from Allesø appears merely to be that much as *t* and *z* have become dislocated from their (partly reversed) charm word *(t)awō(z)* at Allesø and come instead to frame *alu*, at Darum and Nebenstedt they have moved further along and now more heavily disguise the reversed charm word *laþu*.[38]

Similar reasoning, i.e. allowing for coding or a maker's error, presumably explains the legend ᛚᚠᚹ (i.e. *law* for expected *laþu*?) on the Anglo-Saxon pendant from Welbeck Hill, Lincolnshire/East Riding of Yorkshire. Some of the pendant legends remain less clearly interpretable, however, presumably because they

---

[38] Krause with Jankuhn, nos 113 and 115; *IK* no. 13.

have undergone so much scrambling and miscopying that they now only hint at
their meanings and original forms. A pendant found at Broholm, Denmark, for
example, bears the legend:

ᚾᛁᚦᚾᚱᚾᚺᛏᛪ
ᚾᛪᛁᚦᚺᚾᛪ

uiþuluhng
uoiwhug

It seems possible that these legends purposefully hide transformed or abbreviated
amulet-element words like *uilald, hagala* or *laþu*. Nonetheless without any
comparable texts to aid in their decipherment, the Broholm legends remain
mostly opaque.[39]

Another, more regular example of coding can be seen in the Nydam shaft letter
sequence where the runes for *a, l* and *u* preponderate; i.e. **adleuþleaelntz-
uladllaanhl** ⚹ or rearranged with the charm-word letters extracted: *alulalulallaal
depeentzdnh* ⚹. Similar legends which appear to represent variations on *alu* are
found on pendants from Danish Maglemose (*aualhz*) and Tønder (*uldaul*), and
Szatmár, Hungary (*tualeltl*), though what the other letters mixed in with these
coded charm-word sequences signify remains a matter of speculation.

A further example of coding occurs on a pendant known since the seventeenth
century that was found somewhere on the Danish island of Fyn. Its legend reads:

ᚺᛪᚾᚠᛦ
ᚱᚠᚦᚾᛁᚠᛞᚾᛁᚠᛁᚱᛁᛁᚾᛁ ᚠᚱᚾ

Hōuaz laþu aaduaaaliiui alu.

'Howaz, invocation, . . . dedication.'

The legend here clearly features a man's name and two charm words, as well as a
letter sequence which, unlike those on most of the other amulets (but rather like
aallatti on the Lund weaving-tablet), appears to be pronounceable. It has thus
been interpreted as glossolalia, i.e. a 'word' taken from magical utterances or
'speaking in tongues'. Moreover, it features three reversed *a*-runes, as if to signal
some sort of special orthographical or magical effect. In fact as the letter sequence
consists solely of the five letters which make up the word *uilald* 'pendant', it
appears to be a coded item description.[40]

A similar method of encrypting probably lies behind the Lindholmen amulet's
sequence *aaaaaaaazzznnn[n]bmuttt* too. In fact this coded sequence, read backwards, almost spells a word, *tumbnza*, or rather more intelligently *tumbnaz*, a
term which in early Germanic would mean '(something) turned'. This word,
related to English *tumble* and German *tummeln* 'turn', may indicate an item
description '(something) bent' or 'rounded' here, as the Lindholmen bone amulet
is smoothly carved and crescent-shaped.

---

39 *IK* nos 47 and 388.
40 Krause with Jankuhn, no. 119; *IK* no. 58.

One of the other purposes of the letter sequences was not merely to hide charm words or item descriptions within them, but seems also, occasionally, to have been to fill out an amulet legend to a certain number of runes. The letter sequence on the Fyn legend appears to have deliberately been extended out to 12 letters in order to make the whole text 24 runes long. A similar number was achieved for the second side of the text on the Lindholmen amulet where the letter sequence provides a 24-character length. This practice is clearly based on emulating the 24 letters of the older futhark row and has its parallels in ABC-based letter sequences from Mediterranean traditions that are discussed below.

One type of rune-decorated Germanic pendant also displays a related ABC-understanding better known from Greek sources. Three examples from the same mould or die are known, all of which were found by chance near Faxe, Denmark, fixed together on the same golden cylinder:

ᛉᛟᛋᛚᚨᚢ

foslau

Although it is not immediately obvious, the first two letters of this text (with the *f*-rune reversed, probably to mark this practice out further) are the first and last letters of the futhark row – they are the runic equivalent of the Greek letter-pairing alpha and omega still used in Christian symbolism today. Similar letter-pairings were often employed in ancient times to represent mystical concepts such as the signs of the zodiac, though they are known to have their origin merely in simple spelling lessons.[41] This sequence probably qualifies as a letter sequence, then. The rest of the Faxe legend is a scrambled form of a charm word *salu*, one that is repeated twice on another bracteate found in a field near Lelling, Denmark:

ᛋᚨᛚᚢᛋᚨᛚᚢ

Salu, salu.

'Invocation, invocation.'

Some of the pendants only bear a single charm word such as *ota* or *groba*, terms whose exact interpretation often remains unclear. At other times it can be hard to distinguish genuine charm words, some of which, like *maga*, are only attested once, from nicknames, coded expressions or letter sequences. It seems likely, though, that terms such as *alu*, *laþu* and *laukaz* represent an early repertoire of amuletic expressions to which more and more words were added over time.[42]

Given the similarity to the use of *laukaz* 'leek', then, it is not too surprising that the term *alu* has often been connected with similar-looking and somewhat

---

[41] Krause with Jankuhn, no. 122; *IK* no. 101. For an introduction to classical alphabet magic in general see F. Dornseiff, *Das Alphabet in Mystik und Magie*, 2nd ed. (Leipzig 1925). The recent brooch find from Aschheim may also represent an alphabetical amulet text inspired by the runic pair *d* and *o*, but it could just as well be, say, doodling based on the German man's name *Odo*; see K. Düwel et al., 'Vereint in den Tod – Doppelgrab 166/167 aus Aschheim, Landkreis München, Oberbayern', *Das archäologische Jahr in Bayern* 1999, pp. 83–85.

[42] Krause with Jankuhn, no. 121; *IK* no. 105.

everyday words such as English *ale*, a term that ultimately stems from a root meaning 'nourish'. *The Lay of Sigrdrifa*, after all, mentions *ǫlrúnar* 'ale-runes' along with leeks in the context of love magic. Runic *alu* has also been connected with a Hittite term *alwanzah-* meaning 'enchant, bewitch', though, and, rejecting the more obvious 'nourish' etymology for *ale*, some scholars have argued that *alu* should be translated as 'beer' which, it is supposed, may have been thought of as a magical draught in old Germanic times. Other investigators have even suggested that *alu* as 'beer' was seen metaphorically in pagan thought as a representation of libations – liquid offerings to the gods. There are crucial linguistic difficulties in connecting *alu* with *ale* (earlier *aluþ*) or the Hittite term, however, or any other word derived from the root *al-* 'nourish'. After all it appears that the word for 'holy' or 'special drink' in Germanic was **waigaz*, Old Norse *veig* (a term related to *wīju* 'I consecrate'). There is no firm evidence to suggest that *alu* had anything to do with *ale* or libations other than a series of linguistic suppositions made mostly in light of the Eddic 'ale-runes'. Indeed the Edda's *All-wise's Sayings* (*Alvíssmál*) records that 'It is called ale among men, but beer by the gods', further suggesting that libations were unlikely to feature *aluþ* 'ale'. Instead a connection with giving and veneration seems more likely given the appearance of *alu* on the Setre comb seemingly in association with the goddess Nanna, an association further suggested by the meaning of comparable charm words like *laþu*, *wīju* and *salu*, as well as what are usually assumed to be the cultic origins of amuletic symbols such as the (pre-runic) sun symbol the swastika which seem to be functionally akin to the charm words.[43]

Rather than just repeating characters or words, however, rarely the charm-word section of the amulet formulism also undergoes some grammatical expansion on the pendants, much as has occurred (although clearly more extensively) on other more-or-less contemporary amulets like those from Vimose and Kragehul. A simple example is a legend on a pendant that was found somewhere on the Danish island of Zealand, though its exact find site is not known. Its fifth- or sixth-century text reads:

ᚺᚨᚱᛁᚢᚺᚨᚺᚨᛁᛏᛁᚪᚠ:ᚠᚨᚱᚨᚢᛁᚺᚠ:ᚷᛁᛒᚾᚠᚾᛏᚠ·:ᛪ

*Hariūha haitika, Farawīsa. Gibu auja.*ᛪ

'Hariuha I am called, Danger-wise. I give good luck.'[44]

A similar expansion, also clearly using charm words as its basis, is found on a pendant from Trollhättan, Sweden:

ᛏᚠᛈᛪᚱ ᚠᚦᛪᛗᚾ

Tawō laþōdu.

---

[43] Markey, 'Studies in runic origins 2', pp. 189–90 and cf. Nowak, pp. 208ff. In fact an amulet pendant found near Karlino (German Körlin), Poland, records a form of **waigaz* as *waiga* (which is usually interpreted as a name).

[44] Krause with Jankuhn, no. 127; *IK* no. 98.

'I offer an invocation.'[45]

This amulet legend obviously features grammatically variant forms of the charm words *tuwa* (or *tawōz*) and *laþu*. We should probably treat other pendant-legend expansions of the five-part formulism in this manner, then, for example the following pendant text from Tjurkö, Sweden:

ᛈᚾᚱᛏᛗᚱᚾᛏ᚛ᛃᚠᛏᛈᚠᚱᚺᚠᚲᚾᚱᛏᛗ··ᚺᛗᚠᛗᚠᛃᚲᚾᛏᛁᛗᚾᛈᛁᚾ···

Wurte rūnōz an walhakurne Heldaz Kunimundiu.

'Wrought runes on foreign corn (did) Held (i.e. warrior) for Kunimund.'

The appearance of the inflected man's name *Kunimundiu* 'for Kunimund' along with what might either be a description or another man's (nick)name seems aberrant in light of how names usually appear on these pendants. In fact if Held (or 'the warrior') is to be understood as the fashioner of the pendant, the legend would be expected to read *Heldaz wurte rūnōz an walhakurne Kunimundiu*. It has been suggested that the Tjurkö text is poetic, though, showing instances of alliteration (*wurte . . . walha-* and perhaps *-kurne . . . Kunimu(n)diu*) and presumably expressive word order. 'Wrought runes on foreign corn' seems to have been prioritised over the name or description Held by being moved into sentence-initial position.[46]

More obviously poetic in nature is the expression 'foreign corn', seemingly a reference to the gold of the pendant, a metal quite rare in the North until Roman money-diplomacy began. Thus the legend suggests that Kunimund's pendant may have been made from imported gold dust. This part of the text at first appears, then, to be an elaborated item description. The use of the term *rūnōz*, however, points to another interpretation.

A second Germanic amulet pendant from Nebenstedt, Germany, bears a slightly oddly formed legend that also seems to feature the term *rūnōz* 'runes':

ᚷᚠᛃᚠᚾᛉᛁᛃᚢ ᛃᚾᚢᚷᛃᚠ

Glīaugiz wī(j)u r(ū)n(ō)z l(aukaz).

'Gliaug, I consecrate, runes, leek.'

In this text the terms appear to have been progressively abbreviated as the die or mould-maker approached its end, a pattern which probably confirms the expansion *r(ū)n(ō)z* assumed here. In view of the Tjurkö text, the appearance of *rūnōz* might consequently be thought to be a replacement for an item description like *uilald* 'pendant'. Other legends suggest, however, that the Tjurkö legend is in fact a poetic development of a maker's signature such as 'Boso wrote these runes' and that the third element of the Nebenstedt text is a reduction of such an expression.[47] Several maker's legends of this type are, after all, known from other pendant

---

[45] Krause with Jankuhn, no. 130; *IK* no. 189. *Tawō* is a variant of *tuw-* (cf. archaic Italic 'give, offer' forms in *dou-*) and the root from which the causative/iterative verb *taujan* is derived.

[46] Krause with Jankuhn, no. 136; *IK* no. 185.

[47] Krause with Jankuhn, no. 133; *IK* no. 128.

texts. Witness, for example, the following legend, on slightly differently designed pendants found at Väsby and Äskatorp, Sweden:

ᚹᚹᛁᚷᚨᛃᛗᛗᚱᛁᛚᚨᛃᛃᚨᚺᛁᛗᚨᚹᚹᛁᛚᚨᛃᛗ

Uuigaz Eerilaz fāhidu, uuilald.

'Earl Wig adorned, pendant.'

The double spelling of the first letter of the name, title and item description here is apparently a form of punctuation marking out these elements from each other (the verb is not marked out in this way presumably as verbs bore less stress than nouns in early Germanic). It seems rather unlikely, though, that an earl actually decorated this pendant – surely Earl Wig had someone else adorn it, rather than, as the legend seemingly maintains, actually designing the pendant himself.[48]

In fact another pendant legend, from Halsskov, Denmark, probably confirms the suspicion that maker's legends were sometimes substituted for owner's names in these texts:

⚡ -ᛏ-ᛗᛏᚾᚱᚠᚨᚺᛁᛗᛗᛖᛖᚦᛩᚦᛗᚺᚦᛰᛁᛁᚨᛗᛁᚠᚾᛪᚱᛀᚦᛏᛒᛪᛗᛁᚠᛃ

⚡ . . .*etur fāhide laþōþ mhlïiiaeiaugrsþnbkeiaz.*

'. . .etur adorned, invocation . . .'

This pendant legend shows how far variation on the five-part scheme could go. Firstly, the owner's name here is coded or otherwise unreadable today. Secondly, the verb *fāhide* 'adorned, coloured' clearly comes from a typical maker's formula, not one usual for amulets. The charm word *laþu* appears next in an irregular form, too, one reminiscent of the variant, though grammatically regular, form *laþōdu* on the pendant from Trollhättan. Moreover, the letter sequence which follows may have a (further) charm word encoded in it: *l()au()k()az* ← *mhljiiaeiaugrsþnbkeiaz*, i.e. separated out by groups of two runic consonants (before the *l*), six vowels and semi-vowels (before the *a*, one rune for each letter in *laukaz*), six consonants (before the *k*) and a further two vowels (before the final *a*). Like the futhark rows, however, although built around the charm word *laukaz*, the Halsskov letter sequence appears to be formed by principles of orthographical knowledge: in this case the differentiation of runic vowels from consonants.[49]

Similar extensions of the five-part formula may be found in some texts from after the Migration Period too. Often, however, these inscriptions are not so readily interpretable at first even though they apparently are amuletic texts. One example is an inscription on a whalebone *t*-shaped or 'tau' staff found at Bernsterburen, Holland, late in the nineteenth century. Although today broken in several pieces, some of which are now lost, the staff, which was probably a crosier or sceptre, is decorated with stylised horse heads at its cross-piece, and its body with rows of triangular and rectangular markings as well as the runic text.

---

48   Krause with Jankuhn, no. 128; *IK* no. 241.
49   *IK* no. 1.

Dating to about the year 800 its legend was first noticed only as late as 1989; written on three otherwise undecorated sections of the body of the staff it reads:

ᛏᚢᛞᚨ ᚫᚹᚢᛞᚢᚴᛁᚱᛁᚦᚢ ᛏᚢᛞᚨ

Tuda. Æ wudu kiri þu. Tuda.

'Tuda, from wood you turn, Tuda.'

The two names seem to flank a central text, apparently a short two-line rhyme which appears to be similar to the enabling charms found on the Vimose wood-plane or the Strøm whetstone. The flanking by the man's name Tuda is similar to that found on the Thames sword mount, and the verb *kiri* 'turn' is reminiscent of the apparently coded word *tumbnaz* '(something) turned' (i.e. shaped or worked with a tool) on the Lindholmen amulet.[50]

A significantly more difficult text also seemingly of this sort features on another Frisian object, a 12cm-long staff or wand made of yew-wood. From Westeremden, Holland, it probably dates to the late eighth century, and its magical nature seems to be indicated by its use of many variant letterforms along with its clear naming expression and what appears to have been meant as an item description:

ᚩᛈᚻᚪᛗᚢᛡᛁ⊠ᚫᛞᚨᚪᛗᛚᚢᚦ:
ᚹᛁᛗᛟ⊠ᚪᚻᚦᚢᛋᚫ
ᛁᚹᛁᚩᚳᚢ⊠ᛞᚢᚾᚪᛚᛖ:

Op hāmu ji⊠æda amluþ.
Wīmœ⊠ āh þusæ.
Iwiocu⊠dunale.

'At home . . . causes bother (?). Wimœd (?) owns this. Yew . . . (?)'

The only absolutely clear part of this difficult inscription is its naming section: 'W. owns this.' This text has been interpreted, however, as a third example of a *bada* inscription, though such an interpretation relies on the rather implausible reading of the irregular graph ⊠ as an idiosyncratically formed mirror-rune of *b* (usually ᛒ) in the first part of the inscription, and as an irregular *d* (ᛞ) or a phonologically unlikely *b* in the second line. The word ending the first line also appears to be the verb found in the root of the Old Norse name *Amlóði* 'Hamlet', the modern Norwegian descendant of which means 'struggle with yourself'. This suggests that the troublesome letterform might be an idiosyncratic runic *r*, then, as this would give us *jiræda* 'talk' bothering (or the like) at home and a linguistically plausible owner's name Wimœr. But it must be admitted that little of the text can clearly be made sense of – the third line is even less obviously interpretable than the difficult first line of runic text. Like the other rune-inscribed Frisian example, it shows some parallels to the five-part amulet formula of the early inscriptions, though: a naming expression, what may be an expanded charm-

50 A. Quak, 'Nachtrag zu Bernsterburen', *Amsterdamer Beiträge zur älteren Germanistik* 36 (1992), 63–64; Looijena, pp. 314–16.

function description, and what seems to be a reference to the (yew-wood) amulet appear to be the basic elements of the text here. The odd characters, one even apparently in the form of an amuletic symbol, may also have served to make the inscription seem more magical, much as such amplifications more clearly do in some of the golden pendant legends.[51]

A much more striking example of variation from the basic five-element pattern, and one where this decoration seems to have been taken to a further extreme still, is the inscription found on the sixth-century bone amulet from Ødemotland, Norway. Physically similar, given its crescent form, to the Lindholmen amulet, it bears the following mostly perplexing sequences of runes and amuletic symbols featuring runic letterforms in multiple outline similar to those found on the amulets from Lindholmen and Kragehul:

ᚾᚺᚠᚾᚱᛗᚠᛒᚾᚲᛁᛏᚺᚾᛁᛩᛉᛟᛁᛏᚾᚢ
ᚾᛗᚤᚾᚾᚦᚠᚲᛁᚼᚾᛏᛈᛈᛁᛯᛁᚦᚲᛟᛩᛏᚾᚾ

uhaureabuKinuᚦiᛩdþinuu
ueᛩuubaKichnfþiᛉᚦᚲᛟᛩnuu

No doubt this amulet's inscription meant something to its carver, but it seems quite inscrutable today except for its hints of names such as *Buginu* (?), its wealth of amuletic symbols and its futhark row-like sequence *upaKichn*. It bears strong similarities to amulet texts of the five-part type, but like the Frisian amulets contains elements that may stem from a more recent (and more obscure) amuletic tradition too.[52]

The basic five-part system seems to have been employed well into the medieval period, then: both in the regular manner seen on examples like 'Absalon's' ring and the Dublin amulet against the walking dead, but also in somewhat variant forms, both on everyday items like rings and staves, as well as on objects deliberately made to be periapts. Developments in this tradition such as the use of decorative runes and rune-like forms are mirrored by the emergence of other visual additions such as coding and flanking, and ultimately also by the influence of other standard types of runic expressions such as carver's signatures too. Eventually, however, the decorating and encoding seems to have become so common and so complex that even the basic five-part form is hard to discern in some of these inscriptions – several of the later texts apparently of this general type are just too obscurely expressed for much to be made of them linguistically. All that is clear is that, given their permutations and patterns typical of the inscribed pendants of the five-part type, they were almost certainly meant to be amuletic.

Rarely, the five-part system that underlies these texts undergoes some expansion.

---

51 Looijenga, pp. 312–14. Interpreting the ᛘ symbol as a mirrored form of *p*, Looijenga follows E. Seebold, 'Die Inschrift B von Westeremden und die friesischen Runen', *Amsterdamer Beiträge zur älteren Germanistik* 31/32 (1990), 408–427, who reads 'may it also grow by the yew and up on the terp' with an instrumental or locative reading of *iwi-* based on a suggestion in T.L. Markey, *Frisian* (The Hague 1981), p. 121. It seems preferable to insist that 'yew' (perhaps with the *-i-* an agentive suffix) refers to the amulet itself, however, given the propensity for amuletic (and other) runic texts to include descriptions of the items they are written on.

52 Marstrander, review of Arntz and Zeiss, pp. 292–94.

These expansions typically seem to be one-off constructions, however, and do not seem to provide much of a guide to the thinking that lay behind the great majority of unexpanded legends. Instead, the reasoning behind the inscriptions of this basic type is better revealed in a consideration of the origin of the five-element formula and the original function of the runic charm words, item descriptions, names, letter sequences and symbols.

Rather than an indigenous Germanic creation, though, the five-part formula seems to have had its origin in the same area as the runes may well do themselves: in the north and especially north east of Italy, the region where the most examples of North Etruscan inscriptions have been found. Inscriptions similar to those found on runic amulets are known in this region hailing from the centuries BC, most stemming from religious sites and centres where a local version of the Greek goddess Artemis was worshipped.

One of the forms in which the ancient Greeks venerated Artemis was as Artemis Orthia, literally Artemis the 'wordy'. This cult, especially associated with the Spartans, spread at an early date into north-eastern Italy probably via early trading centres such as those of the upper Adriatic. In Italy, though, Artemis Orthia came to be known under another one of her epithets: as Reitia, the divine mistress of words.

Ancient sanctuaries to Reitia sprang up subsequently throughout a region stretching from the plains of the lower Po up into the Alps as far north as Austria. Many of these pre-Roman sites, so archaeologists have discovered, also preserve the remains of inscribed votives. Sometimes written on writing tablets or styli, other times on bronze statuettes or carved (and often burnt) pieces of staghorn or bone, the dedicatory inscriptions of the Reitia cult broadly follow an archaic votive style, but are typically complemented by a local addition. Reitia was clearly worshipped as a goddess of writing in this region and many of the votives offered to her are accompanied not just by written dedications, but also by basic spelling exercises and magical signs, much like those which appear on runic amulets.[53]

Moreover, in the northernmost tradition of Reitia worship, that of the Eastern Alps, the inscriptions often take on a pidgin-like form. The grammatically fairly regular votive messages found further south are often reduced to a sort of short-hand in the northern finds, one where the individual elements seemingly do not form proper, continuous sentences, i.e. they appear to become isolated or non-syntactic. Rather than just a reflection of the physical need for inscriptions on portable objects to be brief, this development seems to have something to do with the grammatical nature of Rhaetic, the local language. Moreover, if we exclude the appearance of the name of the goddess on these votives, they are essentially of five parts – each features one or more of the following elements: the name of the

---

53 For the Reitia cult, especially in the Veneto, see, most recently, A. Mastrocinque, *Santuari e divinità dei Paleoveneti* (Padua 1987), though R.S. Conway et al., *The Prae-Italic Dialects of Italy* 1 (Cambridge, Mass., 1933), pp. 85–92, is the only available survey in English. *Orthia* (earlier *Worthaia*) clearly developed from *wordh-* 'word' and the name *Reitia* appears to be derived from Greek *rêtheisa* (dialectal *reitheisa*) '(she who) is asked'; see T.L. Markey, 'Early Celticity at Rhaetic Magrè (Schio)', forthcoming.

dedicator, a votive verbal noun ('gift', 'offering' etc.), an item description, a spelling exercise and a holy symbol. In fact one of the dedicatory terms often used in Rhaetic texts is *alu* where the word clearly means 'dedication' – the local word even seems to have been loaned into runic use. The five-part runic-amulet formula probably developed out of a grammatically reduced form of a typical Reitia dedication; i.e. an inscription such as 'N dedicated this statuette to Reitia' became merely 'N, dedication, statuette, Reitia', which furthermore might be accompanied by a spelling exercise (or written code), demonstrating the worshipper's orthographic skills to the goddess, and perhaps a magical symbol or two.[54]

There is also clear evidence that Germanic-speakers visited these early sites, though there is no firm evidence to suggest that Germanic visitors to the Alpine Reitia sanctuaries went so far as to bring her cult back with them when they returned into the North. But they do seem to have learned how to express themselves when composing amulet texts in the style of votives of the tutelary goddess.

Once this divine way of writing lost its connection with Reitia devotion, though, it had clearly become amuletic; an *ex voto* used in a personal, everyday context is by definition an amulet. The original function of the runic-amulet formula, then, seems to have been to render the object that bore it blessed or consecrated, an aspect which also explains the formulaic similarities between the five-part texts and inscriptions apparently addressed to gods like those on the Værløse brooch or the Setre comb. This clearly explains the nature of charm words such as *alu*, *laþu*, *salu* and *tuwa*; terms such as *laukaz* may have become associated with amulets through metaphor or a similar development, whereas others such as *maga* 'strong' or *hagala* 'hail' are more clearly later accretions stemming originally from the martial sphere.

The amuletic symbols, similarly, had diverse origins. Swastikas and triskelia were used as holy symbols by the Germanic peoples long before they first learned how to write. Tamgas, on the other hand, were first encountered by the Goths after they had begun their migrations into the south and east – they are usually claimed to be Sarmatian (i.e. of an ancient Iranian people of the Ukrainian steppes) in origin. The tree-like symbols, ᚠ, ᚠ, ᚠ, however, are most similar to cultic markings (typically described as fish-bone symbols) that often appear on votive items from the Italian north east. And lastly, the letter sequences found on Reitia votives – demonstrations of literacy offered to the goddess of words and writing – are often much the same as the uncoded ones found on early runic amulets. Nevertheless, the complex forms of coding and framing used in some of the runic letter sequences seem to be an indigenous Germanic development – although a logical extension of the five-part system nonetheless.

Consequently, the basic system underlying runic amulets of the five-part type seems to have been votive in nature – much as several of the short early texts described in chapter 2 were. The basic repertoire of votive charm words was soon

---

54 See MacLeod and Mees, 'On the **t**-like symbols' and chapter 7. The most useful edition of the Rhaetic inscriptions is Morandi, *Cippo di Castelciès*, and for their translation see, fundamentally, Mees, 'Gods of the Rhaetii'.

expanded, however, to include terms signifying more specific amuletic features, such as protection and strength, a practice that seems to have been expanded even further in Christian contexts. Much as with the more explicitly pre-Christian religious texts, then, other types of expansions on the basic format developed. These are mostly rare or happenstance features, though, such as linking two or more elements together in a short narrative, or including elaborations typical of similar texts, a development seen most clearly in the inclusion of stock expressions like maker's signatures in some of the pendant legends or later amuletic inscriptions. The system came also to be influenced by the addition of features such as flanking and codes, and eventually the employment of strategies reminiscent of cryptic runes. The use of the earliest charm words like *alu* does not long survive the Migration Period, however; many appear to have been lost with the Christian conversion. But in Scandinavia the protective and enabling inscriptions of the five-part type often retained their original pidgin-like character throughout the Viking era and well into the High Middle Ages.

5

Fertility Charms

SYMPATHETIC magic in runic amulet texts was not confined to rhetorical 'just as . . ., so too . . .' inscriptions or even to metaphors (or metonyms) like the charm word 'hail', but also extended to more nuanced and complex symbolic expressions. A common place where sympathetic magic was used in Germanic tradition was in customary medicines which often feature certain types of vegetables, animal stuffs, flowers or herbs chosen because of the beneficial attributes associated with them. Leeks, for instance, were widely used in medieval medicine in order to revive and heal, and they are recorded both in curative recipes preserved in Old Norse literature as well as in Anglo-Saxon medical works. But this property connected with the leek clearly developed out of its association with male sexuality – the leek was the phallic herb in old Germanic tradition. This is not always made clear in medieval descriptions of the leek, however, because describing explicitly this aspect of its nature appears to have been regarded as slightly too embarrassing for many Christian authors. Thankfully, though, not all medieval writers proved so bashful. The most direct description of the phallic nature of the leek derives from a late medieval German source. In the middle of the fourteenth century, Konrad von Megenberg recorded the following about the leek in his *Book of Nature*:

> it brings urine and the intimacy of womankind and brings lack of chastity and most of all its seed . . .[1]

This sexual aspect of the leek can also be seen peeping through in some medieval English sources. In the *Prologue* to Chaucer's *Reeve's Tale*, for example, it is recounted of old men that:

> We hoopen ay, whyl that the world wol pype
> For in oure wil ther stiketh ever a nayl,
> To have an hoor heed and a grene tayl,
> As hath a leek; for thogh our might be goon,
> Our wil desireth folie ever in oon.[2]

---

[1] K. von Megenberg, *Buch der Natur*, Von dem pforren 63. A comprehensive survey of leeks in Germanic tradition is due to appear in a forthcoming study by T.L. Markey, though cf. also W. Heizmann, 'Lein(en) und Lauch in der Inschrift von Fløksand und im Vǫlsa þáttr', in H. Beck (ed.), *Germanische Religionsgeschichte* (Berlin 1992), pp. 365–95.

[2] Chaucer, *Canterbury Tales*, lines 3878–79.

Perhaps the earliest reference of this sort appears, however, in an Anglo-Saxon herbal, the Old English *Herbarius*, whose authorship was ascribed by medieval authors to Apuleius of Madaurus, a second-century writer who was famously persecuted in Roman times for his magical beliefs. The Anglo-Saxon *Herbarium* glosses a herb called *satyrion* as the 'raven's leek' and comments further that:

> This is the herb which some call *temolum* and others *sengreen* (i.e. houseleek) ... and its root is full of sin and evil, much like that of the leek.[3]

The ancient Germanic peoples, in contrast, held the leek in high esteem and as we have already seen its name was widely used in amulet inscriptions as a charm word. The early German word for leek, although highly abbreviated, seems to appear in an amatory context in the runic leading charm from Bülach. On the other hand, in the earlier pendant legends it usually appears to have no specific purpose apart from indicating a generally helpful sort of magic. Given the charm words of a military nature, though, this may be a reflection of other qualities ascribed to the plant: Old Norse sources, after all, sometimes use the leek as a metaphor for virility, for example describing the Eddic hero Sigurd in the *Second Lay of Gudrun (Guðrúnarkviða in forna)* as 'a green leek grown from the grass'.

There are some instances, however, where the name of the leek is obviously being used in another context. The clearest early example is in a runic inscription on a bone instrument for preparing meat, a meat-scraper, from Fløksand, Norway, which reads:

ᚱᛁᛏᚠᚠᚾᚲᚠᛉᚴ

Līna, laukaz, f(ehu).

'Linen, leek, wealth.'

This text, first uncovered in the 1860s, comes from a mid-fourth-century woman's cremation grave, making it contemporary with the earliest pendant or medallion-imitation texts and over two centuries older than the Bülach brooch. The appearance of *laukaz* 'leek' along with the word *līna* 'linen' here, though, at first seems to suggest just a series of generic charm words. Yet this combination is also known from a much later Norse story, *Volsi's Tale (Vǫlsa Þáttr)*, a title which might also be rendered as the *Tale of the Prick*.

This early-fourteenth-century story recounts how a farmer's wife in northern Norway prepared a fetish by covering a horse's penis with leeks and then wrapping both in linen. Each evening in the autumn she passed the fetish around the meal table, and each person who received it was required to say a strophe over it, one of which was:

> You're distended, Volsi, and picked up.
> Endowed with linen and supported by leeks.

Volsi is Norse slang for a penis, and horses' pricks, linen and leeks were obviously

---

3   *Old English Herbarium*, 16 and 49.

associated with fertility magic.[4] But it is clear from the tale that the purpose of the fetish was not to encourage sexual fertility in each of the diners who held it and spoke a charm over it. Instead it conveyed a more general sense of fertility – that associated with autumn, the time of harvests and the slaughtering of animals for meat. In fact the Old Norse *Seeress's Prophecy* similarly seems to record the leek used allusively to refer to chthonic fertility:

Before Bur's sons	lifted the bottoms,
when they Midgard,	the mighty, created
the sun shone from the south	on the stones of the hall,
then was the ground grown	with green leek.

The upside-down *f*-rune on the Fløksand knife is apparently a later addition to the inscription. It seems to be an abbreviation of the runic letter-name *fehu* which meant 'wealth' and is related to the Modern English word *fee*. Wealth was measured in livestock in early Germanic societies, however, and the old Germanic term *fehu* is also related to words like Modern German *Vieh* 'cattle'. Given that the Fløksand meat-scraper was an implement used to prepare meat (presumably by women), the single *f*-rune here probably also refers, much like 'linen' and 'leek' do then, to fertile abundance, an abundance of wealth in live-stock (or meat).

The inscription on the Fløksand scraper also helps to explain another, more difficult inscription on a further bone meat-scraper from Gjersvik, also in Norway. Its damaged runic text reads:

ᚺ--ᚠᛁᛩᚦᛁᛚᛚᛚᛚᛚᛚᛚᛚᛚ

D--fioþi lllllllll

This inscription, also stemming from a cremation grave, but this time dating to the mid-fifth century, is difficult to restore in its entirety. The damaged sequence seems to be a grammatically feminine form, though, and could represent a woman's name. Moreover, given the appearance of 'leek' earlier at Fløksand and the common appearance of *l*-abbreviations elsewhere on runic amulets, the ten repeated *l*-runes seem to represent a tenfold invocation of the power of the leek. In fact the sequence *līna laukaz* is 10 letters long and in one medieval Scandinavian source the name of the *l*-rune is even recorded as 'linen' which further suggests that the 'linen' and 'leek' pairing known from Fløksand was associated with (abbreviation by?) *l*-runes. The Gjersvik knife was probably also a woman's fertility amulet, then, one whose purpose was to ensure food in abundance.[5]

Yet the question remains whether all repetitions of *l*-runes that appear on Germanic amulets can automatically be associated with fertility magic. A pendant found on Fyn bears the legend *nh tbllll* with four repeated *l*-runes. Is it,

---

4   Krause with Jankuhn, no. 37. The name *Vǫlsi* is obviously a derived form of Old Norse *vǫlr* 'rod', and is continued today in modern Norwegian *volse* 'thick, long muscle, thick figure', and cf. Icelandic *völstur* 'cylinder', dialectal Swedish *volster* 'bulge', Old High German *wulst* 'bulge', and the English dialectal word *weal* 'penis'.

5   Krause with Jankuhn, no. 38.

then, a fertility bracteate? The other runes here appear to be pairs from the futhark row, the first pair from the third family and the same pair from the second (although reversed). So can a legend like this be safely interpreted as a letter sequence plus the charm word 'leek' abbreviated four times? A more recent pendant find from Roskilde, Denmark, bears a legend that reads *nhuþull✝ auþrkf* (i.e. *nh laþu ✝ fuþark?*). This suggests that the *l*-runes may instead stand for *laþu* in the legend on the Fyn pendant.[6]

It is still tempting, though, to extend a similar interpretation to repetitions of other letters found on runic amulets. Most commonly these are *z*-runes (or their later Norse descendants *R* and *y*). There is some debate, however, as to what the original name of the *z*-rune actually was. Yet it is hard to see what interpretation we might otherwise give to the following inscription on an antler amulet made in a form reminiscent of the Lindholmen and Ødemotland finds. It stems from Wijnaldum, the Netherlands, and the other side of the piece is decorated with symbols such as crosses, squares and triangles. It is a stray find without a datable context, it is slightly weathered, and the runes are probably of Frisian make:

---ᛜᛁᛝ\ᚤᛜᛁ-

. . . *ŋziŋuzŋz*

The name of the *ŋ*-rune is Ing (older Inguz or Ingwaz), the old Germanic god of fertility who heads medieval genealogies of the kings of the Angles and Swedes. He is also associated with Frey (as Ingvi-Frey) in Old Norse sources such as the *Saga of the Ynglings*, the saga of the descendants of Ing. So if the *z*-rune can also be linked with fertility magic, then surely the Wijnaldum find can only be a fertility amulet. But it is not always clear in these 'nonsense' texts whether we are dealing with abbreviations based on runic letter-names, magical gibberish, incompetent or pseudo-texts, or even different forms of coding derived from other types of runic letter-play. It has been suggested, for instance, that this inscription is essentially a (threefold) elaboration on the divine name Inguz (i.e. *(I)ng(u)z Inguz (I)ng(u)z?*) and hence the appearance of the *z*-runes would have no other special significance. Apart from *alu*, some of the Nydam arrow-shafts bear only single *z* and *l*-runes, though, presumably indicating that there was a magical meaning behind abbreviations of this sort. Nonetheless, the Nydam arrows also suggest that single-rune abbreviations like this, although perhaps originally linked with fertility magic, could readily be employed in a more general decorative or amuletic sense, too, just as charm words like 'leek' are on the old Germanic bracteates and the crosses, squares and triangles evidently are also on the Wijnaldum antler amulet.[7]

The leek was not the only plant or animal associated with old Germanic fertility, however, that came to feature repeatedly in runic amulet texts. The connection between horses and fertility suggested by the Volsi story and the

6   K. Hauck and W. Heizmann, 'Der Neufund des Runen-Brakteaten IK 585 Sankt Ibs Vej-C Roskilde (Zur Ikonologie der Goldbrakteaten, LXII)', in W. Heizmann and A. van Nahl (eds), *Runica, Germanica, Mediaevalia* (Berlin 2003), pp. 243–64.
7   Looijenga, p. 325.

Fløksand find has another reflection in runic pendant amulets, those which carry legends that are comprised solely of forms of the old Germanic word *ehwaz* 'horse'. None of the pendant legends of this type that are known today have the full form *ehwaz*, however, but instead show variations such as *ehwu*, *ehw* and *ehu*.[8] And though horses occasionally appear in bracteate decoration, there is no correlation between the appearance of this term and equine decoration on the golden pendants. Yet this word for 'horse' (which is related to Latin *equus* and English words such as *equine* and *equestrian*) does not appear in connection with 'leek' or give any other indication what its precise meaning is, so it might be thought merely to be a charm word like *hagala* 'hail' or *maga* 'strength', i.e. signifying strength or virility rather than fecundity. It was, after all, also the name of the *e*-rune. But there are several terms for 'horse' common to the old Germanic languages, and it is striking that only variations of the *eh(w)*- form appear on the golden amulet pendants.

There are two old Germanic terms for 'horse' that seem to be associated with warriors and martial prowess. One survives today in English words like *marshal* and the feminine description *mare*, and appears to have originally represented an imported breed of warhorse. The other served as the name of the early English hero *Hengist*, and in Modern German and the Scandinavian languages today means 'stallion'.

Hengist's brother *Horsa* was also a man called 'horse'. But the term which underlies his name was that used most commonly for the common man's animal. In contrast, the only modern descendant of *ehwaz* still employed in a Germanic language is Icelandic *jór*. Moreover, when it is used in early Norse literature, it usually only signifies horses ridden by kings or describes fantastic mounts such as Odin's eight-legged steed Sleipnir, or Hrimfaxi, the horse that carried the Moon across the sky in Old Norse mythology.[9]

Early Germanic	Old Norse	Old English	Old German	Modern English	Early meaning
ehwaz	*jór*	*eoh*	*ehu-*		special horse
marhaz	*marr*	*mearh*	*marah-*	*mar-*	warhorse, steed
hanhistaz	*hestr*	*hengist*	*hengist*		stallion, steed
hrussan	*hross*	*hors*	*hros*	*horse*	common horse

The discovery of the remains of horses sacrificed in prehistoric bogs shows that an association of horses and the divine was very old in the Germanic North. But it was also evidently a long-lasting one too. In the Old Norse *Flateyjarbók*, for instance, it is recounted that Olaf Tryggvasson destroyed a pagan sanctuary in Trondheim, Norway, where sacred horses were kept in honour of the fertility god

---

8   For instances, see Nowak, pp. 274–78. Antonsen, no. 57, interprets these forms as feminines (i.e. *ehwū*, putatively equivalent to Latin *equa* 'mare'), which though not verifiable might be thought further to bolster the connection with the equine sovereignty rituals elucidated in the next few pages.

9   Markey, 'Studies in runic origins 2', pp. 159–76.

Frey. Frey's horses were kept there to be used in sacrifices, and it was forbidden for anyone to ride them. Another connection between Frey and sacred horses appears in *Hrafnkel's Saga* where Hrafnkel is called 'Frey's friend' and has a special stallion named Freyfaxi (i.e. Frey's mane) who is dedicated especially to the god.

The use of the word *ehwaz* on the 'horse' amulets suggests they have something to do with kings, gods and the supernatural, then, rather than warriors, virility or the common man. It is well known, after all, that the horse was a traditional Germanic symbol of sovereignty. In fact in the *Saga of Hakon the Good*, it is recounted that King Hakon was required to drink from broth made from the flesh of a sacrificed horse as part of a pagan ritual. Moreover, like the Celtic Arthur, Old Germanic kings were also thought to be magically connected with their kingdoms, so much so that a troubled kingdom is represented in sources like *Beowulf* by means of the sickness or premature ageing of a king. Clearly in old Germanic tradition sovereignty was not just a matter of keeping the peace, but also of ensuring fertility, fecundity and abundance. *The Saga of the Ynglings* recounts that a failed Swedish king, Olaf Tree-cutter, was even sacrificed to the gods because:

> there came hard times and famine, which [the people] ascribed to their king, as the Swedes always used to judge their kings by whether their harvests were good or not. King Olaf was sparing in his sacrifices and this upset the Swedes as they believed that this was the reason for the hard times. The Swedes therefore gathered troops together, marched against King Olaf, surrounded his house and burnt him in it, giving him to Odin as a sacrifice for good crops.

Similarly the *Saga* also recounts that during the reign of another early Swedish king called Domaldi:

> there was great famine and distress in his day, so the Swedes made great offerings of sacrifice at Uppsala. The first autumn they sacrificed oxen, but the succeeding season things did not improve. The following autumn they sacrificed men, but the next year was even worse. The third autumn, when the offering of sacrifices was due to begin, a great multitude of Swedes came to Uppsala and their leaders . . . agreed that the times of scarcity were the fault of their king Domaldi, and they resolved to offer him up for good seasons, and to assault and kill him, and redden the place with his blood. And so they did.

And as the accompanying *Song of the Ynglings* further recounts:

It happened before	that warriors
reddened the earth	with their king's blood,
and the army of the land	took the life
of Domaldi	with bloody weapons
when the Swedes	were to sacrifice
the ruler	for good harvest.

A related practice is also reflected in the *Saga of Hervor* where a Swedish king by the name of Ingi was driven out of his realm because he was a Christian and had banned the old sacrifices. He was replaced by his pagan brother-in-law who

became known as Blot-Svein, 'Sacrifice-Svein'. Blot-Svein quickly reinstituted
his people's ancient sacrifices, the *Saga* recalling that 'a horse was led up to the
thing and sliced up and shared out for eating, and the sacrifice-tree was reddened
with the blood.' Ingi returned in force three years later, however, killed
Blot-Svein, and banned the pagan ceremonies again.

Horses and their sacrifice thus appear to have been connected principally with
the maintenance of fertility in pagan Germanic tradition. The horse bracteates
were probably thought to guarantee fecundity and abundance, then, much as the
distended Volsi was supposed to do in the Norwegian tale of the horse's prick.

Consequently, it is perhaps not surprising to find that a connection between
horses, fertility, sovereignty and kings is common to other early European traditions. In ancient Rome, for example, horses' blood was smeared about the city in
a fertility festival known as October Equus. And not only did some Irish kings
perform rituals with horse broth similar to those ascribed to the Norse king
Hakon, one early Irish equine sovereignty ritual even featured actual physical
consummation between the king and a sacred mare according to one scandalised
Christian observer. These Celtic and Roman examples are usually compared with
an ancient Indian ritual known as *aśvamedha*, where a horse was smothered by a
woollen or linen blanket, after which the king's chief wife pretended to mate with
the corpse under the blanket. But it is in the North Italian Reitia cult where horses,
fertility and leeks seem to have their most striking connection. One of the most
common types of votive figurines found in the remains of centres of Reitia
worship are those which take the shapes of horses, and the goddess is even
depicted in a figurine found at one of her Alpine sanctuaries with horses' heads
instead of arms. As Artemis Orthia she was clearly a goddess of animals as well as
spelling and words. In fact one of Reitia's titles was *Pora* 'leeky', a description
that clearly refers to fertility. This aspect is seen most clearly in her Roman equivalent Carmentis, the Roman goddess of magic (Carmentis' name comes from
Latin *carmen* 'song, poem, prophesy'), who under her title Porrima (cf. Latin
porrum 'leek') was also known as a goddess of childbirth.[10]

It is perhaps not too surprising then that in most instances of *laukaz* appearing
on bracteates, it does so, like the 'horse' word, as the sole term to be found. The
charm word *ota* similarly only ever appears in isolation on the old Germanic
pendants. It may well be, then, that rather than *ōta* 'smell, odour' (the most
obvious reading), the term *ōtta* 'wealth, fortune' (cf. the German man's name
Otto) was intended by these texts.[11] Moreover, the description *groba* '(something) dug, ditch' which appears once on a bracteate from Hitsum in the Netherlands in combination with a man's name, *Fozo*, might also be thought to belong to

---

10 For the other ancient horse ceremonies see C. Watkins, *How to Kill a Dragon* (New York 1995),
    pp. 265–76 and M. Egg, 'Die "Herrin der Pferde" im Alpengebiet', *Archäologisches
    Korrespondenzblatt* 16 (1986), 69–78 on the Reitia votives.

11 See Nowak, pp. 226–38 and 250–52, for the instances of *laukaz* and *ota. Otto* is an expressive
    form of *ōd-* 'riches, fortune'; **ōt-* 'smell' is the only root with this form attested in Germanic
    otherwise. A derivation of *ota* from **ōhtan* 'terror' (so Düwel, *IK* I, 2, p. 104) is phonologically
    implausible given only North Germanic dialects lose **-h-* in this environment and the word is not
    limited to Scandinavian finds.

this category of fertility charm words – although it is related to *grave* and *engrave*, it is also comparable to *groove*, and in medieval German can also indicate a furrow made by a plough. Recently *līna* 'linen' (or perhaps *wīna* 'wine') has been discerned in combination with *sima* 'cord (i.e. binding)' and *alu* 'dedication' on a pendant from Uppåkra, Sweden, though, which once again points to the suggestion that the charm words on bracteate texts were often taken only as generically magical, not for their specific meanings as is more obviously the case when they appear on finds like the old Scandinavian meat-scrapers.[12]

Other charm words which appear on the amulet pendants have been linked with fertility in the past too, perhaps most notably the often-controversial term *alu*. It is far from clear, however, that *alu* has anything directly to do with fertility. Nonetheless as the commonest of the early Germanic charm words, it appears on all manner of objects, often in isolation. Its appearance on weapons, such as those recovered from the Nydam bog, makes sense in light of the East Germanic spear finds which fit rather more clearly into the five-part formulism described in chapter 4. Similar reasoning also makes clearer the motive for the appearance of *alu* on a (now lost) sixth-century ring found near the town of Karlino (German Körlin), Poland, and even stamped (in the form of decorative mirror runes) on three early Anglo-Saxon funeral urns of a similar date excavated in the 1980s at Spong Hill, Suffolk. Its occurrence as the sole decoration on an undatable, 172cm-high granite stone from Elgesem, Norway, similarly suggests, then, that rune-stones could also bear amuletic texts. This particular example was found in a burial mound, however, and may have been a magical funerary stone.[13]

Nonetheless huge stone monuments rising up from the earth are often considered to be phallic symbols – whether literally as representations of gigantic stone penises, or merely symbolically as signs of the dominance of man over the landscape. In fact in pagan times in the North fertility and abundance were often symbolised by erect penises. One only has to remember Adam of Bremen's description of the image of Frey at Uppsala from shortly before the year 1200 as having 'a much exaggerated penis' to realise how far removed old Germanic thought was from that of the Christian missionaries on manners of sex and fecundity.[14] It should come as little surprise, then, to discover that between the years 200 and 700 the early Norse set up 'holy white stones' carved in the shape of huge erect penises. Nineteenth-century antiquarians could only see mushrooms in these objects, but such obviously phallic monuments help explain the origin of a series of rune-inscribed stones which also seem to have been meant as expressions of fertility magic.

Most rune-stones were clearly funeral monuments – gravestones or memorials – and the erection of funerary rune-stones was particularly common during Viking times. Many of the earliest rune-stones also appear to have had a magical role, however, one closer to that of uninscribed standing stones and other more clearly cultic monuments like the white penis stones and other earlier stone

12 *IK* no. 76; M. Axboe, 'To brakteater', in W. Heizmann and A. van Nahl (eds), *Runica, Germanica, Mediaevalia* (Berlin 2003), pp. 23–26.
13 Krause with Jankuhn, nos 46 and 57; Page, *Introduction*, p. 93.
14 *History of the Archbishops of Hamburg-Bremen*, trans. F.J. Tschan (New York 1959), iv, 26–27.

monuments from the ancient North. In the Bronze Age early Scandinavian people erected what today are called cup-stones, shaped stone monuments with small holes in them. These 'cups' are usually thought to have once held offerings, ones made either as part of funereal practices or as devotions associated with fertility rites. Plainer Scandinavian standing stones were also obviously venerated in pre-Christian times, as laws were enacted after the conversion to Christianity that specifically forbade sacrificing to such stones. The medieval Icelandic *Saga of Christianisation (Kristni saga)* even tells of a *landvætti* or 'guardian spirit' that lived in a stone – many such stones must have been held to be the dwelling places of sacred land spirits. Rune-stones that are not clearly funerary monuments or similar types of memorials need to be understood in light of the full range of beliefs that were associated with uninscribed Scandinavian monumental stones.[15]

Apart from the occurrence of the charm word *alu* at Elgesem, the five-part formulism common in early runic amulets also crops up in several other early rune-stone texts that are not obviously connected with commemorating the dead. It is not always immediately evident, though, what precisely they were intended for. One from Krogsta, Sweden, which may date to about the sixth century, bears runic inscriptions on either side of the stone, one of which is accompanied by the naively formed outline of a man:

ᛊᛏᚨᛁᚾᚨᛉ
ᛗᚹᛊᛇᛖᛁᛃ

Stainaz
mwsïeij

'Stone . . .'

Found in the context of several other (uninscribed) standing stones, this 170cm-high shaped granite slab is clearly not a tombstone. Instead, one of the texts is an item description, the other a letter sequence of the same length. The sequence appears to be a spelling lesson: it contains the two runes for semi-vowels (*w*, *j*), and forms which seem to have been chosen because they make the distinction between otherwise similar-looking vowel and consonant runes clearest. Obviously featuring two elements of the five-part amuletic formula, the Krogsta rune-stone was probably considered to be magical, even though the text does not make its purpose at all clear.[16]

A more elaborate example of an amuletic rune-stone text appears on a 110cm-long stone of carved gneiss found by chance digging at Ellestad, Sweden, during the 1930s. Discovered along with several other large shaped, presumably formerly standing stones, it probably dates from the seventh century. Its tripartite text, both in amuletic terms and in the way the inscription is arranged, reads:

ᛖᛉᚨᛋᛁᚷᛁᛗᚼᚱᚼᛘᚼᚠᛋ-ᛉᚼᚱᚼᛁᛋᛁᛞᛟᛉᚼ

15 For Scandinavian penis, cup and other forms of standing-stones see the first chapter of F. Ström, *Nordisk hedendom*, 3rd ed. (Gothenburg 1985).

16 Krause with Jankuhn, no. 100. The raised arms of the figure suggest it may have been meant to depict a man praying, perhaps a priest; see, further, chapter 7.

ᚼᛏᛣᛁᛏᛣᛚ
ᛉᛉ·ᛉᛁᛁᛁᛁ·ᛉᛉᛉ

Eka Sigimāraʀ afs[a]ka raisidōka, stainaʀ, kk kiiii kkk.

'I, Sigimar the blameless raised (this), stone . . .'

Although clearly an inscription of the amuletic, five-element type, it is easy to see why such a stone is often confused with a funerary monument today, even if it was not found in an ancient graveyard or similar site such as a burial mound. But the naming sequence seems to have deliberately been composed in a stylised manner, with regular rhythm, assonance and rhyme. Moreover the letter sequence seems to be some sort of code as yet unbroken. But what exactly do inscriptions of the amuletic type mean when they appear on rune-stones found among (other) standing stones?[17]

If a penis stone or any other type of fertility monument were to carry an inscription, then it might be expected to be something like that which appears on a stone from Vercelli, Northern Italy. Dating to the last century BC, the inscription on the Vercelli stone is bilingual, partly Latin, partly Celtic, and clearly indicates what it once was:

> Boundary of the field that Acisius Argantocomaterecus gave to be in common for gods and for men, where four stones have been erected accordingly.
>
> Acisios the money-patrician dedicated this depth of gods and of men to him.

Obviously the Vercelli stone was formerly one of a group that marked out the borders of a consecrated site, presumably one dedicated to a chthonic god. Moreover, the second, Celtic line of the inscription is a typical archaic religious dedication, not too dissimilar to those which appear on Reitia votives: it contains the dedicator's name Acisios, an offertory verb, a subject description (i.e. of what has been dedicated) and what seems to have been a pronoun substituting for a divine name. Given the votive origin of the five-part runic amulet formula, it seems likely, then, that stones like those from Krogsta and Ellestad, which are not clearly memorials and cannot be linked with burials, were similarly religious in intent; they indicated that the stones were somehow holy, much like the earlier cup-stones or contemporary white penis stones (to judge from their shape) were also thought to be, or were even possibly closer in purpose to the example described here from Celto-Roman Vercelli.[18]

More obviously pertaining to fertility, however, are two of a collection of stones from the region about the Lister peninsula, southern Sweden, a promontory that in medieval times was an island. Usually described under the local provincial name Blekinge, four rune-stones are known from this area today, all of

---

[17] Krause with Jankuhn, no. 59. The trochaic nature of much of this inscription is noted by M. Schulte, 'Early Nordic language history and modern runology, with particular reference to reduction and prefix loss', in B. Blake and K. Burridge (eds), *Historical Linguistics 2001* (Amsterdam 2003), p. 398.

[18] Lambert, pp. 76–79, albeit with *eu* interpreted as a late form of *eiu* 'to him'.

which seem to be somewhat interdependent. Each can only loosely be dated to perhaps about the seventh century.

The first to be considered here is that from a field known as Gommor, the former site of a village called Gummarp. Neither the village nor the rune-stone exists today; the Gummarp stone was carted off to Copenhagen in the seventeenth century and was subsequently destroyed during a fire in 1728. From the reproductions made before it was lost, though, the following text can clearly be made out:

ᚺᚼᚦᚢᚹᛟᛚᚼᚠᚼ
ᛋᚼᛏᛖ
ᛋᛏᚼᛒᚼᚦᚱᛁᚨ
ᚠᚠᚠ

Haþuwolfa[R] satte staba þria fff.

'Hathuwolf set three staves (here): *fff.*'

The repetition of *f*-runes is immediately reminiscent of the repeated *l*-runes on the Gjersvik meat-scraper as well as that from Fløksand with its single inverted runic *f*. In fact it is hard to see what else could be signified by the three runes other than three abbreviated charm words: 'wealth, wealth, wealth'.[19] Moreover, Hathuwolf is mentioned on another of the Blekinge stones making a comparable statement. The 118cm-tall stone of weathered gneiss comes from a site just north of the Lister peninsula known as Stentoften. First found in the nineteenth century along with five other large (formerly standing) stones, it has a much longer and more complicated inscription on it:

ᚾᛁᚢᚺᚼᛒᛟᚱᚢᛗᛦ
ᚾᛁᚢᚺᚨᚷᛖᛋᛏᚢᛗᛦ
ᚺᚼᚦᚢᚹᛟᛚᚼᚠᚨᛦᚷᚼᚠᛃ
ᚺᚼᚱᛁᚹᛟᛚᚼᚠᚼᛦᛗᚼᚷᛁᚢᛋᚾᚢᚺᛁᛖ
ᚺᛁᛞᛖᛦᚱᚢᚾᛟᚾᛟᚠᛖᛚᚼᚺᛖᛉᚼᚺᛖᛞᛖᚱᚼᚷᛁᚾᛟᚱᛟᚾᛟᛦ
ᚺᛖᚱᚼᛗᚼᛚᚼᛋᚼᛦᚼᚱᚼᚷᛖᚢᚹᛖᛚᚼᛞᚢᛞᛋᚼᚦᚼᛏᛒᚼᚱᛁᚢᛏᛁᚦ

*Niuhabōrum*R, *niuhagestum*R *Haþuwolfa*R *gaf j.*
*Hariwolfa*R *magiusnu* (?) *hlē.*
*H(æ)ide*R *rūnō (ru)no felheka hedera, ginnorūnō*R.
*Hermalās (ūti) æ*R *ærgiu; wēladūds sā þat briutiþ.*

'To the new farmers, to the new guests, Hathuwolf gave *j*.
Hariwolf protection to (your) descendants (?)
A run of bright runes I commit here: mighty runes. Protectionless (because of their) perversion; an insidious death to he who breaks this.'

This time Hathuwolf is described as actually giving something signified by a single runic letter, *j*, which thus seems to be an abbreviation, much as are the *f*'s of Gummarp. Moreover, as the name of the *j*-rune is *jāra* 'bountiful year', both the setting of three *f*-runes and the giving of a *j* seem to be references to fertility or

19 See Krause with Jankuhn, nos 95–98 for the Blekinge group, and Birkmann, pp. 114–42 for summaries of more recent scholarship.

abundance. Both of the first two Blekinge rune-stones are probably fertility stones.[20]

The Stentoften stone also bears two additional sequences, however, one that is slightly damaged, and another that is clearly a curse. In the first Hariwolf also seems to be granting *hlé* 'protection', although this word, related to *lee*, much as in the Vimose wood-plane inscription, could also mean 'fame' here. The difficult expression most commonly read as *magiusnu* following Hariwolf's name appears to be a collective form of *magus* 'son' in an oblique form. We can probably translate *magiusnu* as 'to the descendants' or 'to the youth', though given the present deteriorated state of this part of the inscription, we cannot really be sure.[21]

The last section of the Stentoften inscription continues with a cursing expression that alliterates and is clearly poetic. The text is deficient in some aspects, though: haplography has reduced the alliterating expression *rūnō runo* 'a run of runes' to *rūnōno*, and the expected preposition *ūti* 'out, from, because of' has been left out. But the same curse is repeated on another of the Blekinge stones, that from Björketorp, which reads from bottom to top:

```
ᚢᚦᚨᚱᛒᚨᛋᛒᚨ
ᚺᚨᛁᛞᛉᚱᚢᚾᛟᚱᚢᚾᛟ
ᚠᚨᛚᚺᚨᚺᛖᛞᚱᚨ
ᛁᛏᚱᚢᚾᚾᚨᚱᚢᚾᚨᛉ
ᚺᚨᛗᚱᛗᚨᛚᚨᚢᛋ
ᚢᛏᛁᚨᛁᚱᛈᚨᛏᛒᚱᚢᛏ
ᛉᚨᚢᛈᛒᚨᚱᚢᛏᛉ
```

Ūþarba spā.
Hæidʀ rūnō runo falheka hedra, ginnarūnaʀ.
Ærgiu hermalausʀ ūti æʀ; wēladauþe sāʀ þat brȳtʀ.

'Baleful prophecy:
A run of bright runes I commit here: mighty runes. Protectionless because of (their) perversion; an insidious death to he who breaks this.'

Found along with two other large standing stones, this granite rune-stone is a full four metres high. Here, though, an additional part of text is found on the reverse of the stone, one that describes the curse as a 'baleful prophecy'. There are also several spelling differences that separate the Björketorp from the Stentoften rune-stone, either indicating different spelling traditions, incompetence, or more probably developing or different dialects. The Stentoften stone seems to indicate

---

[20] The 'by nine bucks, by nine stallions' interpretation of L. Santesson, 'En blekingsk blotinskrift', *Fornvännen* 84 (1989), 221–29, although a development on the notion that the Stentoften stone is a fertility monument, is problematic grammatically. *Niuha-* in each case may more straightforwardly be accepted as featuring the sporadic Germanic glide-strengthening (< *niuja-*) also found in runic *Frōhila* (< *Fraujila*; see chapter 4), and realised slightly differently in the Old English variant *nīge* (of *nīwe*) and its Old Saxon equivalent *nigi* 'new'.

[21] The sequence *magiusnu* (if this is the correct reading) appears to be morphologically similar to a collective like Gothic *hlaiwasnos* 'tombs'; see T.L. Markey, ' "Ingveonic" *ster(i)r-* "star" and astral priests', *NOWELE* 39 (2001), 92–105 on similar count and mass collectives.

Fig. 8. Björketorp stones

that Hathuwolf had welcomed foreigners to Lister, so perhaps this explains some of the differences between the Björketorp and Stentoften texts.[22]

The fourth and last of the Blekinge inscriptions is from a village called Istaby and it again mentions Hathuwolf and Hariwolf. This time the 140cm-tall granite stone does not mention fertility, however, but instead, although it was not found in the vicinity of a medieval grave, it is clearly a funeral monument:

ᛋᛈᚠᛏᛦᚾᚺᚱᛁᛈᛁᚠᛈᚠ
ᚺᚢᚦᛁᛈᛁᛚᚠᛈᛦᚾᚺᛗᚱᛁᛈᛁᚠᛈᛁᛦ
ᛈᚠᚱᚺᛁᛏᚱᛁᛏᚺᛦᛈᚺᛁᚺᛦ

Aftr Hariwulfa Haþuwulfaʀ Heruwulfiʀ wrait rūnaʀ þaiaʀ.

'Hathuwolf son of Heruwolf wrote these runes in memory of Hariwolf.'

This is a fairly standard memorial text – hundreds of similar 'after' or 'in memory of' inscriptions are known from Viking times. And to judge from their names, Hathuwolf and his father Heruwolf seem to have been descendants of Hariwolf. This text is written with different forms of *a*-rune from those which are used in the Gummarp and Stentoften inscriptions, so some have thought there may have been two different Hathuwolfs at Blekinge. The term *magiusnu* suggests this is an over-interpretation, though. Nonetheless, Hathuwolf as a giver of fertility appears to have been a kinglet of Lister who was descended from Heruwolf and Hariwolf

---

22 The evidence for dialectal divergence in the texts is considered by M. Schulte, 'Nordischer Sprachkontakt in älterer Zeit', *NOWELE* 38 (2001), 55–57.

with his name based on those of his two ancestors as was traditional in early Germanic times.

Thus it seems that far from being exclusively memorial, rune-stones also played a significant part in the fertility beliefs of the early Scandinavians. They had a role perhaps analogous to the cup and penis stones, as well as the sacred pagan stones mentioned by Christian writers and the folklore of rock-dwelling spirits of the local land. The similarity of the type of inscription found on amulets of a portable nature to those which appear on some early rune-stones once again underlines the religious aspect of the early Germanic amulet tradition. It under-scores how the religious aspect of writing learned from Mediterranean custom came to complement all manner of what were in origin probably very ancient northern magico-religious beliefs. In fact southern traditions seem to be reflected even more clearly in the leek and horse amulets, fertility charms that may well have been inspired by magico-religious associations first learnt at sites of the archaic Italian Reitia cult.

6

Healing Charms and Leechcraft

THE Ribe cranium, whose inscription invokes a divine triad for help against dwarfstroke, seems to be the earliest datable example of a runic charm against some form of pain or disease. The use of runes in explicit healing magic thus appears to be comparatively late. Most examples of such finds are also Scandinavian, although some restorative formulas and healing charms are recorded in runic letters in England and other parts of Europe. Nonetheless leechcraft, the medieval art of healing, often seems to have had less to do with modern notions of medicine than with the supernatural.

In the Middle Ages, after all, sickness was commonly ascribed to the intervention of evil spirits who were thought to enter the body via any available orifice or shoot invisible darts of poison. The Anglo-Saxon metrical charm for a sudden stitch discussed in chapter 2 contained a spell to expel 'elf shot' repeating the phrase: 'Out little spear, if herein it be.' Other Anglo-Saxon charms recorded in medieval manuscripts invoke the agency of disease they are attempting to drive out, e.g.:

> Wen, wen, little wen,
> here you shall not build, nor have any abode,
> but you shall go north, hence to the neighbouring hill.

Flying venom, i.e. airborne contagion, and evil-minded elves, trolls and dwarfs were thought to roam the landscape, and once a person had succumbed to the spirits of disease and become infected, the sickness was commonly conceived of as a malevolent spirit which had to be cast out from the body. This belief in possession, characteristic also of the New Testament, is evident in later Scandinavian charms such as one entitled *For Trolls in People*:

> You, Troll
> Who is in here
> You must go out
> You must flee.

Such exorcisms of evil spirits are paralleled in the works of early Latin medical writers who sometimes refer to them as *carmen idioticum* 'the charms of laypersons'. Not infrequently in Germanic charms, Christ himself is cast in the role of avenging agent, as in the following example from Anglo-Saxon England:

Fly, devil, Christ pursues you!
When Christ is born the pain will go.

The Anglo-Saxon charms, drawing on a number of traditions, including native Germanic folklore and belief in flying venom and malevolent nature sprites such as elves, were modified by the teachings of classical medicine, the liturgy and herb-lore, as well as contemporary Celtic Christianity. Anglo-Saxon herbals and medical manuscripts include scientific treatises translated directly from Graeco-Roman sources and more eclectic popular compilations of charms and herb prescriptions betraying a variety of origins. The only two written in Old English to have come down to us, *(Bald's) Leechbook* (from about the middle of the tenth century) and *Lacnunga* (from about a century later), conflate native pagan charms and rituals, Graeco-Roman medical lore and expressions of Irish-English Christianity. And although the cultural contacts of the Scandinavians were different to those of the Anglo-Saxons, Scandinavian charms similarly represent a synthesis of classical, Christian and ancestral pagan lore. The blend and interaction of pagan and foreign tradition is evident in many of the runic charms, even those which are superficially Christian, and we see Christian prayers, psalms, benedictions, exorcisms and even biblical stories used in the same way as the ritual words, supplications and divine narratives of the pagan charms. Magic, of course, readily absorbs foreign elements, particularly written words or characters, the original significance of which is often long forgotten. Runic charm inscriptions, in Scandinavian or the Latin of the Church, also include vocabulary drawn from Greek, Hebrew and even Irish sources.[1]

Anglo-Saxon leechcraft was based on Germanic (and perhaps Celtic) herb-lore and folklore as well as the works of various Greek medical writers, filtered through Latin authors and often modified by them. These include particularly the *Natural History* of the Elder Pliny, a vast first-century encyclopaedic collection of ancient knowledge, and late classical compilations or abstracts largely derived from it, such as the more superstitious treatise *On Medicine* of the Gaulish writer Marcellus Empiricus (written in about the year 400) who is also sometime referred to as Marcellus of Bordeaux. Several other works of Mediterranean pagan origin, consisting largely of deteriorated Greek medical teaching, were known too, including works ascribed to Dioscorides, Apuleius of Madaurus, Antonius Musa, Hippocrates, Galen, Priscian, Oribasius and Paul of Ægina. After the Norman conquest of England and on the Continent too, classical medical texts continued to be copied, revised and circulated in large numbers, with medical

---

[1] The Anglo-Saxon charms are collected in Storms and the medical background and medical manuscripts of the Anglo-Saxons discussed there as well as in W. Bonser, *The Medical Background of Anglo-Saxon England* (London 1963) and J.H. Grattan and C. Singer, *Anglo-Saxon Magic and Medicine* (London 1952) though cf. the critique of M.L. Cameron, *Anglo-Saxon Medicine* (Cambridge 1993). Norwegian charms are most conveniently collected in A.C. Bang, *Norske hekseformularer og magiske opskrifter* (Oslo 1901–1902), Danish charms in F. Ohrt, *Danmarks Tryllefomler* (Copenhagen 1917) and a useful collection of Swedish charms occurs in E. Linderholm, 'Signelser och besvärjelser från medeltid och nytid', *Svenska landsmål och svenskt folkliv* 41 (1917–40), 1–479. The wen charm is Storms, no. 4, the devil one no. 41, whereas the Norwegian wolf charm is Bang, no. 57.

treatises often forming sections of larger scientific compendia. These works were complemented by the popular natural histories known as bestiaries and lapidaries (cataloguing magical and medical properties of animals and stones or minerals), and fanciful, fantastic manuscripts detailing exotic marvels and curiosities. The cross-cultural contact documented in Anglo-Saxon leechcraft and similar Germanic writings is also evident in the Scandinavian runic charms, which include a mixture of pagan Teutonic magic, often with a Christian veneer, and Latin liturgical elements. They freely borrow learning, tradition and even the words themselves from a variety of foreign sources.

Pagan and Christian exorcism spells are found scratched into a variety of medieval runic amulets. An almost rectangular copper amulet from Sigtuna, Sweden, perforated so that it could be appended to some part of the body, addresses the sickness demon as 'wolf', a term regularly applied to common criminals and those outside the laws of civilised society. The reading starts clearly enough, curving around the two lines of the first side, while the second side has three horizontal lines also in so-called boustrophedon style.[2] Reading of the final line, which is in a mixture of different runic alphabets, is more contentious:

ᚦᚢᚱᛂᚿᛏᚱᚱᛁᚦᚢᛂᚦᚢᚱᛌᛏᛏᚱᚿᛏᛁᛂᛈᚱᛁᚿᚦᚿᛏᚿᛈᚿᛁᛂᛏᛁᛂᛁᛌ'
ᛏᛈᚦᛁᛣᚦᚱᛁᛏᛣᚦᚱᛏᛣᚿᚱᛈᛂ
ᛏᛈᚦᛁᛣᛏᛁᚿᛏᛂᚦᛁᛣᚿᚱᛈᛌᛁᛁᛁᛂ
ᛁ'ᛁᛣᛁᛘᛁᛚᛁᛣᛂᛃᚱᛁᛌᛏᛁᛣᚿᚱᛈᛌᛂᛁᚿᛏᚱᚿ
ᛈᛁᛂ

Þurs sārriðu, þursa drōttinn! Flīu þū nū! Fundinn es(tū).
Haf þær þriāʀ þrāʀ, ūlfʀ!
Haf þær nīu nauðiʀ, ūlfʀ!
iii isiʀ þis isiʀ auki (e)s uniʀ, ūlfʀ. Niūt lyfia!

'Ogre of wound-fever, lord of the ogres! Flee now! (You) are found. Have for yourself three pangs, wolf! Have for yourself nine needs, wolf! *iii* ice (runes). These ice (runes) may grant that you be satisfied (?), wolf. Make good use of the healing-charms!'

In this amulet, probably from the mid-to-late eleventh century, the spirit responsible for the disease is cursed with three pangs and nine 'needs', presumably tribulations of some sort. A *þurs* is an unpleasant giant or ogre: the healing-stick considered in chapter 2 inveighed against the elves, trolls and ogres (*þursir*), in Old English poetry Beowulf's opponent Grendel is a *þyrs* (the early English equivalent) and the very phrase *þursa drōttinn* 'lord of ogres' which appears on this amulet is also found in Eddic poetry where it applies to the evil giant Thrym, famous for his theft of the god Thor's hammer.[3] The wolf is regarded as an agent of evil in Scandinavian folklore (compare modern tales of werewolves) and

---

2   The last three runes are found between two runes back on the first side – apparently the inscriber ran out of room; see M. Eriksson and D.O. Zetterholm, 'En amulet från Sigtuna', *Fornvännen* 28 (1933), 129–56.

3   Many scholars in fact prefer to identify the first word as the name of the god Thor rather than *þurs*, 'ogre'.

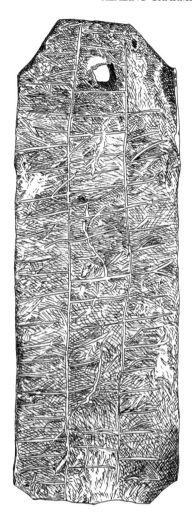

Fig. 9. Sigtuna amulet

several charms address the 'wolf' or charge him to leave a sick person, as in the following Norwegian example:

Mr Wolf, Mr Wolf, Mr Wolf!
If you are in here,
Then you must come out,
North to Klubenmo,
And straighten all the crooked trees,
And bend all the straight ones.[4]

It is also worth remembering that *tuss* and *tusse* (the modern descendants of *þurs*) in some Swedish dialects have the twin meanings 'giant, ogre' and 'wolf'; in some parts of Norway the term even appears to describe a kind of sickness akin to nightmare.

[4] Bang, no. 51.

A close parallel to the runic amulet from Sigtuna has been found in a runic Norse charm against blood poison recorded in a manuscript from Canterbury, also expelling a named agent of disease, addressed as 'wound-causer' rather than 'wolf', and here augmented by an explicit invocation of the pagan god Thor.[5] The Canterbury charm was inserted into the margin of an Anglo-Saxon manuscript finished in the year 1073 and runs as follows:

ᛈᚢᚱᛁᛙᚼᛏᚱᛈᚢᛏᚱᛏᛈᛧᛏᚱᛈᚢᛏᚾᛈᛧᚾᛏᛏᛁᛏᛁᛙ᛬ᛏᚾᛈᚢᚱᚾᛁᛈᛁᚦᛁᛈ
ᚦᛈᚱᚼᛏᛏᚱᚾᛏᛁᛏᛁᚾᚱᛁᛙᚼᛏᚱᛈᚢᛏᚱᛏᚾᛁᚦᚱᛏᚦᚱᛏᚾᛏᚱᛁ᛬

Gyril sārðvara, far þū nū! Fundinn es-tū. Þorr vīgi þik,
þursa dróttinn! Gyril sārðvara. Viðr œðravari.

'Gyril wound-causer, go now! You are found. May Thor bless you, lord of ogres! Gyril wound-causer. Against blood-vessel pus.'

This charm, against a specified ailment (blood-vessel pus), follows the pattern laid out above: discovery ('you are found') of a named agent (Gyril, perhaps related to *gor* 'gore, pus') and banishment ('go now!'). Although not celebrated for his medical prowess, Thor was certainly renowned for his enmity against the giants. He was also conceived of as a protector of mankind as is evident from his role in the sagas and notably in the Kvinneby amulet discussed in chapter 2 (which also featured a banishment formula).

It seems that the effect of the Sigtuna curse lay in a magical formula; at any rate, the runic sequence towards the end of the charm (written in a mixture of runic alphabets, including some rare staveless runes) defies easy interpretation. The closing command 'make good use of the healing-charm!' is reminiscent of the injunction 'make good use of the monument!' found on some Danish rune-stone inscriptions and commonly supposed to bind the corpse to a final place of rest (as is discussed in chapter 9). Here it is probably ironically employed to ensure that the wolfish spirit cannot escape the effects of the charm, or perhaps is addressed to the wearer of the periapt. Several Scandinavian charms end with a plea that the wearer's health be restored: 'Give NN back his health!' or some such phrase.

In fact another parallel to these charms occurs on a runic rib-bone recently found in Sigtuna and dated to the late eleventh or early twelfth century. The text, featuring both normal and cryptic runes, has not been fully deciphered, but seems to read:

ᛁᛉᚱᛁᛚᚾˣᛉᚾᚱᛁᛈˣᚾᛏᛈᚾᛏᛏᚾᚱ᛬ᛈᚱᛉᛈᛂˣᛒᛏᛏᛉᛏᛏˣᚱᛁᛈᚾˣᛒᛏᚱ-
ᛉᛏᛏ᛬ᚱᛁᛈᚾˣᛏᛉᛈˣᚾᛁᛈᛏˣᚾᛏᚱᛈˣᚾᛏᚱᛏᚱᛏᛏˣᚾᛏᚱᛏˣˣᛏᛈᛁᚱˣᛈᚾᚱᛏ
ᛈᛁᛈᛁᛏˣᛈᛏᚾ᛬ᛒᚱᛏᛉᛏ ᚱᛁᛈᛏ

Ioril sār-riða vaxnaur (?) kroke (?).
Batt hann riðu, bar[ði] hann riðu, ok sīða sarð.
Sārāran-vara hafir fullt fengit.
Flȳ braut riða!

<hr/>

5   *DR* no. 419. The Canterbury charm is mentioned in Moltke, *Runes and their Origin*, p. 360.

'Ioril wound-fever . . . He bound the fever, he fought the fever and fucked the sorcerer. Wound . . . has taken full. Fly away, fever!'

Clearly, this is a similar charm and Canterbury's Gyril and the present amulet's Ioril (or Yoril) are evidently the same sickness-causing spirit.[6]

Curiously enough, the final word, *lyf* 'healing-charm, cure', of the Sigtuna copper amulet also opens an unintelligible inscription inscribed in late medieval runes on a stone-age Danish axe. A two-faced copper plate from Skänninge, Sweden, also has the sad residue of a healing charm; its remaining runes read: ᛚᚢᚠᚱᚢᚾᛅᚱ. . . ᚴᛒᚢᛏᚱᚢᚾᛅᛦ, perhaps *lyfrūnaʀ [rist ia]k, būtrūnaʀ*, 'charm-runes (I carve), cure-runes'. The latter expression, as Old Norse *bótrúnar* 'cure-runes', is also encountered on the *skag*-valkyrie stick as well as, probably, in the *Lay of Sigrdrifa* as was indicated in chapter 2; and compare the encouraging runic inscription on a rune-stick from Bergen: *Bót haf þú, velkom(inn)*, 'You shall have a cure, welcome.' *Lyfsteinar* or 'healing-stones' are commonly described as being attached to swords in Old Norse literature and the use of such a stone is detailed in the *Saga of Kormak*. Clearly, then, they refer to a special kind of healing amulet in Norse experience, and in fact the verb *lyfja* 'heal' is one of the most commonly used words in Norse healing spells. Moreover, a healing-tongue (*lyf-tunga*) is also referred to in a runic exorcism from Denmark, discussed below.[7]

Three pangs and nine needs are wished upon the Sigtuna 'wolf'. Nine needs, or perhaps nine *n*-runes, are also invoked in some later Icelandic spells discussed below, and on a similar runic amulet from Sigtuna which seems to be directed against a revenant dead. Like the first runic periapt from Sigtuna and of approximately the same size, the second Sigtuna amulet also bears an inscription, probably from the late twelfth century, carved over both sides of a sheet of copper plate.[8] An idealised reading is as follows:

ᛁᚴᛆᚴᚢᚴᚱᛁᛋᛏᚢᛁ:ᚢᛂᚵᛆᚿᚦᛦ.ᛏᚢᚿᚵᛚᚿᚢᛘ
ᛋᛁᚠᚵᛂᚠᚿᚢᛘ ᛁᛁ
ᚯᚱᚦᛆᛏᛆᚿᚵᛂ.ᛂᚤᚦᛆᛏᛋᚴᛁᚿ
ᛂᚴ.ᚦ.ᛋᛁᚵᚦᚱᛁᛆᚿᛆᚢᚦᛦᚿᛁᚢ
ᚢᛁ

*Ik ak uk. Ris þū ī veg undi***ʀ** *tunglunum,*
sifgefnum!
Ør þat angi! Eyð þat skīn!
Ek þ(urs) seg þriu, nauðr nīu.
Vīurr nān'k (?)

'*Ik ak uk.* Rise and go away beneath the benevolent stars! Make this crazy (i.e. confused), mist! Destroy this, (sun)shine! I say three ogres, nine needs. (As) overseer of the sanctuary, I conjure (?)'

6 For the Sigtuna bone curse see H. Gustavsson, 'Verksamheten vid Runverket i Stockholm', *Nytt om runer* 13 (1998), 19–28.

7 The Skänninge copper plate was published by H. Gustavsson, 'Verksamheten vid Runverket i Stockholm', *Nytt om runer* 16 (2001), 19–34. The Bergen cure-stick is N B203.

8 The second Sigtuna amulet is discussed by A. Nordén, 'Bidrag till svensk runforskning', *Antikvariska studier* 1 (1943), 154–70 and it is his interpretation which is presented here.

Although the translation provided above is not unproblematic, the invocation of 'three ogres, nine needs' is clear enough. The word *þurs* 'ogre' is ideographically represented by the rune Þ whose name was 'ogre'. The expression 'I say three ogres, nine needs' can obviously be compared not only with that of the other Sigtuna amulet but also with the similar maledictions on the Bergen curse-stick and in the Eddic poem *Skirnir's Journey* that were discussed in chapter 2: the stick's 'wolfish evil and hatefulness', cut 'thrice against the ogres' and more directly the *Lay*'s 'I carve for you an ogre (*þurs*) and three staves: evil and madness and hatefulness'. Nine need(-runes) also feature in an erotic Icelandic spell to compel a woman to love the caster: *risti eg þér ása átta, nauðir níu*, 'I carve for you eight ᚨ and nine ᚾ'. They also appear among 'fart runes' in the *Galdrabók* in a spell calling for an inscription in blood and the recitation: 'I carve for you eight *a*-runes, nine *n*-runes, thirteen *þ*-runes' (*Otte ausse Naudir Nije þossa ðretten*) which will 'torment your stomach with terrible farting'.[9]

The *n*-rune is further referred to in the Eddic poem the *Lay of Sigrdrifa* where it is supposed to be marked 'on the nail' in connection with an amatory charm (see further chapter 10). The three *i*-runes on the first amulet have also been thought reminiscent of the three ᚱ, *n* and *t*-runes on the Lindholmen amulet (chapter 4), the triple *f*-runes on the Gummarp stone (discussed in chapter 5) or even the three staves threatened by Skirnir or the three pangs wished upon the wolf in the runic curse. Further similarities between the two amulets include the apparent banishment formula in the imperative ('Flee now!' or 'Go away!'), the mention of three monsters or miseries or nine needs and the untranslatable sequences, presumably magical formulas, in a mixture of runic alphabets.

The word *nauðr* 'need' is apparently found on one end of a rune-stick from Bergen featuring largely unintelligible text, although perhaps containing the words *vas* 'vessel', *lavare* 'wash' and the name *Maríu* 'Mary', and which is thus somewhat suggestive of a ritual of some kind. The ideographic invocation of Þ *þurs* 'ogre' and ᚾ *nauð* 'need' may be further encountered on a small, carved stick from twelfth-century Lödöse, Sweden. The stick's nine runes at first seem to read *þþþnnnooo*, but carefully cut inside the *þ*-runes are monograms of *n* and *o* (i.e. *þnoþnoþnonnnooo*). The inscription thus appears to consist entirely of a complicated *þ(urs)*, *n(auð)*, *o(ss)*, 'ogre, need, god (?)' sequence repeated as some kind of magical formula (the attested names of the latter rune are contradictory, but a reading *áss* 'As, god of Asgard' rather than *óss* '(river) mouth' seems preferable here). Another stick inscription from Bergen simply consists of a nine-fold monogram of the runes Þ (*þ*) and ᚾ (*n*); yet another merely reads *nnþnnþ* (and a monogram of *nþr*, presumably an abbreviated *n(au)ðr* 'need' or ideographic 'need, ogre, ride', is repeated eight times on another Bergen stick, alongside other magical symbols). The Roskilde pierced rune-stick bafflingly repeats the runes *u* 'aurochs' and *þ* 'ogre' (perhaps an abbreviation *þu(rs)*?) nearly a hundred times over four sides. These do not seem to be spelling lesson-based sequences, then, of

---

9   The Icelandic love spell (*kvennagaldur*) is recorded in Árnason, *Íslenzkar þjóðsögur* 1, p. 449; the fart runes in the *Galdrabók*. Fart runes of a different kind might be identified on a stick from Bergen discussed in chapter 3. See also McKinnell and Simek, pp. 140–44.

the type described in chapter 4, but instead appear to be based on the ideographic meanings of the runic letters *þ* and *n*. Furthermore, a much earlier Swedish runic find, an early-eighth-century pierced copper amulet from a Gotlandic grave, appears to read ᚦᚢᚾᚢᚱᚦᚢᚱᛋ, and, from the opposite direction, ᛁᛁᛁᚼᚨᛏᚱᚾᛁᛉ. The beginning of this might be transcribed as *þunur þurs*, i.e. starting with a word reminiscent of *Þunarr*, possibly an early Nordic form of the name Thor (cf. Old English *Þunor*). Given his name literally means 'thunderer', though, the expression may equally mean 'thundering-ogre', followed by what may be read as another negative expression, *iii hatr nem*, '*iii* take hate (or persecution)', the three repeated *i*-runes being reminiscent of those found on the Sigtuna 'ogre' amulet. Moreover, the Norwegian *Runic Poem* continues this theme when it warns that 'the ogre (rune) causes women torment' and the Icelandic version similarly explains that 'the ogre is women's torment and crag-dweller and Valrun's husband'. Clearly the ogre rune had unpleasant significance for Scandinavian women; its use in threatening amatory magic and sickness curses suggests it was considered to have powerful negative magical connotations (and in fact the love spell from the *Galdrabók* considered in chapter 2 used the staves *molldþuss* and *mann*, 'earth-ogre' and 'man'). A further runic amulet from Köpingsvik, Sweden, as yet unpublished, reads *þrymiandi þurs*, 'noisy ogre' and also seems to be aimed at expelling a sickness demon of some sort. The phrase *(þ)urs rist-ik fra*, 'an ogre I carve' has also been identified on an amulet from Vassunda, Sweden, though it is a much more degenerate specimen and its testimony is correspondingly less trustworthy.[10]

A similar kind of pagan exorcism, although with Christian interpolations, from about the year 1300 is found on a piece of wood from Ribe, Denmark, which is covered on five sides with runes:

+ᛁᛆᚱᚦ:ᛒᛁᚦᛆᚴ:ᚢᛆᚱᚦᛅ:ᛆᚴ:ᚢᛒᚼᛁᛘᛅᚿ:ᛌᛆᛚ:ᛆᚴ:ᛌᛆᚿᛏᛅᛘᛆᚱᛁᛆ:ᛆᚴ:ᛌᛁᛆᛚᚠᛅᚿ:ᚠᚢᚦᚱᛆᛏᛅᚿ:ᚦᛅᛏᚼᛆᚿ:
ᛚᛅᛘᛁᚴ:ᛚᛅᚴᚿᛅᛌ:ᚼᛆᚿᛏ:ᛆᚴᛚᛁᚠ:ᛏᚢᚴᚴᛅ:ᛆᛏᛚᛁᚢᛅ:
ᚢᛁᚢᛁᚿᛏᚿᛅ:ᚦᛅᚱ:ᛒᛆᛏᛅ:ᚦᛆᚱᚠ:ᛆᚱ:ᛒᛆᚴ:ᛆᚴᛆᚱᛒᚱᛦᛏ:ᛆᚱᛚᛅᚴᛅ:ᛆᚴᛆᚱᛚᛁᛘ:ᛆᚱ:ᛆᚢᛅᚿ:ᛆᚴᛆᚱᛆᚱᛅᚿ:
ᛆᚱ:ᛆᛏᛚᛅᚦᛁ:ᚦᛅᚱ:ᛁᛚᛏ:ᚠᛆᚿᛁᛆᛏ
ᚠᚢᛘᛅ:ᚢᛆᚱᛏ:ᚼᛁᛏᛅᚱ:ᛏᛁᚿ:ᚼᛆᚿ:ᛏᛅᚱ:ᛁ:ᚼᛆᚴᛅ:ᚢᛏᛅ:ᚦᛅᚱ:ᛚᛁᚴᛅᚱ:ᛆ:ᚦᛁ:ᚿᛁ:ᚿᛆᚢᚦᛅᚱ:ᚦᛅᚱ:ᛚ---
ᚱᛆ:ᚦᛁᚿ:ᚿᚦᚦᛅᚦᛁᚠᚢᛚᚼᚢᛅᚱᚠᛁ
ᚠᚢᛚᛅ:ᚼᚢᛅᚱᚠᛁ:ᛆᛏᛅᚿ:ᛆᚴᛅ:ᛅᚦ:ᚢᛆᚱᛘᚿᛅᚿ:ᚢᛆᚴᛅ:ᚠᛆᚱᚱᛅᚿ:ᚦᚢ:ᚦᛅᛅ:ᛒᛆᛏ:ᛒᛁᚦᛅᚱ:ᚦᛅᚱ:ᛆᚴ
ᛆᚱᚦ:ᛆᛏᚴᛅᚦᛅ:ᚱᛆᚿᛏᛁ:ᛆᛘᛅᚿ:ᛆᚴ:
ᚦᛅᛏ:ᛁ+

Iorð biðak varðæ
sōl ok santæ Marīa
þæt han læ mik
ok līf tungæ
þær bōtæ þarf.

ok uphimæn,
ok sialfæn Guð drōtæn,
lǣknæs hand
at livæ bivindnæ

10 Ideographic invocations of 'ogre' and 'need' are found on the Bergen sticks N B332, N B476 and N B504, and the Lödöse stick, for which see Svärdström and Gustavson, 'Runfund 1974', pp. 166–77. The Hallbjäns copper plate is presented in H. Gustavson and T. Snædal Brink, 'Runfynd 1980', *Fornvännen* 76 (1981), 186–191 and the other Gotlandic amulet is mentioned ibid., p. 189. A reading of the Vassunda amulet (which does not command much support) is in Nordén, 'Bidrag', pp. 183–86. On the Norwegian runic poem see A. Liestøl, 'Det norske runediktet', *Maal og minne* (1948), 65–71 and Page, *Introduction*, pp. 65–73.

Ōr bak ok ōr bryst,   *ōr lǣkǣ ok ōr lim,*
ōr øvǣn ok ōr ørǣn,   *ōr allǣ þe þǣr ilt kanīat kumǣ.*

Svart hetǣr stēn,   *han stǣr ī hafǣ ūtǣ.*
þǣr ligǣr ā þe nī nouðǣr,   *þǣr ... þen ... þǣ þes skulǣ hvǣrki,*
skulǣ hvǣrki søtǣn sofǣ   *ǣþ varmnǣn vakǣ,*
førrǣn þū þǣssǣ bōt bīðǣr   *þǣr ak orð at kvǣðǣ rōnti.*
Amǣn ok þǣt sē.

'I pray earth to guard   and high heaven,
the sun and holy Mary   and the lord God himself,
that he grant me   leech-hands
and a healing tongue   to heal the trembler
when a cure is needed.

'From back and from breast,   from body and from limb,
from eyes and from ears;   from wherever evil can enter.

'A stone is called Svart (i.e. 'black'),   it stands out in the sea,
there lie upon it nine needs,   who ... then ... should,
shall neither sleep sweet   nor wake warm,
until you pray this cure   which I have proclaimed in runic
                                  words.

Amen, and so be it.'

This so-called 'healing stick', just under 30cm long, evidences a five-part incantation. The opening lines are in the *fornyrðislag* metre typical of Eddic verse and contain an invocation of the powers of the universe: earth, high heaven and the sun, as well as God and Mary. This precedes an alliterative exorcism of 'the trembler', i.e. the trembling disease, malaria. A narrative stage then ensues, followed by a threat and a bilingual conclusion (Hebrew *amen* and its Old Danish translation *þæt se*). Although found in Denmark, various linguistic affinities indicate that the charm was either inscribed by a Norwegian or perhaps by a Dane copying from a Norwegian exemplar. Ribe, after all, was a thriving trading town.[11]

Despite the superficial veneer of Christianity in the form of an appeal to God and the Virgin, the text sounds patently heathen with its invocation of the power of the earth and sun. A similar hymn to the sun, 'high heaven' and the earth forms part of the famous Anglo-Saxon *Æcerbot* or *Field Remedy*, an agricultural ritual for blessing and fructifying the fields, part of which reads:

Eastwards I stand, for favours I pray.
I pray the glorious Lord, I pray the great prince,
I pray the holy guardian of the heavenly kingdom.
Earth I pray and high heaven,
and the true holy Mary,
and heaven's might and high hall
that I may pronounce this charm,

11 The Ribe stick is discussed by Moltke, *Runes and their Origin*, pp. 493–96 and more extensively in idem, 'Runepindene fra Ribe', *Fra Nationalmuseets arbejdsmark* (1960), 122–36; cf. also L.L. Hammerich, 'Der Zauberstab aus Ripen', in H. Kuhn and K. Schier (eds), *Märchen, Mythos, Dichtung* (Munich 1964), pp. 147–67. McKinnell and Simek, p. 142, propose reading *at lyf binda*, 'to bind/construct a charm' rather than 'to heal the Trembler' (*at livǣ bivindnǣ*): in any case, an emendment of some kind is required as the charm actually has *uiuindnǣ*, a word which not only ruins the alliteration but which is not known in Norse.

by the grace of the Lord, by firm thought,
awaken these plants to our worldly use,
fill this earth by firm belief,
beautify this grassy turf . . .
Erce, Erce, Erce, mother of earth,
may the all-ruler, eternal Lord, grant you
fields growing and thriving . . .

This charm and its accompanying rituals, despite Christian overtones, betray an undeniably pagan origin for many of the rites and formulations. The name Erce is not Old English and is usually regarded as a pre-Christian name for Mother Earth, an Old British fertility goddess. A Latin prayer to the earth has also survived from Anglo-Saxon England and belief in the power of the earth is evident in various Germanic charms and practices, including the old Scandinavian custom of laying a child on the earth as soon as it is born.[12]

In fact, it is a commonplace of magic that enchanters call on higher powers to give them strength. The Ribe staff has also been compared with a charm recorded in an eleventh-century Anglo-Saxon manuscript which begins:

I secure myself by means of this staff and commend myself to the protection of God, against the painful stitch, against the painful blow, against the grim horror, against the great terror which is hateful to everyone, and against all the harm that may go into the land.[13]

As well as recalling the earlier English charms, the Danish spell is also strongly reminiscent of local Scandinavian verse. The poetic Norse concept of *upphiminn* 'high heaven' or 'heaven above' (cf. the *upheofon* 'high heaven' in the Anglo-Saxon text) recurs in a Viking Age memorial rune-stone from Skarpåker, Sweden, which ends with the versified phrase *Iarð skal rifna ok upphiminn*, 'Earth shall be riven and high heaven', presumably evoking the final catastrophe of Ragnarok, the final doom of the gods, to express the grief-stricken father's dismay at the loss of his beloved son. The lines recall further fragments of Eddic poetry, e.g. the creation myth as described in the *Seeress's Prophecy*:

There was no sand, no sea,	no surges cold.
There was no earth	nor high heaven;
the void was gaping,	but grass nowhere.

'High heaven' is also referred to in three other Eddic poems, as well as Old Saxon and Old English religious poetry. Thus 'earth and high heaven' seems to have been a Germanic poetic commonplace, equivalent to the expression 'heaven and earth' still used today.[14]

---

[12] The Anglo-Saxon field remedy is in Storms, pp. 172–87. *Erce* means 'furrow' in Celtic (Ogham Irish); see G. Nagy, 'Perkúnas and Perenŭ', in M. Mayrhofer et al. (eds), *Antiquitates Indogermanicae* (Innsbruck 1974), pp. 113–31 on similar theonyms developed from the same root.

[13] Meaney, pp. 18–19. On staves in magic practice see Hammerich, pp. 153–54.

[14] On the use and possible significance of 'high heaven' see L. Lönnroth, '*I rð fannz æva né upphiminn*', in U. Dronke et al. (eds), *Speculum Norroenum* (Odense 1981), pp. 310–27.

After its evocative opening, the Ribe runic charm then makes reference to a further ancient trope, healing with hands (leech's hands) and healing with words (or, rather, healing with the tongue). Similar formulations are common in Norse mythological literature and like 'earth and high heaven' seem to represent very old, certainly pre-Christian rhetorical tradition. The Ribe runic charm then continues with an enumeration of the parts of the body from which the demon is to be exorcised, a strategy characteristic of magical practice in general. The Anglo-Saxon charm against elf shot considered earlier similarly continued, for instance: 'If you were shot in the skin, or were shot in the flesh, or were shot in the blood, or were shot in the bone, or were shot in the limb, never may your life be torn apart'. A charm *Against Worms* from Germany in a like manner also begins: 'Go out worm with nine little ones, out from the marrow to the bone, from the bone to the flesh, out from the flesh to the skin, out from the skin to the arrow.' Such enumerations are strongly reminiscent of classical curse spells, however, some of which even had small human figurines attached to them with nails piercing each of the areas to be affected. Protective prayers known as *loricae* naming various parts of the body are also well known from Christian liturgical manuscripts and have been claimed originally to have been charms to counter classical binding curses. Described by a term at first denoting a leather cuirass and later a breastplate, a *lorica* provided metaphoric armour repelling demons and sins. In fact the earliest *loricae* were early Irish prayers invoking protection for body and soul from various diseases and afflictions, and they seem to have first been introduced to England directly from Ireland. In view of their popularity in Anglo-Saxon times, it is not surprising to find that exorcising spells in other Germanic traditions are infused with such elements. The following example against 'elf sickness' from England, recorded in Latin and ultimately traceable to the so-called *Lorica of Gildas* (probably written in Ireland in the seventh century), is one of the earliest of such recorded works:

> Almighty God, Father of our Lord Jesus Christ, by the imposition of this writing, drive out from your servant (name) every attack of spirits, from the head, the hair, the brains, the forehead, the tongue, from under the tongue, from the throat, from the pharynx, from the teeth, the eyes, the nose, the ears, the hands, the neck, the arms, the heart, the soul, the knees, the hips, the feet, the joints and all limbs within and without. Amen.

Loricae continued to be popular in Germanic leechcraft: one is found in the Icelandic *Galdrabók* and later Scandinavian examples continue to show several points of similarity with the Ribe inscription.[15]

Subsequent to the listing of the parts of the body from which the disease is to be expelled, the ensuing narrative stage of the Danish charm has a mostly obscure reference to nine needs lying upon a stone, Svart, which stands in the sea (where they perhaps were banished). Nine needs also featured in the previous runic

---

15 On the origin of the *loricae* and the *lorica* of Gildas see M.W. Herren (ed.), *The Hisperica Famina II* (Toronto 1987). The *lorica* reproduced here is Storms, no. 17, the *Galdrabók* spell is no. 21; cf. also Moltke, 'Runepindene fra Ribe', pp. 130–31.

curses where they were wished as an affliction upon the demons of disease. In fact the number nine plays a significant role in Germanic folklore: charms frequently contain nine ingredients or specify a ritual to be performed nine times (e.g. the *Field Remedy* requires the speaker to turn to the east and bow nine times) and in fact the needs have also been compared with the nine sisters of 'Noththe' described in a charm against a 'kernel' considered later in this chapter. We can also recall Woden's connection with nine twigs in the *Nine Herbs Charm* for snakebite from the *Lacnunga* (where similarly an allusion is made to the herb *stune* which grew 'on stone', while the final herb of the charm, *wergule*, was sent by the seal 'over the sea's ridge': perhaps the nine stone- and sea-based needs are a Northern version of the nine powerful Old English herbs).

In fact, however, the needs may not have originally belonged in the spell at all. The Ribe text is comparable with an Icelandic formula to staunch bleeding, part of which reads:

> A stone called Surt stands in the temple. There lie nine vipers. They shall neither wake nor sleep before this blood is staunched. Let this blood be staunched in the name of the Father and the Son and the Holy Ghost. *Filium Spiritum Domino Pater.*

Similarly, a German formula exorcises worms from various parts of the body to a great stone far away in the sea. Originally, then, the stone seems to have been a remote place of expulsion for whatever was thought responsible for causing a sickness.[16]

Whatever the significance of the need-infested stone, the Ribe runic charm specifically claims to heal or ward off 'the trembler', i.e. malaria, the scourge of medieval Denmark. Fever is also alluded to in a much earlier Danish charm found on a larger, decorated ashen rune-stick, approximately 50cm long, from Hemdrup, North Jutland:

> ᚢᛅᚾᚦᛁᚴᛁᛒᛅ·ᚠᛁᚢᚴᛅᛏᛁ·ᚭᛋᛅ·ᛅᚢᛅᚭᚢᛒᛁ
> ᚠᚢ⁝ᚾᛁᛚᚢᛁᛅᛁ. . .
>
> *Van þik æfa fiūkandi, Āsa æy ā ā ūfi (?) . . .*
>
> 'The storming one never overcame you, Asa . . .'

The end of the inscription is uncertain, perhaps 'Asa has luck in strife', and trails off into a sequence of cryptic runes as yet undeciphered. The 'storming one' (*fiūkandi* can mean 'the whirling', 'blowing', 'driving' or 'storming') obviously refers to an illness of some sort, although it is not certain exactly which disease is being referred to here. Grammatically, the same *-nd-* (present participle) construction is found in the 'trembling one' (*bifanda*) in the Ribe wand text, discussed above, and the formulation is somewhat reminiscent of the present participles in the Swedish Högstena amulet, considered below.

The Hemdrup inscription, probably dating from the ninth century, is carved in

16 Árnason, *Íslenzkar þjóðsögur* 3, 2nd ed. (Reykjavík 1958), p. 470. Further parallels are discussed in Hammerich, pp. 158–59.

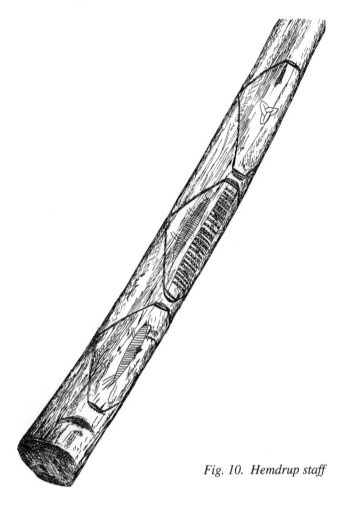

Fig. 10. Hemdrup staff

elaborate contoured runes with double outlines and filled with pointed prick marks, enclosed in a crudely shaped polygon along with some sketches of a human being and an animal, usually identified as a dog. Alongside, another polygon contains an elegantly incised symbol, a form of the knot-like triquetra (⚶) that symbolises the Trinity, which here, in an inscription from pre-Christian Denmark, may be being used merely as a magical sign. A further polygon contains what appears to be another inscription in cryptic writing almost resembling cuneiform script. The stick also features two further polygons enclosing the canine (or rather beetle-like) animals. Thus the magical effect is probably not confined to the inscribed runic formula, but extends to the magic signs and squiggles which ornament most of the wooden surface. Large decorated sticks reminiscent of the Hemdrup staff are also known from elsewhere in Denmark and Germany, although their function remains unestablished.[17]

---

[17] Moltke, *Runes and their Origin*, pp. 350–53; Nielsen, *Danske runeindskrifter*, pp. 58–62.

It is also tempting to compare the swarthy stone of the Ribe text with another Norwegian runic amulet describing some form of magic ritual involving a stone. The late-thirteenth-century Norwegian runic text, which is also metrical, but seems more like a round than a piece of Eddic verse, runs as follows:

ᛁᛋᛁᛌᛏᛁᛁᛍᚴᛏᛁᛁᚿᛁᛏᚨᛏᚱᛁᚱᛋᚼᛈᚱᚱᛁᚿᛈᛁ᛬ᚨᛏᚨᚱᛁᛌᛏᚼᚦᛁᚱᛌᚨᛈᛁᛁ᛬ᚿᛁᚨᛏ᛬ᛁᚠᚠᛈᚨᚱᛁᛁᛁᛌᛏᛁᛁᚴᛏᛁᛁᚿᛁ᛬

Ími stein heitti.
Aldri reykr rjúki.
Aldri seyðir soðni.
Út yl, inn kyl!
Ími stein heitti.

'Imi heated the stone.
Never shall the smoke smoke.
Never shall the cooking be cooked.
Out heat, in cool!
Imi heated the stone.'

This rhetorically complex charm features alliteration and rhyme as well as stylistic framing ('Imi heated the stone' twice) and two *figurae etymologicae* or grammatical figures ('smoke smoke' and 'cooking be cooked'). Its purpose remains rather mystifying, although it has been regarded as a spell to spoil someone's cooking, i.e. a kitchen curse, with Imi perhaps a cooking-sprite or smoke demon. The literal meaning of *ím* is 'embers, ashes, dust' and the derived form Imi or Imr is a Scandinavian man's name as well as that of an Eddic giant and a poetic term for 'wolf'. The use of vapour baths ('stone baths') and the smoke of certain herbs to drive out spirits of disease in animals and humans is well-attested in Germanic folklore and leechcraft, though, and might be compared with the use of steam and steam-baths typical of classical medicine, the Christian ritual of burning away the ashes or embers of sin, or the fumigation practices of medieval necromancy and astral magic.

The Norwegian runic text recalls the story related in the *Prose Edda* of how Odin, Loki and Hoenir were unable to cook their meal because it had been enchanted by the giant Thjazi so that, until he had been promised his share, *eigi soðnaði á seyðinum*, 'it did not cook in the pit-fire' (i.e. expressed again with a similar grammatical figure based around the verb *sjóða* 'cook'). The words are also echoed in a (similarly rhyming) curse against fever recorded in a Norwegian book of black magic from 1815 which reads:

Ud, Ølen,
og ind Kjølen! I 3de N.

'Out, ale,
and in, cool! In the third name.'

Here it seems that an original *yl* 'heat' has been garbled to *øl* 'ale'. Presumably, then, the Imi text was originally much more than merely a carefully composed round. In fact a recently discovered fragment of rib-bone from Lincoln, England bears an Old Norse runic inscription comparable to this Norwegian one, with a similarly baffling legend: ᛒ----ᛁᚠ+᛭ᛁᛏᛁᛦ+'ᛏᛁᚻ+, *B. . . il heitir stein(n)*, 'B. . . heats the stone' or perhaps 'A stone is called B. . .'. [18]

Like other Germanic peoples, the Scandinavians believed in malignant spirits of disease floating around the atmosphere, attacking the unwary. To protect themselves, Scandinavians carved runic charms to ward off these insidious beings. A twelfth-century bronze amulet from Högstena, Sweden, for instance, contains such an alliterating spell against roaming spirits of disease:

ᚷᛏᚱᛏᚻᛏᛏᚾᛁᛑᚱᛏᛏᚻᚱᛏᛏᚾᛁᛑᚱᚱᛁᛑᛏᛏᛏᛏᚾᛁᛑ
ᚾᛁᛑᚱᚱᛁᛏᛏᚻᛏᛏᚾᛁᛑᚱᚻᛁᛏᛁᛏᚻᛏᛏᚾᛁᛑ
ᚱᚻᛁᚠᛏ--ᛁᚾᛁᛑᚱᛏᛏᚱᛏᚻᛏᛏᚾᛁᛑᚱᛏᚠᛁᚾ᛭
ᚠᚻᛏᛏᚻ-ᚠᛏᚠᛏᛏᛦᚾ--ᚻᛏᚾᚠᚾᛏᚾᛏᚾ-ᛏ

Gal anda viðr, gangla viðr, rīðanda viðr, viðr rinnanda, viðr sitianda, viðr sign(and)a, viðr f(a)randa, viðr fliuganda. S[kal] alt fyrna (?) ok um døyia.

'I incant against the spirit, against the walking (spirit), against the riding one, against the running one, against the sitting one, against the signing one, against the travelling one, against the flying one. It shall completely wither (?) and die.'

As the amulet was found in a grave, it has been suggested that it was directed against a revenant spirit, but it seems more likely to have been a talisman that was supposed to protect its owner from the agencies of sickness which roamed the country at large, and was buried with the owner after death. In this case, the runes were explicitly carved to ward off the evil spirits of disease which were thought to prey on the unprotected, and after enumerating seven means of transport available to the malignant spirits, the enchanter commands them to shrivel and die, robbing them of the very life-force they seek to deprive their victims of. The laboured repetition of ideas contained in the means of transport is comparable to the rhetoric of the Irish and English *loricae* discussed earlier, but has, perhaps, an even closer parallel in a German witch's explanation that there were nine sorts of spirits or sprites: riding, splitting, blowing, wasting, flying, swelling as well as deaf, dumb and blind. Furthermore the plea for protection from various forms of evil is also reminiscent of the fourteenth-century rune-stick from Bergen discussed in chapter 2 in which the carver cuts runes as a form of security against elves, trolls and ogres.[19]

At least one instance of a rune-inscribed healing amulet is known from the Continent, however, a comparatively early example that was discovered at Britsum, Holland, in 1906. Found on a 12.5cm-long smoothed wand of yew

---

18 On this text see Liestøl, 'Rúnavísur frá Bjǫrgvin', pp. 32–33 or idem, 'Runic voices', p. 25. A slightly different translation is presented in Liestøl, *Runer frå Bryggen*, pp. 38–41. McKinnell and Simek, p. 133, prefer to translate 'Let a stone be called Ími (Sooty)'. The Norwegian spell is Bang, no. 21. On the Lincoln bone see J. McKinnell, 'A runic fragment from Lincoln', *Nytt om runer* 10 (1995), 10–11 and McKinnell and Simek, p. 133.

19 The Högstena amulet is *SR* V, no. 216. The bulk of the text is clear, although slightly different translations of the opening and closing phrases have been proposed, e.g. in H. Jungner, 'Högstena-galdern', *Fornvännen* 31 (1936), 278–304 or Krause, *Runen*, p. 55. See also J. Grimm, *Teutonic Mythology*, trans. J.S. Stallybrass 3 (London 1883), pp. 1156–57 for the nine sorts of *holdlichen*.

wood, it features a mix of runic and a few Roman characters. Some of the runes, which are written with decorative multiple stems, though, are too worn to be made out today. What can be read of its text, written in an early form of Frisian, is:

ᚦᚠᛏᛁᚠᛒᛗᚱᛗᛏᛥᚢᛥ
LID
--ᛏᛒᚠᚱᚠᛥᛗᛁ

Þon iæberet: dud lid.
. . .n borod mi.

'This may you (?) bring about: numbness gone away.
. . .n bored me.'

The Britsum amulet probably stems from about the eighth century, and features a runic letterform ᚠ (obviously representing a vowel) and terms whose proper interpretation, as is the case with many Frisian inscriptions, has proved a matter of some controversy. It appears likely that *dud* is an early form of Old Frisian *dud* 'numbing, deadening', a word related to English *dodder* – i.e. presumably a signification of some sort of debilitative condition or disease. The term that follows it, written in Roman letters, is also quite evidently an early form of Old Frisian *lid* 'gone away' and may well have been written in this manner so the presumably prestigious Roman letters might have the effect of bolstering the charm.

The two verbs *(iæ)beret* and *borod* have also been the cause of some dispute, but the first seems to be a form of the verb meaning 'bring about' (or even 'conceive a child') known from all of the Germanic languages. The second line is also obviously a naming expression 'N . . . me', with the 'talking' probably intended to represent the 'voice' of the shaped stick. What must have been the owner's name, then, is mostly lost, but the verb, which may have referred to the carved nature of the wand rather than literally a bored hole, suggests this line was simply intended as a maker's signature. Overall the text is reminiscent, then, of the contemporary or slightly later Ribe cranium text. The Britsum inscription does not make explicit reference to whatever agency it was (unlike Ribe with its divine triad), however, that was supposed to ensure that the ailment would go away. Taken together, the Britsum and Ribe texts appear to be more typical of early runic amulet texts, very much like the early protective and amatory runic charms. Consequently, the later examples, such as those of the sickness-banishing type, seem to represent a differently evolved sort of charm, perhaps ones more heavily influenced by classical or Christian rites and beliefs, especially in the form of the exorcisms so common in ancient times.[20]

---

[20] Looijenga, pp. 309–10 reads the *i*-rune and *æ*-rune as representing individual words *i(w)* 'yew' and *ǣ(w)* 'always' as was first done by S. Bugge, 'Das Runendenkmal von Britsum in Friesland', *Zeitschrift für deutsche Philologie* 40 (1908), 174–184. The sequence *iæ* might more plausibly be read as a verbal prefix to *ber-*, however, i.e. < **ga-ber-* 'bring about, conceive'. Old Frisian *dud* is ultimately a zero-grade development of the root **dwe-* found in words like English *dull* and German *toll* 'mad'; and note that the interpretations of *lid* proffered by Looijenga are forms derived (and with meanings unattested in Frisian) from the Germanic verb *l þan 'go (away), journey'.

More explicitly Christian, however, is the following rather mangled charm from Bergen, probably from the late fourteenth or early fifteenth century. The runes cover four sides of a square wooden amulet, pierced at one end, whose inscription reads:

·⁝· ᛁᚽ:ᚽᛆᛘᛂᚴᛆᛏᚱᛁᚿᛆᚦᚠᛁᛚᛁᛆᚦᛌᚴᚱᛁᛏᚢᚿᛆᚽᛏᛁᛆᛘᛂᚽ:ᛧᚢᚱᚱᛆᛆ
ᚤᛆᛚᚱᚠᚢᛁᚠᚢᛂᛐᛂᛁᚿᛁᚽᛘᛂᛐᛁᛧᛁᚽᛆᚿᛁᚽᛘᛂᛐᛁᛧᛁᚽᛆᛘᛁᛁᛆ
ᚴᛁᛆᛧᚱᚢᚿᛆᚦᚴᛆᛧᛁᛆᛧᚱᛁᚿᛏᛂᚠᚢ-ᛁᛘᛆᚴᛆᚿᛘᛆᚢᛁᛏᛆᚦᚿᛆᛧᚱᛆᛒᛆᛏ
ᚿᛆᚠᛁᚽᛂᛚᛆᚢᛁᛏᚠᛂᛒᚱᛆᚿᛆᛐᛁᚠᛆᚢᛁᛆᛐᚠᚢᛁᛘᛆᚢᛂᚿᚿᛆᚱᛂᛚᚱ

In nomine Patris et Filii et Spiritus sancti, amen. Cura!

Vulner[a qu]in[qu]e Dei	*sint medicina (mei)*
sint medicina mei	*pia crux et passio Christi,*
[Qu]i me plasmavit et sacrabat	*sanguine lavit,*
febres adigovit	*qui me vexare l(abo)r(avit).*

'In the name of the Father and of the Son and of the Holy Spirit, amen. Cure!

'May God's five wounds	be (my) medicine.
May my medicine	be the holy cross and Christ's passion.
He who moulded and washed me	with holy blood,
expelled the fever	which strove to torment me.'

This text is extant in a number of variants; fragments have survived in several versions in Scandinavia and elsewhere in Europe, including the *Galdrabók*, although this is the earliest known example from Norway. Some of the graphemic features point to a Danish origin for this inscription and the closest parallel is in fact a mid-fifteenth-century formula against malaria found in a manuscript now in Copenhagen. This opens with an appeal to the Trinity and the following rhymed hexameters:

Qui me plasmavit	*et sacro sanguine lavit*
febres compellant,	*qui me vexare laborant*
vulnera quinque dei	*sint medicina mei*
Sit medicina mei	*pia crux et passio Christi*
Vulneribus quinis	*me Christi salva ruinis*

Then follows a blessing of the sick person, followed by a near-repetition of two of the lines:

Febris depellant,	*qui me vexare laborant*
vulnera quinque dei	*sunt medicina mei.*

Last comes a list of seven names (Piron, Pupicon, Diron, Arcon, Cardon, Jadon and Ason) usually regarded as the names of the evil spirits causing the fever, followed by another appeal to the Trinity and a further blessing. The number seven is frequent in Middle Eastern magic and had astrological implications (there were seven planets, after all, which orbited in seven heavens). Seven is also, of course, significant in the Bible: it is the number of days of creation in Genesis; Revelation describes seven seals, seven angels, seven plagues and the seven-headed beast; there were seven deadly sins and so on. Thus it is no surprise to find some Anglo-Saxon charms requiring seven masses to be sung or an act to be performed for seven days, and seven sisters are in fact invoked on a Danish runic amulet discussed below.

The Norwegian runic text focuses instead on the number five, though, acquiring its potency through its explicit reference to Christ's suffering on the cross and his five wounds. Devotion to the five wounds of Christ, reaching an artistic and literary peak in the fifteenth and sixteenth centuries, found its way into healing charms as well as those asking protection from sorcery, weapons, thieves and for tracing missing people. The charm appeals to Christ to expel the fever, rather than commanding the fever itself to depart. Whether the fever from which relief is sought refers to malaria (although this is not expressly mentioned, and was rather more common in Denmark than in Norway at this time), however, or even the bubonic plague (ravaging Europe in the middle of the fourteenth century) is not made explicit.[21]

Just as the Danish manuscript charm discussed above invoked the suffering of Christ and enumerated seven spirits of disease, we find a list of what were probably originally seven names occurring on a late runic charm inscribed on a lead amulet from Blæsinge, Denmark:

Xᛍᚮᚿᛁᚢᚱᚮᚢᚮᛋ.ᛋᛂᛒᛏᛂᛘ:ᛋᚮᚱᚮᚱᛂᛋᛂᛏ--ᛆᚱ-------ᛋ:ᚱᛂᛋ...
ᛂᛚᚠᚠᚱᛁᛍᛆ:ᛆᚠᚠᚱᛁᛍᛂᛆᛋᚮᚱᛁᛆᛆᚠᚠᚮᛍᛆ:ᛆᚠᚠᚱᛁᛍᛆᛚᛆ:ᛍᚮᚿᛁᚢᚱᚮᚢᚮᛋᛂᛏᛍᚮᚿ:ᛏᛂᛋᛏᚮᚱ:ᛒᛂᚱᛒᛆᛏᚱᛂᛘ:
ᛂᛏᚠᛁᛚᛁᚢᛘᛂᛏᛋᛒᛁᚱᛁᛏᚢᛘ:ᛋᛆᚿᛍᛏᚢᛘ:ᚢᛏᚿᚮᚿ:ᚿᚮᛍᛂᛆᛏᛁᛋ:ᛋᛏᛆᛘᚠᛆᛘᚢᛚᚢᛘ:ᛑᛂᛁ:ᚿᛂᚹᚢᛂ
ᛁᚿ.ᚮᛍᚢᛚᛁᛋ:ᚿᛂᚹᚢᛂᛁᚿᛘᛂᛘᛒᚱᛁᛋ:ᚿᛂᚹᚢᛂᛁᚿᛘᛂᛑᚢᛚᛚᛁᛋ::ᚿᛂᛍᛁᚿᚢᛚᛚᚮᛍᚮᛘᛒ
--ᛁᚿᛂᛘᛂᛘᛒᚱᚮᚱᚢᛘᛂᛁᚢᛋ:ᚢᛏᛁᚿᚼᛆᛒᛁᛏᛆᛏ:ᛁᚿᛏᛂᚢᛁᚱᛏᚢᛋᛍᚱᛁᛋᛏᛁ:ᛆᛚᛏᛁᛋᛋᛁ
ᛘᛁ:ᛂᛍᛍᛂᛍᚱᚢᛍᛂᛘ:ᛑᚮᛘᛁᚿᛁ:ᚠᚢᚵᛁᛏᛂ:ᛒᛆᚱᛏᛂᛋ:ᛆᛑᚢᛂᚱᛋᛂ:ᚢᛁᛍᛁᛏᛚᛂᚮ:ᛑᛂᛏᚱᛁᛒᚢᛁᚢ
ᛑᛆᚱᛆᛑᛁX:ᛑᛆᚢᛁᛏ:ᛁᚿᚿᚮᛘᛁᚿᛂᛒᛆᛏᚱᛁᛋᛂᛏᚠᛁᛚᛁᛁ:ᛂᛏᛋᛒᛁᚱᛁᛏᚢᛋᛋᛆᚿᛍᛏᛁᛆᛘᛂᚿX...
ᛍᚱᛁᛋᛏᚢᛋ:ᚢᛁᚿᛍᛁᛏ: ᛍᚱᛁᛋᛏᚢᛋ:ᚱᛂᚵᚿᛆᛏ: ᛍᚱᛁᛋᛏᚢᛋ:ᛁᛘᛒᛂᚱᛆᛏ: ᛍᚱᛁᛋᛏᚢᛋ:ᛚᛁᛒᛂᚱᛆᛏ+
ᛍᚱᛁᛋᛏᚢᛋᛏᛂᛒᛂᚿᛂᛑᛁᛍᛆᛏ:ᛆᛒᚮᛘᚿᛁ:ᛘᛆᛚᚮ:ᛑᛂᚠᛂᚿᛑᛆᛏ:ᛆ:ᚵ:ᛚ:ᛆ:ᛒᛆᛏᛂᚱ:ᚿᚮᛋᛏᛂᚱ:X:

Coniuro vos, septem sorores. . . Res[tilia(?)]
Elffrica, Affrica, Soria, Affoca, Affricala.
Coniuro vos et contestor per Patrem et Filium et Spiritum sanctum,
ut non noceatis istam famulum Dei,
neque in oculis, neque in membris, neque in medullis,
nec in ullo comp[ag]ine membrorum eius, ut inhabitat in te virtus Christi altissimi.
Ecce crucem Domini! Fugite partes adverse! Vicit leo de tribu Juda, radix David.
In nomine Patris et Filii et Spiritus sancti, amen.
Christus vincit, Christus regnat, Christus imperat, Christus liberat,
Christus te benedicit, ab omni malo defendat. AGLA. Pater noster.

'I conjure you, seven sisters . . . Res[tilia(?)] Elffrica, Affricca, Soria, Affoca, Affricala.
I conjure and call you to witness through the Father, the Son and the Holy Spirit, that you do not harm this servant of God, neither in the eyes nor in the limbs nor in the marrow nor in any joint of his limbs, that the power of Christ

21 The 'five wounds' stick from Bergen is *NIyR* no. 632. Its many parallels, including the Copenhagen manuscript version, are discussed there, though we have chosen a slightly different interpretation (involving less textual restructuring) of the inscription to the one given in *NIyR*.

most high shall reside in you.
Behold the cross of the Lord! Begone, ye enemy powers! The lion of the tribe
of Judah, the root of David, has conquered.
In the name of the Father, the Son and the Holy Spirit, amen.
Christ conquers, Christ reigns, Christ commands, Christ delivers, Christ
blesses thee (and) from all evil defends. *AGLA*. Our Father.'

This late medieval Christian amulet seems to address the seven spirits of disease
as seven sisters and to banish them through the power of the cross. It was
commonly held at the time that disease was caused by seven (or nine) female
demons, often sisters, and a sixteenth-century Danish formula against sickness
names them as Illia, Reptilia, Folia, Suffugalia, Affrica, Filica, Loena or Ignea.
Variants of these names are encoded in an eleventh-century German text (Ilia,
Restilia, Fagalia, Subfogalia, Frica, Iulica, Ignea) and different and equally fabulous names are also recorded elsewhere.

In the runic charm we see a conflation of the familiar banishment of disease
spirits with an explicit appeal to the Christian powers for intercession. The *Ecce
crucem Domini* (*Behold the Cross of the Lord*) antiphon is a typical Christian
exorcism prayer and recurs on several Scandinavian amulets, runic and otherwise, as is further discussed in chapter 8. The Blæsinge text also emphasises the
triumph of Christ, repeating the jubilant 'Christ conquers, Christ reigns' *Laudes*
litany of the early Carolingian court, which is commonly encountered in prayers,
exorcisms, charms and all sorts of Christian amulets (including further runic ones
discussed in chapter 8). Also recurrent on magical amulets of a late or high medieval date in Scandinavia is the holy acronym *AGLA*, a protective formulation of
Cabbalistic origin usually thought to represent the letters of the Hebrew exhorta-
tion *attah gibbor le'olam adonai*, 'thou art strong to eternity, Lord'. Employing a
strategy typical of medieval charms, this runic amulet also enumerates the parts of
the body which are to be rendered invulnerable (the eyes, limbs, marrow, joints)
in a *lorica*-like formulation.[22]

This charm may be compared with a similar charm against specified illnesses
found on a non-runic lead amulet from Schleswig, Germany. In a somewhat
emended version, the Latin text reads:

The beginning of the Holy Gospel according to John. In the beginning was the
Word and this Word has no beginning and remains without end. In the name of
our Lord Jesus Christ I conjure you, demons and elves, and all the infections of
all illnesses, and all obstructions, by the one God, the almighty Father and his
son Jesus Christ and the Holy Spirit, that you may not harm this servant of God
by day or by night, nor at any hours. Behold the cross of Christ! Begone, ye
enemy powers! The lion of the tribe of Judah has triumphed, the root of David,
amen. May the cross bless me, name, amen. May Christ's cross protect, may
Christ's cross deliver me, name, from the devil and from all evils, amen. *Sator
arepo tenet opera rotas. Sator arepo tenet opera rotas.*

22 On the Blæsinge lead amulet and parallels see M. Stoklund, 'Runefund', *Aarbøger for nordisk
Oldkyndighed og Historie* (1986), 189–211. On *AGLA* see S.A. Horodezky, 'Agla', in J. Klatzkin
(ed.), *Encyclopaedia Judaica*, 10 vols (Berlin 1928–34), I, pp. 1042–43, although cf. H.-U.
Boesche in Düwel, 'Mittelalterliche Amulette', pp. 289–90.

Another non-runic charm on a lead amulet from Danish Romdrup similarly runs:

> In the name of the Father and the Son and the Holy Ghost, amen. I adjure you elf-men or elf-women and demons through the Father and the Son and the Holy Spirit, that you do not hurt this servant of God, Nicholas, neither on the eyes nor on the head nor on the limbs. But the strength of Christ the highest will dwell in him, amen. Christ conquers, Christ reigns, Christ commands. May Christ bless these eyes together with the head and the other limbs. In the name of the Father and the Son and the Holy Spirit, amen. *AGLA* . . .[23]

A not dissimilar Christian runic charm is found on the Danish Odense lead tablet, which was found in a graveyard, a circumstance which has led to the supposition that it was placed to transfer sickness from the suffering victim, Asa, named in the text, to the buried corpse: the transference of disease by a formula or ceremony to another object, animate or otherwise, is well attested in Germanic leechcraft. It may instead have been placed there in order to protect the dead Asa in her grave; or was perhaps buried with her as a treasured possession. The folded lead roll contains a mixture of pious Christian sentiment and what appears to be runic gibberish:

```
✝ ᚢᚾᚴᚿᛏᚿ ᚴᛁᚿᚿ:ᛒᚱᛁᛘᚴᛁᚿ✝ᚼᛁᚱ:ᚹᛏᛁᛏᛁᚱᛁᚿ
ᛏᛘᛏᚱᛁᚴᛁᛁ:ᛏᛘᛒᛁᚴᛁᛁᚱᛏᚱᛏᚾᚱ:ᛘᚱᛏᛁᛏᚱ
:ᛁᛒᛏᛏᛁᛏᚱ:ᚱᚱᛁᚴᛏᚾᚴᚾᛁᛏᚱᛁᛏᚱᛁᚴᛏᚾᚴ ᚱᛏᚱ
ᛏᛏᛁ:ᚱᚱᛁᚴᛏᚾᚴᛁᚤᛒᛏᚱᛏᛁ. ᚱᚱᛁᚴᛏᚾᚴᛁᛒᛏᚤᛁ
ᚤᛏᚱᛏᚤᛏᛘᛏᚤ:ᚱᛁᛒᛏᚱᛏᛁ:ᚱᚱᚾᚴᚱᛁᚴᛁᛁ
ᚴᛁᛁ:ᚴᚾᛒᛏᚱᚤᛏ.ᛏᚴᛁᚤ.✳ᛁᚱ.ᛏᛁ ᚾᛒᛁᚱᚿᛏ.
✝ᚱ✳ᛏᚱᛏᛁ.✝ᛁᛁᚱ✳ᛏᚱᛏᛁ✝ᚱ✳ᛏᚱᛏᛁ
✝ᛏᚱᛘ ✝ ᚴᛏᛁᚱᚾᛁᚴᚱᛁᚴᛁᛁ ᚴᛁᚱ ᛏᛏᛁᚤᛏ✝
```

Unguen (?) sine prīmsigna (?) sal condolor (?)
Anakristi anapisti kardur nardiar ipodiar.
Christus vincit, Christus regnat, Christus imperat,
Christus ab omni malo me Āsam liberet.
Crux Christi sit super me Āsam, hic et ubique.
Khorda inkhorda khordai.
AGLA. Sanguis Christi signet me.

'Ointment without prime-signing (?), salt, great sorrow (?)
Anakristi anapisti kardiar nardiar ipodiar.
Christ conquers, Christ reigns, Christ commands,
may Christ deliver me from all evil, Asa.
May the cross of Christ be over me, Asa, here and everywhere.
Khorda inkhorda khordai.
AGLA. May the blood of Christ bless me.'

Despite a rather baffling opening which, if not meaningless gibberish, apparently

---

[23] For the Schleswig amulet see C. Gastgeber and H. Harrauer, 'Ein christliches Bleiamulett aus Schleswig', in V. Vogel (ed.), *Ausgrabungen in Schleswig* 15 (Neumünster 2001), pp. 207–26 and, with further parallels, Düwel, 'Mittelalterliche Amulette', pp. 237–55.

alludes to the Christian ceremony of preliminary baptism (*prima signatio*) and perhaps salt and (holy) oil, widely used in baptismal ceremonies (and other rites), the amulet text is largely comprehensible. It repeats a variation on the *Laudes* litany 'Christ conquers, Christ reigns, Christ commands', a formula that is widely encountered in Germanic charms. The words 'may the cross of Christ be over me', from a common medieval prayer, and 'may Christ deliver me from all evil' appearing here also find a close parallel in a Norwegian cross from Gaular parish, considered below. These standard Christian invocations are supplemented by what appear to be magical pseudo-Latin rhyming formulas: *anakristi anapisti*; *kardiar nardiar ipodiar*; and *khorda inkhorda khordai*. Such formulas were already known to early writers like Marcellus of Bordeaux and often have their origin in key words, either of Latin or foreign origin. Marcellus, for example, includes some charms written in the dying Celtic tongue of Gaul in his treatise, one of which, recommended for expelling an object blocking the throat, is reminiscent of some later Germanic charms. Invoking the name of the Gaulish god Esus as well as assonating elements probably referring to hoarseness or phlegm, it reads:

> *Exu cricon! Exu criglion! Aisus scrisumio velor! Exu cricon! Exu grilau!*

> 'Out *cricos*! Out *criglios*! Esus, I want to spit! Out *cricos*! Out *grilau*!'

Gaulish *cricos* 'hoarseness, phlegm' appears here along with words that seem to have become linked in the same way an expression like 'pick a peck of pickled peppers' is formed. Similarly, then, the *anakristi* sequence looks like it might have the words *Christ* and *anapaest* in it, while the *khorda* sequence can be read as more-or-less intelligible Latin: *chorda, in chorda, chordae*, 'a string (of a musical instrument) in a string of string' almost as if it were a tongue twister or a grammatical exercise. In fact a group of assonating sounds similar to the *khorda* sequence, replete with the preposition *in*, but this time quite meaningless in Latin, also occurs on a flat, pierced wooden amulet from Bergen which dates to the early thirteenth century:

⊹ᚠᛆᚱᚦᛁᚼ:ᚠᛆᚱᚦᛁᚼ:ᛁᚼᚠᛆᚱᛒᛆᚱ
ᚾᚼᛏᚠᛁᚠᚱ

Gordin, kordan, inkorþar. . .

Here what may have initially been *khord-* has become *gord-* in the first word, much as *cric-* becomes *crigl-* and then *gril-* in the Gaulish medical charm recorded by Marcellus many centuries before.[24]

Moreover, a small lead amulet from Lurekalven, Norway shows another

---

24 The Odense lead tablet (*DR* no. 204) is discussed in Moltke, *Runes and their Origin*, pp. 492–93, the *kordan/gordin* rhyming formula is also discussed by Düwel, 'Mittelalterliche Amulette', pp. 256–57 and J.E. Knirk, 'Runic inscriptions containing Latin in Norway', in K. Düwel (ed.), *Runeninschriften als Quellen interdisziplinäre Forschungen* (Berlin 1998), pp. 482–83. Marcellus' Gaulish is covered in Lambert, pp. 177–78 and see W. Meid, *Heilpflanzen und Heilsprüche* (Innsbruck 1996) more generally.

variation on the *khorda* sequence. Tightly pressed into a package, it has not yet been unfolded and thus cannot be read in its entirety, although the third line apparently reads:

-ᚨR11ŀ·PᚨR11ŀ·1ŀPᚨR. . .

[g]ordan, gordin, ingor. . .

The significance of this particular rhyming formula is unknown, although the *khorda* rhyming variants seem to find a further, somewhat older parallel in a manuscript from Uppsala, Sweden. Probably of German origin, this features a charm against elves which was supposed to be written in lead.[25] Similarly, the three terms are found, perhaps as names or as a magical formula, in a Latin metrical text, *Omne genus demoniorum* (*Every Phantasmal Creature*). More recent parallels are also found in Norwegian books of black magic, including some using the word *cordi* against snakebite or to protect against thieves. They might be further compared with the inscription found on a small runic stick from Swedish Lödöse which has been archeologically dated to the second half of the thirteenth century. The inscription appears to read:

PᚨR11ŀ:PᚨR11ŀ
ƗᚦPᚨR11ŀ
ⁿPᚨⁿ:ⁿPᚨ1:ⁿPᚨᚦ

Gordin, gordan
et gordan
ufau ufai ufao.

This may be a modified form of the *chorda* or 'string' sequence (perhaps originally *cordis* 'heart'), followed by what may be a magical formula, *ufau ufai ufao*, a variant of which is discussed below.

It is not in fact uncommon to find unintelligible magical formulations repeated throughout the Germanic world and beyond. As well as the ones mentioned above, we have of course the fairytale expressions *abracadabra*, *fee fi fo fum* and *hocus pocus*, familiar to children everywhere. Often in runic texts such expressions are corruptions of well-known Latin liturgical phrases, as are *hocus pocus* from *hoc est corpus (meus)*, 'this is (my) body' or the Swedish children's rhyme *arje marje grase* from *Ave Maria gratia*, 'Hail Mary (full) of grace'. A runic sequence of this broad type is *maksnaksbah* which is recorded on a flat stick from Oslo; it may be built around Latin *pax* 'peace'. Another recurring runic formulation is in fact a variation on the well-known magical word abracadabra found on two Norwegian amulets and dating back to classical and Middle Eastern precedents. A lead plate from Bergen, Norway, dated to the fourteenth century, reads:

ᚠBRᚠB-ᚱRᚨBᚨ
----BᛏR--Rᚨ-

---

[25] The long German formula appears to conjure the elves Gordin (Gord'i), Ingordin and Cord'i; see Düwel, 'Mittelalterliche Amulette', pp. 248–49.

abrabalraba
. . . barkalrar (?)

This is presumably some kind of magic based on the *abra* expression. The expression (*abakalaba abakala*) also seems to appear on a lead plate from Tårnborg, Denmark along with the words *libera* 'free', *Andreas* and *Alpha*. The similar *abracalara* is also encountered in an amuletic text on a lead cross from Gaular parish, Norway:

+ᛀ.ᛈ.ᚱ.ᛀ.ᚲᛀᛂᛁᚱᚼ
ᛀ'ᛂᛁᚱ.ᚢᛁᚼ'ᛁᚼ
ᚼᛁᚱᛁ''ᛁᚼᛀᛁᛈᛁᚼᛀᛁᛂᚱ
ᛂᛅᚤᛁᚼᛁᛂᛂᚤ.ᛀᛀᛂᛁᛁᛁ
ᛁᚦᚱᛁᛈᚼᛆᚤᛁᛂ
ᛗᚤᛈ-ᚦ
ᛗᛀᚱᛗᛂᛀᛀ'ᛁᛂ
. . .ᛈᛂᛁᚦᛁᚼᛀᛀᛁᚦ
. . .ᚱᚱᛀ.'ᛁᚦ'ᛗᚲᚼ
ᚱᛂᛀ'.ᛀᛒᛀᚤᚼ
ᚼᛁᚤᛀᚱᛀᛀᚤ
ᚤᛁᛂᛀᛈᛀ.ᛀᛁᚦᛀᛂᛁ.+ᛀ
ᛒᚱᛀᚼᛀᚱᛀᚱᛀ.+ᛀᛒᚱᛀᚼᛀ.
+ᛀᛒᚱᛀᚼᛀ.+ᛀᛒᚱᛀ.
ᚲᛀᛉ.ᛂᛀ
ᛒᛁ'.ᛀᛒᛀᚤ
ᚼᛁᚤᛀᚱᛀᛀᚤ
ᚤᛁᚼ

AGLA. Pater noster, qui es in caelis, sanctificetur nomen tuum. Adveniat regnum tuum. Fiat voluntas tu[a si]cut in caelo, et [in ter]ra. Sit super nos. Ab omni malo, amen. Alpha, Adonai. Abracalara, abraca, abraca, abra. Pax nobis! Ab omni malo, amen.

'*AGLA*. Our Father who art in heaven, hallowed be thy name. Thy kingdom come. Thy will be done, on earth as it is in heaven. May this (the cross?) be over us. From all evil, amen. Alpha, Lord. *Abracalara, abraca, abraca, abra.* Peace be with us! From all evil, amen.'

This double-sided runic crucifix has nine lines of runes on each side. Like the inscription on the original cross of Christ, the Norwegian runic cross evidences a mixture of Latin, Hebrew and Greek, being predominantly in Latin, but featuring the Hebrew *Adonai* 'Lord' and Alpha, the first letter of the Greek alphabet, commonly used to refer to God, the beginning and end (alpha and omega) of all things. The powerful charm contains not only the beginning of the *Lord's Prayer*, but also a call for protection from evil powers, 'May this (the cross?) be over us. (Protect us) from all evil, amen', similar to that on the Odense lead roll considered above. Reference to the power of the cross is found in a number of Christian runic amulets considered in chapter 8. Both the Odense and Gaular amulets also have the mystic acronym *AGLA* and a magical formula; where the Danish example featured nonsensical rhymes, on the Norwegian cross we encounter the reducing formula *abracalara, abraca, abraca, abra.* This 'counting down' method was popular as it was thought to symbolise the gradual reducing to nothing of symptoms of disease and was especially commonly used with the magic word abracadabra, which was sometimes written down as follows:

abracadabra
abracadabr
abracadab
abracada
abracad
abraca
abrac
abra
abr
ab
a

Counting down is frequent in charms and magic, and remains popular in contemporary nursery rhymes and children's songs (*10 Green Bottles* among others). One Anglo-Saxon diminishing charm was supposed to be sung nine times on the first day, eight on the second and so on, while another against a 'kernel' or swelling reads:

> Nine were Noththe's (Node's? Need's?) sisters, then the nine became VIII and the VIII became VII and the VII became VI and the VI became V and the V became IIII and the IIII became III and the III became II and the II became I and the I became none.

Reducing remedies are also found in the sources on which much of Anglo-Saxon leechcraft is based, e.g. Marcellus Empiricus' *On Medicine* has a charm against swollen glands (similarly referred to as 'sisters') which involves counting down the glands in much the same manner, while another of Marcellus' charms begins with the name of an eye-problem *cucuma* and counts it down: *cucuma, ucuma, cuma, uma, ma, a.*[26]

The Norwegian runic cross ends with a prayer and a repetition of its apotropaic formula. It is further considered together with other Norwegian crosses in chapter 8, as are also other Christian formulas which recur in a number of amulets, including *AGLA*, references to the power of the cross, various epithets of God and such standards as the *Hail Mary*, the *Lord's Prayer* etc.

A late-twelfth-century rune-stick, also from Bergen, contains a similarly well-stocked protective charm:

ᛁᛉᛁᚨᚱ᛬ᛁᚱᛁᛒᚨ᛬ᛏᛁᚻᛁᚦ᛬ᚨᛒᛁᚱᛁ᛬ᚱᚨᛏᚻᛁ
ᛏᛁᚱᛏᚱ ᚠᚱᛁᛏᚱᚤᛁᚻᚻᛅᛁᚤᛏᚻᛁᛁᚠᚻᛅᚤᛏᛏᚱᛁᚤᚱ
ᛏᛁᚱᛏᚱ᛬ ᚠᚱᛁᛏᚱᚤᛁᚻᚻᛅᛁᚤᛏᚻᛁᛁᚠᚻᛅᚤᛏᛏᚱᛁᚤ
ᚱᛁᚻᛅᛅᚤᚤᛁᛏᛅᛅᚤᛏᚻᛅᛁ ᚠᚱᛅᛁᚻ

---

[26] On the Tårnborg amulet see Düwel, 'Mittelalterliche Amulette', p. 259. The Norwegian lead cross is also discussed ibid. and by A.M. Knudsen and H. Dyvik, 'Et runekors fra Sogn og Fjordane', *Maal og Minne* (1980), 1–12. The English charm is Storms, no. 3.

Sator arepo teneth opera rotas.
æekrær kreærman numen signum terram.
æekrær kreærman numen signum terram.
Consummatum est. Klas á.

'*Sator arepo tenet opera rotas. Acre, acre, ærnem*, divine will, sign, world (repeated). It is done. Klaus owns (this).'

The charm opens with the popular *sator arepo* magic square formula, found on a number of Scandinavian runic inscriptions (for more on which see below), and concludes with a mark of ownership, preceded (in the opposite direction) by the Latin words of Christ as he died (one of many religious expressions typical of Scandinavian runic amulet inscriptions composed after the conversion). The stick also seems to record three apparently unconnected words in Latin: *numen* 'divine will', *signum* 'sign' and *terram* 'world'.[27]

Of especial interest here are the second and third lines of the inscription containing a charm formula (carved on different sides and in opposite directions) and followed by some apparently unconnected Latin words. Close parallels to this *acræ ærcre ærnem / acre arcre arnem* text are found in a variety of Old English manuscript charms (for staunching blood, against flying venom, against black ulcers, to make holy salve, etc.) and have been variously identified as containing Latin, Greek, Hebrew, Arabic or (more convincingly) Celtic words. In fact one tenth-century leechbook's table of contents declares the charm to be Irish and some of the recurrent sounds can indeed be associated with Old Irish words: *ar* 'against', *cró* 'blood, gore' and perhaps, though less certainly, *ne(i)m* 'poison'. The sequence, punctuated in the Bergen inscription in a manner which indicates that a proper understanding of the original meaning of the words has been lost, perhaps represents a very debased version of an originally Irish charm for staunching blood, although the creator of the runic text seems to have had little idea of exactly what was being recorded. Nevertheless, the notion of a blood-staunching charm is perhaps supported in the runic version by 'It is done', the words uttered by the pierced and dying Christ on the cross, which were common in charms for staunching blood. In fact even the *sator arepo* formula used here may support this notion as it constitutes part of a fifteenth-century Icelandic charm against heavy menstrual bleeding which records it is to be written on a stick and tied to the thigh of the sufferer.[28]

Variants of the *acre arcre* text also occur on three much earlier Anglo-Saxon runic rings which probably all date to the ninth century or thereabouts.[29] A gold ring from Bramham Moor, West Yorkshire, bears the text:

✝ᚠᚱᚪᚱᛁᚾᚣᛁᛏᛦᚪᚱᛁᚾᚱᛁᚦᚠᛦᛏᛦᚯᚷᛚᛂᛋᛏᛂᛈᚩᚾᛏᚩᛚ

ærkriufltkriuriþonglæstæpontol.

---

[27] On the rune-stick (*NIyR* no. 640) see also Düwel, 'Mittelalterliche Amulette', pp. 230–31.

[28] Cf. H. Larsen (ed.), *An Old Icelandic Medical Miscellany* (Oslo 1931), p. 51.

[29] The Anglo-Saxon runic rings are discussed in Gosling, 'The runic material from Tønsberg', and D.M. Wilson, 'A group of Anglo-Saxon amulet rings', in P. Clemoes (ed.), *The Anglo-Saxons* (London 1959), pp. 159–70; cf. also H. Meroney, 'Irish in the Old English charms', *Speculum* 20 (1945), 172–82.

This sequence is echoed in the legend of the golden Greymoor Hill (Kingmoor, Cumberland) ring (the last three runes of which are inside the hoop):

+ᚠᚱᛆᚱᛁᚾᚠᛁᛏᛆᚱᛁᚾᚱᛁᚦᚠᛏᛉᚾᚠᛏᚠᚴᚠᛏ
ᛏᚠᛏ

ærkriufltkriuriþonglæstæpon tol.

Similar, but more distantly related is the legend of an agate ring, probably from Linstock Castle, Cumberland:

ᛉᚼᚳᛗᚱᛘ·ᚱᛁ·ᚾᚠ·ᛞᚠᛏ·ᛗᚱᛁ·ᚾᚱᛁ·ᚦᚠᛏ·ᛈᛏᛗᚼ·ᛏᛗ·ᚴᚠᛏᛗ·ᛏᚠᛏ

eryriufdolyriuriþolwlestepotenol.

Although these inscriptions, like the manuscript charms they resemble, contain no clearly identifiable Anglo-Saxon words, some forms and rhyming patterns in them are strongly reminiscent not only of two versions of an Anglo-Saxon charm for staunching blood (with *æ-ryn.thon*, *ær grim thonn*, perhaps medieval Irish *greann* 'irritation' and *tonn* 'skin', i.e. 'against skin irritation'), but also the much later Norse amulet. Further developing the Irish analogy, we can perhaps identify *þon* (*tho(n)n* in the manuscript blood charms) with Irish *tonn* 'skin'; manuscript *ffil, fil* (cf. runic *fl*, or possible alternative of *fel* on Bramham Moor) with Old Irish *fil* 'it is' or *fuil* 'blood'; runic *enol* or manuscript *leno* with the Old Irish oblique form *léunu* 'hurts'; although again it is doubtful how far such analogies should be pursued when the original meaning was doubtless lost on the charm copyists themselves. The pattern of rhyming or repeating syllables (e.g. *kriuriþon glæstæpon tol*), after all, is quite common in gibberish charms runic or not: examples from Anglo-Saxon literary sources include *geneon genetron catalon*, *beðegunda breðegunda elecunda, caio laio quaque uoaque, gise ges maude leis bois eis audies maudies, leta lita tota tauta* among others. Runically, we encounter *kales fales agla hagla* on a square wooden amulet from Oslo or the similar gibberish pseudo-Latin magic *ales tales arfales* on a wooden measuring-stick handle from Lödöse, Sweden. Though doubtless many originated as corruptions of foreign phrases, others, still, once such expressions had become common in medieval magic, may never have begun in any linguistically sensible word or text, but perhaps relied instead mostly on the euphonic effect and the notion that such sequences had mystical meanings.[30]

The use of outlandish phrases or words was not unique to the Germanic world, of course. Classical writers of herbals and other medical texts, including the influential Alexander of Tralles, had long ago introduced magical formulas and rites to their work, many of which were probably of Middle Eastern origin. Marcellus of Bordeaux evidently delighted in recording gibberish charms of this type. For instance he records a charm against toothache that was to be repeated seven times on a Tuesday or Thursday when the moon was waning which reads: *argidam, margidam, sturgidam*. Another similarly unintelligible text he recorded against stomach-ache similarly runs: *adam bedam alam betar alam botum*. Whether

---

[30] The 'ales' rune-charms are N A321 and Svärdström, *Runfynden i Gamla Lödöse*, pp. 11–12.

these were originally based in Gaulish, corrupted Latin or another language, their literal meaning seems to have played little or no role in their use as (or acceptance in) healing charms.

The final, unintelligible line of a wooden amulet from Bergen, shaped like a flat-bottomed rowing boat and pierced at one end, undoubtedly contains another magical formula of this type, which also to some extent parallels that evidenced on the Anglo-Saxon rings:

ᚾᛁᚺᚠᚻᛁᛁᚿᛁ·ᛁᛃᛉᚴᚻᛁᛁ·ᛁᚱᛃᛈᛁᛉᚴᚠ
--ᛣᚿᛁᛃᛁᚤᛃᛁᛈᛁᚴᚻᛁᛁᚿᛁ:ᚾᚺᛁᛁᛁᚿᛁ ᛃ
ᛁᚿᛁᛁᛒᛁᛁᛁᚿᛁᛒᛁᚱᚿᛃᛏᛈᛏᛁᛃᚠᚻ

Dionysius, Johannes, Serapion,
[Mal]chus, Maximianus, Dionysius.
sussbissusbirumæþanole.

The amulet, dating from about the year 1250, features the names of five of the legendary Seven Sleepers of Ephesus, as well as the mysterious formula *sussbissusbirumæþanole*, which at first looks as if it might begin with an irregular form of Latin *sospes* 'safe' and perhaps *suspirium* 'sigh, deep breath', while *irumæþanole* might be compared with *kriuriþonglæ* on two of the Anglo-Saxon rings. Yet another example of the formula, however, is found on a pierced wooden amulet from the stave church at Lom, Norway:

ᚤᛃᚱᛣᚿᛁᚤᛃᚦᛁᛃᛁᛁᚾᚿᛣᛃᛁᚱᛃᛣᚻᛁᛁᚻ
ᛣᛃᛣᚻᛁᛁᛣᛒᛁᚻᛁᛁᛃᛉᛃᚻᛁ
ᛣᛃᛃᛣᛃᛁᛣᛃᚿᛣᛃᚿᛃᛃᚻᛁᚤᛃ
ᛁᚿᛁᛣᚻᛁᛣᛁᛁᚿᛁᛣᚿᚱᚿᛁᛁᛈᛁᛉᛁᚿᛁᛃᚤ

Marcus, Mattheus, Lucas, Rafelesen,
Gafeles, Gabeles, Johannes.
faofaifaufau. onima.
suspespisus crucifixus (?) am(en?).

'Mark, Matthew, Luke, Raphael (?), Gabriel (?, twice), John.
faofaifaufau. soul (?)
suspespisus crucifix (?) am(en?).'

Here we have no less than two magic formulas alongside the names of the four evangelists and slightly strange forms of what appear to be those of the archangels Raphael and Gabriel; in fact the runic *rafelesen* of the first line and *gafeles gabeles* of the second may be rhyming sequences based on the archangel names. These are followed by what seems to be a slightly erroneous form of Latin *anima* 'soul'. After the sequence *faofaifaufau*, the now-familiar *sospes*-like formula appears slightly more intelligible here, apparently containing the word *crucifixus*. It thus seems it might be a botched attempt to render an expression such as the *Nicean Creed*'s *sub Pontio Pilato passus, crucifixus*, 'was crucified under Pontius Pilate'. In any case, a probably liturgical source seems to have degenerated into pure hocus pocus here, producing an expression of no more linguistic significance than the magic sequence *faofaifaufau* (which is discussed below), although the reverse may also be the case, i.e. an attempt may have been made to read religion into an originally magical non-Christian sequence.[31]

Another instance of the presumably botched Christian formula opens the inscription on a flat, well-carved rune-stick from Bergen, with a mid-thirteenth century dating:

ᛍᚢᛂᛒᛍᛁᛋᚢᛁᛍᚢᛒᛁᚱᛁᚢᛘᛂᚦᚮᚿᛚᛁᚢᛘ
ᛆᚵᛚᛆᛑᛂᛚᛆᚮᚿ.

Suebsicuisubiriumeþonlium
AGLA delaon.

Consisting largely of unintelligible sequences, the purpose of the amulet remains obscure, although we can discern a formula like the one above, followed by the Cabalistic word *AGLA* and the incomprehensible *delaon* (which has been suggested to be a distortion of two Hebrew letter-names, *daleth* and *nun*, as they often appear in similarly distorted forms in mystical works of the time). Also from Bergen, a small folded lead plate, with a probable dating of c. 1350–1400, contains four lines of runes, two on each side:

ᛍᚢᛍᚴᛁᛍᛍᚢᛍᚴᛁᚱᛁᚢᚱᛂᛍᚿᚮᛚᛁᚮᚴᛆᚱᛆᚱ
ᛙᛆᚽᛏᛁᛁᛆᚼᛆᚽᛁ'ᛘᛆᚱᚴᚢᛍᛘᛆᚦᛁᛆᛍᛚᚢᚴᛆᛍᛆᚱᛏᛂᛁ
ᚦᛆᛣᛍᛆᛁᚴᛁᛂᛏᛂᚦᚽᚽᚴᛆᛆᚴᚽᛆᛋᛍᛁᛆ
ᛆᚢᛂᛘᛆᚱᛁᛆᛏᛁᛍᚢᛍᚴᚱᛁᛍᛏᚱᛆᚢᛂᛘᛆᚱᛁᛆ

suspissuspiriuresnoli ok arr(e)tôn.
Johannes, Marcus, Mattheus, Lucas. Orate.
þoysoipieæeþnnkoapnacsia.
Ave Maria et Jesus Kristr, Ave Maria.

'*suspissuspiriuresnoli* and The Unsayable.
John, Mark, Matthew, Luke. Pray.
þoysoipitætþnnkoapnacsia.
Hail Mary and Jesus Christ, Hail Mary.'

The small amulet, probably from before the year 1413, similarly opens with the magical formula, following it by a litany of holy names. The Greek word *arretôn* 'the unsayable, secretive, most secret', was often employed as a divine epithet, and the amulet is probably asking God and the four evangelists to pray for the bearer.[32]

Another version of this formula (*susbiristæ*, although this may also reflect Latin *spiritus*) may occur on a fragmentary lead roll from a Danish grave at Viborg, which was probably thought to ward against some kind of fever (*febris*). Unfortunately the amulet is sadly damaged and largely unreadable, although some few words such as *[Al]fa O, no[mine?], susbiristæ, nomine Spiri[tus], febri[s], amen, AGLA* and *Maria* can be discerned. In any case, the amulet's

31 *NIyR* no. 637; see also Knirk, 'Runic inscriptions containing Latin', p. 488 and A. Liestøl, 'Runefunn under golvet i Lom kyrkje', *Foreningen til norske minnesmerkers bevaring årbok* 132 (1978), 183–85.
32 *NIyR* nos 638–39.

inscription consists of protective formulas of some sort: perhaps the idea was to transfer the fever to a corpse, or perhaps the amulet was carved in an unsuccessful bid to restore the feverish victim to health.[33]

The gradual degeneration of once intelligible formulas can probably account for several otherwise apparently meaningless texts which nevertheless recur in various guises. For example, an incomprehensible line following the Old Norse sentence 'you are crazy' is found on a rune-stick from Bergen:

ᚦᚢᛁᚱᛏᚡᚱ
ᛒᚨᛒᛁᛗᚠᛁᛒᚨᛒᛏᛁᚷᚨᚠᛁᛒᚨ...

Þú ert ær(r). bobinafibobæshafibo.

This text invites comparison with one from a slightly more meaningful perforated beech staff from Borgund church:

+ᛒᚨᛗᛒᛁᛗᚠᛁᚻᛒᚨᛗᛒᛁᛗ
ᛒᛏᛁᚨᚠᛏ

Bona benigna . . . bona benigna . . .

'Good bone . . . good bone . . .'

The Borgund amulet has also been compared with magical formulas of the *buro, berto, beriora* type, some of which were used in staunching blood and may originate in the name of Veronica, the woman who wiped the sweat from Jesus during his passion, or Berenice, the wife of the Graeco-Egyptian king Ptolemy III, who sacrificed her hair to give her husband victory.[34]

The other magical formula found on the Lom rune-staff, *faofaifaufau*, is to an English speaker immediately reminiscent of the charm spoken by the giant in the fairytale *Jack and the Beanstalk*: 'Fee, fi, fo, fum, I smell the blood of an Englishman.' A similar formula is found on a cruciform wooden amulet from Bergen, pierced at one end; here again with magic of an apparently Christian sort:

ᚠᚨᛁᚠᚨᚨᚠᚨᚾᛁᚠᛁᚠᚱᚾᛁᛁᚤ
ᛁᚨᚤᛁᚻ.ᚨᚻᚨᚠᛗᚻ

Faifaofau.
Ecce crucem Domini!
Aea, AGLA.

'*Faifaofau.* Behold the cross of the Lord! *Aea, AGLA.*'

The amulet has been dated to about the year 1300. Its Latin text reminds the reader of the crucifixion of Christ, the *Behold the Cross* antiphon also appearing on the Seven Sisters lead leechcraft amulet (see above) and some runic lead crosses discussed with other Christian inscriptions in chapter 8, which also employ the lucky acronym *AGLA*. *Aea* may derive from *Eia*, one of the holy

---

33 The Viborg lead strip is presented by M. Stoklund, 'Runer 1995', *Arkæologiske Udgravninger i Danmark* (1995), 275–94.

34 These 'bone' sticks are *NIyR* nos 349 and 644.

words (originally just a Latin exclamation indicating delight) that appear in medieval lists. The *faifaofau* formula, appearing here and on the Lom stick considered earlier, also occurs, interspersed with magical symbols, on a runic eye-charm from Bergen to be discussed later in the chapter, and is not dissimilar to *ufau ufai ufao* on the Swedish rune-stick described above. Like many of the unintelligible words and phrases considered here, it presumably represents the corrupt remnants of a once-intelligible (but probably foreign) expression. Such debased versions often came to rely on rhyme, alliteration or assonance, rather than linguistic meaning, for their mystical significance.[35]

More distant parallels, showing similar vocalic variation, are probably no more than nonsense writing or didactic runic spelling exercises, although they have been connected with alphabet magic. These include the text *fifafufofyfi* on a wooden wheel and the legend on a tabletop which reads: . . . *nam ek þetta því: fefufafø. fuþorkhnieøsbpmtlæy. fatatratkatnatpatbatmat*, 'I learned these: *fe fu fa fø fuþork* etc.' Two further rune-sticks contain the futhark row plus various syllabaries, e.g. *fu:fo:fi:fy, fofafi*, while a third, presumably evidencing letterplay or early word-formation practice, has: *fufafefifoþoþaþiþu. fund, þund, rund, gund, lund, hind, sund, þond*. Just as in the case of the use of letter pairs in Gnostic mysticism, magical significance could presumably still be thought to exist in sequences that were still patently formed originally just as spelling lessons.[36]

More overtly pagan is the rhyming 'thistle, mistletoe' formula which occurs in various guises throughout Sweden, Denmark, Norway and Iceland. It generally occurs in a cryptic runic sequence requiring some kind of shuffling of the runic characters to make them readable. What appears to be the original version of the charm occurs in two Viking Age rune-stone inscriptions. The more straightforward of the two, the Ledberg stone, from Sweden, depicts scenes from the Norse apocalypse of Ragnarok, but bears a standard memorial text: *Bisi satti stæin þannsi æftiʀ Þorgaut* . . . *faður sinn. Ok þau Gunna baði*, 'Bisi placed this stone in memory of Thorgaut . . . his father. And Gunna, both'. This is followed by the cryptic runic sequence:

:ᚦᛘᚴ:ᛁᛁᛁ:ᛋᛋᛋ:ᛏᛏᛏ:ᛁᛁᛁ:ᛚᛚᛚ

þmk iii sss ttt iii lll

i.e. *þistill, mistill, kistill.*

'Thistle, mistletoe, casket.'

The same mysteriously encoded sequence is encountered on a Danish memorial stone. The Gørlev rune-stone bears a magical memorial text which is analysed fully in chapter 9, though its mysteriously encoded section similarly reads: ᚦᛘᚴᛁᛁᛁᛋᛋᛋᛏᛏᛏᛁᛁᛁᛚᛚᛚ, *þmk iii sss ttt iii lll*, 'thistle, mistletoe, casket'.

35 The *feefifo* inscriptions include this one, N B646, as well as N A71 from Lom, *NIyR* no. 633 from Bergen, and the previously discussed stick from Lödöse.

36 On runic syllabaries see K.F. Seim, 'Runes and Latin script', in K. Düwel (ed.), *Runeninschriften als Quellen interdisziplinäre Forschungen* (Berlin 1998), pp. 508–12.

An unencoded version of the formula is scratched into the wall of Borgund stave church in Norway. The inscription reads:

ᛏᛁᛌᛏᛁᛚᛘᛁᛌᛏᛁᛚ ᛆᚴᚼᚽᚦᛁᚱᛁᚦᛁᚦᛁᛌᛏᛁᛚ

Tistill, mistill ok hinn þriði, þistill.

'*Tistill* (?), mistletoe and the third, thistle.'

The sonorous rhyme of the formula presumably led to its expansion with linguistically meaningless sounds, as with *tistill*, above. In any case, the same kind of encoded formulation is found on another rune-stick from Bergen:

ᛘᛏᛕᚴᚱᚵᛒ ᛁᛁᛁᛁᛁᛁᛁ ᛌᛌᛌᛌᛌᛌᛌ ᛏᛏᛏᛏᛏᛏᛏ ᛁᛁᛁᛁᛁᛁᛁ ᛚᛚᛚᛚᛚᛚᛚ

Mistill, tistill, pistill, kistill, ristill, gistill, bistill.

'Mistletoe, *tistill*, epistle (?), casket, ploughshare (?),[37] *gistill, bistill.*'

This yields a string of mainly nonsensical rhyming words, as does the encoded runic variant on a chest found in Lomen church, Norway:

ᚱ⁝ᛕ⁝ᚴ ᛁᛁᛁ ᛌᛌᛌ ᛏᛏᛏ ᛁᛁᛁ ᛚᛚᛚ

ristill, pistill, kistill.

'Ploughshare (?), epistle (?), casket.'[38]

Further botched versions of the formula can probably be identified in a half-dozen Norwegian inscriptions. A version of the same formula, still written in runes, is even encountered in an Icelandic tale, the *Saga of Bosi and Herraud*:

ᚱ.ᚯ.ᚦ.ᚵ.ᛘ.ᚢ ᛁᛁᛁᛁᛁᛁ. ᛌᛌᛌᛌᛌᛌ: ᛏᛏᛏᛏᛏᛏ ᛁᛁᛁᛁᛁᛁ ᛚᛚᛚᛚᛚᛚ

In the saga, the sequence forms part of a powerful runic curse which forces the king of Götaland to comply with the demands of an old woman. Similarly, the curse in *Skirnir's Journey* has 'be like the thistle, which is crushed at the end of the harvest'. The original purpose of the 'thistle, mistletoe' charm is not known, however, but given the nature of similar sequences and its mention of mistletoe, it presumably originated in some kind of herb-lore which degenerated over time into a powerful magic formula. Mistletoe continues to play a part in bringing couples together at Christmas; it was also used in the weapon responsible for the death of the beloved Norse god Balder and was widely used in magic ritual – 'mistletoe of the oak', for instance, to be pounded small and dry and put in the best wine, is employed in one complicated Anglo-Saxon charm against shingles. During the Middle Ages, mistletoe was often used as a cure against epilepsy, it is invoked in various manners in European folklore and continues to play an

37 Other possible meanings include 'lady' or 'ringworm'; see McKinnell and Simek, p. 136.

38 Following an older (discredited) reading ᛏᚱ rather than ᛏ, McKinnell and Simek, p. 136, suggest reading *þristill*, cf. *þristr* 'a three' thus 'Trinity' (?), and suggest a Christian parody or adaptation of the traditional formula.

important role in homeopathic medicine. It was also venerated by the Celts and the solemn rites attending the gathering of the mistletoe by the Druids of Gaul and Britain are described by Pliny in his *Natural History* where he claims it was used as a cure for infertility. The power of herbs was increased by singing charms over them and performing magical actions as they were being gathered, prepared and administered, and the thistle, mistletoe formulation may have originated in such a practice.[39]

We also encounter the expanded, encoded version of the thistle, mistletoe formula on a thirteenth or fourteenth-century rune-stick from Tønsberg, Norway, where it appears in company with a variety of good-luck devices. The stick inscription seems to be the work of several different carvers and in its entirety the partly versified charm reads:

ᚾᛁᛚᛁᚠᚱ.ᚢᛁᚱᛁ.ᚢᚾᚼᚱ.ᛆᛘᚾᚴ.ᛘᛁᛏ:'ᛏᚾᛁᚽ:ᚴᚱᛁᛘᚱ:ᚼᛆᚠᚢᛘ:ᛘᚾᛚᛏ:ᛘᛆᚱᛏ:ᛆᚠᚴᛆᚱᛁᛘᛁᛚᛚᛁ:ᚠᛁᚱᛁᚱ:ᚦᛆ
'ᛆᚴ:ᛆᛏᚾᚴ: ᚢᛁᛚ:ᚽᛘᛆ:ᛆᚠᚦᛁ:ᚱᚢᚽᛆᚱ:
ᚽᛆᚢᛆ:ᚴᚽᛆᚱ:ᚾᚴ:'ᛒᚢ:ᚱᚦᚾᚴ:ᚢᛁᛚᛏ.ᛏᚢ.ᚴᛁᚠᛏᛆ.ᛘᚾᚱ.ᚾᛁᚽᛆ.ᚦᛆ.ᚾᚽ:ᚦᛆᚱᚾᚱ:ꝺꝺꝺꝺꝺᛘᚱᛏᚼᚴᛁᛁᛁᛁᛁ'''''
ᛏᛏᛏᛏᛏ ᛚᛚᛚᛚᛚ.
ᚾᛏᚦᚠᚠ''ᛆᚽᛏᚾᛏᚦᚠᚠ''ᛆᚽᛏ
:ᚦᛆᚢ:ᚾᚱᛆ:ᛒᚾᚦᚾ:ᛁᛒᚢᚦ:'ᛆᛘᛆᚽ:ᚴᛚᛆᚢᚠᛆ:ᚴᛆᚱᚾ:ᛆᚠ:ᚴᛆᚽᛆ:ᚢᛁᛚᛁᛆᛚᛘ':ᚼᚾᛁᛚᛚᚦᚢ.ᚼᚾᛁᛚᛚ.'ᚾᛚ.ᚦᚢ.ᚦ
ᛆ...

Eilífr virðivægr á mik. Með Steingrímr hǫfum mælt mart okkar í milli fyrir þá sǫk at ek vil nema af því rúnar.
eaauo (?) knǫrr. Ek spyr þik: vilt þú gipta mér eina þá? En þar eru þessar, m r t h k iiiii ttttt lllll
e(inn), t(veir), þ(rír), f(jórir), f(imm), s(ex), s(jau), á(tta), n(íu), t(íu), e(llifu), t(ólf), þ(rettán), f(jórtán), f(imtán), s(extán), s(jautján), á(ttjan), n(ítján), t(uttugu)
nir a (?)

Þau eru bæði   *í búð saman*
Klaufa-Kári   *ok kona Vilhjálms . . .*
Heill þú!   *Heill, sæll þú þá . . .*

'Eilif the worthy owns me. With Steingrim, we have spoken much between ourselves for the reason that I want to learn runes from it.
eaauo Knorr. I ask you: will you give me one of these to marry? And they are these: mistletoe, ploughshare (?), *tistill, histill*, casket.
O(ne), t(wo), t(hree), f(our), f(ive), s(ix), s(even), e(ight), n(ine), t(en), e(leven), t(welve), t(hirteen), f(ourteen), f(ifteen), s(ixteen), s(eventeen), e(ighteen), n(ineteen), t(wenty). *nir a.*

[39] The 'thistle, mistletoe' runic inscriptions include the stones *SR* II, no. 181, *DR* no. 239 and further inscriptions found in Norwegian churches, *NIyR* nos 75 and 364 (and cf. *NIyR* nos 365–67), as well as the rune-sticks N B391 and N A39. The formula is discussed in C. Thompson, 'The runes in Bósa saga ok Herrauðs', *Scandinavian Studies* 50 (1978), 50–56, Liestøl, *Runer frå Bryggen*, pp. 18–19, S.A. Mitchell, 'Anaphrodisiac charms', *Norveg* 38 (1998), 19–42 and M. MacLeod, 'Bandrúnir in Icelandic sagas', *Scripta Islandica* 52 (2001), 35–51. Mistletoe is widely used as magical protection; see K. von Tubeuf, *Monographie der Mistel* (Munich 1923). On the significance of the thistle in *Skirnir's Lay* see W. Heizmann, 'Der Fluch mit der Distel', *Amsterdamer Beiträge zur älteren Germanistik* (1996), 91–104 and Von See et al., pp. 118–26.

'They are both lodging together,
Clumsy-Kari and William's wife.
Hail to you! Hail and good fortune to you then!'

This runic stick is replete with protective formulas. Even the conclusion might be compared with the greeting on the Bergen rune-stick naming Odin and Thor considered earlier: 'Hail to you and be in good spirits!' (see chapter 2). As well as a casual statement of ownership, an apparent proposal of marriage and some gossip in the Eddic *fornyrðislag* metre, we have cryptic runes encoding the word *þessar* 'these', the expanded mistletoe, casket formula and a system denoting the numbers 1 through 20 with each initial rune appearing two or four times.[40]

This same system of numerical abbreviation is found in some further Norwegian inscriptions. One is carved into the walls of Gol stave church (now in Bygdøy, Oslo):

ᚾᛐᚦᚠᚠᛌᛌᛆᚿᛐᚾᛐᚦᚠᚠᛌᛌᛆᚿᛐ

E(inn), t(veir), þ(rír), f(jórir), f(imm), s(ex), s(jau), á(tta), n(íu), t(íu), e(llifu), t(olf), þ(rettán), f(jórtán), f(imtán), s(extán), s(jautján), á(ttjan), n(ítján), t(uttugu).

The same sequence for encoding the numerals is also found on three rune-sticks from Bergen, one of which starts with an unpronounceable letter sequence and further encodes the days of the week in a manner similar to the numerical one:

ᚼᚢᚱᚦᚱᛚᛌᛚᚱᚦᛌᚱ ᛚᛆᚠᚱᛆ͡ᚿᛋ ᚱ ᚱᚱ ᚦᚱ
ᛌᛘᛐᚯᚦᚠᛚᚾᛐᚦᚠᚠᛌᛌᛆᚿᛐᚾ

hurþrlslrþsr Lafranz r(eist) r(úna)r þ(essa)r . . .
s(unnudagr), m(ánadagr), t(ýrsdagr), ó(ðinsdagr), þ(órsdagr), f(reyjudagr), l(augardagr), e(inn), t(veir), þ(rír), f(jórir), f(imm), s(ex), s(jau), á(tta), n(íu), t(íu), e(llifu) . . .

'*hurþrlslrþsr* (magic letter sequence?) Lawrence c(arved) t(hese) r(unes) . . . S(unday), M(onday), T(uesday), W(ednesday), T(hursday), F(riday), S(aturday), o(ne), t(wo), t(hree), f(our), f(ive), s(ix), s(even), e(ight), n(ine), t(en), e(leven) . . .'

The opening sequence is somewhat similar to the recurrent unpronounceable ones from Bergen, Tønsberg and Iceland considered earlier, and not entirely unlike the Æbelholt sequence *horþl*.[41]

Runic cryptography was widespread in medieval Bergen and did not necessarily imply occult practices were at work. The numerical futhark code was particularly popular in the harbour town, inscribers pictorially representing various runes as scales on a fish, hairs in a beard, or bodily appendages. Various ciphers occur in runic inscriptions from the earliest to the latest time periods and

40 The Tønsberg rune-stick is discussed by Gosling, 'Runic material', pp. 181–83; cf. also McKinnell and Simek, pp. 137–38, who describe it as a set of writing exercises. The word *kn rr* might be either a personal name or the name of a kind of trading ship (*knarr*).

41 The Gol inscription is *NIyR* no. 573; the Bergen sticks are N B46, N B89 and N B287.

probably served a variety of purposes – usually as a form of game or linguistic challenge, although sometimes a more secretive or sinister purpose may be suspected.

The encoded 'thistle, mistletoe' formula is not the only one which might betray pre-Christian origins, however. The Bergen rune-stick considered earlier, with repeated *acre, acre ærnem*, also contained the recurrent *sator arepo* formula which was well known throughout the ancient and medieval worlds, and in fact, known as the 'Devil's Latin' or the 'Devil's Square', remained popular in Scandinavia into the nineteenth century as a protection against theft and various illnesses. The magical effect of the formula lies in the fact that if properly spelt and laid out, it constitutes a twenty-five letter word-square, reading the same horizontally and vertically, left to right and in reverse:

```
S A T O R
A R E P O
T E N E T
O P E R A
R O T A S
```

The earliest documented occurrences of the formula are found in the ruins of Pompeii, which suggest it is ultimately pre-Christian; some researchers maintain it originated as symbolic of the wheel (*rotas*) or was associated with agrarian rites. There have been many interpretations of the rather nonsensical sequence: most attempts founder on the term *arepo*, which is not standard Latin, and the most straightforward translation runs 'The sower Arepo holds the wheels at work'. The use of the words of the square in magic of many sorts ensured that any linguistic sense was evidently lost early, however, the words valued more for their apotropaic effect (frequently appearing alongside other palindromes, powerful names, symbols and magic formulas) or re-interpreted, as in Coptic and Ethiopian Christianity, where they were regarded as the names of the five wounds of Christ or of the five nails of the cross, or later as divine epithets or the names of angels, or even (in Byzantine tradition for example) as the shepherds who visited the newborn Christ at Bethlehem. Other attempts to explain the sequence regard it as an anagram and in fact one popular derivation is that this may be based on the letters of the *Lord's Prayer* in Latin plus the Greek letters a(lpha) and o(mega):

```
                A
                P
                A
                T
                E
                R
  P A T E R  N O S T E R  O
                O
                S
                T
                E
                R
                O
```

This cryptological solution, first developed in the 1920s, however, may be little more than a modern fiction, as there are manifold other ways of rearranging the letters to render religious expressions both Christian and otherwise. In fact a number of alternative anagrammatic rearrangements invoking Satan made their way into books of black magic.[42]

Whatever its origin, the formula is found all over the Roman world and, from about the ninth century, the words of the square featured regularly in medieval European charms and talismans, occurring in Norwegian and Danish black magic as late as the nineteenth century. It was used in blessings, as general protection, or sometimes specifically against lightning, fire, theft, sickness, madness, pain or heartache.

Runically, the *sator arepo* formula is found eight times in Sweden, Norway and Iceland, often set out as a palindrome or word square. We encounter it in incomplete form, with only the words *sator arepo tenet* remaining, on the bottom of a fourteenth-century coopered bowl from Örebro, Sweden:

ᛋᛆᛐᚮᚱ
ᛆᚱᚾᛕᚮ
ᛐᚾᚽᚾᛐ

Sator
arepo
tenet.

In this instance each of the 15 remaining runes is neatly boxed, indicating an understanding of the original 'magic square' layout. The full palindrome, again in a boxed arrangement, is also found carved into the inner bottom of a gilded silver chalice from Dune on the Swedish island of Gotland. The inscription is a later addition to the chalice:

ᛋᛆᛏᚮᚱ
ᛆᚱᛂᛒᚮ
ᛐᛂᚽᛂᚦ
ᚮᛒᛂᚱᛆ
ᚱᚮᛐᛆᛋ

Sator
arepo

42 H. Hofmann, 'Satorquadrat', in G. Wissowa et al. (eds), *Paulys Real-Encyclopädie der Altertumswissenschaft*, 2nd ed., 59 vols (Stuttgart etc. 1894–1980), 15th supplement volume, pp. 477–565. Perhaps inevitably due to the difficulties of translation, the formula has thus been widely resolved into different solutions, both pagan and Christian and nonsensical, by reshuffling the letters or by identifying various abbreviatory encodements or cryptograms, acronyms or even anagrams (again resulting in a myriad of possibilities, of which the most popular is the *Pater Noster* explanation given above). While the background of the square has been variously defended as letter magic (created in Pythagorean mystical circles) or alternatively as Christian, Jewish, Gnostic, pagan, numerological and geometrically symbolic, its use in Christian amulets is incontestable. The use of the formula in magic was condemned by the seventeenth-century Icelandic cleric Guðmundur Einarsson who provided several instances of its use; see Daviðsson, p. 161.

teneth
opera
rotas.

Interestingly enough, this inscription employs a spelling mistake repeated in several Norwegian examples (i.e. ᚦ for ᛏ in *teneth*, reflecting contemporary Norse pronunciation of Latin), thus unintentionally destroying the palindromic effect and indicating that the words had taken on a magical meaning independent of the quadrilateral principle that originally informed the sequence. Another secondary runic inscription from Dune, this time inscribed on a pendant, also reveals a spelling error, reading:

ᛋᛆᛏᚮᚱᛆᚱᛂᛏ
ᛒᚮᛏᛂᚾᛂᛏ
ᚮᛒᛂᚱᛆᚱᚮᛏᛆᛋ

sator aret
po tenet
opera rotas.

In Norway, the final part of the formula further occurs on a flat, broken rune-stick from Trondheim, dated to the twelfth or thirteenth century:

. . .ᛒᚮᛏᚾᚦᛏᚮᛒᛂᚱᛆᚱᚮᛏᛆ'

[sator are]po t(e)n(e)th opera rotas.

The formula is also found on a much later rune-stick from Bergþórshvoll, Iceland, tentatively dated to the seventeenth or eighteenth-century, along with an incomplete runic alphabet:

ᛆᛒᛌᛑᛂᚠᚵᚼᛁᚴᛚᛘᚾᚮᛕᛩᚱᛋᛏᚢ
ᛋᛆᛏᚮᚱ:ᛆᚱᛂᛕᚮ⁝ᛏᛂᚾᛂᛏ⁝ᚮᛕᛂᚱᛆ⁝ᚱᚮᛏᛆᛋ

abcdefghiklmnopqrstu
sator arepo tenet opera rotas.

Although the sequence is not definitely attested in runes in Denmark, it is found carved in Roman letters in the limestone ashlars of Skellerup church, North Jutland, and on the lead amulet from Schleswig discussed earlier.[43]

The sequence is also found in the context of some longer runic inscriptions. A broken thirteenth-century rune-stick from Bergen is a veritable treasure-trove of protective, mainly Christian formulas (albeit often misspelled ones) with, in the final line, a more personal prayer in Norse. It reads:

43 On runic *sator arepo* see Düwel, 'Mittelalterliche Amulette', pp. 228–37, and on the Swedish bowl see H. Gustavson and T. Snædal Brink, 'Runfynd 1978', *Fornvännen* 74 (1979), 233–35. The Gotlandic inscriptions are *SR* XI, nos 145 and 149 respectively, the Trondheim stick *NIyR* no. 820, and for the Icelandic stick see A. Bæksted, *Islands Runeindskrifter* (Copenhagen 1942), p. 206.

ᛁᛆ᛬᛬ᛒ᛬᛬ᚱ᛬᛬ᛆ᛬᛬ᚠᚢᚦᛏ᛬᛬ᛳᛁᛏᛡᚱ᛬᛬ᛡᚱᛏ...
ᚱᛡᚠᛡᛁᚠ᛬ᚠᛡᛒᚱᛁᛁᚠ᛬ᚣ...
ᛁᛁᛂᚾᚤᚱᛂᛁ᛬ᚣᛡᚱᛁᚾᛡ᛬ᚠᛏᚤᛁᛁ ᚠ...

AGLA. Guð. Sator are[po].
Raphael, Gabriel, M[ichael],
Jesus Kristr. María gæt mín. F. . .

'*AGLA*. God. *Sator are[po]*. Raphael, Gabriel, M[ichael], Jesus Christ. Mary,
protect me. *F. . .*'

The formula also opens an inscription on a square rune-stick from Bergen, which
has been dated to the thirteenth or fourteenth century:

'ᛆᛂᚪᚱᛂᚪᚱᛁᚴᛆᛂᛏᛁᛁᚦᛂᛆᚴᛁᚱᛆᛂᚱᛆᛏᛡᛁᛂᚴᛆᚠᛁᛂᚴᛆᚱᛡᚠᚠᛁᛁᛒᚾᛁᛁᛆᛁᚾᛁᛆᛒᛁᚠᚠᛁᛁᛒᚾᛁᛂᛆᛂᛂᚠᛂᛂ
ᚠᛂᛂᛆᛂᛂᛁᛆᚼᛆᚠᚠᛁᛂᛁᚾᚤᛆᛁᛂᚣᛆᚦᛁᚾᛁᛂᚣᛆᚱᚤᚾᛁ
'ᛁᛁᛆᛁᚱᛆᚣᚣᛁᛁᛁᚤᛆᛖᛁᛁᚠᛁᛖ

Sator arepo teneth opera rotas. Pax portantibus, salus habentibus! AGLA.
Johannes, Lucas, Mattheus, Marcus.
Svá erum mit skyld til Sl. . .

'*Sator arepo tenet opera rotas*. Peace to the bearers, health to the owners!
AGLA. John, Luke, Matthew, Mark. Such is my debt to Sl. . .'

The unfinished third line of this inscription is in a different hand and bears no rela-
tion to the rest of the text. As can be seen, though, the *sator arepo* formula often
occurs in company with other good-luck phrases, such as *AGLA* and the names of
the evangelists, archangels or saints, or generally benevolent wishes such as
'Peace to the bearers, health to the owners!'[44]

The 'peace to the bearer' formula is also found on two further runic inscriptions. The first is on a soapstone spindle-whorl from Swedish Jämtland, found
along the pilgrim route to the shrine of St Olaf in Trondheim. Its text reads: *Pax*
portanti, salus (h)abenti! Ingiwaldr, 'Peace to the bearer, health to the owner!
Ingivald.' The second, on a pierced wooden amulet found in Lom stave church in
Norway, reads:

ᚠᛆᚱᛁᚱᛆᛏᛁᛁᛆᚪᛁᚠ
ᚼᚠᛂᚣᛆᚱᚼᚾᛂᛁᚾ
ᚼᛁᛂᚣᛂᛆᚦᛁᚼᛂᚴᛆᚪ
ᚴᛆᚱᛡᚠᛡᛁᛂᛂᛁᚾᛂ

Kyri(os?), rota(s?), Johannes, Marcus, Lucas, Mattheus. Pax portanti! Salus!

'Mercy (?), *rotas* (?), John, Mark, Luke, Matthew. Peace to the bearer!
Health!'

Runic talismans such as these are obviously designed to ensure or preserve good
luck or good health.

Similar in spirit is the cheerful Latin verse on an unfortunately broken birch
stick from thirteenth-century Bergen:

---

44 These are *NIyR* no. 636 and N B583; cf. Dyvik, p. 2.

ᛁᚿᚼᛚᛁᛏ:ᛁᛁ�ᚱᛁᛏ:ᚿᛁᛏᚼᛁᛃ:ᚱᚿᛁ:--ᛏ-...
ᚿᛏᛁᚱᛁ:ᛘᛁᚿᛁ᛬ᛃᚼᛁᛏ᛬ᛁᛁᛒ:ᚼᛏᛀᛁᛏ:...

Ducite discrete vitam, que . . .
Vestra salus mete sit ne(s)cia . . .

'Lead a life discreetly, which . . .
May your (good) health know no bounds . . .'

The runes which remain are decoratively double-cut and well finished, so some care was taken in their execution. Originally, the text was probably a couplet written in hexameters with internal rhyme, much like the five wounds inscription considered above. The runic Latin indicates, though, that the text was written to reflect pronunciation rather than following regular Latin spelling. The verse may have been copied from a collection of poems, but it is otherwise unknown, although verses expressing similar sentiments are attested in regular Latin.

A more urgent plea for healing may be evidenced on a rectangular fourteenth-century rune-stick from Bergen, which may perhaps be read as *Medet huc* 'heal this', followed by the Norse form of the name John. The reading is fairly uncertain, however, and the text too short to yield much information on healing runes or rituals. The third side of the stick is also filled with rune-like signs, though this may be in imitation of runic writing rather than represent an assortment of magical symbols.[45]

Nevertheless, it may be that the very act of writing was thought to cure afflictions, if one interpretation of a rune-inscribed sheep-bone, found in Fishamble Street, Dublin, is to be credited. The Viking-Age shoulder-bone has the following inscription:

ᛁᛁ- ᚱᛁᛏᛁᛁᛁᛏᛀᛏᛁᛈᛀᛀᚿᚼᛃᛏ-...
ᛀᛁᛈᚿᛀᛁᛏᚿ

The second side remains uninterpreted (it is perhaps a magical formula: *aikuaitu*; cf. *iurlurukiaikuaitu* on a batten of wood from Trondheim). A possible interpretation of the first, ending with *ame[n]*, is *riti sanat gálu*, 'by writing heals the crazy woman'. The use of magic writings or runes in healing is a popular theme in Norse literature and magical runes for curing illness are described in some Norse sagas, notably that of the Viking warrior and rune-master Egil Skallagrimsson. In one celebrated episode of *Egil's Saga*, Egil arrives at the house of Helga, a Swedish peasant girl who is confined to her sick bed and has lost her mind, bewitched by misapplied runic spells. A local lad, trying to win the love of the maiden, had carved runes to this effect on a piece of whalebone placed in the girl's bed, but the flawed inscription had instead caused the girl's illness to worsen. Realising that the runes had been miscarved, Egil burns the bone and lays

---

45 On the 'Peace to the bearer' inscriptions see Knirk, 'Runic inscriptions containing Latin', p. 487 and Liestøl, 'Runefunn under golvet', pp. 186–87. The other Latin texts are *NIyR* nos 604 and 608.

a new, beneficial runic inscription under her pillow. The grateful girl then recovers swiftly.[46]

Another well-attested medieval method of conquering sickness was based on the idea of magical similarity, relating (or alluding to) a mythological story in which the same problem had been overcome. Many Germanic healing remedies contain such a storytelling element and the narrative charms they attest usually describe the circumstances in which something analogous to what the victim was suffering from was overcome by a holy or legendary figure. We have already seen that this form of charm was known in the ancient world and one example, that of Antaura the headache mermaid, was related at the outset of chapter 2. We also encountered this approach in the *Nine Herbs Charm*, which relates how Woden smote a poisonous serpent with his nine glory twigs, and in the runic amulet describing Thor's fishing expedition from South Kvinneby. Sympathetic narration is also the principle behind one of the most famous relics of Germanic paganism, the second Merseburg charm, later versions of which survived to recent times in various forms in Scandinavia, England, Scotland and Germany.[47]

The ninth-century German version of the charm reads:

> Phol and Wodan rode to the wood;
> then Balder's foal sprained its foot.
> Then Sinthgunt sang over it and Sunna her sister,
> then Frija sang over it and Volla her sister,
> then Wodan sang over it, as he well knew how,
> as for this bone-sprain, so for blood-sprain, so for limb-sprain,
> bone to bone, blood to blood, limb to limb, as if they be glued together.

This sort of charm seems to have been very popular in Germanic tradition and many later versions of it are known. In later texts the Germanic gods are generally replaced by Christ, Mary and the apostles. The second Merseburg charm has occasioned a great deal of interest among linguists as a very similar verse employing a comparable rhetorical form (mentioning 'marrow to marrow' and 'joint to joint') is also known from an ancient Indian source. Like the Merseburg charm and later examples, the Atharva-Veda, nearly fifteen hundred years earlier than the German text, features a god healing fractured bones and an enumeration of the various body parts. The similarities are striking, but it is not entirely clear they are linked. Anglo-Saxon charms for sick cattle, sheep, horses and for sudden death in swine, however, are well attested and German investigators have even sought to establish a link between some of the Old Germanic bracteates, which they claim depict the scene of Balder's injured foal, with similar curative magic.[48]

---

46 The Dublin bone is Barnes et al., no. 10.
47 On the Merseburg charm see now H. Eichner and R. Nedoma, 'Die Merseburger Zaubersprüche', *Die Sprache* 42 (2000/1), 1–195 and H. Eichner, 'Kurze "indo"-"germanische" Betrachtungen über die atharvavedische Parallele zum Zweiten Merseburger Zauberspruch (mit Neubehandlung von AVS. IV 12)', *Die Sprache* 42 (2000/1), 211–33.
48 K. Hauck, 'Völkerwanderungszeitliche Bilddarstellungen des zweiten Merseburger Spruche als Zugang zu Heiligtum und Opfer', in H. Jankuhn (ed.), *Vorgeschichtliche Heiligtümer und Opferplätze im Mittel- und Nordeuropas* (Göttingen 1970), pp. 297–319.

But runic charms for animal health are controversial, although a piece of bone from Lund, dated to the first half of the twelfth century, may refer to veterinary magic of some kind. The fragmentary text reads:

> . . .ᛅᚱᚦᛁ-⁝ᛘᛂᚦ⁝ᚼᛂᛋᛏᛁ⁝ᚱ͡ᚯᚦᛆ. . .
> . . .ᚼᚴᛁ⁝ᛋᛒᛅᛏᛅ⁝ᛅᚱᚴᚱ⁝. . .
>
> . . . *arði með hæsti røða* . . .
> . . .*hki spata argʀ* . . .

This rather obscure text appears to represent some form of ritual magic. The first line seems to refer to ploughing (*arði*) with a red horse (*með hæsti røða*), a formulation which suggests magical significance as red animals are often supernatural in European folklore. The second line is even more puzzling, but *spata* may be a German loanword referring to spavin (a disorder of a horse's hock), while the word *argʀ*, found in several rune-stone curses, has a number of meanings, usually to do with sexual deviancy or harmful magic (see chapter 9). Perhaps the text, like those that appear on several Danish rune-stones, was to curse someone with perversity or to infect their crops or livestock. In its lamentably fragmentary state, however, we have no sure way of knowing what was really intended here.[49]

More concrete examples of narrative charms are found on several Scandinavian runic amulets featuring the names of the Seven Sleepers of Ephesus. A popular Christian legend, familiar in Western Europe by the end of the sixth century, it told of a gruesome persecution of Christians by the emperor Decius in the middle of the third century. Seven noble young men refused to forswear their faith and voluntarily retired to a cave in Mount Celion, near Ephesus, in what is now Turkey. The enraged emperor ordered his men to seal up the entrance to the cave and thus entomb the sleeping men, who miraculously re-emerged during the reign of the Christian Emperor Theodosius (either the Great, regnant 379–395, or the Younger, 408–450), thus proving the doctrine of the resurrection of the dead. The names of the Seven Sleepers, of the mountain where they slept and the duration of their sleep, vary considerably, although in Roman martyrology they are commemorated as Maximianus, Malchus, Martinianus, Dionysius, Johannes, Serapion and Constantinus. All seven names occur in Norse material, including Norse translations of the legend, the Swedish and Norwegian runic inscriptions discussed below, and in an Icelandic magic formula against insomnia.

The names of the Seven Sleepers also occur in several Anglo-Saxon charms, usually in connection with sleep or fever. Their help is related to their mythological story: just as their power enabled them to sleep untroubled for decades, the invocation of their names is supposed to grant the sufferer the power to sleep unaffected by insomnia or illness. Although the Seven Sleepers are frequently encountered in Scandinavian runic inscriptions, whether they were invoked as a non-specific kind of blessing or were meant to help against sleeplessness after a fever or provide a long respite from disease (or perhaps the seven spirits of disease) is not usually made clear.

49 Moltke, *Runes and their Origin*, p. 464.

One of the earliest runic occurrences of the sleepers seems to be on a lead amulet from Alvastra, Sweden. Its creation, however, like several of the sleeper amulets, may even precede the publication of Jacobus de Voragine's *Aurea legenda* (*Golden Legend*) in about the year 1260, which is subsequently supposed to have widely popularised the tale. The text on this amulet, found in a sarcophagus, relates the story of the sleepers and ends with a pious appeal to the Trinity. It bears the following fairly lengthy text:

ᛁᚠᛃᛆᛘᛏᚿᛏᚱᛁᛆᚽ:ᛏᛁᛁᛦᚿᛁᛚᛁ-ᛏᛏᚿ:ᛆᚿᛏᚿᛁᛆᚱᛚᚤ:ᛁᛒᛁ:ᚱᛏᚿᛚᛁᛏᚿᚤᛚ
ᛖᛁ:ᚿᛏᛒᛁᛏᚤ:ᚿᛃᛤᚤᛁᛁ:ᛏᛆᚱᚤᛁᛏᛏᛏᚿ:ᚤᛆᚱᛁᚤᚿᚿ:ᚤᛏᛃᛏᚤᛁ
ᚤᛁᛆᛏᚿᚿ:ᚤᛆᚱᚤᛁᛆᛏᚿᚿ:ᛏᛁᛆᛁᚿᛁᚿᚿ:ᚿᛏᚱᛆᛒᛁᛆᛏ:ᚤᛆᛏᚿᛃᛁᛃ
ᚱᛁᚿᚿ:ᛁᛤᛆᛏᛃᛁᛏᛏᚿ:ᚿᛁᚤ:ᚱᛏᚤᚿᛁᛏᚤᛃᛏᛤᛁᚤᚤᛃᚤᚿᚪᛏᛏᛃ
ᚤᛁᛁᛁ:ᛏᛃᚿᚿᛏᚱᛁᚤᛏᚿᚿ:ᚤᚱᛁᚿᛁᛁᛒᛏᛏᛁᚤᛁᛁᛃᚤᛆᚱᛒᛃᚿᛁᚿ
ᚿᛃᚤᚿᚤᛆᛒᛏᛁᛁᛏᛃᚤᛁᛏᛏ:ᛒᛃᛏᚱᛁᚿᛏᛁᚤᛁᚿᛁᛁᛏᛏᚿᛒᛁᚱᛁᛏᚿᚿ
ᚿᛃᛤᚤᛁᛁ:ᛏᚤᛁᛏ

In monte Celion et in civitate Ephesiorum ibi requiescunt septem sancti dormientes: Malchus, Maximianus, Marcianus, Dionysius, Serapion, Constantinus, Johannes. Sic requiescat hic famula Domini nostri Jesu Christi Benedicta, a morbo si occumbet. In nomine Patris et Filii et Spiritus sancti, amen.

'In Mount Celion and in the city of Ephesus there rest seven holy sleepers: Malchus, Maximianus, Marcianus, Dionysius, Serapion, Constantinus, Johannes. So may Benedicta, a handmaid of Our Lord Jesus Christ, rest here, if she should die from illness. In the name of the Father and the Son and the Holy Spirit, amen.'

More condensed versions of the narrative charms simply list the names of those involved. A difficult Norwegian rune-stick from early thirteenth-century Bergen contains a variety of holy names, many in rather corrupt forms, including those of some of the sleepers:

ᚦᛁᛁᛁᛏᛃᚴᚱᛁᚿᛏᛏᚱᛏᛏ.ᛏᛁᚱᛏᚤᛏᛏᚿᛤ:ᛁᛤᛏᚱᚿᛏᚱᛒᛁ:ᛖᛃᚱ
ᚤᛏᚿᚤᚱ.ᚤᚤᚤᛏᛏᛁᛃᚤᛁᛏᚿ.ᚤᛆᛏᚤᛆᚱᛁᛁᚿᛁᛁᛏᚿᛁᚤᚿᛁᛦᛏᛏᛏᚿᛃᛁᚿᛁ
ᛃᚤᚿᛃᛏᛏᛏᛁᚦᚦᛏ:ᛏᛁᚱᛆᚤᛁᛁᛃᚤᛏᛏᛏᛁᛃᛁᚤᛏᛃᚤᛆᚤᛃᚤᛏᛏᚤᛏᛁᛃᛃᛏ
ᛁᛁᚿᛁᛁᚱᛏᛏᚱᛃᚤᚱᛏᛏᛆᛤᛁᛁᚤᚿᛏᛏᛃᛁᛤᚤᛃᚱᚤᚿᛁᛏᚦᚦᛏᛁᛁᛃᛏᛃᛏᛁᛁ
ᛖᛃᚱ
ᛖᛃᚱ

... dux (?)... Maximianus, Malchus (?), Martinianus...
... dirige (?), Domine, Deus meus. Consummatum est...
Tíu nætr eru frá Jóhnesiku (?)... Marcus, Lucas (?), Johannes (?)...

'... leader (?)... Maximianus, Malchus (?), Martinianus... govern (?), Lord, my God. It is done... Ten nights are from... Mark, Luke (?), John (?) ...'

In this in parts quite uninterpretable amulet text, the names of at least two of the sleepers (Maximianus, Martianus and perhaps Malchus?) can be made out in company with what seem to have been intended to be those of the four evangelists (only Mark's name is absolutely clear) plus the words *Deus meus*, 'my God' and *Consummatum est*, 'It is done', the cry of the dying Messiah, the latter a common element in charms (particularly those to staunch bleeding). The text also refers to *tíu nætr . . . eru frá Jóhnesiku* (i.e. *Jónsvǫku*?), presumably 'it is ten nights since St John's Vigil' (23 June), giving a date of 3 July. But we lack the fuller context that would allow determination of what motivated the carving or the reasoning behind the more impenetrable sections of the text that only hint at words like *dux* 'leader', *dirige* 'govern' and *Domine* 'Lord!' at various points.

The names of some of the sleepers and at least two of the evangelists are also inscribed in the wooden walls of Vågå stave church, Norway:

> ᛒᚽᛏᚱᚢ'. . . ✝ ᛘᛆᚱᚴᚢ'ᛆᚢᚴ. . . 'ᛋᚱᛆᛕᛁᚭᚿᚴᛆᚿ'ᛏᛆᚿᛏᛁᚿᚢ'
> ᚼᛁᛆᛚᛒᛁᛘᚽᚱᛆᛚᛚᚽᚱᚦᚽᛁᚱ✝ᛆᚢᚦᚢᚿᚱᚽᛁ'ᛏᛘᛁᚴ
>
> *Petrus . . . Marcus auk . . . Serapion, Constantinus*
> *Hjálpi mér allir þeir. Auðun reist mik.*
>
> 'Peter . . . Mark and . . . Serapion, Constantinus. May they all help me.
> Audun carved me.'

The inscription has not yet been properly published, but apparently the names Maximianus, Martinianus and probably Malchus can also be discerned. Another wooden amulet from Bergen, discussed earlier, evidences the names of the sleepers, albeit in a somewhat corrupt form (Dionysius, Johannes, Serapion [Malch]us, Maximianus, Dionysius), alongside a spell of some sort which finds parallels in several runic amulets from Norway and Anglo-Saxon England. The names Maximianus and Malchus may also be written backwards on a rather incoherent but well-worn pierced wooden amulet from Bergen.[50]

While none of the Norse sleeper inscriptions is explicit as to its purpose, there is undoubted evidence of magical practice at work in some. We may suppose that they were all motivated by the desire to confer some form of health or happiness. Charms describing a fabulous legend or narrative occur frequently in Anglo-Saxon leechcraft texts as well as in their Latin and Greek sources. A Greek charm to remove a bone sticking in the throat, for instance, alludes to the resurrection of Lazarus and the miracle of Jonah; in Germanic charms, Longinus, the soldier who pierced Christ's side upon the cross, is frequently encountered in charms for staunching blood. Other Christian stories are alluded to in various runic charms. The names of the three men who escaped unscathed from the fiery furnace of King Nebuchadnezzar, for example, are found on two Norwegian runic amulets, the first representing a charm for the eyes. The inscription is from Bergen and it is carved on a flat rune-stick, rounded at one end, which has been dated to around the year 1335:

> ᛡ ᚢᛁᚦᛆᚢᚼᚢᛘ:ᛏᚭᛒᛁᛆ':'ᛆᚿᛆᛏ:ᚭᚴᚢᛚᚢ':ᛁ'ᛏᛁ'ᚭᛘᛁᚿᛁ' ᚠᛆ-ᛯᚠᛆᚢᛯᚠᛆᚭᛯ ᛯ
> 'ᛁᛏᚱᛆᚴ:ᛘᛁ''ᛆᚴ:ᛂᚦᛆᚴ:ᛒᚽᚿᛆᚴᚭᚴ ᛘᛦᛚ ᛆᚢᚢᛘ:ᚽᚭᛘᚭ' ᚢᛁᚦᛒᛚᚭᚦ
>
> ᛡ *Við augum. Tobias sanat oculus istius hominis fa[i]* ᛯ *fau* ᛯ *fao* ᛯ ᛯ.
> *Sidrak, Misak et auk Abdenago. myl (?) augum (?) eomeos (?) Við blóð.*

50 The Seven Sleepers amulets include *NIyR* nos 54 and 637, *SR* I, no. 248, N B596 and possibly N B593; see Dyvik, pp. 4–5 and J.E. Knirk, 'Arbeidet ved Runearkivet, Oslo', *Nytt om runer* 13 (1998), 18–19.

Fig. 11. Bergen stick

'For the eyes. Tobias heals the eyes of this person. *fa[i]faufao*. Shadrach, Meshach and and Abednego (?). Salve (?) the eyes (?) *ameos* (?). For the blood.'

The inscription opens with the sign ᛏ known from a late Icelandic manuscript as *tvísteyptr maðr*, 'twice-dunked man (i.e. *m*-rune)' or *harðsól*, 'heavy-sun (i.e. *s*-rune)' which is found in several runic texts. A single-barred variant is more common in (magical) manuscripts and, although it is sometimes identified as a Christian cross, presumably, to some carvers at least, it had some magical significance – a tenfold sequence occurs on a lead plate from Borgund, Norway, together with a fairly corrupt runic text. Similarly, the first line of the inscription considered here concludes with a magical formula interspersed with a series of decorative rune-like symbols (⍟) such as are found on the Kingittorsuaq stone from Greenland along with ᛨ (the latter symbol also occurs in some Swedish inscriptions).

The runic text is in a mixture of Old Norse and Latin. It opens typically enough with a statement of the purpose of the charm: 'for eyes'; yet oddly closes with what is evidently the next charm in the inscriber's exemplar: 'for blood'. This is probably an indication that runic legends could be copied from books at this time, rather than just reflecting epigraphic or oral traditions, which is hardly surprising at such a late date. The sense of the runes immediately preceding these words is less certain, although *myl* may perhaps be linked with Greek *mylphe* 'eye-ointments' and *eomos* may refer to the medicinal plant *ameos* (bishop's weed).

The Latin text which follows the heading is somewhat distorted, but obviously refers to the apocryphal story of Tobias who, on the advice of the archangel Raphael, smeared fish gall on the eyes of his blind father, Tobit, who thereby recovered his sight. Similar formulas against eye infection based on this story are found all over Scandinavia and further afield, with a particularly close parallel surviving in a Danish manuscript: *Sana, quaeso Domine, oculos istius, cui benedicimus, sicut sanasti oclos Tobie!*, 'Heal, I beseech you Lord, the eyes of this man whom we bless, just as you have healed the eyes of Tobit!'

The linguistically incomprehensible culmination of the first line, *faifaufao*, has several parallels and was discussed earlier in the chapter. The formula may derive from a form of alphabet magic using the names of Hebrew characters, perhaps to represent divine epithets. A singular *fau* or *fao* also appears, perhaps based on the Hebrew letter-name *vau*, which in some mystical texts signifies 'life', in some further Norwegian amulet inscriptions. A distorted list of Hebrew letter-names and the single-barred ᛏ is in fact found in an Icelandic formula dealing with ophthalmia, while a mid-fifteenth-century Danish spell against shingles employs

Hebrew letter-names and the three biblical names, Shadrach, Meshach and Abednego, found here.

The second line of the eye charm names the three men cast by the Babylonian King Nebuchadnezzar into flames for refusing to worship a golden image in the Book of Daniel. This was a popular story in the Middle Ages and the names of the youths, as well as the hymn they are supposed to have sung, were employed not only in the liturgy and private prayers, but also in charms against fire as well as incendiary diseases such as shingles. Some twelfth-century Swiss formulas to ignite the fires of love feature the names of the three men as well as divine epithets, magic words and Hebrew letters. Here the names are probably invoked to deliver relief from the burning pain of ophthalmia, or perhaps to induce some other form of miracle.[51]

These three names probably also occur on a broken rune-stick from Tønsberg, Norway, dated to the later half of the thirteenth century. Here the entire text comprises the following runes:

-ᚱ.ᚤᛁᛐᚱ.ᛁᚦᛁᛒ1ᛁᛘᛐᛅ

[Sidra]k, Misak et Abdenago.

Without more context it is impossible to determine the purpose underlying the inscription, perhaps another eye-charm, although a Swedish runic lead cross, using the words of the Catholic funeral rite, begs Christ for deliverance from flames as the three youths were saved.[52]

Another charm for eyes is found on a five-sided pierced wooden amulet from Bergen, probably from about the year 1400:

⫶·ᛅᛏᛅᚤᛁᛂᛁᛂᛐᚦᚼᚱ--1-ᚢᚾᛁᛅᛰᛁᚱᚾᛁᛐᛅᚼᚾᚦᛅᛌᚼᚼᛁᛂᛐᛚᛂᛐᚢᛅᛅᚼᚾᚦᛅᛁ
ᛁᛂᛐ1ᚾᛂᚷᛅᛰ----ᚾᚤᛐᚾᛐᚤᛁᛂᚱᛁᚼᛅᚱᛐᛁᛅ⫶ᚤᛐᛂᛐᛅᛐᛅᛐᛜᚱ
ᚠᚤᛅᛂᚾᛐᚷᛁᛒᛅᛅᛐᛅᛅᛰᛁ⫶ᚠᛅᛐᛰᛅᚱᛁᚠᛅᛒᛅᚠᛁᛂᛰᛅᚱᛅᚼᛐᛐᚾᛂᚼᚼᚤᛐᛐᛐᛅᛜᚱ
ᛁᛂᚤᛐᛂᛐᚾᛁᛰᛅᛐᛐᚱ-ᚠᚤᛐᛂᛐᚾᛁᚥᛁᚱᛐᚾᛁᛂᚤᛐᛂᛐᚾᛁ
ᛂᚻᛁᚱᛁᛐᚾᛂᛂᛐᛂᛐᚾᛂⰗ⫶·

O Domine Jesu Chr[is]t[e], qui apervit oculos caeci nati, salva oculos,
istius hom[inis c]um tua misericordia!
Messias, Soter, Emanuel, Sabaoth, Adonai. Fons et origo bonis, paraclitus ac
mediator.
Immensus Pater, [i]mmensus Filius, immensus Spiritus sanctus.

'O Lord, Jesus Christ, who opened the eyes of the blind newborn, save the eyes of that man with your mercy!
Messiah, Soter, Emmanuel, Sebaoth, Adonai. Source and origin of goodness, comforter and mediator.
Immeasurable Father, immeasurable Son, immeasurable Holy Spirit.'

This narrative charm, relating the anecdote of Jesus opening the eyes of infants, is

---

[51] This stick is *NIyR* no. 633; the plate with the symbols is N A5. On this symbol see *NIyR* VI, pp. 63–64 and 239.

[52] The inscription is N A292. McKinnell and Simek, p. 148 further cite an unpublished inscription on a lead plate from Sarpsborg, Norway, featuring the names of the three youths.

known in several variants. A long Danish version from the mid-fourteenth century runs as follows:

> *Qui apervit oculos ceci nati per sanctam misericordiam suam, oculos istius famuli Dei N. illuminare dignetur, amen! Increatus Pater, increatus Filius, increatus Spiritus sanctus. In mensus Pater, in mensus Filius, in mensus Spiritus sanctus. Eternus Pater, eternus Filius, eternus Spiritus sanctus.*

Written in Latin, the runic charm also employs to amuletic effect several divine epithets from a popular medieval hymn, the *Alma chorus Domini*, to refer to God, as is discussed in more detail in chapter 8, as well as containing the phrase 'immeasurable Father, immeasurable Son, immeasurable Holy Spirit' taken from the liturgy. It is worth remarking that Anglo-Saxon herbals and leechbooks prescribed more remedies for eyes than for anything else (although curiously enough, ears seem to be referred to in a late medieval manuscript runic formula against jaundice to be carved on wood and burnt: *Pollux, index, medius, medicus, auricularis*, 'Pollux, forefinger, middle, doctor, ear').[53]

Divine miracles are also alluded to in a charm for childbirth found on a double-sided rune-stick from Bergen, archeologically dated to around the fourteenth century:

ᛘᛆᚱᛁᛆ:ᚲᛁᚲᛁᚱᛁᛐ:ᚺᚱᛁᛌᛐᚿᛦ:ᚽᚱᛁᛌᛒᛐᛐ ᚲᛁᚲᛁᚱᛁᛐ:ᛁᛆᚼᛆᚠᚼᚿᛦ:ᛒᛆᚲᛐᛁᛌᛐᛆᛦ:ᛁᚽ:ᛁᚠᚠᛆᚱᚿᛦ
ᚿᛁᚽᛁᚱᛆᚺᛁᛆᚽᛖ:ᛌᛁᛌ:ᛆᛒᛌᛆᚿᛐᛆᛌᛖᛖ:ᛐᚺᛌᛁ:ᛁᚽᚠᛆᚠᚿᛖ:ᛐᛆᛦᛁᚽᚿᛌᛐᛖ:ᚿᛁᛆᚺᛆᛐᛐ:ᛐᛐ:ᚠᚿ

> *Maria peperit Christum, Elisabet peperit Johannem Baptistam. In illarum veneratione sis absoluta. Exi, incalve! Dominus te vocat ad lu(cem)/lu(men).*

> 'Mary bore Christ, Elisabeth bore John the Baptist. May you be absolved in veneration of them. Out, unhairless one! The Lord calls you into the light.'

This parturition charm, revealing a high degree of Latin literacy, refers to the miraculous conceptions of Mary, the virgin mother, and the aged Elisabeth who begot John the Baptist. The charm is well known, in a variety of versions, from all the Scandinavian countries as well as Germany and Britain. The closest parallel seems to be a (much longer) Icelandic example found in an early-sixteenth-century manuscript, the first part of which reads:

> *Mulier ista N de partu liberetur. Elizabeth peperit Johannem Baptistam et beata Maria peperit Deum exi calve, exi calve, ad lucem Dominus te vocat in nomine Domini nostri Jhesu Christi amen. Maria peperit Christum Elizabeth peperit Johannem Baptistam. In illa veneratione sis absoluta sancta Maria quae portasti Christum, sancta Elizabeth quae portasti Johannem Baptistam succurite famule vestre N que capilli capitis eius omnes trementes camille exi foras, lux te expectat Anna peperit Mariam, Maria peperit salvatorem Jhesum Christum. Ventrem huius mulieris aperi N exi tenebris et transe ad lucem salvator te vocat, amen.*

---

53 Cf. Dyvik, pp. 7–8. On the runic formula against jaundice see Bæksted, *Islands Runeindskrifter*, p. 221.

Uniquely, the runic example addresses the child as *incalve*, the 'not-hairless one', in calling it to come forth; the Icelandic calls upon the opposite (and less usual newborn state), *calve* the 'hairless one', both of which (*Exi, (in)calve*) may represent corruptions of an original address *exinanite*, 'tear down', as is found in some recorded manuscript versions. Usually the charm would be written down and placed on some part of the labouring woman's body: an early-sixteenth-century book of magic from Vinje, Norway (reflecting Danish tradition), instructs that it should be written on a letter long enough to wrap around the belly, while a Swedish version, also to be laid on the belly, contains the added precaution of recommending immediate removal of the charm after delivery to prevent the expulsion of the intestines! The charm could also be written on food for the woman to ingest. The state of the Norwegian rune-stick, however, showing traces of a probably identical text which has been cut away, has given rise to the speculation that the original text was swallowed by the woman (cf. the runic potion described in the *Lay of Sigrdrifa* in the *Poetic Edda*, where runes are scraped off and mixed into mead). In fact the idea that labour could be helped by supernatural means is recurrent in the *Edda*, occurring in *Oddrun's Lament*, the *Lay of Fafnir* as well as in the *Lay of Sigrdrifa*.[54]

Despite a lack of runic parallels to the childbirth charm, we do have instances of Scandinavian spell-sticks being tied to the body of a sufferer. An Icelandic charm against severe periods was supposed to be cut on a stick (*kefli*, usually translated as 'rune-stick') and tied to the thigh of a heavily menstruating woman. But despite this spell for stemming blood and a reference to a charm *For the Blood* at the end of the runic spell *For the Eyes*, we actually have no extant runic charms explicitly for staunching blood from medieval Scandinavia, although 'thin blood' is referred to in a perplexing message on a wooden stick from Lödöse, Sweden: *Hagormʀ (?) helgar. . . þunnt blōð ūʀ rinn ūʀ a[-]r blōð ūʀ rinn ūʀ a. . .* As well as what is probably the name Hagorm and the adjective *helgar* 'holy', we have here the words 'thin blood, run out, out of . . . blood, run out, out of . . .', but what this may have meant to the people who carved it, some time in the late twelfth or early thirteenth century, we now have no way of telling.[55]

The medical charms considered in this chapter employ a variety of strategies to achieve their effect. Some address the spirits of sickness directly in banishing or exorcising them, or simply warning them away; some attempt to transfer the disease to corpses; others appeal to God or other higher powers to intervene on their behalf. A mixture of beliefs of different origins is evident in many if not most of the charms, some of which, though Christianised, retain a pagan aspect. Runic inscribers continued to enchant their inscriptions with potent words or names or even whole formulas, often linguistically debased versions of exotic chants or charms where the magical power largely relied on the feeling of awe and impotence on the part of the recipient. Alternatively, the sympathetic narrative charms relate names or anecdotes familiar from pagan or Christian legend, associating events or ideas from the epic past with a present situation. Gradually what

---

[54] The Bergen childbirth charm is *NIyR* no. 631; cf. also Liestøl, *Runer frå Bryggen*, p. 19.

[55] H. Gustavson et al., 'Runfynd 1982', *Fornvännen* 78 (1983), 224–43.

seems originally to have been a largely oral healing tradition became increasingly bookish until many of the texts seem almost to have been copied out of spell and charm collections, in quite the reverse manner from what we might have expected given the growing condemnation of the use of runic sorcery evident in some parts of Christendom. In the apotropaic and exorcising runic amulets, traditional Germanic magic was freely mixed with Christian rites and prayers, and such syncretism of profoundly pagan and deeply Christian aspects is evident also in the charms considered in chapter 8.

7

Pagan Ritual Items

THERE are several more early runic inscriptions found on objects that may have been amulets, but they are carvings which often more clearly represent aspects of pre-Christian religious thought and belief. Many of these items might well have been similar to phylacteries then – i.e. items with inscriptions that were partly votive in nature rather than exclusively amuletic. These may still have been expressions which were thought to convey protective or remedying powers, however, in addition to their general sense of sacredness. There seems little other reason why an object like the Vimose buckle (considered at the outset of chapter 2) would bear such an obviously votive text, especially in light of other rune-inscribed buckles like the more regularly amuletic Pforzen find. It may even be that the early Germanic brooches which appear to feature the names of old Germanic divinities should also be accorded the status of pagan phylacteries. But they seem best classed just as regular amulets given the dozens of more typical talismanic inscriptions of Iron Age and early medieval date found on similar items.

These more overtly religious or cultic inscriptions appear on all manner of items, from rune-stones to jewellery, other forms of personal accoutrement and even simple wooden objects. Often they are found without much discernable context and are creations that have not attracted the kind of comparative study that commoner objects have been subjected to. This is frequently because they represent the only example of a rune-inscribed object of this nature or are otherwise contextually isolated or odd. Yet a broader perspective is sometimes required in order to present these texts and the items which bear them in any sort of meaningful context.

The basic form of an archaic votive inscription is essentially fourfold.[1] A surprisingly large number of archaic religious inscriptions belong to this general type, whether written in early Latin, Greek, Etruscan or one of the other ancient languages of the ancient Mediterranean world. No matter the peculiarities of the language in question, the basic, full style is to mention the dedicator, the deity to whom the object has been offered, a verb indicating the act of offering and a

---

[1] On archaic and classical votives see T. Homolle, 'Donarium', in C. Daremberg and E. Saglio (eds), *Dictionaire des antiquités grecques et romaines*, 5 vols (Paris 1877–1917), II.1, pp. 363–82 and W.H.D. Rouse, *Greek Votive Offerings* (Cambridge 1902).

description of the object the inscription is found upon. One fairly typical example of this full type is the following text found on a bronze ladle (technically called a *simpulum*) presumably once used to pour libations, found at Settequerce, near Bolzano in north-eastern Italy. Unearthed in the late 1880s, it clearly dates to the fifth or fourth century BC, i.e. to the pre-classical or archaic period. Written in North Etruscan letters of the usual Bolzano type, it is Rhaetic (an Alpine form of Etruscan) in language and reads:

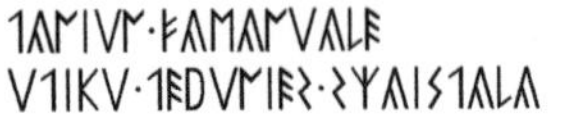

ꓘꓘꓲꓦꓲ·ꓞꓮꓠꓮꓲꓦꓮꓡꓞ
ꓦꓲꓲꓘꓦ·ꓲꓐꓦꓨꓲꓞꓲ·ꓝꓯꓯꓲꓝꓯꓠꓯ

Paniun Vaśanuale upiku Perunies Sχaispala.

'Bronze dedicated to Vesuna by Perunius Scaispa.'[2]

These four basic elements of the votive type may be supplemented in various ways, most commonly by expanding upon one of the four elements, for instance by adding to the verb or perhaps to the name of the divinity. The following much-embellished example is found on a votive pin, an oversized writing stylus, unearthed in the late nineteenth century from the largest-known centre of the Reitia cult, that found in the ruins of the ancient city of Ateste (now Este, near Padua). Inscribed with typical Venetic letterforms, its perhaps fourth-century BC text runs:

� (votive inscription line 1)
ꓮꓔꓝ·ꓲ·ꓲꓐꓡ·ꓲ·ꓫꓲꓲꓯ·ꓲ·ꓲ·◇·ꓲꓝ◇·ꓲ·ꓫꓲꓲ◇ꓲꓔꓡꓦ◇
XXX-XXXXXXXXXXXXXXXXXX
>>>>>>>>>>>>>>

Mego doto Fugsia Votna Sainatei Reitiai op voltio leno. ttt[t]tttttttttttttttttt.
>>>>>>>>>>>>>>

'Fugsia Votna dedicated me to Sainati Reitia, willingly, deservedly. . .'

This type of archaic inscription is known as a 'talking text' as the inscription refers to the object it is found on by means of a first-person pronoun – in this case *mego* 'me'. It is clearly of the basic four-part archaic votive type, but the action of dedication is complemented by an adverbial expression, *op voltio leno,* 'willingly, deservedly.' The goddess is also described by an additional name or epithet: Sainati, a functional title which may mean 'the apportioner of sex'. Moreover, though perhaps unsurprisingly given this is a Reitia dedication, it also features additions typical of the tutelary-goddess sanctuary finds: a letter sequence and a long herring-bone-like votive symbol (one commonly found on Venetic votives). Few archaic votive inscriptions are quite as effusive as this example, however. In fact the general four-part style is often abbreviated, sometimes even just to the name of the dedicator, and most archaic votive inscriptions

---

2 Morandi, *Cippo di Castelciès*, no. 10, reads the inverted *v* of Settequerce's *Vaśanuale* as an *l*, though the same goddess is clearly mentioned (as *Vaśunu*) in the Sanzeno inscription described above in chapter 2; see Mees, 'Gods of the Rhaetii'.

usually only feature a selection of the constituent parts described here, much as do the texts of the runic five-part amulet type.[3]

Early Latin dedications essentially accord to the archaic four-part style, too. But by the Imperial period a standard Roman monumental formula had been established which represents a very different sort of votive text. Instead of including a dedicatory verb linking the offerer to the figure being venerated, they usually only display a supplementary expression, a justification detached from the name of the god and that of the offerer. Roman dedications also typically omit item descriptions which are, in effect, redundant – they are usually supplied merely by looking at the item the inscriptions appear on.

The essential form of any Roman votive inscription is usually quite plain and standardised, then. Especially when found in the Roman provinces, they are almost relentlessly of the same style as the following inscription from Cologne. Dating like most of the ancient altar inscriptions of the Rhineland to the second or third century AD, it is quite typical in terms of its use of the basic Roman votive style:

MATRIB--
MEDIoTAVTEH--
IVL꒒PRIMVS
VETRANVS
LEG꒒I·M
P·F•V·S·LM

Matrib[us] Mediotauteh[is].
Iul(ius) Primus vet(e)ranus leg(ionis) I M(inerviae) p(iae) f(idelis).
V(otum) s(olvit) l(ibens) m(erito).

'To the Mediotautic Mothers.
Julius Primus, veteran of the legion I Minervia (whose motto is) "Dutiful, Loyal".
In fulfilment of a vow; willingly, deservedly.'

This is clearly quite a different form of votive text from the archaic examples considered above. It is not utterly unremarkable as a Roman votive, however. Linguistically, the adjective *Mediotauteh[is]* is Germanic or Germanicised as are many other descriptions of deities mentioned in similar votives stemming from the Roman-occupied parts of ancient Germany. Yet more strikingly and to date uniquely, this Germano-Roman dedication also features some additional symbols. Two of them are triskelia – religious symbols which sometimes appear in association with runic amulet inscriptions. Unlike in runic texts, though, the triskelia are employed here as word-dividers much like ivy-leaf decorations (known in Latin as *hederae*, i.e. 'ivy dividers') are at times in similar inscriptions from all over the Roman world. The triskelia on this Germano-Roman altar seem just to serve as holy decoration – a visual Germanic addition to an otherwise quite

---

3   G.B. Pellegrini and A.L. Prosdocimi, *La lingua venetica* 1 (Padova 1967), no. Es 44. The explanation of Reitia's title *Sainati* as related to Greek *saina* 'pudenda (both male and female)' is due to T.L. Markey.

staid and typical Roman expression. Like the appearance of the adjective *Mediotauteh[is]*, the influence in this text appears to be from Germanic tradition to standard Roman votive practice, then, not the other way around.[4]

Conversely, examples such as the Vimose buckle inscription, much like the Germanic amulet formula, seem to continue the archaic four-part (or rather, its extended six-part northern Italian) votive form. Indeed the Vimose find is a poetic but otherwise fairly regularly archaic type of formulation: 'I dedicate (this) end ring to the As.' On the other hand, it and other examples like the Setre comb inscription are strikingly unlike typical Roman votive texts.

Archaic Italian dedications do evince a tendency to include poetic or stylised language, however, if not outright formal poetry as do many early Greek and runic magico-religious texts. One example is the *donum dedit* 'gift given' etymological figure even known from some Latin votive inscriptions. Other characteristic stylistic aspects, including the feature of 'talking' (which is often dismissed as somehow just a primitive characteristic in both traditions) are also common to both archaic Italian and early runic (but not imperial Roman) inscriptions.[5]

In fact we even have one clear instance of an early pagan priest writing in runes using the common runic 'talking' style. An early rune-stone from Nordhuglo, Norway, bears the following short, seemingly fragmentary message in 8 to 10cm-tall runic characters:

ᛗᚲᚷᚨᛗᛁᛜᚠᚨᛏᚷᚠᛖᛗᛁᚤᛁᚺ. . .

Ek gudija Ungandiz ih. . .

'I, Ungand the priest *ih. . .*'

The Nordhuglo stone was found on the island of Huglo in 1905 being used as part of a bridge and it is unclear, unfortunately, what the stone was used for at the time the priest Ungand left his name in runes here. The forms *gudija* and *Un-gandiz* assonate and alliterate; yet though it literally means 'un-magical', the same name, in the later Latinised form Ongendus, is also recorded for a Danish king from about the year 700, so it would be misleading to read too much into his name. The final sequence *ih* is often thought to be some sort of abbreviation, perhaps of a geographical indication 'in Huglo', but there are no clear parallels that might confirm this particular interpretation. Equally, the final *ih. . .* may simply now be incomplete, however – a sizeable chip appears in the stone immediately after the mysterious sequence. Pagan priests are also mentioned in some funerary rune-stone dedications that can clearly be ascribed to the Viking Age, and the Nordhuglo stone may well once have been a memorial of this kind. The Nordhuglo find, though, can only roughly be dated to the early runic period, i.e. sometime before the sixth century.[6]

---

4   The Cologne inscription is *CIL* XIII, no. 8222 and is pictured in B. and H. Galsterer, *Die römischen Steininschriften aus Köln* (Cologne 1975), table 23. See also Mees, 'Early Rhineland Germanic' for an explanation of *Mediotautehis*.

5   L. Agostiniani, *Le "iscrizioni parlanti" dell'Italia antica* (Florence 1982); W. Euler, *Dōnum dō-* (Innsbruck 1982).

6   Krause with Jankuhn, no. 65.

There are many hundreds of texts known from Roman Germany that feature the names or epithets of goddesses which are clearly Germanic or Germanicised, many of which are reflected in inscriptions as old as the earliest runic texts. Scores of Germano-Roman divinities are represented in thousands of votive altar texts, ranging from uniquely evidenced figures named on formerly freestanding stones to the ruins of temples literally packed with engraved altars all dedicated to the same Germano-Roman cult. But little of what we know about early Germanic religion from Roman sources has proved obviously of much use in explaining rune-inscribed votive and cultic objects. In fact only one passage recounted by a Roman writer seems to have any hint of runic tradition, one where a divination by a tribal priest is described. Tacitus, the Roman concerned, only actually uses the term *nota*, i.e. 'sign, indication, mark', however; and although there are good grounds upon which we might connect this term with the use of writing in divination (e.g. the employment of the same term for what were clearly letters of the alphabet in divinations recounted by Virgil and Cicero – Tacitus' main literary models), it is not clear that this interpretation of his passage from AD 98 is absolutely reliable, or whether it has any relationship with runic practice attested in inscriptions from later times.[7]

The rune-inscribed items which have come down to us appear unexpectedly un-Roman then. But this does not seem merely to be a reflection of the fact that we have no clear examples of more portable items inscribed with Roman-letter religious inscriptions that are clearly to be connected with Germanic speakers either. In fact dedicatory inscriptions on loose items are generally rare in Roman contexts – religious epigraphy of Imperial date is substantially restricted to monumental epigraphs like altar-stones. Those which do appear on such items often seem only to parrot the better-known monumental tradition at any rate, often featuring stock formulas of the *libens merito* type. Instead, for many religious and cultic runic inscriptions, the clearest connections again seem to be with similar expressions that come from the area in which the North Etruscan inscriptions are found, a region and tradition where the archaic style of votive inscription remained in use often until the early years AD. Germanic religious and cultic life seems to have more in common with archaic European practice, then, than it does with that of the more refined and idiosyncratically formularised pieties of Roman (and Germano-Roman) experience.[8]

In fact one of the late North Etruscan texts is even clearly connected with an early Germanic priest, seemingly an early predecessor of Ungand. Although it is not written in runes, the inscription is composed in one of the archaic alphabets that have so much in common with the runic letters they may well represent the source from which the runes originated. The inscription is obviously very rune-like, it dates to the middle of the last century BC and was inscribed with letterforms typical of inscriptions found in the environs of Bolzano.

---

7 Tacitus, *Germania* 10; cf. B. Mees, 'Runes in the first century', forthcoming.
8 One striking, though still markedly un-rune-like, exception is an engraved silver ring from Xanten (*CIL* XIII, no. 10024.34) which bears a full military naming expression and an abbreviated variation on the *donum dedit* formula: 'The double and time-and-a-half cohort veteran Flavius Simplex, formerly a double-pay veteran of the same cohort, gave as a gift.'

In 1811 a collection of ancient helmets was unearthed in the remains of what at first seemed to have been a merchant's depot on the border of the ancient Roman provinces of Noricum and Pannonia Superior. At least two clearly bore inscriptions on their brims, and although discovered in what is now Slovenia, the helmets appear first to have been inscribed further to the west, and are proudly displayed today in the Fine Arts Museum of Vienna.

The inscription on the helmet dubbed Negau B was subsequently to become famous as the oldest native testament of a Germanic language, and many scores of interpretations have since been promoted as the correct reading of the inscription. The find site is actually known as Ž-enjak – Negau was the name of the local lordship in imperial Austrian times. Much of what has been written on the Negau B helmet until recently, though, has paid little or no attention to the fact that one of the accompanying helmets was also inscribed, and the inscriptions on the Negau A helmet clearly indicate how the text on Negau B is to be interpreted.[9]

A recent survey photo taken of the Ž-enjak site has shown that the helmets were deposited at the edge of a large Celtic archaeological complex, probably an ancient ritual site. The helmets seem to have been deposited purposefully – in fact in a ritual manner well known throughout the Celtic world. But how did a Germanic legend come to appear in a predominantly Celtic context?

The earliest that Germanic-speaking peoples are known to have been in this area is the late second century BC when the invading Cimbri and Teutones advanced into what is now Austria from the east. These tribes seem originally to have been of Jutlandic origin, and it has long been surmised that the Danish place-names Himmerland and Thyth record their former homelands. The fear that these foreign warriors inspired was subsequently to be termed the *furor Teutonicus*; thus the English word *Teutonic*. Yet it is clear there were other Germanic visitors to the East Alpine region in the last centuries BC. Besides the evidence of the Negau B inscription, a belt-buckle of Germanic make has been found in Sanzeno, northeast Italy, and an early Germanic brooch has been discovered on the Austrian Magdalensberg (Mt Magdalen). Both items are of such poor workmanship it seems unlikely that they were brought this far south as a result of trade – instead it appears that the eastern Alps were frequented by early Germanic folk in the last centuries BC.

Yet it was not until the middle of the first century BC that the term *German* first appears in a Latin account, and it was probably about this time that the Negau B helmet was inscribed by a Rhaetic-speaker for a man with a Germanic name, possibly one living among Rhaetii and Celts. The inscriptions on helmet A are of a similar nature to that on Negau B and represent a linguistic mixture of both Rhaetic and Celtic. The Negau B inscription clearly reads:

ᚾADIYA⟨ᛏIᛏᚠIFA\\\I⊦

Harigasti teiwa \\\il

'Harigast the divine . . .'

---

9   The Negau inscriptions are comprehensively surveyed in Markey, 'A tale of two helmets'.

The region about Bolzano features several of the centres of Reitia devotion that evidence the general six-part formulism apparently continued in the five-part Germanic tradition of amulet inscriptions. It should come as no surprise, then, to discover that the name Harigast, literally 'Army-guest' has often been interpreted as that of a god in the past. But a similar inscription appears on Negau A that suggests Harigast was a mortal. In fact a later form of this name, Hergest, is known from medieval German sources where it clearly belonged to an ordinary man.

The other inscribed helmet bears four separate texts showing at least two separate hands which read:

ᛜV᛾ᛘᛁᛈᚨᛘVᚨᛈᛁ ᛋIDAKV:ᛏVD1ᛁᛁADᛘᛖᛁᛣᚠᛁ
ᛉᚦDV1

Dubni banuobi.
Sīragu turbi.
Iarśe eiswi.
Cerub(ogios).

'Of Dubnos the pig-slayer (i.e. sacrificer?).
Astral priest of the troop.
Iarsus the divine.
Cerubogios.'

The first two naming expressions and the last are purely Celtic, while the third appears to be the Rhaeticised form (much as *Harigasti* is) of a Celtic man's name followed by a purely Rhaetic title. This (third) text seems to be almost precisely the same as the Negau B inscription, then, though with a Rhaetic word for 'divine' appearing where the Rhaeticised Germanic form *teiwa* does on Negau B. The description *teiwa* 'divine' thus seems to have been an early way to signify a priest.

It is clear from Danish bog finds that wooden copies of helmets of the Negau type were still being made for Germanic warriors in the last few centuries BC. But it was an altogether different situation in the Mediterranean area. There, such helmets had long since stopped being made for military use; instead depictions from Northern Italy and the Alpine regions suggest that helmets of the Negau type were only used by priests at the time of the deposition of the Slovenian finds. We even have an example of a Negau-style helmet unearthed from a site near Ravenna with only the letters *aev*, the first three letters of the Rhaetic alphabet, inscribed on its rim. The Negau helmets were clearly left behind as part of a religious ceremony, and although the texts seem at first only to represent the names of the various owners of the helmets over time, the *aev* inscription as well as the letter sequence-like markings following *teiwa* on the Negau B find suggest that these texts had some other religious purpose too: that is, adding writing to them in a manner reminiscent of runic amulet texts was thought to make them (or indicate clearly that they were) holy items.

An archaic Italian and decidedly non-Roman connection also seems to explain some of the earliest runic finds on what appear to have been pagan ritual items. In the late 1970s, for instance, archaeologists began to unearth a horde of military accoutrements from what was formerly a lake in the Illerup river-valley,

Denmark. Finds of masses of Iron Age spears, shields and similar items are well known from Jutland – they probably represent sacrifices of war-booty – and similar finds had often produced examples of rune-inscribed weapons before. Classical sources record war-booty being deposited in rivers and such as sacrifices to war-gods by Germanic war-leaders. So evidently the Danish bog finds represent the fulfilment of vows to offer booty to the war-gods after the winning of battles. But the Illerup finds were to prove to be the most spectacular of all such discoveries. The number of rune-inscribed items unearthed by Danish archaeologists soon easily surpassed those discovered in comparable hoards, and a great number of bejewelled bandoliers, brooches and similar items were also found at the site. All manner of inscriptions were found there, on metal shield-fittings, spearheads and other military gear. But the oddest of all was surely the discovery of a wooden rune-inscribed handle of a fire iron. Over a hundred fire irons were discovered at Illerup among over a thousand weapons, hundreds of shield bosses and grips as well as other military items. Yet no rune-inscribed fire irons are known from other sites. The Illerup fire iron seemed to be an inexplicable runic oddity, a unique item without any comparable context or explanation.

One example of a linguistically Latin fire-iron inscription is known from Merovingian Germany, but it is just a boastful maker's mark: '(Though) from iron, I shine (like) a work of silver.' Yet inscribed fire irons are well known in archaic Italian archaeology, especially in Etruscan and Rhaetic (i.e. North Etruscan) contexts. Fire irons were used in religious rituals to carry incense and prepare burnt offerings, so it should not come as a surprise to find religious dedications on some of them. A clear Etruscan example is a richly decorated bronze ember-scoop that dates from the late sixth or fifth century BC. It records on its handle, in typical Etruscan manner, 'I (am) Silvanus's', Silvanus being a well-known Italian deity. Another such example is the so-called 'Verona sword', a damaged ember-scoop from the fifth century BC with a Rhaetic dedicatory inscription of the six-part type on its haft.

A similar inscription is also found on another type of ritual fire iron from Ca' de Cavri, Italy, the so-called 'Padua shovel', a small fourth- or third-century BC ritual shovel or scoop. It also bears a Rhaetic inscription of the usual archaic type (very similar to that on the Settequerce ladle, but also including two votive symbols: Ⅴ and ✻) on one side of its blade, and it seems to be dedicated to Vesta, the Italian goddess of the hearth. In fact many of the Reitia *ex voto* finds – especially those of stag horn – are so-called holocaustic votives, i.e. they were burnt as part of their offering to the goddess of the word.

The inscription on the Illerup fire-iron handle was first noticed in 1992 and archaeologists have dated the find to about the year 200. The inscription is clearly legible and reads:

 XↃↃↃ

Gaunþz.

'Gift.'

This sequence has been interpreted as a man's name *Gauþ*, 'Barker' or 'Mocker' (i.e. an imitative expression similar to the Mos spearhead's *Gaois* 'Howler'), a supposition clearly based on the notion that this should be a maker's or owner's inscription. There are grammatical problems with such an interpretation, however, and given the type of item it appears on, the legend is more sensibly explained as a short, linguistically regular votive expression deriving from a verb *gaunnan* which in later contexts (e.g. Modern German *gönnen*) means 'to grant' or 'allow' and is related to a Gothic word for 'favour' or 'grace'. So although the inscription is extremely short, both etymology and context suggest it should be considered a dedicated item, similar to archaic Italian votive fire-iron finds. In fact *gaunþz* is virtually a homonym of *alu* or one of the other dedicatory charm words, all of which seem to be old votive verbal nouns. The inscription is probably confirmation that the Illerup fire iron was considered to be holy, the property of the gods, though determining whether it was used for purification, making burnt sacrifice or another religious use of fire probably awaits further archaeological analysis.[10]

A further rune-inscribed find often not recognised as religious in nature first came to light in 1865 when an ancient warrior's grave was discovered at Frøyhov, Norway. Apart from the usual remains of swords, spears and shields, the grave, which dates to about the year 160, also contained a 7.5cm-high bronze figurine in the shape of a man. It has since been interpreted as a decoration from a destroyed bandolier, but the style of the figurine is of a votive type well known in archaic Italian contexts. The arms of the figurine are outstretched and the only forearm that remains today is raised. This type of representation is known as *orans*, Latin for 'one who prays', in Mediterranean archaeology, and represents someone praying with arms outstretched – the usual manner of praying in pre-Christian times – and inscriptions are always dedications when they are found on Mediterranean *orans* figurines.

Some of the letters on the Frøyhov figurine are somewhat oddly shaped, however, and seem almost to be closer to North Etruscan characters than runes. They are written on the lower abdomen of the figurine and can clearly be made out, though their interpretation remains contested:

ᛟᚠᛜᛁ

?ada.

The first rune is odd in shape, but if taken as an *ŋ*, the inscription seems to be unpronounceable and little more is gained from reading it in reverse. But if the first character is interpreted as an archaic *w* or even a *g*, the presumably mid-second-century text can be read either as *Wanda* 'Slav, Wend', *gada* 'companion'

---

[10] M. Stoklund, 'Neue Runeninschriften um etwa 200 n. Chr. aus Dänemark', in E. Marold and C. Zimmermann (eds), *Nordwestgermanisch* (Berlin 1995), pp. 209–10 (with an onomatopoetic interpretation), but see MacLeod and Mees, 'Triple binds', n. 14, for the formal linguistic reasoning behind the interpretation given here. The Merovingian-era fire iron is G. Waurick (ed.), *Gallien in der Spätantike* (Mainz 1980), no. 341, the Etruscan example is S. Haynes, *Etruscan Bronzes* (New York 1985), no. 104 and its inscription is translated in A. Morandi, *Nuovi lineamenti di lingua etrusca* (Rome 1991), pp. 149–50, while the Verona and Padua finds are Morandi, *Cippo di Castelciès*, nos 51–52, and see Mees, 'Gods of the Rhaetii' for translations.

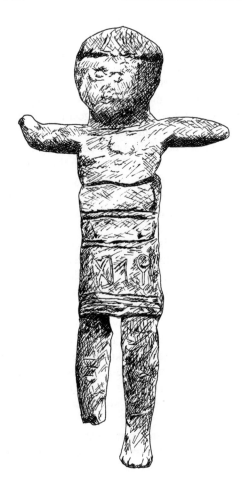

Fig. 12. Frøyhov figurine

or perhaps even *ganda* 'magical'. The ending *-ada* strongly suggests we are dealing with a name, though whether this is that of the dedicator or the deity to be honoured is not completely clear. The name of a divine recipient would be expected to appear in an oblique (i.e. 'to, of, for') or addressing (vocative) form, however, so interpreting this as an owner's name seems more probable here. In fact it is often only the offerer's name that appears in similarly laconic dedications in Mediterranean votive settings; the dedicatory nature of an elliptical text is often indicated only by the type of item it appears on.[11]

Reminiscent of the Frøyhov find and similarly controversial is a rune-inscribed bronze figure that was discovered in 1907 near Køng, Denmark.

---

11 Krause with Jankuhn, no. 44; Markey, 'Tale of two helmets', p. 96. Several *ex voto* of the *orans* type are pictured in L. Zemmer-Plank (ed.), *Culti nella preistoria delle Alpi* (Bolzano 1999), including ones wearing helmets of the Negau type. The reading of the first rune here possibly as a *g* relies on the notion that the *ŋ*-rune was originally employed to distinguish plosive [g] from the usual realisation of structural Germanic /g/ as a fricative [ɣ] and the likely origin of the *ŋ*-rune in an archaic qoppa; see Mees, 'North Etruscan thesis', p. 62.

Nine-and-a-half centimetres tall and a stray or isolated discovery probably dating to the fifth or sixth centuries, the figurine's arms are stretched out downward this time as is more typical, for example, of archaic Italian representations of divinities. Its inscription is quite damaged, however, and only the following can be made out today:

-- ᚠᛉ

..ngo.

Appearing on the back of the figurine, this is almost certainly a short name, perhaps *Thingo*, *Lango* or the like, presumably, again, that of the owner or dedicator of the figurine. It also appears to be a religious find, then, though without any more context we cannot really be sure.[12]

Another runic find, one almost universally declared as votive, but with no immediately obvious classical parallel, was found on a large ring discovered in the nineteenth century as part of an ancient treasure hoard. There is talk of sacred oath-rings in Old Norse literature, as well as temple-rings upon which the blood of animal sacrifices was showered, and collections of neck-rings have been discovered in Scandinavian bog and river deposits. But the golden ring from Pietroassa, Romania, seems to be the only possible runic testimony of such a holy ring.

The ring clearly dates from the late fourth century and is of East Germanic manufacture. It was originally discovered along with three other large golden rings, but it was damaged shortly after being displayed at the Exhibition universale in Paris in 1872 upon its return to Romania. It was cut in two after being stolen by a thief and part of the text was damaged by the thief's knife, which has led to some controversy as to part of the inscription's correct reading. Yet a photograph of the inscription was taken in 1872 and published by London's Arundel Society in one of their renowned folio art editions. The photo shows that the inscription clearly reads:

ᚷᚢᛏᚨᚾᛁᛉ ᛈᛁ ᚺᚨᛁᛚᚨᚷ

Gutanio wīh hailag.

'Gutanio, sacred, holy.'

The Pietroassa inscription does not seem to fit any recognised votive formula precisely, but rather is expressed in a terse manner reminiscent of early runic amulet texts. The term *Gutanio*, evidently a name, literally means 'Gothic female' and grammatically could be either a singular or a genitive plural. It is reminiscent in form of some of the epithets of the Rhenish mother goddesses – the Cologne inscription, for example, is clearly dedicated to the mother goddesses of the Mediotautic tribe, and similar inscriptions to goddesses described as 'Swabian mothers' and even 'Germanic mothers' are known from the Roman Rhineland. Another rune-inscribed neck-ring of a similar date, a diadem-like

---

[12] Krause with Jankuhn, no. 45.

piece of jewellery found in a grave at Strårup, Denmark, bears only a name, and Gutanio looks just to be an agentive form, similar to Gaios 'Howler' and the other (misleadingly suggestive) forms that appear on early Germanic spears and the like. The four Romanian rings were discovered along with a decorated dish of provincial Roman make that seems to include a representation of three Germano-Roman mother goddesses on it and Jordanes records that the Goths were descended from Gapt, who may literally have been 'the (great) Goth'. In fact there are sculptured reliefs of the mother goddesses (who are usually depicted in threes) where they are sometimes shown as wearing neck-rings or torques. But it is not only deities in Romanised contexts that are represented wearing neck-rings: one of the early Germanic wooden idols, a masculine figure from Rude Eskilstrup, Denmark, also wears a carved torque around its neck; and in fact many smaller early Germanic wooden statues are represented wearing necklaces.

The form Gutanio is followed by the two old Germanic terms for 'holy', though, and some have seen the influence of a Christian expression like *sacrosanct* (i.e. sacred + sanctified) at play here. Yet most of the Germanic languages tend to use one or the other of these two terms to mean 'holy' in the Christian sense and the other only in a marginal way. In the Gothic Bible it is the *wīh* word that is used to indicate the Christian notion of 'holy', whereas in English it is obviously the *holy* (from earlier *hailag*) form that has prevailed – in Old English the *wīh* form meant 'idol' and it appears regularly in early, apparently cultic Anglo-Saxon place-names like Willey or Wye (and cf. Danish Vimose the 'holy moor'). The Pietroassa inscription may indicate that something associated with Gutanio was holy in one sense, then, and that something else was holy in another – the distinction may well originally have been that *wīh* was originally the type of holiness connected with gods and goddesses (and hence holy sites) and *hailag* that of sacred or consecrated (i.e. essentially human-fashioned or used) objects in Gothic. Unlike Gutanio, the 'holy' words are clearly both grammatically neuter singulars, however, and the usual Germanic word for 'ring' is masculine. 'Necklace' is a neuter in Latin and Greek, though, so the inscription may have been intended to read: '(necklace) of the Gutanio (i.e. the Gothic mother-goddesses?) sacred (and) holy'. The two terms may have functioned much like regular amulet charm words, but it is hard to be rid of the impression that the ring inscription was votive in nature. It might have been a holy item upon which oaths were sworn or the blood of sacrifices was sprinkled, although it is also just as possible that it was, rather, once worn as an amulet, perhaps even as a pagan phylactery belonging to a Gothic priestess (who had the title or name Gutanio?), if not, as some of the early wooden idols from the North suggest, worn by a statue once kept in a place holy to the mother goddesses of the Goths.[13]

There is at least one rune-inscribed ritual find, however, that bears an inscription that much like the Vimose buckle's text appears to be more clearly of the regular archaic Italian votive type. One of the most impressive of all the runic

13 Krause with Jankuhn, no. 41 and cf. no. 42; see also B. Mees, 'Runo-Gothica', *Die Sprache* 43 (2002–3), 70–73 and T. Capelle, 'Ringopfer', in H. Jankuhn (ed.), *Vorgeschichtliche Heiligtümer und Opferplätze im Mittel- und Nordeuropas* (Göttingen 1970), pp. 214–18 on (uninscribed) votive ring finds.

discoveries from the Old Germanic North was surely that which appeared on the second of the golden horns that were found near Gallehus, Denmark. The two early-fifth-century horns were discovered in the seventeenth and eighteenth centuries respectively, and as the finest examples of ancient Germanic gold-work known to date, were held as two of the greatest treasures of the royal collection in Copenhagen. They were too tempting for thieves, however, and both were stolen one night in 1802 never to be seen again. Poems were written bemoaning the thefts and they remain dear to Danish hearts and minds. Eventually replicas were made based on the illustrations of Danish antiquarians. The unscrupulous destroyer of two of Denmark's greatest national treasures, however, also robbed the world of the most impressive of all expressions of pagan Germanic votary practice.

The horns themselves were clearly of ritual function – they are covered with representations of warriors, knights, a horn-carrying old man (perhaps a priest), men with animal horns on their heads, serpents, rosettes, stars, horses, dogs, fish, goats, and even apparently monstrous beings: animal-headed men, centaurs, a two-headed ('pushmi-pullyu') horse, a three-headed axe-wielding humanoid figure and a head imposed over an animal skin. Some of the figures appear to be dancing, though it is difficult to judge the function or importance of the Gallehus decoration. Two-headed (or 'Siamese') horses appear among East Alpine votive statuettes where they are clearly figuratively associated with Reitia, and some of the other Gallehus representations may have later Northern and Celtic parallels. Frieze-like decorations of this type seem to have had a story-telling aspect to them – they 'narrated' in a manner reminiscent of modern-day cartoons. But much of what has been written on the horns in the past has been speculative, if not outright fantastic. It is not at all clear what their decoration represents except that it has strong parallels with some earlier, though less fabulous, friezes of Germanic make that also show animals, stars and humanoid figures in what may have been narrative scenes.[14]

The inscription on the 75cm-long second horn (or horn B) has been well studied in the past and it might seem there is little controversy over the linguistic analysis of the text. In fact it is frequently quoted in Germanistic literature not merely for the impressive physical properties it once enjoyed, but also for its literary style – its text clearly alliterates and constitutes a full poetic line. What has escaped most observers, however, is the votive nature of the inscription. From the eighteenth-century reproductions of the horns, the lost inscription evidently once read:

---

[14] Foreign influence in early Germanic styles is usually ascribed principally to the Celts either directly (via, e.g., the Thraco-Celtic Gundestrup cauldron) or by a nebulous 'Einstimmung oder einer inneren Aufnahmebereitschaft' to quote H.J. Eggers et al., *Kelten und Germanen in heidnischer Zeit* (Baden Baden 1964), p. 157. More recent contributions, e.g. M. Todd, *The Early Germans* (London 1992), pp. 126ff., though, stress the influence of Roman and Imperial provincial styles. The early Germanic friezes and frieze-like works, after all, have close thematic and stylistic parallels in Italian zoomorphism – they are not at all Celtic in their 'narrative' arrangement. See also Zemmer-Plank (ed.), no. 131 (pl. xxii) = Morandi, *Cippo di Castelciès*, no. 19 for the inscribed 'Siamese horse' votive.

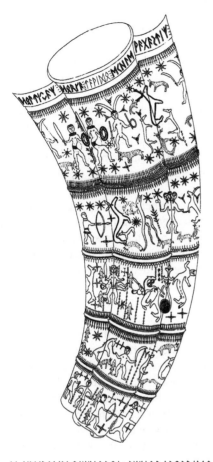

Fig. 13. Gallehus horn

ᛗᚲᚺᚾᛗᛈᚠᚷᛉᛏᛁᛃᚺᛟᛁᛏᛁᚾᛖᚱᛃᚺᛟᚱᚻᚠᛏᚠᛈᛁᚾᛟ

Ek Hlewagastiz holtijaz horna tawido.

'I, Hlewagast, from the holt, dedicated the horn.'

Along with its alliteration (*Hlewagastiz holtijaz horna*) the choice of words here indicates this is a carefully composed text. It is strange, then, that it has usually been interpreted merely as a prosaic maker's inscription. The verb *tawido* is typically translated as 'made'. Yet this interpretation is based on the meaning that the equivalent form of this word has in Old English, Old Saxon and Gothic. Its closest Scandinavian relatives mean 'grant, bestow, assist, help' and its original meaning was 'reward, offer, dedicate'. As the verb *do* eventually lost its original meaning 'to make', each of the Germanic dialects developed a new way of signifying 'making': Gothic used *taujan*, German and English now have *machen* and *make*, and the word 'to make' in Scandinavian contexts is *garwjan* (Danish *gera*, Swedish *göra*), a common verb in runic inscriptions from Viking times. The Scandinavian 'make' word *garwjan* seems originally to have meant 'to make food, to cook' but lost its specific connection to food preparation over time; evidently a similar generalising also occurred in some other Germanic dialects for *taujan* 'reward, offer, dedicate'. In fact a rune-inscribed spear from Illerup uses *tawide* in what is usually thought to be a maker's signature, though it could easily have meant 'dedicated' or 'rewarded' – swords, after all, were often presented as rewards by Germanic chieftains to favoured retainers. Given that other forms of the verb *tawido* are found on Scandinavian bracteates where they do not seem to mean 'make' or 'made' (cf. *tuwa*, *tawo* etc.), a better translation of the Gallehus verb *tawido* would surely be 'offered, dedicated'. Although it is possible that *tawido* may have developed the general 'make' sense attested in Old English, Old Saxon and Gothic in Hlewagast's dialect, a dedicatory meaning of the verb here is required by the obviously religious nature of the decoration of the lost golden horns. After all, objects associated with libations (like the Settequerce ladle) in archaic Italian practice commonly bear texts of a similar form.[15]

The religious function of horns in Germanic tradition appears to be essentially separate from that of the classical cornucopia or horn of plenty, the Graeco-Roman symbol of abundance, though. Early Northern European graves often feature items connected with the preparation and consumption of liquor, and drinking evidently had a ritual function in the pagan Germanic tradition. Literary sources like *Beowulf*, for example, describe the offering of mead to warriors at kings' halls in what appears to have been a ritual manner – and there are two early medieval Christian mentions of consecrated drinks or drinking vessels in early saint's lives, where the saints concerned destroy the apparently devilish brews. In Jonas of Bobbio's *Life of St Columban the Abbot*, the Irish missionary encounters German pagans with a vat or a tun whose contents they intended to offer to Wodan. Similarly, in the same author's *Life of St Vedast the Bishop*, the French saint (who is sometimes also called Foster or Waast) causes a drink presented at a royal feast that had been 'consecrated in the heathen manner' to spill by making a sign of the cross over it. Rather than just a Christian hagiographical cliché, then, the Gallehus inscription appears to support the testimony of these two tales told of Merovingian-era saints.[16]

Moreover, the ritual associations of horns in early Germanic tradition are also indicated in another runic inscription, but this time only pictorially. An inscription on a 1.25m-high rune-stone from Snoldelev, Denmark, seems to be a memorial text:

ᚴᚢᚾ·ᚢᛡᚨᛚᛋᛏᛡᛁᚾ·ᛋᚢᚾᚨᛦ
ᚱᚢᚺᛡᛚᛏᛋ·ᚦᚢᛚᚨᛦ·ᛜᛋᚨᛚᚺᚨᚢᚴᚢ
卐 ᘓ

Gunwal(d)s stain, sunaz Ruhalts, þulaz ą Salhaugu(m) 卐 ᘓ.

15 Grønvik, 'Runeinnskriften på gullhornet', reaches similar conclusions independently to Markey, 'Dedicatory formula', about the votive nature of the Gallehus inscription and the runic verb *taujan*, which is distantly related to *donate* and *dedicate*. We prefer to translate the ambiguous *holtijaz* as 'from (the) holt' rather than '(son) of Holt' on the model of the Nydam axe-haft's *sīkijaz* 'from the sike' as such early runic forms seem more commonly to be ablative constructions rather than patronymics, and it is not clear that Holt is an anthroponym at any rate; see Mees, 'Runic **erilaʀ**', p. 52.

16 M.J. Enright, *Lady with a Mead Cup* (Dublin 1996), pp. 86–87.

'Gunwald's stone, Ruhalt's son, sage on the Sal-mounds.'

Below the eighth-century text, however, there are two amuletic symbols, a swastika and a strange form of triskelion consisting of three interlocked drinking horns. Horns were so strongly associated with ritual in Scandinavia it seems that they could even have a role in amuletic symbolism.[17]

A further runic find clearly to be associated with drink appears on a silver straining-spoon that was found in the nineteenth century at Oberflacht, Baden-Württemberg. We do not know what context the Oberflacht strainer was discovered in, but silver straining-spoons are typically found in women's graves from both Germany and Anglo-Saxon England. It has variously been declared a Christian ritual object or compared with finds of silver spoons which bear Latin amuletic inscriptions in Roman letters like 'Posenna (long) may you live!', the names of saints, crosses or Christograms. The Oberflacht strainer has been dated to the last third of the sixth century, the runes are carved on the back of the item and seem to read:

ᚷᛒᛁ:ᛗᚢᛚᚦᚨᚠᛞ

G(i)ba dulþ afd.

'Gift (?), feast, after/behind (?)'

The term *dulþ* 'feast', the only one that can clearly be read here, has been interpreted as referring to a Christian festival. But the item is so early and the find context so obscure that it is not at all clear what the words were supposed to indicate. The object looks like it may be an amulet, as silver spoons are found commonly enough in the graves of Merovingian noblewomen (and we still speak of silver spoons in a similarly privileged context today). Moreover silver straining-spoons are often found in combination with other high-value items such as crystal baubles in early Anglo-Saxon women's graves. Silver utensils of this sort were clearly symbols of the role played by early Germanic noblewomen as mistresses of leading houses (another find of this type is symbolic keys), so it may be that culinary (and hence prestigious) associations are reflected in the word *dulþ* 'feast' here. Yet strainers are particularly concerned with the preparation of liquor as early mead and wine were often rather coarse and required much straining as well as decanting before they were drunk. The Oberflacht inscription features terms that are otherwise unparalleled in a Merovingian runic context and its expression is rather laconic, but there is an example of an inscribed sieve written in North Etruscan characters where its cultic associations are more immediately evident. A find dating to around the birth of Christ from Cles, near Bolzano, is a strainer that bears a clearly cultic legend. The appearance of what seems to be an abbreviated form of the verb 'to give' (or perhaps a verbal noun 'gift'), points to a similarly dedicatory reasoning behind the Oberflacht

---

17 Moltke, *Runes and their Origin*, pp. 158 and 183. Another inscribed horn which may have been intended as a votive was found during the Illerup excavations; see Stoklund, 'Neue Runeninschriften', pp. 210–11. Its inscription is so poorly preserved, however, it is hard to tell what it may have originally signified.

inscription: it appears to be a pagan votive text linked to the cultic aspects of Germanic drinking. How it was used, its precise meaning, and especially what the elliptical sequence *afd* indicated, though, remain unclear.[18]

The use of the verb *tawido* at Gallehus suggests that another rune-inscribed item, which though often considered to be mundane, may also represent a pre-Christian cultic item. It is a rather plain yew-wood casket that was found at Garbølle moor, Denmark, and it is a stray find. Similar in form to an old pencil box, the 17cm-long casket was found without any context; even its contents are long lost. Its runic inscription is clear, though, and reads:

ᚺᚨᚷᛁᚱᚨᛗᚨᛉ᛬ᛏᚨᚹᛁᛞᛁ᛬

Hagiradaz tawide.

'Hagirad dedicated.'

This is obviously an early inscription, perhaps from the third or fourth centuries, but it is not entirely unique. There are several, often decorated boxes or caskets inscribed with Anglo-Saxon runes of Christian date, for instance, that appear to have served as reliquaries – repositories for holy items. For example the runic text on the Anglo-Saxon Mortain casket reads *God helpe Æada þisne cismēl gewarhtæ*, 'God help Æada (who) wrought this chest-counsel (i.e. inscription).' A medieval Danish rune-inscribed box, mentioned in the chapter on amatory finds, even bears what appears to be a Latin love charm. So though *tawide* is often translated as 'made' or 'prepared' here, the Garbølle box seems to have been another religious find – perhaps a pagan reliquary of some sort – though what the box once held remains a mystery.[19]

A similar admixture of Christianity and paganism may have been at work in the two cases of runic inscriptions found on parts of models of swords, both stemming from the remains of mound dwellings in Dutch Frisia. The first is miniature in size, it is made of yew-wood and was found at Arum; dating to the late eighth century, the blade of the wooden sword features some ornamentation and the following runic message:

ᛖᛞᚨᛒᚨᛞᚨ

Edæboda.

The inscription appears at first to be no more than a name. *Edæboda* seems to

---

[18] The Oberflacht inscription is compared with silver spoons by K. Düwel, 'Runische und lateinische Epigraphik im süddeutschen Raum zur Merowingerzeit', in idem (ed.), *Runische Schriftkultur in kontinental-skandinavischer und -angelsächsischer Wechselbeziehung* (Berlin 1988), pp. 239–45, though see Meaney, pp. 82ff. for their fuller context. Cf. A. Mancini, 'Iscrizioni retiche', *Studi etruschi* 43 (1975), 249–306, no. 75, for the inscribed Roman-type sieve from Cles. Its inscription, which is paralleled by one on a statuette of Mars from Sanzeno, seems to mean 'bronze offering' or the like; see Mees, 'Gods of the Rhaetii'.

[19] Krause with Jankuhn, no. 30. The Mortain casket's description *cismēl* is analysed here as (Anglian) *cis(t)-mēl*, a compound comparable to Old Norse *málfár* 'counsel-adorned', with the final term a dialectal form of Old English *mæl* 'council, meeting, speech etc.'; cf. Page, *Introduction*, pp. 162–63.

mean 'oath-messenger', however, a description that appears remarkable in light of what ceremonial swords were often used for. Ceremonial swords, often over-sized (though usually made of steel rather than wood), were used to represent men of high office, kings, mayors and such, in public processions in medieval times. Swords were also generally considered in Christian contexts to be symbols of virtue, justice and light. It has been suggested, consequently, that much like modern Bibles, the Arum sword may have represented an item upon which people swore oaths. It seems possible, then, that the inscription is a description of the sword, not the name of its owner.[20]

A second example of a rune-inscribed, albeit full-sized, model of a sword came to light at Rasquert in 1955. This time, though, all that remains of the item is a whalebone handle. Of late-eighth-century date, its runes are rather difficult to make out as the whalebone surface has weathered badly, but seem to read:

ᛗᚲᚾᛗᚠᛨᛁᛏᚠᚲᚠ

Ek Unmædi toka.

All that remains beyond dispute with this inscription is that it begins with a naming sequence of the first-person 'talking' type well known among runic amulet texts. The following sequence should be a name, then, and perhaps ends with a verb meaning 'made' or the like. The sequence *toka* is reminiscent of *tuwa* and *taujan*, and though similar to *took*, this word is usually thought to be a late loanword to Frisian from Norse. At the very least, this seems, then, to be a naming expression 'I Unmædi . . .', which presumably indicates a similar interpretation is to be preferred for the legend on the Arum sword. The name *Unmædi* has been translated as 'not-mad' which is as suggestive as 'oath-messenger'. But little has been won in the past by focusing on the literal meanings of names which appear in runic inscriptions. Both of the sword texts mention males and look to be little more than minimal legends of the votive or five-part amuletic type. Small weapon-shaped objects are sometimes found in German and Anglo-Saxon women's graves of early medieval date, and similar miniature finds (including shields) from Viking Age Scandinavia are also often found in women's graves and so have also been explained as protective amulets given by warriors to their wives. Unlike the German, Anglo-Saxon and Scandinavian objects, however, there is nothing to link the Frisian examples particularly with women – the names suggest that the opposite may be the case – although they might also have been thought to symbolise notions of virtue or status. The Frisian weapons do seem at least to be amulet-like, but like oversized ceremonial swords may have had a public function, which if so would also set them apart from most (other) runic amulets. At the very least they seem to be magico-religious in function and presumably have something to do with (masculine) virtue.[21]

A further aspect to ritual is of course the erection and dedication of altars. After

[20] Looijenga, p. 309.
[21] Looijenga, pp. 316–17. See also R. Koch, 'Waffenförmige Anhänger aus merowingerzeitlichen Frauengräber', *Jahrbuch des Römisch-Germanischen Zentralmuseums Mainz* 17 (1970), 285–93, Meaney, pp. 153ff. and Zeiten, pp. 15ff. for miniature weapon amulets.

all, the commonest place to find runic votive texts, following the Roman model, might have been thought to be on rune-stones. There are some rune-stone inscriptions that seem like they might be votive – recall the stone of Ungand, for instance, considered earlier in this chapter, and the Blekinge fertility stones – but they are composed in such a manner that they are not obviously dedicatory. In fact some later rune-stone texts even make clear references to Thor blessing something, though these all seem to be funerary stones. Nonetheless one early rune-stone religious inscription has been found that more clearly displays a form of cultic expression, though admittedly a quite complicated one, which bears some similarities to those often found on pagan altars from the Mediterranean world.

A relatively clear example of a rune-stone dedicatory inscription is that which appears on a stone found in 1894 at Noleby, Sweden. An irregularly shaped, roughly 70cm-long piece of gneiss, it was reused as part of a wall sometime after it was first inscribed, however, so we are not aware of why and where it was originally situated. The following legend can be read, clearly marked out in 6 to 7cm-high runic letters along one of the flat edges of the stone:

ᚱᚢᚾᛟᚱᚹᚨᚠᛁᚱᚨᚷᛁᚾᚨᚲᚢᛞᛟᛏᛟᛃᛖᚲᚨ
ᚢᚾᚨᚦᛟᚢ:ᛋᚢᚺᚢᚱᚨᚺ:ᛋᚢᛋᛁᚺᛗᚺᚾᚹᛁᛁᛏ
ᚺᚨᚲᚢᚦᛟ

Rūnō fāhi raginakundō tōjeka.
Unaþou suhurah susihe hwatin.
Hakuþo.

'A rune I paint, of the gods made known, I offer.
For satisfaction *suhurah susihe* may they whet. Hakutho.'

This at first semantically strange-seeming inscription is set out in a poetic form, with alliteration and even regular measures, and seems to record ritual phrases. It appears to begin with a tightly composed expression – what linguists often call a 'squish' – that shows signs of being formulaic. After all, not only does it feature a late form of the votive verb *taujan* (i.e. as *tōjeka*), the alliterating expression *rūnō. . . raginakundō*, 'rune. . . of the gods made known' (separated here by the verb *fahi* for poetic effect) is also found on another rune-stone, probably of eighth or ninth-century date, from Sparlösa, Sweden. The Sparlösa stone similarly records *rūnaʀ . . . rægi[n]kundu* 'runes . . . of the gods made known' along with a memorial message, perhaps recording (rather than being part of) some sort of a ritual (see further chapter 9). Less expectedly, though, more-or-less the same expression 'runes . . . by gods made known' is also found in a later form (in what seems to be an expansion of the 'squish') in the Eddic *Sayings of the High One*:

Þat er þá reynt, er þu at rúnum spyrr
inum reginkunnum,
þeim er gærðu ginnregin
ok fáði fimbulþulr.

It is proven when you ask about runes
by gods made known,

those which the great gods made
and the awesome sage (i.e. Odin) painted.

It is striking that two early Swedish inscriptions should record what is essentially the same alliterating expression as recurs in a later Icelandic poem – the best explanation seems to be that 'rune(s) . . . by/of the gods made known' was an important phrase, perhaps because it was part of a well-known early Norse charm or prayer. Offering runes to the gods seems to be a reflection of the sacred characteristic associated with runic writing also seen in the spelling exercises which appear in runic amulet texts. It is interesting, too, that *ragina-* or (later Norse) *reginn-* is a term that originally meant 'counsellor' or 'adviser'. In fact Regin is the name variously of a dwarf, giant or dragon who appears in several Norse sagas and lays, and who is eventually killed by the hero Sigurd. The word is also often used in connection with Odin, for example in another passage from the *Sayings of the High One*, 'and the great gods made / and Hropt of the gods carved' (*ok gærðu ginnregin / ok reist Hroptr rǫgna*), where Hropt is a byname of Odin meaning 'Singer' or 'Squawker'.[22]

Odin was the god who first discovered the runes according to Norse myth and his epithets include many descriptions like Hropt, for example Ómi 'Shouter'. In normal use, though, *hroptr* typically signifies animal noises (like cawing etc.) and is probably related to the Norse word *hrafn* 'raven, crow'. This name seems to reflect Odin's role as the lord of what was once another meaning of *wood* in English, i.e. 'madness, inspiration, magic, poetry, rage'; his animal nature is realised more physically in his two pet ravens Hugin and Munin ('Thought' and 'Memory'). He is the adviser or inspirer, the maker of weird noises, and the chanter of magical sounds. The rune-lore section of the *Lay of Sigrdrifa* even mentions 'mind-runes' (*hugrúnar*) conceived of by Odin the squawker (*um hugði Hroptr*). Thus offering 'rune(s) . . . of the gods made known' is probably a form of supplication to Odin, the divine master of northern writing. The first line of the Noleby text, then, appears to be a complicated form of dedicatory expression.

The next line contains two unintelligible words, probably alliterating magical gibberish similar to that found in medical charms (*su-hu-rah, su-si-he*). And the other slightly irregularly spelled terms of this line seem to indicate that the inscription was made to whet (in the figurative sense) satisfaction, i.e. perhaps to help make amends for some sort of misdeed or misfortune. This expression has been connected with funerary magic – i.e. sharpening the enjoyment of a dead person (so they will rest happily in their grave) as many rune-stone memorial texts feature statements of this sort. But the Noleby stone does not exhibit any of the characteristic features of Scandinavian funerary stones (it is relatively small after all) and its first line seems to be a votive, rather than a commemorative expression. In fact the stone's second line is reminiscent of the justifications which often appear in Roman votive texts like 'in fulfilment of a vow'. We seem

---

22 The singular *rūnō* 'rune' at Noleby seems to have been chosen in order to rhyme with *-kundō* 'known' and may represent a collective use of *rune* for 'runic message'. See Markey, 'Dedicatory formula' for the most recent analysis of the Noleby stone.

to have here, then, a complicated runic dedication to the gods, probably to Odin, by Hakutho in order to right or make amends for some unspecified wrong.

The formulaic language seen on the Noleby stone appears to be part of a vocabulary of religious lore not only replicated at Sparlösa and in Eddic sources, but which is probably also represented in the 'run of bright runes' and 'mighty runes' mentioned on two of the Blekinge stones. In fact the Blekinge expression *ginna-rūnaʀ* 'mighty runes' is also reminiscent of the *gagaga gīnu gahellija*, 'A roar I cry (i.e. gape) resoundingly' of the magical chant written on the Kragehul spear. The element *ginn-* (which originally meant 'yawning' or 'gaping') is found in Old Norse in the compounds *ginnheilagr* 'very holy' (cf. Kragehul's use of *wīju* 'I consecrate') and *ginnregin* 'great gods' (cf. Noleby's *rūnō . . . raginakundō* and the stanza from the *Sayings of the High One* cited above), as well as *Ginnungagap* the 'mighty gap' that the *Seeress's Prophecy* recounts existed before the world was made. The elements *ginn-* 'gaping, mighty' and *ragina-* 'counsellors, gods' crop up in the same circumstances often enough that they seem to have been key terms in the Old Germanic religious vocabulary. Thus their use in compounds connected with runes probably indicates that formulaic texts like that on the Noleby stone represent merely the tip of the runic iceberg when it comes to an early Germanic use of writing in votive contexts. It is an iceberg, however, that has otherwise mostly been lost.

Formulaically, then, the text on the Noleby stone seems to witness reflections of archaic, Roman and indigenous types. The first line is clearly poetic, both in terms of features such as alliteration and rhythm, as well as in its elusive, figurative language. Its use of a dedicatory verb also seems to point to a retained archaic feature such as appears on the Gallehus horn, though one not found on inscribed Roman altar-stones. Noleby's justification, however, although also obliquely expressed seems close to a typical Roman element – a feature not commonly found in comparable archaic texts, even those on engraved stones. In fact the seemingly linguistically meaningless sequences *suhurah susihe* appear to have their nearest parallel in leechcraft texts. The Noleby inscription may ultimately represent a blend of all four of these traditions, rather than the idiosyncratic and mostly inscrutable expression that it is often supposed to be.

Rather than obviously being influenced by Roman norms and practices, then, early Germanic cultic practice appears to have had much more in common with the pre-Roman traditions of the Alpine regions and Northern Italy. The influence of archaic religious tradition seems to go beyond the probable North Etruscan origin of the runes and the five-part amulet formulism so similar to that of Reitia votives (as was discussed in chapter 4). The cult of the divine word represented by Reitia, Artemis of the Word, also has parallels in the runic aspect of the cult of Odin. In fact the two-headed horse on the Gallehus horn may indicate that Reitia's role as the goddess of animals, especially the horse, was remembered for a time in Germanic tradition. Northern religious life seems very un-Roman and equally very unlike that reconstructed by many archaeologists in the light of the testimony of rune-inscribed ritual items.

8

Christian Amulets

W ITH the piecemeal conversion of the Germanic kingdoms a new influence becomes apparent in runic amulet texts. Old runic standards such as the charm words *alu* or *laukaz* begin to be usurped by recognisably Christian elements and features – especially, as we have already seen, in healing charms. The first Germanic groups to convert were the emigrant continental tribes, the Goths then the Franks, Burgundians and the Lombards. Irish missionaries then began the conversion of the Anglo-Saxons which was completed as a result of St Augustine's mission that emanated directly from Rome. Irish monks again partic- ipated in the conversion of the Germans, as also did Englishmen like St Boniface, though the conversion of all the remaining continental tribes was not completed until the time of Charlemagne and his military defeat of the continental or 'Old' Saxons. The Scandinavians were last as the Christian faith finally spread to the northernmost reaches of Europe – the first signs of Christianity become evident in Denmark in about the ninth century when Christian symbols first begin appearing on rune-inscribed memorial stones.

Yet the conversion did not mean the overnight destruction of pagan culture. As is still often the case today, Christian conversion usually meant the retention of many local customs and cultural expressions. This in turn sometimes led to a syncretism of Christian belief and pre-Christian tradition. As long as this did not mean outright return to the worship of pagan gods, the retention of many of the old practices and traditions was usually tolerated by the Church.[1]

Christianity, however, also brought with it its own mystical traditions and its own types of amulets. Although Gnosticism was frowned upon as a heresy, some echoes of Gnostic practice nevertheless survived into early Christian use. The focus of the Gnosts on the power of supernatural names and the mystical associa- tions of letters also found in Jewish mysticism came to be reflected in Christian religious life and superstition. Typically, though, Christian mysticism had its own language derived from its own sources, ones usually recognisably different to those used by the Gnosts and in Jewish Cabalistic belief.

Early medieval Christian amulets typically record short benedictions or prayers, or snatches of biblical or liturgical tracts. Often written on parchment, they were sometimes carried in small cases and were worn about the body.

---

[1] J.C. Russell, *The Germanization of Early Medieval Christianity* (New York 1994); R.A. Fletcher, *The Conversion of Europe* (London 1997).

Known as phylacteries, these were essentially unofficial and often secular expressions. A growing number of Christian texts on brooches and pendants are also known that are typically repetitions of words like 'holy' or indirect ways of referring to God. Over time the type of expressions found on Christian amulets developed in keeping with the emergence of new trends in Christian mysticism, such as the development of litanies of the various names and epithets of God, popular themes like the five wounds of Christ or the Seven Sleepers of Ephesus (discussed in chapter 6), prayers used in exorcisms or other Church rites, to even key doctrinal terminologies and the like. The great majority of these were written in Latin or less commonly Greek – the principal two languages of the Church – although occasionally a word or two from Aramaic or Hebrew might also appear. Yet there is no evidence that the use of runes was incompatible with Christianity as is sometimes averred. As the appearance of Christian symbols and eventually phrases on Scandinavian rune-stones indicates, the contrary often seems to have been the case.[2]

There is some evidence for Christian amulets inscribed in runes from the Continent, but these often appear to be syncretic expressions. The mid-sixth-century Lombard brooches from Bezenye, Hungary, which were discussed in chapter 4, for example, bear what seem to be wishes for joy and blessing, the latter using a term, *segun*, often thought to have had an exclusively Christian sense. But it is not clear that these inscriptions represent any more than the Christianisation of an old Germanic tradition. Although *segun* undoubtedly derives ultimately from the Latin verb *signo* 'mark' used in the sense 'mark as holy, mark with a sign of the cross', these amulets seem to fit the ancient runic five-part amulet formulism better than they do any early Christian one.

As was discussed in chapter 2, the two sequences, *kr* and *ïia*, on the Charnay brooch also may represent abbreviated mystical names typical of Gnostic amulets, Christ and Iaô respectively. A more clearly and seemingly more regularly Christian inscription, however, comes from Chéhéry, north-eastern France, and is found on a golden disc brooch that dates to the about the year 600. Rather worn, it was found in a woman's grave in 1978 and is a mixture of both Roman and runic letters, as well as apparently also a linguistic blend of Latin and a Germanic tongue. Given the find location it is presumably Frankish both in language and in manufacture, and its in parts unclear text reads:

DEOꙄ:ÞE
ᛁᛏᛁᛗ:E
ᛊᚾᛗ. . .

Deo s(ancto) . . .
-tid . . .
sum . . .

'To holy God. Thehtid (?) . . . I am. . .'

---

[2] For a brief survey of non-runic texts see R. Favreux, *Les inscriptions médiévales* (Tournhout 1979), pp. 98–101. K. Thomas, *Religion and the Decline of Magic* (London 1971) deals in general with magic and medieval Christianity as does V.I.J. Flint, *The Rise of Magic in Early Medieval Europe* (Princeton 1991).

Reversing a letter, although a common enough mistake, is also a typical way of signalling abbreviation in Latin, so we can be fairly sure that the text begins in a typically Christian manner – it is probably part of a short benediction similar to *Deo gratias* 'thanks be to God'. What should be made of the next few elements is not so clear, however – the runes and Latin letters may even have been inscribed at different times – although the runic sequence *-tid*, terminated by a typically runic form of punctuation mark, appears to be the last part of a Germanic name, perhaps *Thehtid* or the like. The Latin verb *sum*, then, seemingly followed by what has been read as including *ik*, the Germanic pronoun 'I', presumably indicates a 'talking' owner's expression: 'Thehtid I am' (or the like). In fact the Chéhéry find is reminiscent of a sixth-century similarly part-Latin, part-Germanic inscription in Roman letters on a buckle found in an old cemetery at Monnet-la-Ville in the Haute Jura. This Burgundian text also seems to be amuletic and reads: *Tonacius vivas! maxote, fecit, mic, me, feci, facio*, i.e. 'Donatius, (long) may you live! made, made, me, me, I made, I make'. It is hard to be sure the Chéhéry brooch also bears an amuletic text, although it certainly does seem like one with its pious opening words and what appears to be a mixed Latin and Frankish naming expression.[3]

Numerous Christian amulets in Roman letters are known from Germany, too, but there are no clear examples of rune-inscribed amulets (even only partially so) that are obviously Christian. The Nordendorf brooch has been considered a record of a Christian renunciation of the pagan gods, of course, as was mentioned in chapter 2 and the inscription on the silver strainer from Oberflacht has also been supposed to reflect a Christian context. But most claims of Christian influence in early German runic texts usually turn out to be equally as tendentious or unclear as the swearing off interpretation of the Nordendorf inscription or the Eucharistic explanation of the Oberflacht strainer. The mid- to late-sixth-century *bada* texts are also often thought to be of this type as the term later comes to refer to the Christian sense of comfort, i.e. the consolation of faith in God. Yet there is nothing in them to indicate that this is necessarily the case; and in fact formulaically, much like the Bezenye inscriptions, the German *bada* texts seem quite pagan.

Another German example of a runic inscription usually thought to be Christian is that which appears on a brooch from Osthofen, a town in the district of Worms. The gilt bronze disc brooch dates from the mid-seventh century and was found in 1854 in an ancient Frankish cemetery. The brooch is broken, however, a large part of it is lost, and what is left is not particularly well preserved. Nonetheless it has traditionally been read as:

ᚷᛟ:ᚠᚢᚱᚠᛝ-ᚾᛝ-ᛟᛈᛁᛏᛗ✚

Go[d] fura d[i]h d[e]ofile!

---

3   Düwel, 'Runische und lateinische Epigraphik', pp. 235–36, S. Fischer, 'Merovingertida runfynd i Ardennerna, Frankrike', *Nytt om runer* 14 (1999), 12–13, S. Fischer and J.-P. Lémant, 'Epigraphic evidence of Frankish exogamy', in E. Taayke et al. (eds), *Essays on the Early Franks* (Groningen 2003), pp. 241–66 and C. Mercier and M. Mercier-Rolland, *Le cimetière burgonde de Monnet-la-Ville* (Paris 1974), pp. 62–63.

'God before thee, devil!'

Unfortunately it is not at all clear whether this text ever included the words 'God' or 'devil', or even the early German word for 'thee'. An Old High German version of the inscription would be expected to read *Got fora dich tiuval*, an earlier one probably *God fora þih diubal*, and though the *o*-spelling in *fora/fura* might be allowable on idiomatic grounds, both the final *e* and the *i* in *d[e]ofile* cannot be reconciled with the early German word for 'devil' (Latin *diabolus*). It has been argued instead then that this sequence is an obliquely inflected man's name *Theophilus*, which would be Greek and hence presumably suitably Christian. But this interpretation again is based upon debatable phonological ground and scarcely makes the inscription any more readily comprehensible. The text may start with the word *God*, but it could equally begin with *gôl* 'sang' (cf. the Freilaubersheim inscription considered in chapter 3) or several other old German or Frankish names or words.[4]

Christian influence has also been identified in some further early German inscriptions, but in each case problematically.[5] More obviously, though, individual supplications also occur on at least two probable amulets from Anglo-Saxon England. A bone comb from Whitby in North Yorkshire perhaps dating to the eighth century or thereabouts has a personal plea, rendered in a mixture of Latin and the Anglian dialect of Old English. The inscription, whose linguistic mix makes it reminiscent of the Chéhéry and Monnet-la-Ville finds, reads:

ᛗᛖᚢᛋᛗᛖᚢᛋ ᚷᛖᚪᛚᛚᛈᛖᚪᛚᛞᚪᛈ ᚻᛗᛈᛁᚳᚠᛚᛗᛏ. . .

Deus meus. God eallwealda helpe Cyn. . .

'My God. May God Almighty help Cyn. . .'

The Whitby inscription almost seems to be a partial translation of a typical Latin amulet text into Old English. *Deus meus*, after all, is both the opening words of several medieval prayers and a biblical expression – one of the pleas made by Christ during his passion, repeating the opening of one of the Psalms. A similar runic 'God help X' message is also found on the Mortain casket, as was mentioned in chapter 7. A less clearly Latin-predicated inscription also appears, however, on what was once probably part of another Anglo-Saxon amulet, on a bone plate this time, which confines its language to the native vernacular:

ᚷᛖᚻᚷᛖᚳᛈᚠᛈᚠᚱᛈᚻᚠᛗᚻᛈᚦᛁᚦᛁᚾᚱᚱᚪᛏ

God gēcaþ āræ Hadda þi þis wrāt.

4   Krause with Jankuhn, no. 145 and cf. W. Jungandreas, 'God fura dih, Deofile', *Zeitschrift für deutsches Altertum und deutsche Literatur* 101 (1972), 84–85, the final *-e* makes this part of the inscription look like it was supposed to read 'for Deofil', though, so it may well have been originally intended as an amatory text.

5   E.g. on a brooch from Soest according to U. Schwab, 'Runen der Merowingerzeit als Quelle für das Weiterleben der spätantiken christlichen und nichtchristlichen Schriftmagie?', in K. Düwel (ed.), *Runische Schriftkultur in kontinental-skandinavischer und -angelsächsischer Wechselbeziehung* (Berlin 1988), p. 378 and on a silver sword-fitting from Eichstetten in Kaiserstuhl by Düwel, 'Runische und lateinische Epigraphik', p. 268.

The Derby panel was once riveted to another object, long since lost, and has no known context; even its precise find location is a matter of some dispute. A probable translation of its text is 'God preserves the honour of Hadda who wrote this', although other meanings have been suggested, all along similar lines. Nevertheless, despite several Christian rune-stone memorials which invite prayers for the deceased and even what seems to be a runic version of the passion poem *The Dream of the Rood* on a lavishly decorated stone cross at Ruthwell, in south-western Scotland, few demonstrably Christian sentiments occur on Anglo-Saxon runic amulets.[6]

The situation is quite different in Scandinavia, however, where the greatest number of runic amulets which postdate the Viking period are overtly Christian. Many contain protective formulas, implicitly or explicitly invoking the aid of God, his angels or his saints. These appear in Latin, the language of the learned clergy, and the more familiar Norse vernaculars, and cover a diverse field. We have recognisable quotations from the Bible or Christian liturgy, more homely personal prayers and a long line of inscriptions featuring what has been termed 'holy quack' – a largely random collection of Christian and magical words and names, usually in Latin, Greek or Hebrew, and often in garbled form.

The medieval idea that sickness was a punishment for sin led to fear and superstitious practices among the laity. Thus, scattered throughout the magical and medical runic amulets are numerous liturgical words and phrases. The apotropaic use of the names of saints, often in semi-gibberish phrases with foreign liturgical words, is already familiar from the leechcraft amulets, and is common in Christian magic.

The most popular of these holy 'words of power', and already familiar from its regular occurrence in leechcraft inscriptions, is the Cabalistic acronym *AGLA* (the Hebrew invocation 'Thou art strong to eternity, Lord'). Popular in medieval Christian spells from throughout Europe, it is found in around 30 runic inscriptions, sometimes even spelt out with the cruciform punctuation commonly used when it appears in Roman-letter texts: i.e. *A⁘G⁘L⁘A∴*. Despite its literal meaning, there is no doubt that *AGLA* was valued principally as a magical formula. As we have seen, it regularly occurs in the context of longer inscriptions, although these sometimes comprise no more than a jumbled collection of magical protective words. The ubiquitous *AGLA* also regularly appears alongside prayers or expressions of affirmation such as *amen*. A church bell from Saleby, Sweden, dating from the year 1228, invokes St Dionysius (Denis) and informs its readers:

+ᚦᛆ:ᛁᛆᚴ:ᚢᛆᚱ:ᚴᛆᚱ:ᚦᛆ:ᚢᛆᚱ:ᚦᚢᛋᚼᚢᚿᛏᚱᛆᚦ:ᛏᚢ:ᚼᚢᚿᛏᚱᛆᚦ:ᛏᛁᚢᚼᚢ:ᚢᛁᚿᛏᚱ:ᛅᚴ:ᛆᛏᛏᛆ:ᚠᚱᛆ:
ᛒᛦᚱᚦ:ᚴᚢᛋ:+ᛆ+ᚴ+ᛚ+ᛆ+:
:ᛆᚢᛂ:ᛘᛆᚱᛁᛆ:ᚴᚱᛆᛏᛆ:ᛒᛚᛂᚿᛆ:
:ᛏᛁᛆᚿᛁᛋᛁᚢᛋ:ᛋᛁᚦ:ᛒᛂᚿᛂᛏᛁᚴᛏᚢᛋ:

Þā iak vaʀ gar, þā vaʀ þūshundrað tu hundrað tiugu vintr ok ātta frā byrð Gu(ð)s. AGLA. Ave Maria gratia plena! Dionysius sit benedictus.

6 Page, *Introduction*, pp. 130ff. and 163–65; cf. J.M. Bately and V.I. Evison, 'The Derby bone piece', *Medieval Archaeology* 5 (1961), 301–5.

'When I was made, then was one thousand, two hundred and twenty-eight years from the birth of God. *AGLA*. Hail Mary full of grace! May Dionysus be blessed.'

Medieval church bells were rung to ward off evil and even sometimes thunderstorms, and in Scandinavia were often inscribed with the futhark row or parts of the *Hail Mary*, texts evidently aimed at an otherworldly audience rather than the church congregation. Sometimes their messages were even more explicit, as on a rune-inscribed church bell from Hardeberga, Sweden:

ᛔᛅᚱᚴᚱᚢ'ᛁᛌᛆᚴᛌᛁᚼᚭᚢᛘ:ᚠᚠᛁᛆᚦ:
:ᛔᚱᛆᚴᚢᛚ:ᛆᛘᚿ:ᛘᛆᛚᛁᚼᚭᚢᛘ✠

Per crucis hoc signum fugiat	*procul omne malignum.*
'By this sign of the cross	all evil shall flee far away.'

This hexameter is often encountered in sickness charms. A similarly authoritative proclamation in Roman letters is the inscription on the Danish Jydstrup bell: *Vocor Maria demonum victrix melodia*, 'I am called Mary, vanquisher of demons by my melody.'[7]

The *AGLA* invocation also occurs on its own, e.g. on a wooden spatula from Tønsberg, Norway preceded and followed by a small incised cross. It also occurs in repeated form on a thirteenth-century wooden cross from Trondheim, for instance, interspersed with inscribed crosses to read *AGLA AGLA AGLA*, or on a square wooden amulet from Oslo which reads *kales fales AGLA* ✻ *AGLA* – i.e. two magical rhyming words, what was probably supposed to be a Christogram or a cross and *AGLA* twice. Reinforcing its magical connotations, the word is frequently encountered anagrammatically, too, as on the Revninge gold ring which features the text *arota AGLA GALA LAGA*. The same scrambling is found among unreadable runes on a lead amulet from Tårnborg, Denmark (*AGLA GALA LAGA*), introducing a longer inscription on the Selsø lead roll (see below) and in similar form on a thirteenth-century horn clasp from Söderköping, Sweden, which carries the legend *AGGALA LAGA GALLA*. We have already seen *AGLA* combined with *sator arepo, fai fao fau, khorda inkhorda* or other magic words or formulas in chapter 6 and it also appears alongside prayers and holy names. In fact *AGLA* frequently occurs in company with magical phrases or the names of saints or archangels. Representative is a fragmentary lead piece from Glim, Denmark, perhaps originally a cross, where a scrambled form of *AGLA* is found along with the names of the evangelists John, Mark and Matthew: *Johannes, Ma[rkus ?], Mattheus . . . AGLA GALA*.[8]

7 *SR* V, no. 210; *DR* no. 299; cf. also Moltke, *Runes and their Origin*, p. 444.

8 Unless otherwise indicated, the lead amulets discussed here can be found in Düwel, 'Mittelalterliche Amulette', pp. 227–302; cf. also Knirk, 'Runic inscriptions containing Latin', pp. 476–507. See also the spatula N A8, the wooden cross *NIyR* no. 821, the Oslo amulet N A321 and the ring (the first word of which is often restored to *Arretôn* 'The Unspeakable' or *aretê* 'virtue', or even part of the *sator, arepo* formula) *DR* no. 203. The Söderköping clasp is discussed by J.P. Strid and M. Åhlén, 'Runfynd 1985', *Fornvännen* 81 (1986), 217–23, who point out the symmetry in the spelling.

A number of amuletic inscriptions occur on lead rolls, tablets and crosses of varying size. Several of the latter, often but not inevitably found in graves, bear inscriptions in runic or Roman minuscule. The Osen cross, for example, considered in the chapter on leechcraft, contained the *abracalara* formula as well as pious Christian messages such as are found on several runic charms. Nearly all the Scandinavian rune-inscribed lead objects appear to be in Latin or pseudo-Latin, although many of them are incomprehensible, comprising rune-like signs rather than readable runes, which may feasibly represent a form of alphabet magic, if not simply the process of decay.[9]

Many such runic talismans consist solely of a collection of divine epithets or similar expressions assumed to confer protection, ones often similar to those found on ancient Gnostic amulets. Particularly common among runic examples are *Adonai* 'Lord', *Agios* 'Holy', *Arretôn* 'The Unspeakable', *Athanatos* 'Immortal', *Eia* 'Aha! (or Good!)', *Em(m)anuel* 'God with us', *Hely* 'My God', *Messias* 'Messiah', *Pantocrator* 'Almighty', *Sabaoth* '(Lord) of Hosts', *Soter* 'Saviour' and *Tetragrammaton* 'the four letters (which spell Yahweh in Hebrew, YHVH)'. A lead amulet from Kaupanger in Norway, as yet unfolded, so with most of its text still obscured, reveals a list of such words: *Jacob, Credo, Hely, Soter, Agios, Eia, Deus* and *AGLA AGLA AGLA* (the last three expressions arranged in the shape of a cross), i.e. 'Jacob, I believe, My God, Saviour, Holy, Aha!, God, *AGLA* (x3)'. Similarly, a thirteenth-century pierced lead cross from Trondheim, Norway, has five-fold *AGLA, Agios* and perhaps *fau*.

The act of placing a formula of absolution or exorcism on the breast of the deceased, often in the form of a cross, was widespread in the early Anglo-Norman world and may have influenced Scandinavian practice. On the other hand, two runic lead crosses from Bru, Norway, are generally presumed to have been placed in Bronze Age burial cairns in order to ward off the walking dead. These are in a sadly fragmentary state: one seems to include a list of sacred words and perhaps abbreviations: *Adonai . . . Ecce, Credo . . .*, 'Lord . . . Behold, I believe . . .' On the second Bru cross various words and perhaps abbreviations in runes and Roman letters can be discerned, i.e. *Athanatos* 'Immortal', *crux* 'cross', *Domini (?)* 'of the Lord', *serpens* 'serpent', *aries* 'ram', *leo* 'lion', *vermis* 'worm', *Arretôn* 'The Unspeakable' and the name *Olaus* (Olaf), with the animal symbols representing fragments of at least one early medieval hymn: the *Alma chorus Domini* (*Dear Chorus of the Lord*). Also featuring liturgical text is the Roman-letter inscription on the Krossvold cross which reproduces most of the first four verses of the *Christ the Saviour* sequence from the Christian liturgy, another series of enumerations for God. A further Norwegian lead cross from Alshus evidences only a conglomeration of unreadable rune-like signs.[10]

In fact rather than represent a continuation of Gnostic practice, lists such as

---

9   On the use of lead in magical practice see Düwel, 'Mittelalterliche Amulette', pp. 252–55.

10 The Bru lead crosses are *NIyR* nos 262 and 263 respectively (cf. also Düwel, 'Mittelalterliche Amulette', pp. 279–80). 'Fragments' of another medieval prayer, *Deus Pater piissime*, are often suggested to appear in these sequences, but this identification is based on the appearance of only one word, *arretôn*.

those on the Bru crosses seem to have developed from hymns like the *Alma chorus* which are essentially enumerations of names for God:

Alma chorus Domini nunc pangat nomina summi:

Messias, Soter, Emanuel, Sabaoth, Adonai,
Est unigenitus, via, vita, manus, homousion,

Principium, primogenitus, sapientia, virtus,
Alpha, caput finisque simul vocitatur et est o,

Fons et origo boni, paraclitus ac mediator,
Agnus, ovis, vitulus, serpens, aries, leo, vermis,

Os, verbum, splendor, sol, gloria, lux, et imago, Panis, flos, vitis, mons,
janua, petra, lapisque,

Angelus et sponsus, pastorque propheta, sacerdos,
Athanatos, kyrios, theos, pantocrator, Iesus,

Salvificet nos, sit cui saecla per omnia doxa. Amen.

'Dear chorus of the Lord, now follow the main names:

Messiah, Soter, Emmanuel, Sabaoth, Adonai,
He is the only begotten, the way, the life, the power, the same as (the Father),

The beginning, the first-born, the wisdom, the strength,
Alpha, he is usually called the beginning and the end at the same time, and he is Ω,

Source and origin of good, comforter and mediator,
Lamb, sheep, calf, serpent, ram, lion, worm,

Mouth, word, magnificence, sun, glory, light and likeness,
Bread, flower, vine, mountain, beginning, rock and jewel,

Angel, and sponsor, and pastor, prophet, priest,
Immortal, lord, god, almighty, Jesus.

Save us; so be it forever for all glory. Amen.'

Fragments of the *Alma chorus*, the office hymn for the compline of Whitsunday in the Sarum rite, recur on several runic amulets. The hymn, used in Norwegian masses since the twelfth century and popular in Norwegian and Icelandic literature and epigraphy, was said to have been sung by the Norwegian King Sverrir during a battle near Nordnes in the year 1181. The most complete version occurs on the eye-charm amulet examined in chapter 6 which contained not only a familiar biblical formula against eye-disease, but also an extended sequence from the *Alma chorus Domini*. In fact such lists are well known from medieval Christian exorcisms, benedictions, warding charms and such from most parts of Western as well as Northern Europe.[11]

---

[11] On the *Alma chorus Domini* and the similar *Deus Pater piissime* hymn in Norse tradition see L. Gjerlow, '*Deus pater piissime* og blykorsene fra Stavanger bispedømme', *Stavanger Museums Årbok* 1954, pp. 85–109. For further notes and editions of the *Alma chorus Domini* and *Deus Pater piissime* see G.M. Dreves and C. Blume (eds), *Analecta hymnica Medii Aevii*, 55 vols (Leipzig 1886–1922), XV, no. 2 and LIII, no. 87.

Another, this time unprovenanced, Norwegian amulet in the form of a lead tablet employs the typically magical strategy of extending from the specific to the sweeping: it reads *aaa þþþ aaaaaa AGLA, Michael, Gabriel, Rafael, Raguel, omnes angeli et archangeli, pantaseron, Gunnlaug, P(ater) n(oster), a(men)...*, '. . .*AGLA*, Michael, Gabriel, Raphael, Raguel, all the angels and archangels, Almighty, Gunnlaug, O(ur) F(ather), a(men)' (followed perhaps by a misspelt *AGLA*). Only the fragmentary text . . . *Patris* . . . *[Tet]r[a]grammaton, Christ[us](?)...*, 'of the Father, *Tetragrammaton*, Christ (?)' can be discerned on the highly corroded lead amulet from Allindemagle, Denmark, while a small lead roll from the cemetery at Høje Taastrup, Zealand, has the following names: *[Johan]nes, Marcus, Lucas, Dionysius(?), (Tetra)grammaton*, i.e. 'John, Mark, Luke, Dionysius, *(Tetra)grammaton*'. A more cohesive text occurs on a small lead roll, probably a reliquary, which seems to have contained a kind of bone powder, from Västannor, Sweden. This runic text also incorporates the ever-popular *Hail Mary* in the usual medieval form, i.e. that derived directly from the archangel Gabriel's greeting to the Virgin:

> +ᛆᚢᛂᛘᛆᚱᛁ-ᚵᚱᛆᚴᛁᛆᛔᛚ-ᚿᛆᛑᚮᛘᛁᚿᚢ'ᛏᛂᚴᚢᛘ+
> ᛒᛂᚿᛂᛑᛁᚴᛏᛆᛏᚢᛁᚿᛘᚢᛚᛁᛂᚱᛁᛒᚢᛌᛂᛏᛔᛂᚿᛂᛑᛁᚴᛏᚢᛌ
> ᚠᚱᚢᚴᛏᚢᛌᚢᛂᚿᛏᚱᛁᛌᛏᚢᛁᛆᛘᛂᚿ+ᛆᛚᚠᛆᛂᛏᚮᛆᚵᛚᛚᛆ+
> ᛑᛂᚢᛌᛆᛑᛁᚢᛆᚠᛂᛌᚢᛌᚴᚱᛁᛌᛏᚢᛌᛑᚮᛘᛁᚿᚢᛌᚿᚮᛌᛏᛂᚱ

> *Ave Maria, gratia plena! Dominus tecum. Benedicta tu in mulieribus et benedictus fructus ventris tui. Amen. Alpha et O(mega). AGLA. Deus adiuva! Jesus Christus Dominus noster.*

> 'Hail Mary, full of grace! The Lord is with thee. Blessed art thou amongst women and blessed is the fruit of thy womb. Amen. Alpha and O(mega). *AGLA*. Help, God! Jesus Christ our Lord.'

God, as we saw earlier, was often referred to in poetry, benedictions and magical spells as 'Alpha et Omega' or simply 'Alpha', a divine title from the Book of Revelation symbolising the beginning (and end) of everything.[12]

Miscellaneous runic collections of powerful names or words are not confined to lead rolls or crosses, however; rather they are found on almost every conceivable kind of Scandinavian runic talisman. The names of the archangels (Raphael, Gabriel, Michael) functioned as powerful protection, as did those of the four evangelists. Here might be recalled the protective Norwegian *sator arepo* rune-stick discussed earlier with its many invocations: *AGLA, Guð, Sator are[po], Rafael, Gabriel, M[ichael], Jesus Kristr, María, gæt mín...*, i.e. '*AGLA*, God, *Sator arepo*, Raphael, Gabriel, Michael, Jesus Christ, Mary, protect me . . .'. A runic inscription cut into a plank in Tonstad church, Norway, in about the year 1200 similarly contained a litany of holy words and names – some familiar from the medieval prayer *Deus Pater piissime (God the Father Most Pious)* – rendered in Latin, but ending with a supplication in Norse:

12 On the Västannor lead roll see H. Gustavson and T. Snædal Brink, 'Runfynd 1979', *Fornvännen* 75 (1980), 229–39.

ᛕᛂᛐᚱᚢᛌ:ᛕᛆᚢᛚᛚᚢᛌ:ᛆᚿᛑᚱᛂᛆᛌ:ᛘᛆᚱᚴᚢᛌ:
ᛘᛆᚱᛁᛆ:ᛘᛆᛐᚼᛂᚢᛌᛚᚢᚴᛆᛌ:ᛁᚭᚼᛆᚿᚿᛂᛌᛌ:
ᛐᛂᛐᚱᛆ:ᚵᚱᛆᛘᛆ:ᛐᚭᚿ:ᛆᚵᛚᛆ:ᛆᚵᛁᚭᛌ:
ᛆᚿᚿᛆᛁᛚ ᛘᛂᛌᛌᛁᛆᛌ:ᛁᛂᛌᚢᛌ:ᚴᚱᛁᛌᛐᚢᛌ:ᚵᚢ . .
ᛘᛆᚱᛁᛆᛘ.ᚼᛁᛚᛦ ᚼᛁᛚᛦ ᛁᛂᛌᚢᛌ ᚴᚱᛁᛌᛐᚢᛌ:ᛐᛂᛐᚱᚼᛆᚵᚭᚿ

Petrus, Paulus, Andreas, Marcus, Maria, Mattheus, Lucas, Johannes, Tetragrammaton, AGLA, Agios, Annail, Messias, Jesus Christus, Gu[ð], Maria, Hely, Hely, Jesus Christus, Tetrag(rammat)on.

'Peter, Paul, Andrew, Mark, Mary, Matthew, Luke, John, *Tetragrammaton, AGLA*, Holy, Annael (?),[13] Messiah, Jesus Christ, God, Mary, My God, My God, Jesus Christ, *Tetragrammaton.*'

A similar collection of names is found on a well-shaped and perforated Bergen rune-stick:

ᚭᛆᛚᚠᛆᚴᚱᛁᛌᛐᚢᛌᛂᛐᛆᛚᚠᛆᛁᛂ
ᛌᚢᛌᛂᛐᛘᛆᚱᛁᛆᛘᛆᚱᛋᚢᛌ
ᛘᛆᛐᛂᚢᛌᛚᚢᛋᛆᛌ
ᛁᚭᚼᛆᚿᚿᛂᛌᛘᛆᛐᛂᚢᛌᛚᚢᛋᛆᛌ

O(mega), Alpha, Christus et Alpha, Jesus et Maria, Marcus, Mattheus, Lucas, Johannes, Mattheus, Lucas.

'O(mega), Alpha, Christ and Alpha, Jesus and Mary, Mark, Matthew, Luke, John, Matthew, Luke.'

An even more exotic collection of epithets, interspersed with crosses and ending with what are probably corrupt forms of *AGLA* (x3), appears on a wood-piece from Borgund church, Norway:

ᛘᛂᛌᛌᛁᛆᛌᛌᚭᚦᛂᚱ
ᛂᛘᛆᚿᚢᛂᛚᛌᛆᛒᛆᚭᚦᛆᚦᚭ
ᚿᛆᛁᚢᛌᛁᚭᚿᛆᚵᛁᚭᛌᚭᚦᛆᚿ
ᚿᛆᚦᚭᛌᛂᛚᛂᛁᛌᚭᚿ✠✠✠✠✠✠
ᛆᛚᚠᛆᛂᚦᚭ✠✠✠✠
ᚠᛁᛚᛂᚼᛌᛆᚱᛐᛁᚠᛂᚼᛌ
ᛑᛂᚢᛌᛁᛂᛌᚢᛌᛌᛆᛚᚢᛆᛐ
ᚭᚱᛆᚵᛁᚭᛌᚭᚦᚭᚿᛆ
ᚦᚭᛌᛂᛚᛂᛁᛌᚭᚿᛆᛂᛚ
ᚵᛆᛆᚵᛂᛚᛆᛁᛆᚵᛂᛚᛆ

Messias, Soter, Emanuel, Sabaoth, Adonai, (Homo)usion (?), Agios, Athanatos, eleison!, Alpha et O(mega), Filex, Artifex, Deus, Jesus, Salvator, Agios, Athanatos, eleison!, AAELGA, AGELAI, AGELA.

'Messiah, Soter, Emmanuel, Sabaoth, Adonai, The same as (?), Holy, Immortal, have mercy!, Alpha and O(mega), Fortunate, Maker, God, Jesus, Saviour, Holy, Immortal, have mercy!, *AGLA, AGLA, AGLA.*'

The order of at least the first five words corresponds to that of the *Alma chorus*

[13] Perhaps a corruption of *Hosanna in* or the Old Testament name Han(n)iel.

Domini, quotations from which are also found on the lead crosses discussed above. The names of the evangelists (*Mattheus, Lucas, Marcus, Johannes*) are also found on the Nesland church crucifix placed together with their symbols at the end of the cross arms, as was usual in Gothic sculpture.[14]

Many of the extant Christian amulets are in a poor state of preservation and their texts are often largely illegible. Incomprehensibility may also indicate, however, that the carvers had little or no understanding of what they were writing (particularly if it was in Latin or another foreign language) and many texts remain wholly or partly unintelligible despite their runes being perfectly clear. Thus while sometimes we can attribute our lack of understanding to the state of the amulet's preservation, in at least some cases the suspicion must instead fall on the carver. Sometimes, however, only pseudo-writing may ever have been intended – the amuletic effect lying in the illusion of writing rather than the linguistic message, although it has also been suggested that some deliberately nonsensical texts were carved in order to pre-occupy (and thus disable) the Devil. Sequences of unintelligible text dog the interpretation of many post-Viking-Age inscriptions. A thirteenth-century wooden cross from Bergen, a two-part affair covered on both sides with runes and originally affixed to something else, gives us the names of the saints Benedict and Margaret of Antioch (the patron saint of women in labour), and fourfold *AGLA* amidst incomprehensible runic sequences, while *AGLA* (repeated thrice) remains the only comprehensible word on a flat rune-stick from Bergen and (twice) on a wooden cross from Hermannsverk, Norway. Yet another rune-stick from Bergen yields *Sabaoth* as the only linguistically meaningful word, and perhaps a mangled *Johannes ap(ostolus)* 'the apostle John' is all that is comprehensible today on another Bergen stick. It is tempting, although often probably futile, to set out to try to reconstruct the original text underlying some of the corrupt snatches of Latin which have come down to us, e.g. on a square stick from Oslo which one might suppose was intended to contain fourfold *Tetragrammaton* alongside repeated *AGLA*, with perhaps Old Norse *Guð*, 'God' repeated three times, perhaps even *Eia* and the woman's name *Þora*. Two enfolded lead plates from Ål church, Norway, each contain several lines of mostly unintelligible text where (five-fold) *AGLA* and *Alpha et* remain the only readily discernable elements, but where one might also wish to identify *Tetragrammaton*, a mangled rendition of 'Mark' and 'Matthew', a botched *Kyrie eleison!*, 'Lord have mercy!' and possibly *Christe eleison!*, 'Christ have mercy!' Similarly obstinate is the text on a long lead band from Leiulstad, Norway, presumably a garbled collection of names including that of Mary and some of the evangelists as well as some further liturgical text. An oblong lead plate from Borgund, Norway, appears to have some corrupted evangelist names, and perhaps *Tetragrammaton* as well as *Amen* can be restored, while a carefully cross-sectioned stick from the stave church there seems to yield *Domine!*, *concessum*, 'Lord!, permission'. Reading the runes in such cases often becomes

---

14 The problematic Tonstad inscription (*NIyR* no. 216) is also discussed by Knirk, 'Runic inscriptions containing Latin', p. 481. The Bergen rune-stick, Borgund wood-piece and Nesland church crucifix are *NIyR* nos 173, 348 and 634.

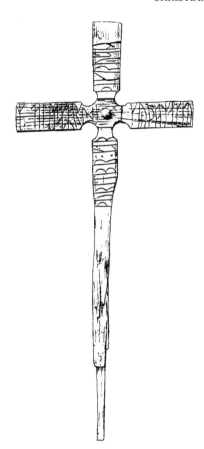

Fig. 14. Ikigaat cross

largely a guessing game. Speculation has been particularly rife about the
messages on a Greenlandic wooden cross from Ikigaat (formerly Herjolfsnes)
whose horizontal limb may be read as *AGLA, Tetragramma[ton], Jesus . . .
Pantocrator*, with the outer panels supposedly containing *P[rincipiu]m A[lpha]
et finis O[mega]* (cf. Revelation's *Ego sum Alpha et Omega, principium et finis*).
The cross's shaft, which apparently belonged originally to a different cross, reads
more intelligibly: *María. Mikael á mik. Brigit(?). Þórir*, i.e. 'Mary. Michael owns
me. Brigit. Thorir (carved me?).'[15]
    Nevertheless, the remote island of Greenland, occupied by Norse settlers from

---

[15] The Bergen cross is *NIyR* no. 642, the *AGLA* Bergen stick is *NIyR* no. 643 and the Hermannsverk
    cross is N A51. The Sabaoth stick is N B218, the Johannes stick *NIyR* no. 647, the Borgund stick
    N A26 and the Oslo stick and lead plates are discussed by A. Liestøl, 'Runeinnskriftene frå
    "Mindets tomt" ', in H.I. Høeg et al., *De arkeologiske utgravninger i Gamlebyen, Oslo* 1 (Oslo
    1978), pp. 214–24; cf. Düwel, 'Mittelalterliche Amulette', passim. The reading of the
    Greenlandic cross presented here is based on *NIyR* VI, p. 82. The Ikigaat crosses are also
    discussed by F. Jónsson, 'Interpretation of the runic inscriptions from Herjolfsnes', *Meddelelser
    om Grønland* 67 (1924), 273–290 (with a different reading of the above); further inscriptions
    from Sandnes and Umîviarssuk are discussed by E. Moltke, 'Greenland runic inscriptions IV',
    Meddelelser om Grønland 88 (1936), 223–32.

the end of the tenth century to around the year 1500 is of particularly interest for its superstitious Christian magic, often encountered on what are usually referred to as 'burial' crosses such as the one just discussed. Several runic examples were found in coffins buried at the cemetery at Ikigaat, but they may have been used as devotional crosses before being buried (as is perhaps indicated by similar crosses from Norway which have no connection with cemeteries and the fact that the name of the deceased is mentioned in only one case). Three examples simply say 'Mary', but longer Greenlandic inscriptions include not only the one discussed above but also the following texts: *Guð almáttigr gœ(ti) Guðleifar vel*, 'May God almighty protect Gudleif well'; *Þórleifr gerði kross þenna til lofs ok dýrkunar Guði almátkum*, 'Thorleif made this cross in praise and worship of God the almighty'; and Latin-Norse hybrids such as: *Jesus Kristr hjálpi. Christus natus est nobis*, 'May Jesus Christ help. Christ was born for us'; and *María, Eloihim, Jo(hannes) Johannes, Faðir, Jesus, Deus meus, Eloi, ok Sonr ok Andi*, 'Mary, God, John, John, Father, Jesus, My God, God, and the Son and the (Holy) Spirit'. Similar collections of holy names, occurring in magic formulas known from all over Western Europe, are remarkably frequent in Greenland. The magic wand from Kilaarsarfik (formerly Sandnes) is a prime example of such Christian quackery, its three sides apparently reading:

```
∴ᛁᚱᛆᛁ:ᚠᛕᚱᛁ ᛁᚿᚿᛦ:ᛁᛆᛁᛁᛦ∴:ᛁᚱᛆᛁ
ᛁᚱᛁᛆ:ᚦ: ᛁᚱᛆᛁ:ᛦ:ᛁᛒᛦᛁᛁᛒᛁᛆᛁ:ᛁᛆᛁ
ᛁᚱᛁᛆᛁ:ᛈᛁᚿᛁ:ᛁᚦ:ᛆᛁᛆᛆ:ᛁᚿᛰ:᛬ᛁᛁᛦᛁ
ᛕᛦᛁᛩᛁᛁᛆᛁ:ᛁᛆᛒᛁ:ᛁᛈ:ᛦᛁᛁᛁᚱ:ᛕᛁᛒᛦᛁᛁᛁ
ᛦᛆᛁᛈᛆᛁᚱ
```

Elon . . . nomen (?) Elon ilim . . . Elon . . . Sabaoth, Zion, Elion . . . Adonai, lux, [T]etragrammaton, Sabaoth (?), Michael, Gabriel, Rafael.

'*Elon . . .* name (?) *Elon . . . Elon . . .* Sabaoth, Zion, *Elion . . .* Adonai, light, *Tetragrammaton*, Sebaoth (?), Michael, Gabriel, Raphael.'

Elon is probably a corruption of Hebrew *'El 'Elion* 'God on high' – it or the more correct *Elion* (and *Ilion*) are frequently employed in magical formulas.

The 'holy quack' inscriptions constitute a small but significant part of the amuletic material. More meaningful are several Christian inscriptions which contain more comprehensible biblical allusions or direct quotations. The use of sacred passages on or in phylacteries is common to many religions and we have already seen the *Lord's Prayer* appearing in conjunction with the *Hail Mary*, *AGLA* and other (magical) formulas such as *abracalara*. The *Lord's Prayer* was part of the Latin catechism familiar to all Scandinavians, along with the *Nicene Creed* and the *Hail Mary*, and many medieval runic gravestones in Sweden, Norway and even Iceland contain the plea to pray the *Our Father* for the soul of the deceased. Versions of the *Lord's Prayer* were also regularly carved into church walls or pillars, whether in supplication, as a pious exercise or simply a signal of boredom during a tedious sermon it is difficult to tell.

The full prayer, in Latin, is inscribed in runes onto a lead plate that was buried at Ulstad, Norway, concluding with the names of the four evangelists:

ᚦᛒᛁᛁᛏᚱᛁᚼᚨᛁᛏᚱᚴᚾᛁᛏᛁᛁᚼᚼᚼᚦᚱᛁᛁ:�
ᚴᛁᛁᛁᚠᛁ�ᚦᚨᚾᚱᛁᚼᚣᚦᛁᚾᚾᚣᚦᛈᚾᚦᛁᛁᚦᚱ
ᛏᚠᚴᚾᚣᚾᚾᚣᚠᛁᚦᛈᚾᚷᚾᛁᛁᛁᚾᛁᚾᛁᛁᚴᚾᚦ
ᛁᛁᚼᚼᚠᚷᛏᚦᛁᛁᛏᚱᚱᛒᛁᛁᚣᚼᛁᚾᚱᚾᚣᚷᛁᛁᛁ
ᛁᛁᚾᚾᚣᚷᚷᚦᛒᛁᚷᚷᚦᚦᚷᛁᚣᛁᚾᚦᛁᛁᛒᛁᚷᛒᛁᚾᚷᛁᛁᛁ
ᚱᚷᛁᚴᚾᚦᛏᚦᛁᚷᛁᚣᛁᚾᚾᚣᚾᚦᛒᛁᚷᚱᛒᚾᛁᛁᛁ
ᚾᚱᛁᛏᚦᛁᛁᚷᛁᛁᚼᚷᚾᚷᛁᛁᛁᛁᛏᚣᚷᚼᛁᚷᛏᚣᛏᚦᚷᛁ
ᛒᛁᚱᚾᚷᚷᚣᚷᚷᚣᛁᚼᚦᛁᚷᚼᛁᚾᛏᚣᚦ
ᚾᚣᚦᚦᛈᚾᚣᚷᚱᚴᚾᚾᚾᚱᚷᛁᛁ

Pater noster qui es in caelis, sanctificetur nomen tuum, adveniat regnum tuum, fiat voluntas tua sicut in caelo et in terra. Panem nostrum cotidianum da nobis hodie et dimitte nobis debita nostra sicut et nos dimittimus debitoribus nostris, et ne nos inducas in temptationem, sed libera nos a malo, amen. Johannes, Mattheus, Mattheus, Marcus, Lucas.

'Our Father who art in heaven, hallowed be thy name, thy kingdom come, thy will be done on earth as it is in heaven. Give us this day our daily bread and forgive us our trespasses, as we forgive those who trespass against us, and lead us not into temptation but deliver us from evil, amen. John, Matthew, Mark, Luke.'

Usually, however, it is not the entire prayer, but a part of it which is scratched onto runic amulets. Parts thereof are found on a couple of Bergen rune-sticks, once with a list of Norse names, presumably of those who were seeking protection. A highly abbreviated version of the *Lord's Prayer* seems to occur on a four-teenth-century leather knife-sheath from Örebro, Sweden, with only the words *Maria, Pater, Pater*, i.e. 'Mary, (Our) Father, (Our) Father'. A late-twelfth-century rune-stick amulet from Trondheim has the beginning of the *Lord's Prayer* along with the first part of the futhark row and the Norse message *Svein Auðunsonar reist rúnar þessar*, 'Svein Audun's son carved these runes.' Another pierced wooden amulet, from Lom church, Norway, has a powerfully devout combination, opening with the *Lord's Prayer*, throwing in some apostles' names and ending with a snatch of the *Hail Mary*. It reads: *Pater noster qui es in caelis. Mattheus, Marcus, Lucas. Ave Maria gratia!*, i.e. 'Our Father who art in heaven. Matthew, Mark, Luke. Hail Mary (full) of grace!'[16]

Parts of the *Hail Mary* appear everywhere in Scandinavia, carved into church walls, on grave stones, on church bells, censers, baptismal fonts, door rings and other church furnishings, the Marian cult being no less popular in Scandinavia than it still is today in other parts of the Christian world. The prayer is a regular ingredient in magic formulas and also appears on several Swedish, Norwegian, Danish and Greenlandic amulets, including wooden rune-sticks, at least some of which were probably used as rosaries (and also, as with the *Lord's Prayer*, are

---

[16] The Ulstad plate is *NIyR* no. 53. McKinnell and Simek, p. 181, note that versions of the *Lord's Prayer* have been found on at least eight lead crosses to date. Parts of the *Lord's Prayer* are found on a few rune-sticks (*NIyR* nos 615–16 and 816), a Swedish knife-sheath (Gustavson and Snædal Brink, 'Runfynd 1978', pp. 235–38; the reading as an abbreviated prayer rather than the names Mary and Peter seems the most likely) and the Lom amulet (Liestøl, 'Runeinnskriftene frå "Mindets tomt"'); cf. also the Osen cross from the previous chapter and *NIyR* VI, pp. 41–43 and 235–36.

sometimes augmented by personal names or longer messages), as well as bases of wooden tankards or bowls, a wooden skewer, a textile implement, probably for winding yarn, a bronze Norwegian ring and some Danish knife-hafts too. A thirteenth-century Danish sword pommel even doubles up by having the opening words of the prayer in runes as well as Roman letters. Sometimes the prayer is condensed to a simple *Ave!* 'Hail!' Many of these inscribed items are food vessels, objects onto which magical words and symbols (including the cross and the pentagram) are frequently cut; compare the *sator* goblets or *fuð/fuþark* tankards and skewers of previous chapters. Such protective magic was presumably thought to prevent the food or drink each contained from being tainted by evil powers or as a form of blessing.[17]

Even more common is the simple invocation *Maria* 'Mary' inscribed on church walls, gravestones and a variety of church furnishings, but also regularly on secular items, often occurring at the bottom of wooden vessels and on spindle-whorls, once even in company with the futhark row. The name Mary (which was not yet a truly secular name, but referred almost exclusively to biblical figures or to Scandinavian royalty) often occurs with litanies of other holy names on rune-sticks.[18] Several Greenlandic wooden cross inscriptions also invoke the Virgin, either by simply writing her name, or in the context of a longer inscription, often no more than a rigmarole of holy names or words.

A fragmentary Bergen rune-stick from shortly after the year 1248 has an invocation of the Virgin, rendering a rather botched version of the *Anthem of the Blessed Virgin*, also known as the *Five Gaude antiphon*:

+ᚠᛁᚾᛏᛁ:ᛚᛁᚼ:ᚱᛁᚼᛁᚱ·ᛁᚾᛁᚱᛣᛅᛁᚼ·ᛣᛅᚱᚾᚱᛏᛏᚼ·ᚠᛁᚾᛏᛁ
ᚱ. . .
ᚠᛁᚾᛏᛁ:ᚠᚾᛁ:ᚠᛁᚼᚾᛁᛁᛁᛁ:ᚼᛏᚱᚼᛁ:ᚱᚾᛣᛁᚼ-
ᚱᚱ-ᚱ. . .

With some correction this reads: *Gaude, Dei genetrix, virgo immaculata. Gaude q[uae]* . . . *Gaude, quae genuisti aeterni lumi[nis] cl[a]r[itatem]*. . ., 'Rejoice, mother of God, immaculate virgin! Rejoice, thou who . . . Rejoice, thou who created clarity from eternal light!' The author of this amulet, ignorant of the finer aspects of Latin, does not seem to have recorded the text for liturgical purposes. It was perhaps an amulet or incantation for childbirth, as is suggested not only by the words of the anthem, but also by a Bohemian spell which opens with 'Rejoice mother of God!' and continues with the childbirth charm discussed in chapter 6. The inscription in its entire state was presumably meant to record:

---

17 The rune-sticks include *NIyR* nos 135, 617, 618, 619, 620, N A63, N A72, N B611 and N B623; wooden food vessels and skewer include *NIyR* nos 621–24 and N B3, and for the yarn-winder see E. Svärdström and H. Gustavson, 'Runfynd 1972', *Fornvännen* 68 (1973), 185–203. The ring is *NIyR* no. 27 and on the knife-hafts see Moltke, *Runes and their Origin*, p. 468 and Stoklund and Düwel, 'Runeninschriften aus Schleswiger Grabungen', pp. 157–59. The pommel is *DR* no. 50; cf. also further, a church bell and a door ring, *NIyR* nos 142 and 347.

18 These include U UR4.4, *NIyR* no. 626, N B362 and N B422; cf. Stoklund and Düwel, 'Runeninschriften aus Schleswiger Grabungen', pp. 161 and 162 and Bæksted, *Islands Runeindskrifter*, pp. 207–8.

Gaude, Dei genetrix, virgo immaculata!
Gaude, quae gaudium ab angelo suscepisti!
Gaude, quae genuisti aeterni luminis claritatem!
Gaude, mater!
Gaude, sancta Dei genetrix virgo!

'Rejoice, mother of God, immaculate virgin!
Rejoice, thou who received the tidings of joy from the angel!
Rejoice, thou who brought forth the clarity of light eternal!
Rejoice, mother!
Rejoice, holy virgin, mother of God!'

The *Anthem*, of eighth century date, became popular at the beginning of the eleventh century and was used both in private and official Church liturgy. Although known from hundreds of twelfth and thirteenth-century manuscripts, it had not been found in medieval Norway prior to the discovery of this rune-stick.[19]

Further Christian inscriptions contain recognisable quotations, including fragments of the Psalms. Psalters, i.e. compilations of the Psalms, were often used as prayer books, and medieval magical spells and ritual incantations frequently employed Psalms, in Latin as well as the vernacular, and these were sometimes expressly directed to be written down rather than chanted or sung.

It is hardly surprising, then, to encounter a runic Psalm decorating a midtwelfth-century church bell from Gjerpen, Norway. Along with a text in Roman letters (*Sanctus Petrus Apostolus bleci os*, 'May St Peter the Apostle bless us') is a runic rendition of a section of Psalm 118:

✠ ⟨runic inscription⟩

Dextera Domini fecit virtutem, dextera Domini exaltavit me, dextera . . .

'The right hand of the Lord did valiantly, the right hand of the Lord raised me up, the right hand. . .'

More baffling is the purpose of a fish-shaped wooden amulet from Umîviarssuk, Greenland, which contains a rather botched version of part of Psalm 119:

⟨runic inscription⟩
⟨runic inscription⟩

Maria. Memor esto verbi tui s(er)vo tuo, in quo mihi s(pe)m (dedisti).

'Mary. Remember thy words to thy servant, through which thou (gave) me hope.'

Different verses of this Psalm are found in the *Galdrabók* in various spells for help in legal matters. The Greenland fish-amulet also has the name Mary and ten notches, which suggests it was a prayer counter. Another Greenlandic rune-stick, from the Western Settlement, reads:

⟨runic inscription⟩

---

[19] *NIyR* no. 629.

Fig. 15. Umîviarssuk amulet

Fledin (?) tudo (?) unus Deus meus omnis Patris et (in) caelo et in terram nominatur(?)

'. . . he is called my one God of all lands in heaven and on earth.'

The wooden handle of a stylus, dated to the end of the twelfth century and found in the urban centre of Swedish Lödöse, bears a verse from Psalm 51 which still forms part of the confession liturgy:

ᛏᛁᛒᛁᛋᛟᛚᛁᛒᛆᚴᚴᛁᚿᛁᛆ�473ᛁᚠᚤᛁᚴᛆᛁᛧᛁᚠᛁᛆᛁᚿᛒᛁᚿᛏᛁᚠᛁ. . .
ᛁᛁᚱᛁᛒᚿᛁ�213ᚿᛁᛆ�b381ᚠᛁᛆᚤᛁᚿᛏᛁᛧᛆᚱᛁᛁ

Tibi soli peccavi et malum coram te feci, ut iustifi[ceris in] sermonibus tuis et vincas cum iudicaris.

'Against thee, thee only, have I sinned, and done this evil in thy sight; that thou mightest be justified when thou speakest and be clear when thou judgest.'

Yet another Psalm is found on the twelfth-century rune-stick discussed in chapter 3, a notched wooded component of unspecified purpose, pierced at one end, which contains the beginning of Psalm 110:

ᛁᛁᛆᛁᛁᛁᛆᛁᛁᛁᛁᛁᚠᛁᛁᛁᛁᚦᛆᚽᛁᚱᛆᚠᛆᛁ
ᛏᛁᛈᛁᛁᛁᛁᚴᛁᚤᛁᛂᛁᛁᛁᛁᚤᛁᛆᛁᛁᛁᚽᛁᛁᛏᛁᛪᛁᛁᚱᛁᛁᛁᚤᛁᛆᛁ

sisesisisesilsisi . . .
Dixit Dominus Domino (meo), sede a dextris meis.

'*sisesisisesilsisi* . . . The Lord said unto (my) Lord, sittest thou at my right hand.'

The section from the well-known Psalm occurring in the second line of this text is found in several medieval masses, and was the opening Vespers Psalm on Sundays. The first line ends with a six-armed hooked star, perhaps a form of Christogram and in any case presumably intended as a holy symbol of some sort (a comparable eight-armed cross is found amidst other magical symbols on one of the Bergen rune-sticks discussed in chapter 6 containing a runic monogram of ᚼ, ᚦ, ᚱ). In this runic charm the star is preceded by an apparently pagan expression reminiscent of the see-see charms, and in fact another one of the see-see charms appears in an apparently pagan-Christian mixture on a square stick from Bergen first mentioned at the end of chapter 3. This inscription begins with an almost direct quotation from the Norse translation of the Latin *Passion of St Andrew the Apostle*. It reads:

Heilagr Andreas postoli fór and at boða orð Guðs, ok gerði han mar[gar] jartegnir í nafni dróttins . . . Sé, sé, Sessi. Sé konu væna. Sé þú hvar sittir.

'The holy apostle Andrew journeyed (throughout Greece) to preach the word of God, and he performed many miracles in the name of the Lord . . . See, see, Sessi. See the beautiful woman. See where she sits.'[20]

More inscriptions repeat snatches from various sections of the liturgy. Prayer fragments from *Commune plurimorum martyrum* (*The Common of Martyrs*), for instance, are carved into part of the choir of Hopperstad stave church, Norway:

. . . ᛣᛁᛉ1ᛁᚱᛁᛒᛆ⁚ᠮ1ᛁᛣᛁᛐᛁ·ᛁᚼᠾᠮᚿ1.ᛁᚾ1ᛁ·ᛣᛁᚱ1ᛒᛁᚿ1ᛁ. . .

. . . *[Gaudeat] martyribus. Letamini exultent iusti mirabilis . . .*

'. . . May he rejoice with the martyrs. The righteous exult with wonders . . .'

Also apparently borrowed from the liturgy is a short sequence on a pierced wooden handle from Trondheim which appears to have served as an owner marking for wares. The runes, which seem to be based on the liturgical expression *miserere mei Deus!*, 'take pity on me, God!' read: *Þórir á. Miserere mín!*, 'Thorir owns. Take pity on me!' This blend of Latin and Norse has been compared with another Norwegian owner inscription, this time from Bergen, also with a bilingual religious addition, reading: *Ari á. Sancti Ólafr . . .*, 'Ari owns. St Olaf . . .' Both of these owner inscriptions are perhaps augmented by religious pleas in order to guarantee protection for the goods they once marked during their transportation.[21]

A quotation from the Psaltery is coupled with a sacramental blessing of a dwelling in a rune-inscribed *Benedictio mansionis* (*House blessing*), appearing on a squarish lead roll from Kävlinge, Sweden. One side of the roll bears a carving of the standard Christian representation known as the *Majestas Domini*: Christ seated on a cushioned bench holding up his right hand with three raised fingers, to his left the jewel-encrusted Book of Life. On the opposite face, inscribed with a sharp tool, is a long runic text (in imperfect Latin) which seems to read:

⨳ᛒ1ᛰᛒ11ᚱᚼᚠ� runic inscription lines

20 The bell is *NIyR* no. 143; on the fish amulet see *NIyR* VI, pp. 45–46. The stylus is described in Svärdström, *Runfynden i Gamla Lödöse*, pp. 30–33. The rune-sticks are *NIyR* no. 628 and N B524.

21 *NIyR* nos 405, 614 and 802.

ᛏᛁᛉᚼᛁᛒᛉᛋᛏᛐᚿᛋᚠᛒᛦᛏᛏᚿᛁᛒᛏᛏᚿᛦᛐᛦ
ᛒᛋᛦᛈᛁᛒᛋᛋᛁᚱᛏᛞᛐᛞᛐᛏᛦᛦᛁᛋᛏᛏᚿᛋᛒᛐ
ᛏᛏᚱᛐᛦᛒᛒᛐ:ᛒᚿᛈᛐᛦᛐᛋᛐᚿᛋᛋᚠᛒᛦᛐ
ᛦᚿᚿᛋᛋᛐᚿᛏᛦᛐᛈᛏᛋ. . . .ᛒᚿᚱᛈᛏᛉᛐᛋᛋ
ᛒᛏᚱᚿᛒᛉᛦᛈᛐᚱᚿᛦᛐᚿᛦᛐᛒᚿᛁᚱᛐᚿᛏᛋᛒᛁ
ᚱᛁᛋᚿᛋᛐᛉᛉᛐᛁᛒᛒᛐᛏᛁᛉᚠᛒᛒᚱᛐᛏᛒᛐᚿᛐ
ᛐᛒᛐᛦᛋᛋᛋᛐᛒᛉᚿᚱᛁᛒᛐᚿᛋᛒᚿᛈᛒᛐᛦ
ᛈᚿᛏᛁᛈᛐᛒᛐᚿᚱᛐᛦᛒᛒᛏᛒᛋᛐᛉ
ᛉᛁᛋᚠᛒᛏᛒᛐᛁᛉᛁᛒᛒᛒᚱᛁᛋᚠᛒᛐᛁᛁᛁᚠᛒᛉᛒᛁ
ᚱᛁᛐᛋᛋᛐᛉᛉᛁᛐᛁᛉᛋᛒᛒᚠᛒᛐᚿᛒᛏᚱᛐᛒᛉ
ᛉᚿᚱᛁᛐᛦᚠᛒᛐᛦᛒᛦᛒᛒᛁᛐᛒᛐᛒᛋᛒᛏᛏᛒ
ᛐᛦᛏᛒ⊠

Pax Patris et Filii Christi crucifixi et Spiritus sancti sit p(erpetuo?) super omnes habitantes et manentes in hoc loco et defensio crucis Christi(?) Christus contra omnes adversiones immundi spiritus iniusti(?). . . Amen. Benedicat nos Deus, Deus noster. Benedicat nos Deus et metuant eum omnes fines terrae. T. Domine Deus, Pater omnipotens famulos tuos et famulas tuae maiestatis(?) purgatos(?) per unicum filium tuum in virtute Spiritus sancti benedice et protege ut ab omnibus(?) securi in tua iugiter laude laetentur. Amen. Benedictio et defensio Patris et Filii et Spiritus sancti dicenda et super hanc curiam et omnes habitantes in ea. Amen.

'May the peace of the Father and the Son, the crucified Christ, and the Holy Spirit be perpetually over all those who live and frequent this place, and the protection of the cross of Christ. Christ against all the enemy powers of the unjust spirit . . . Amen. May God bless us, our God. May God bless us and may all on earth fear him . . . Lord God, omnipotent Father, thy manservants and the maidservants of thy majesty . . . cleansed from sins through thy only son in the power of the Holy Spirit, bless and protect (them) so that they safely into thy. . . from all . . . continually in praise may rejoice. Amen. May the blessing and protection of the Son and the Holy Spirit be poured over this home and all who live therein. Amen.'

This text features a quotation from Psalm 67 ('God shall bless us; and all the ends of the earth shall fear him') and emphasises the peace and power of the Holy Trinity, entreating for the household inhabitants the blessing of the Father, Son and Holy Spirit.[22]

In fact many runic amulets invoke the triune God. An early example is the Bornholm amulet, its runes minutely inscribed on both sides of an Arabic silver coin (which itself dates from between the years 907–913):

ᛏᛒᛏᛋᚿᛋᚿᛋᛦᚱᛁᛋᛏᚿᛐᚪᛁᛐᚿᛁᛋᛏᛁᚠᛁᚠᛁᛁᛏᛉᛦᛁᛏᛏᛒ
ᛏᛏᚱᛁᛋᛏᚦᛈᛁᛐ
ᛁᚿᛋᛁᛐᛋ
ᛏᛞᛋᛒᛁᚱᛁᛏᚿᛋ
ᚠᚱᛁᛋᛏᚿᛋᛒᛁ

---

22 H. Gustavson, 'Verksamheten vid Runverket i Stockholm', *Nytt om runer* 14 (1999), 20–23. He suggests that the cross-surrounded *t* might be read as the prayer opening *te igitur* 'thou therefore'. McKinnell and Simek, p. 183, point out that, as in other liturgical blessings, the myriad small crosses denote pauses where the priest or officiator crossed himself or made the sign of the cross.

ᛒᛁᚾᚴᛏ
ᚠᚾᛁᚼᚱᛁᚠᛁᚦ
ᚱᛁᛏᛦ
ᛏᛁᚱᚠᛏ
ᛦᚠᚾᚼᛏᛪᛏᛏᚦᛁᚴ

(Je)Jesus(us) Christus filius Dei vivi. In nomine Patris et Filii(usia) et Spiritus.
Christus (pi)pius sanguis vivit, vitam aeternam custodiat is.

'Jesus Christ, son of the living God. In the name of the Father, the Son . . . and
the Spirit. Christ . . . the gracious blood is living, may it preserve eternal life.'

Here are reproduced (imperfectly) the words of Simon Peter to Jesus in the
Gospel of Matthew: *Tu es Christus, filius Dei vivi*, 'Thou art Christ, son of the
living God.' The words on the reverse are those of the priest as he receives the
chalice at mass: *Sanguis Domini nostri Jesu Christi custodiat animam meam in
vitam aeternam*, 'May the blood of our Lord Jesus Christ preserve my soul to life
everlasting.' (The words also recall those of the end of the Odense lead-plate
considered earlier: 'may the blood of Christ bless me'.) The small size of the
runes on the Bornholm coin (which has a diameter of only 2.5cm) and the glosso-
lalia-like syllable repetition and lack of regard for textual clarity suggest that the
inscription was intended for the supernatural rather than the human eye.[23]

The *In nomine Patris* formula, familiar from Catholic ritual, is also found, in
more abbreviated form, on a steelyard handle from Ribe, Denmark, which reads
simply *In nomine Patris et Filii et Spiri[tus sancti]*, 'In the name of the Father, the
Son and the [Holy] Spirit'. A perforated rune-stick from Årdal church, Norway,
similarly gives what is presumably the name of its owner, Gudrid, followed by a
pious prayer: *Guðríðr. In nomine Patris et Filii et Spiritus sancti, amen. Dominus
Jesus Christus, amen*, 'Gudrid. In the name of the Father and the Son and the Holy
Spirit, amen. Lord Jesus Christ, amen'. This is paralleled in part by a fragment of
a Swedish lead amulet which reads: *[Spirit]us sanctu[s] [A]lpha et O(mega). . .*,
i.e. 'Holy Spirit. Alpha and O(mega)'. An even more fragmentary form of *In
nomine Patris* may be found on a late-fifteenth-century perforated lead plate from
the cathedral at Trondheim: *Ame[n], [n]omin[e]*, 'Amen, (in) the name.' A
section of a fourteenth-century wooden cross from Bergen bears an incomplete
text which reads: *Rex Judaeorum. In nomine Patris. Nazarenus*, 'King of the
Jews. In the name of the Father. Nazareth'. *Jesus* and *et Filii et Spiritus sancti,
amen* would presumably have been inscribed on the missing vertical arm. After
all, invocation of the Trinity was prevalent in magic and folk-healing throughout
most of Europe through most of the medieval period.[24]

Further recognisable liturgical quotations occur in other Scandinavian amulet

---

[23] The Bornholm amulet (*DR* no. 410) is described by Moltke, *Runes and their Origin*, pp. 361–64
and Stoklund, 'Bornholmske Runeamuletter', pp. 855–63.

[24] The Ribe handle is described in Moltke, *Runes and their Origin*, p. 474, the rune-stick is *NIyR* no.
345, the Swedish amulet is described in H. Gustavson, 'Verksamheten vid Runverket i Stockholm', *Nytt om runer* 9 (1994), 26 and the lead plate is *NIyR* no. 507, although its runic nature is
disputed by Knirk, 'Runic inscriptions containing Latin', p. 498. The Bergen cross is *NIyR* no.
630.

texts. The words *Agnus Dei*, 'Lamb of God', appear in only one inscription, a fragment of a gravestone from Vamdrup, Denmark, and the Greek *Kyrie eleison!* 'Lord have mercy!' is only certainly attested in one runic inscription, a late-thirteenth-century Bergen rune-stick, apparently shaped so that a cord could be tied around one end: *Kyrie eleison! Christe eleison!* 'Lord have mercy! Christ have mercy!' (although in non-runic contexts the petition is also found on a lead strip from Hallingdal). Another well-known expression, *Gloria in excelsis Deo!*, 'Glory to God in the highest!', sung repeatedly during the celebration of the mass, is inscribed on a thin wood-piece from Bergen with traces of decoration dated to the late twelfth century, and might be compared with the runic *Gloria!* cut into the walls of Hopperstad church, Norway.[25]

A rune-inscribed Swedish find with the *Commendatio animae (Recommendatio of a Soul Departing)*, a prayer for the soul of the deceased in the Roman funeral rite, alludes to the fate of the three young men, Shadrach, Meschach and Abdenego, who were spared from the flames of Nebuchadnezzar:

ᚦᚢᛘᛁᚼᛁᚠᛁᚼᛁᚾ... ᛁᛒᛁᚱᚦᛁᚼᛁᚼᛁᚠᛁᛒ... ᚱᛁᛒᛁᚱᚦᛁᚼᚦᛁᛁᚦᛁᚼ... ᚦᛁᚠᚦᚢᛁᚼᚦᛁᚦᛁᚼᛁᚼ·ᚼ-...

Domine Jesu [Christe, l]ibera de ignib[us sicut] liberasti tres [pueros] de camino ignis . . .

'Lord Jesus Christ, deliver (our souls) from the flames, as thou delivered the three [boys] from the fiery furnace . . .'

This prayer is the seventh from twelve which all begin with *Libera animam servi tui, sicut liberasti*, 'Deliver the soul of thy servant as thou delivered . . .', followed by the names of biblical or apocryphal figures. This fragmentary thirteenth-century lead cross from Lödöse, presumably a grave amulet, invites comparison with the Norwegian inscriptions which feature the names of the young men who were saved from the flames (discussed in chapter 6). Another lead cross, from fourteenth-century Gotland, Sweden, invokes the women who followed Jesus from Galilee to Jerusalem and attended his tomb, as well as probably St Catherine of Alexandria, the patron saint of a nearby Franciscan convent. It reads: *Intersede pro nobis semper et sancta Maria, mater Jacobi apostuli, et sancta Maria Magdalena et Salome et sancta Caeri!*, i.e. 'Intercede for us always, and holy Mary, mother of Jacob the apostle, and St Mary Magdalene and Salome and St C. . .!'[26]

Inscribed crosses of this type often feature texts warding off demonic powers in the manner of a famous scene from the *Life of St Anthony the Hermit*. A lead cross from Madla church cemetery, Norway, for instance, even has a text reminiscent of the Danish Seven Sisters charm considered in the chapter on leechcraft, containing, as it does, the *Ecce crucem Domini! (Behold the Cross of the Lord!)*.

---

25 The gravestone is *DR* no. 27, the *Kyrie eleison* rune-stick is *NIyR* no. 627 (although the words may appear also in rather botched form on the Ål lead plate discussed earlier) and the *Gloria in excelsis Deo* wood-piece is N B601 (cf. *NIyR* no. 399 'Gloria' in Hopperstad church).

26 The Lödöse cross is described by Svärdström, *Runfynden i Gamla Lödöse*, pp. 28–30; the Visby cross is described in H. Gustavson, 'Christus regnat, Christus vincit, Christus imperat', in L. Karlsson et al. (eds), *Den ljusa medeltiden* (Stockhom 1984), pp. 61–76.

This prayer, otherwise known as the motto of St Anthony, enjoyed widespread popularity during the Middle Ages and was often used in exorcisms as well as a form of mental or physical protection against the Devil (indeed, some Catholics today continue to wear or carry a copy). The Norwegian lead cross dates from the late thirteenth or early fourteenth century and also features an inscribed figure of Christ on one side. Its text, in a rather baffling arrangement around the cross-limbs, reads:

```
+ᛏᛁᛁᛏ ᚱᚱᚾᚼᛏᛦ
ᛏᚼᛦᛁᚼ ᚠᚾᚱᛁᛏᛏ
ᚲᚭᚱᛏᛏᛁ ᛏᛁᚾᚠᚱᛁᛏ:ᚾᛁ
ᚼᛁᛏ ᚠᛏᛁ:ᛏᛏᚱᛁᛒᚾᛁᚾᛏᛏ ᚱᛏᛁᛁᚱᛁ ᛏᛏᚾᛁᛏ
ᚠᚾᛏᛏᚾᚭᚱ ᚠᚱᛏᛁᛏ:ᛁᛁ ᚲᛏᛁᛏᛁᛏ
ᚾᛦ:ᚱᚾᛏ ᚠᛏᛁ. . .
-ᛁᛏᚱᛏᛁ
ᛁᛏ. ᛁᛁᚾᛁ.ᚱᚱᛁᛁᛏᚾᛁ
ᛦᛏᚱᛁᚠᚾᛁ
ᛦᛏᚦᛏᚾᛁ
ᚠᚾᚱᛏᛁ ᛁᛏᛝ
--ᛝᛏᛁᛏᛏᛁ
ᛏᛏᚱᛏᚠᚱ
ᛏᛦᛏᛏᛏᛁᛁᛏ
ᚲᛝᛏᛏᛏᛏ:
```

Ecce crucem Domini! Fugite partes adversae! Vicit leo de tribu Juda, radix David. Quatuor gramis in pectalon quod fron[te tuli]t Aaron. Jesus Christus, Marcus, Mattheus, Lucas, Johannes, Tetragrammaton, Alpha et O(mega).

'Behold the cross of the Lord! Begone, ye enemy powers! The lion of the tribe of Judah, the root of David, has conquered. Four letters in the *pectalon* which Aaron wore on his forehead. Jesus Christ, Mark, Matthew, Luke, John, *Tetragrammaton*, Alpha and O(mega).'

The stirring *Ecce crucem* antiphon also appears in Roman miniscules on another lead cross from nearby Gruda and the first words follow *faifaofau* on the cruciform wooden runic amulet from Bergen (see chapter 6). The 'lion of the tribe of Judah' and 'the root of David' are messianic titles given to Christ, a descendant via the line of King David of Judah, the fourth-born son of Jacob (Israel) whose descendants make up the twelve tribes of Israel.

Following this expression on the Madla cross are two slightly corrupt verses from the early medieval hymn *Deus Pater piisime* (i.e. *Nomenque anecfenethon / quod fronte tulit Aaron, / sculptumque tetramathon, / quatuor gramis in pectalon*). The Book of Exodus describes the plate of gold engraved with 'Holy to the Lord' borne by Aaron on his forehead as a mark of the guilt involved in the sacred gifts consecrated by the Israelites. A recently found lead cross from a burial mound at Sande in Norway has an almost identical text:

```
+ᛏᛁᛁᛏ ᚱᚱᚾᛁᛦᛏᛏᛦᛁ
ᛁ:ᚠᚾᚠᛁᛏᚲᚭᚱᛏᛏᛁ
ᛏᛏᚾᛏᚱᛁᛏᛁᛁᛁᛏᛏᛏ
ᛏᛏᚱᛁᛒᚾᛁᚾᛏ. . .
```

ᚠᚢᛂᛏᛗᛅᚱ ᚠᚱᛅᛖ ᛁᛁᚴᛏᛁ
ᛂᛁᚠᚢᛤᛁᚠ
ᛈᛅᛖᛁᛏᛗᛁᛁᛏ:
ᛂᛁᚱᛅ ᚴ:ᛁᛂᛁᚢᛁ+
-ᛏᛪᛁᛁᛁᛁᛁ
ᛃᛅᚱᚠᚢᛁ
ᛃᛅᚦᛏᚢᛁ
ᚠᛄᚴᛏᛁ
-ᛅᛈᛖᛂ ᛂᚴ
ᚴᛪᛅ ᛁᛂ
ᛂ + -:

Ecce crucem Domini! Fugite partes adversæ! Vicit leo de tribu Juda, [radix David.] Quatuor gramis in pectalon, (quod), fronte tulit Aaron. Jesus. Johannes, Marcus, Mattheus, Lucas, AGLA, Alpha et O(mega).

'Behold the cross of the Lord! Begone, ye enemy powers! The lion of the tribe of Judah, [the root of David,] has conquered. (There are) four letters in the *pectalon*, (which) Aaron wore on his forehead. Jesus, John, Mark, Matthew, Luke, *AGLA*, Alpha and O(mega).'

The inscriptions on the two crosses are then completed with names of the four evangelists, the Cabalistic acronym *AGLA* (or *Tetragrammaton* on the Madla cross) and Revelation's symbol for God.[27]

The Seven Sisters amulet also contained a further liturgical quotation: the Gallo-Frankish *Laudes* or 'Christ conquers, Christ reigns, Christ commands, Christ delivers' litany which is frequently encountered in ecclesiastical exorcisms as well as in blessings and protective invocations. Artistically it occurs on numerous medieval objects of devotion and it is also recurrent in magical formulas and amulets found throughout Western Europe, both to protect against sickness and (as the so-called German *Wettersegen* or 'weather blessing') to ward off or expel diverse evils such as thunderstorms and drought. The motto even appears on the title page of a French book of black magic. A jubilant acclamation invoking the conquering Christian god, the *Laudes* litany is found on two Danish sickness amulets discussed in chapter 6 and it also recurs on a somewhat earlier runic amulet of copper from Boge, Gotland:

+ᛁᛂᛪᛃᛁᛂᛁᛏᛪᛃᛁᛂᛁᛂᛂᛂᛏᚱᛁᛂᛂᚢᚠᚱ-
+ᛂᛏᛁ+ᚠᚢᚦᚱᛪᛪ+ᛏᛪᛃᛁᛂᛁᛒᛂᛏᚱᛁᛂ+
ᛁᛒᛃᛁᚠᛁ+ᚠᚢᛒᚱᛪᛪ-ᛒᛁᚱᛁᛏᚢᛂ
+ᛂᛂᚠᛃᛏᛁᚠᚢᚦᚱᛪᛪ+ᛏᛃᛁᛂ+ᚠᚱᚢᚠᛂ
+ᛏᛁᛒᛂᛏᛂᚱ+ᚠᚱᚢᚠᛂᛏᛁ ᚠᛁᚠᛁᚢᛂ+
+ᚠᚱᚢᚠᛂᛏᛁᛂᛒᛁᚱᛁᛏᚢᛂ+
+ᛂᛂᚠᚱᛏᛁ+ᚠᚢᚦᚱᛪᛪ+ᛏᛃᛁᛏ+
+ᚠᚱᛁᛂᛏᚢᛂᚱᛁᛪᛁᛂᚦ+ᚠᚱᛁᛂᛏᚢ+
+ᛂᛂ+ᚠᚢᚦᚱᛪᛪ+ᛈᛁᛂᛂᛁᚦ+ᚠᚱᛁᛂᛏᚢᛂ+
+ᛁᛃᛒᛁᚱᛂᚦ+ᛏᛃᛁᛂ+

---

27 The traditional reading of the Madla cross (*NIyR* no. 248) must be reviewed in light of the similar cross recently found in Sande presented by K.J. Nordby, 'Arbeidet ved Runearkivet, Oslo', *Nytt om runer* 16 (2001), 13–18.

In nomine Domini nostri Jesu Christi, Guðlaug, Domini Patris et Filii, Guðlaug, Spiritus sancti, Guðlaug, amen. Crux (Chris)ti Pater, crux (Chris)ti Filius, crux (Chris)ti Spiritus sancti, Guðlaug, amen. Christus regnat, Christus, Guðlaug, vincit, Christus imperat, amen.

'In the name of our Lord Jesus Christ, Gudlaug, of our Lord the Father and Son, Gudlaug, of the Holy Spirit, Gudlaug, amen. Cross of Christ the Father, cross of Christ the Son, cross of Christ, the Holy Spirit, Gudlaug, amen. Christ reigns, Christ, Gudlaug, conquers, Christ commands, amen.'

The repeated expression *crux Christi*, 'cross of Christ' is abbreviated each time in a manner similar to modern Xmas for Christmas, i.e. simply as *crux -ti*. It does seem, then, that repetition, as so often encountered in the *lorica* formulas, remained important in liturgical magic as well; thus conceivably the invocation of 'Father, Son and Holy Spirit' rather than the simple 'Trinity', as well perhaps as the threefold 'Cross of Christ', the tri-verbal 'Christ reigns, conquers, commands' and even the triple naming of Gudlaug here. The *Laudes* formula and a repeated formula of the cross also recur on a Danish lead roll from Selsø: *AGLA LAGA GALA . . . crux Lucas, crux Marcus, [crux] Johannes, [crux Mattheus] . . . artan . . . artan Christus. Christus regnat, Christus imperat, Christus . . . benedi(cat),* 'AGLA LAGA GALA . . . cross Luke, cross Mark, [cross] John, [cross Matthew,] . . . *arretôn* (?) 2 . . . Christ. Christ reigns, Christ commands, Christ . . . blesses'. The cross is also invoked on an unusual four-sided lead wand from Roskilde, Denmark, presumably belonging to the named Christina: *Crux Christi crux . . . crux Johannes crux. Crux Lucas, crux Ma[theus?] . . . Christina*. Reference to the cross is further found on a fragment of rib-bone from Sigtuna, Sweden: *Crux Marcus, crux Lucas, crux Ma[theus, crux Joh]annes, crux Maria, mater Domini*, as well as in a Swedish rune-stick's list of holy names: *Maria, Mathie, Marce(?), filii(?) Bene(dicti), Maria, Maria Magdalena, Jacop, Olafʀ, Laurencius, Maria, Bartholomei Egidii, Maria, kross Mathei, Mikael*, 'Mary, Matthew, Mark, sons of Benedict, Mary, Mary Magdalene, Jacob, Olaf, Lawrence, Mary, of Bartholomew of Aegidius, Mary, cross of Matthew, Michael'.[28]

A further liturgical text is found on a rather damaged copper amulet found in a grave at Vassunda, Sweden: *Pater custodiat te, Jesus Christus benedicat te, Borg. . .,* 'The Father guards you, Jesus Christ blesses you, Borg. . .'. Although many Scandinavians could probably parrot snatches of Latin liturgical text, a proper knowledge of the language of the Church would have been largely restricted to members of the clergy and the educated elite, and most of the Latin texts discussed so far appear to be quotations rather than original compositions. For the laity, Latin belonged to the mystical rituals (and hocus pocus) of the

---

[28] Gustavson, 'Christus regnat', pp. 61–64. On devotional, apotropaic and other magical uses of the widespread motto *Christus vincit, Christus regnat, Christus imperat* see E. Kantorowicz, *Laudes Regiae* (Berkeley 1958), pp. 1–13; some Scandinavian examples are provided in Gustavson, 'Christus regnat'. Details of the Selsø lead strip can be found in Düwel, 'Mittelalterliche Amulette', pp. 264–65 and the Roskilde lead wand is described by M. Stoklund, 'Runer', *Arkæologiske udgravninger i Danmark* (2001), 252–60. The Swedish rib-bone is H. Gustavson et al., 'Runfynd 1988', *Fornvännen* 85 (1990), 23–42; the Nyköping rune-stick E. Svärdström, *Nyköpingsstaven och de medeltida kalenderrunorna* (Stockholm 1966), p. 8.

Church. The high status of Latin is indirectly attested not only by the frequent appearance of Latin or pseudo-Latin in magical formulas, but also by the mid-fifteenth-century observation in the Swedish work of religious edification *Själens tröst* (*Comfort of the Soul*) that Latin prayers were regarded as more effective than those in the vernacular. An irregularly shaped rune-stick from Bergen, dated to about the year 1200, seems to be a prayer of some sort: *Honor Deo veniat meo*, 'Let honour come to my God'; and a damaged piece of soapstone from Ipiutaq, Greenland, has the text: ... *ora pro nobis* ... *Rafael*, '... pray for us ... Raphael'. More obscure is the reference on an elaborate thirteenth-century rune-stick from Trondheim: *Jerusalem! Neque concreditur* (or *congreditur*) *in horreum, amen*, 'Jerusalem! Not even in the barn is it contended/entrusted(?), amen.' Still other pious inscriptions are encountered which, although in the Latin of the Church, seem to contain more personal blessings or supplications. A damaged thirteenth-century rune-stick from Bergen reads: ... *Panto(crator?)* ... *amen ... Nicholas(?) ... Valete in Domino!* ..., i.e. 'Almighty. . . amen. . . Nicholas. . . Fare well in the Lord!'[29]

The majority of personal benedictory inscriptions, however, are rendered in the vernacular. A rather formal prayer appears on a wooden object from late-thirteenth-century Bergen: *Dróttinn um alla fram! Ok þú styrk mik til allra góðra hlut[a]. [Dr]óttinn Jesus Kristr, sá er bæði er guð ok maðr, heyr ákall mitt ... þik ok biðja mér miskunnar viðr þik ok Maríu, móður*, 'Lord above all! And thou strengthenest me for every good lot. Lord Jesus Christ, who is both God and man, hear my invocation ... thee and pray for mercy for me from thee and Mary, (thy) mother.' Another example is found on a late-thirteenth-century rune-stick from Bergen: *Guð, er alt má, blessi Sigurð prest, er mik á*, 'May God, who presides over all, bless Sigurd the priest, who owns me.' Another Bergen rune-stick is more direct: *Guð blessi yðr Rannveig*, 'May God bless you, Rannveig.' Yet another inscribed item invoking the protection of a higher power is an eleventh-century walking stick from Schleswig, with the repeated text: *Krist hialpi Sven Harpara ... Krist hialpi Sven Harpara*, i.e. 'May Christ help Sven the Harper' (x 2).[30]

Some amulets are less specific in nominating who is to receive the blessing, and calls on God, his angels and saints to bless or grant the inscriber mercy also stray into direct calls for protection. A more fragmentary benediction occurs on another Bergen rune-stick, the beginning unfortunately unintelligible: ... *á mik, en Guð blessi þik*, '... owns me, and may God bless you'. Somewhat reminiscent of the 'peace to the bearer' formulation (see chapter 6) is the Norse runic inscription on a thirteenth-century wooden amulet from Oslo which reads: *Guð gæti þess er mik berr ok ... þess er þik*, 'May God protect those who carry me and ... those who for you (?)' In a similar vein, one thirteenth-century Swedish ring is expressly designed to confer protection upon its wearer; its runes read: *Blætsa(ð)r sē sā ær mik bær*, 'Blessed be he who bears me.' We have already encountered a

---

29 For the Vassunda amulet see Gustavson, 'Christus regnat', pp. 68–70. The Bergen and Trondheim sticks are *NIyR* nos 609, 641 and 836.

30 N 289, N B403 and N B431. For the Schleswig stick see Moltke, *Runes and their Origin*, p. 480.

number of amuletic runic rings of course and in fact some medieval sources recount that a vein from the ring finger led directly to the heart, which is perhaps one of the reasons why rings were commonly thought to make especially good amulets. A Danish silver-ring bears an incomprehensible runic inscription and a semi-comprehensible Roman-letter inscription which is familiar from other rings as well as charms against sickness, and seems to be a corruption of some formula referring to the Magi. Another Christian amulet ring, made of gold and from Norwegian Bergen, features an inscription predominantly inscribed with Roman letters mixed with some runes; it consists solely of the names of the four evangelists: Matthew, Mark, Luke and John (MⅠTHEVrᴹⅠRCVSLVS---ᐸNNEr).[31]

A more extensive collection of holy names is found on a rune-stick from Bergen, which also employs a number of cryptic runic devices. The inscription begins with a list of names which is followed by a formula seeking protection: *Mikael(?), Pétr, Jóhannes, Andrés, Lafrans, Tomas, Ólafr, Klemet, Nikulás. Allir helgir menn, gæti mín nótt ok dag, lífs míns ok sálu. Guð sé mik ok signi,* 'Michael (?), Peter, John, Andrew, Lawrence, Thomas, Olaf, Clement, Nicholas. May all the holy men protect me by night and day, my life (i.e. body) and soul. May God see me and bless me.' It then turns to cryptic runes, rendering its futhark code in a variety of runic cryptograms which picturesquely indicate the placement of the runes in the three groups of the futhark row by using scales on the body of a fish and (human) bodily appendages, continuing: *Guð gefi oss býr ok gæfu Mariæ . . . hjálpi mér Klemet, hjálpi mér allir Guðs helgir (menn),* 'May God give us a fair wind and may Mary (give us) good luck . . . Help me, Clement, help me, all of God's holy (men).' Cryptic runes are also encountered on a fragment of a cow rib-bone from Sigtuna, Sweden, archaeologically dated to the thirteenth century. The text opens with a somewhat perplexing message: . . . *Jesus, Jesus, Jesus, kalksins/kalkans gardr/guardian(?), Jesus, Jes[us].* . ., 'Jesus, Jesus, Jesus, guard(ian)? of the (communion) chalice, Jesus, Jes(us)'. The reverse then continues briefly in cryptic runes saying . . . *ráð rúnar,* i.e. 'read the runes'. It is sometimes assumed that the use of runic cryptography is inextricably linked to magical practice, but this is not necessarily the case. In fact all kinds of motivations seem to have prompted the use of cryptic runes – sometimes, undoubtedly, to conceal a clandestine pagan message (see e.g. the 'Thor bless' formula discussed in chapter 9), but more often, presumably, as a simple runic riddle or puzzle.[32]

The Christian amulets in runes from Scandinavia encompass a large and diverse range of inscriptions, from perfectly proficient runic transliterations of liturgical Latin texts, through less fluent or idiosyncratic renderings, to pious gobbledygook where an original liturgical quotation can only with difficulty be discerned behind the magic veneer. Christian rites and traditional Germanic magic were frequently combined to magical effect; *AGLA* and other imported

---

[31] The Bergen rune-stick has the number N B410; the Oslo amulet is N A323. The rings include *SR* XIV.1 no. 2, *DR* no. 20 and *NIyR* no. 635.

[32] On the Clement stick see Liestøl, *Runer frå Bryggen*, pp. 16–18. McKinnell and Simek, p. 35, note that Clement is a patron saint of sailors and link this text to the 'brim-runes' of the *Lay of Sigrdrifa*. The Sigtuna bone is described in Gustavson et al., 'Runfynd 1982', pp. 224–43.

Christian terms, names and titles rapidly acquired a mystical taint, and were frequently employed in runic magic. Although not as common in the other runic traditions, the employment of such expressions on Scandinavian runic amulets is scarcely different from their use in other parts of Latin Christendom at the time, once again underlining the generally unremarkable nature of runic inscriptions at least when it came to magical practices. More personal prayers and invocations were usually rendered in the language of the everyday masses, however, who continued to carve homely runic supplications in the manner of their pagan ancestors. Indeed, the most unpretentious runic amulet which expresses the basic tenets of Christian belief is probably that engraved on a bone from Sumtangen in Norway, which reads simply: *Guð er alls*, 'God is everything.'[33]

---

[33] N A61.

9

Rune-stones, Death and Curses

FOR most Scandinavians, accustomed to stumbling across rune-stones when walking through the countryside, runic inscriptions do not possess the same aura of mystery as they do for many from other countries. In fact, usually to the disappointment of those who first encounter them, most runic inscriptions carved on raised stones and rock faces say little more than 'X raised this stone in memory of Y', with perhaps some formulaic expansion, e.g. 'a valiant man'. Deviation from this standard is rare, and the comparatively humdrum nature of these rune-stones may seem worlds apart from the more colourful messages encountered on runic amulets.

That is not to say that departures from the standard memorial formula are never encountered, however. Rune-stone memorials from the early runic period are much more varied than their later counterparts – it seems that it was only when the erection of rune-stones became very common that memorial texts became stereotypical. Yet even in the highly formulaic world of the Viking-era rune-stones, we do on occasion encounter some more sentimental additions such as: 'The death of a mother is the worst that can happen to a son'; or 'It is better to leave a good foster-son than a wretched son.' Runic epitaphs also occasionally include messages of a darker nature such as: 'Black men betrayed him on a voyage . . . May God betray those who betrayed him.' There are even some instances of memorial poetry, legal entitlements and, perhaps more strikingly, some rune-stone memorials that feature texts which seem to represent cultic or mythological lore.[1]

One rune-stone memorial bearing an inscription often thought to include a cultic element is the Swedish Sparlösa stone. Appearing to date from about the year 800, this 1.62m-long and 60cm-wide slab of worked granite is decorated with various pictures including depictions of animals (such as birds), a house, a ship and two men (one riding a horse and brandishing a sword, the other comprising only a head and shoulders with a raised arm), which may themselves have had cultic significance. Its inscription is written on four of its sides in a mixture of long-branch and short-twig runes, and seems to represent the work of two different hands. Removed in 1937 from the wall of a church where it had been

---

[1] A recent survey of the rune-stones of the Viking era is B. Sawyer, *The Viking-Age Rune-Stones* (Oxford 2000).

serving only as an ashlar, its original context is unknown. It clearly features a memorial text which states the stone was raised by a certain Gisli for Gunnar, but this appears to be a much later addition to its decoration and longer runic sequences. The primary runic text appears on three sides of the stone, is written in much larger characters and appears to relate some sort of dedication featuring three other figures, Evisl, Eric and Alrek, who are seemingly a father, son and uncle or brother-in-law. The stone is quite damaged, however, and the correct reading of many parts of its primary text is disputed. A minimal reading of the inscription is:

⁜:ᛁᚾᚱᚼᛁ᛬ᚨᚠ:⁜ᛁᚱᛁᛁᛁᛋᛋᚾᛂᚨᛁᚨ᛬ᚨᚠ᛬ᚨᚱᚱᛁᛁ--
---1---ᚱᛈᛁᛁᚨᚠᚱ⁜ᚾᚱᚾᛁᚨᛈᛁ⁜ᛚᛁ...
...⁜ᛋᛋ⁜-ᚠᛁᛁᛁ᛬ᚾᚠᛋᛋᛁᛈᛁᚨᛁᛂᛋᚾ⁜ᛈᚨ᛬-⁜-ᚾ--ᚠ⁜
...-ᛂᛁᛁᛋᛋᛁᚾ⁜ᚾᛈᛁᛈᚨᛂ᛬ᚨ·⁜'ᚱᚱᛁᛈᚾᚱᚾ--ᛚᚾᛂᛈ-1⁜ᛁᚾᛁᛋᛁ
...ᛁᛂ---ᛂᚾᛚ-⁜--ᛈ⁜ᚾ'ᛁᛈᚨᛁᚾᚱ⁜ᛁᚾᛁᛈᚨᚾᛚ⁜ᛁᚱᛁᛁᛁᛁ'
ᚨᛂᛁᚾᛁⁱ⁜ᚱᚾ
ᛈᚾᛁᛁ
⁜ᚠᛏ⁜ᛁᚾᛁᛋᚾᛂᚱᛏᛈ
ᚱᚾᛁᛁᛂᛁᛈ⁜ᛂᚱ⁜ᛈᛁ-ᚾᚠᚾᛏᚾᛁᚾᛈ⁜ᚱ'ᚾ⁜ᛈ⁜ᛁᚱᛁᛁᛈᚾᛁᚾᚠᚾᛁᛈ⁜ᛈᛁ·
ᚾᛁᚾ-ᛁᛏ
...-ᚾᛁᚱᛈᚾᛏᚱ'ᛈ'ᛂᚾᛁᛒᛁᛁᛂ-
---ᚠᚾᛂᛁᚾᛁᛁᚾᚾᛂ--
...ᛁᚾ
ᛁᛁᛋᚾᛁ:ᛈᛏᚱᛈᛁ:ᛁᚠᛏᛁᛚ:ᚠᚾᛏᛏᚱ:ᛒᚱᚾᛈᚾᚱ ᚠᚾᛒᚱ ᛈᛁᛋᛁ

Aiv(ī)sl gaf Airīks sunʀ gaf Alrīk[ʀ]
...la gaf raul at gialdi, ... [þ]ā sa[t] faðiʀ Upsal faðiʀ svāð
a[.]a[.]u[..]ba... [.]omas nætʀ ok dagaʀ. Alrīkʀ lu[bu]ʀ ugð[i]t Aivīsl
s[---]nuʀ[-]a[--] þat Sigmarr (h)ǽiti maguʀ Aīriks. Mǽginiaru þuno aft
Aiv(ī)s(l). Ok rāð rūnaʀ þaʀ rǽgi[n]kundu iu þar, svāð Alrīkʀ lubu fāði.
uiu[r]am ... [i]ukrþsarsksnuibin ... kunʀ ok lios ... iu
Gīsli gǽrði ǽftiʀ Gunnar, broður, kumbl þessi.

'Evisl gave, Eric's son gave Alrek. . .
. . . gave . . . as payment. Then (?) the father sat (?) (in) Uppsala (?), the father that . . . nights and days. Alrek Lubu did not fear (?) Evisl.
. . . that Eric's boy is called Sigmar ("celebrated-for-victories"). Mighty battle (?) . . . in memory of Evisl. And interpret the runes of the gods made known there . . ., that Alrek Lubu painted.
. . . and light . . .
Gisli made this monument in memory of Gunnar, (his) brother.'

Apart from the expression 'runes of the gods made known', familiar from the Noleby stone, much of the information given in this text concerning Evisl, Eric and Alrek Lubu is hard to recover. Some interpreters have discerned the name of the god Frey at various points in the text, however, for example in the difficult sequence before *þat Sigmar* reading 'The sax is now Frey's. . .' there, and *gaf raul at gialdi* has been interpreted as 'offered to (F)rey as payment'. A famous temple where Frey (along with Odin and Thor) was worshipped at Uppsala is described by Adam of Bremen in his late-eleventh-century description of Scandinavia.[2] It

2 See chapter 5.

may be, then, that the stone commemorates some sort of religious ceremony with its recording of giving and the painting of runes by Alrek 'there' (at Uppsala?). Another Swedish rune-stone, from Kälvesten, mentions an Evisl 'who fell in the east' and two brothers Eric and Alrek, both early Swedish kings, are mentioned in the *Saga of the Ynglings* where it is recounted they were killed in mysterious circumstances while out riding one day. The Sparlösa inscription clearly evidences alliteration in some sections and it has been suggested that parts of its text may have been versified. But there are too many unknowns and not enough context here for us to really be sure whether the Sparlösa stone does in fact record some sort of pagan cultic practice, perhaps, in light of the Blekinge stones a fertility rite, no matter how suggestive the much-damaged primary inscription seems today. Gisli may have ignored or simply not have understood the stone's original purpose. But the primary inscription might equally well merely have been an elaborate memorial text of some kind given its phrasing 'in memory of Evisl' which is reminiscent of the standard rune-stone funerary formula. If so, the giving commemorated here may well have been payment for something quite mundane – one plausible interpretation of *raul* is merely as a payment of *raut* 'money' (i.e. with the unexpected *l* read as a reversed *t*) perhaps as a commission or a fine. After all, the appearance of a text featuring legendary kings and heroes in a funerary setting is paralleled in a much longer and more famous runic memorial inscription.[3]

The longest rune-stone text, that on the Swedish Rök stone, contains over 700 runes on its five inscribed sides and seems to date to the ninth century. The main text of this 3.85m-high and 1.5m-wide granite monument, however, appears to have little to do with the man the inscription makes clear is being commemorated by the stone. The inscription is mostly in short-twig runes, although it also features a long series of cryptic runes, some of which are similar to older runes, others which are more typical Viking-era expressions. The order of reading some sections of the text, as well as a few of the expressions it contains, are disputed, though a conservative reading is:

```
ᚠᛈᛏᛅᚠᛏᛅᛑ'ᛏᛐᛐᛏᚠᚱᛐᛐᛁᛑᚠᛁ
ᛁᚼᛐᚠᚱᛁᛐᛈᛈᛑᛁᛈᛁᛑᛁᚠᛈ᛫ᛈᚠᛁᚠᛁᚠᛐᛐᚾᛐᚼ
'ᚠᚠᛐᛏᛑᛈᛏᛁᚼᛁᛑᚠᛅᛐᚠᚱᛁᚠᛁᛐᛁᛏᚱᚠᛐᚠᛁᛁᛐᚠᛁᛅᛏᛐᚠᛁ
ᛑᚠᛁᛁᛐᚠᛐᛅᚼᛁᚠᚠᛁᛁᛁᛐᛐᚼᚼᛁᛁᛁᚼᚼᛏᚼᛁᛁᚼᛁᚠᚱᚠᚼᚠᛐ
ᚠᛁᛑᚠᛁᛁᛁᚾᛏᚠᚠᛅᛐᛏᛁᛁᛐᛏᛐᚼᛏ᛫ᛑᚠᛁᛈᚠᚠᚼᛨᛏᚼᚼᚠ
ᚱᛁᛏᚼᚠᛁᚠᚼᚱᚠᛁᛐᚠᛅᛁᛏᛐᛏᚼᛐᚼᚱᛑᛁᚠᛁᚠᚱᛐ
ᛏᛁᛁᛏᚱᚠᛁᛑᚠᛐᛁᛐᛏᚠᛐᚠᛁᛐ
ᛏᛁᛁᛐᛐᛐᛈᛁᚠᚠᛁ
ᚱᚠᛁᛑᛁᚠᚼᚱᛁᚠᛁᛏᛁᚠᛑᚼᚱᛏᚼᛑᛁ'ᛁᛁᚠᛁᛁ
ᚠᛏᚼᛐᚠᚠ'ᛐᚱᛐᚼᛐᚼᛏᚱᚠᛁᛑᛏᚠᚱᛁᛁᛁᛐᛐᚼᛁᛅᛈᚠᛏᚱᚼᛁᚠ
ᚠᛑᛐᚠᛁᛁᚼᛑᛏᛈᛁᚠᛐᛅᛐᛐᚾᛈᛈᛨᚠᛐᛏᚠᛑᛁᛈᚠᛐᛁᛏᚠᚱᛁᚠᚠ
ᛑᚠᛐᛈᚠᚼᛏᛐᚼᛐᚠᛈᛐᚼᛐᛐᚠᚱᚼᛐ'ᛏᛁ'ᛁᛈᚼ
ᚠᚠᛁᛁᛐᚼᛁᛐᚼᛏᚠᛁᚠᛈᚼᛐᚼᛈᚠᛁᛁᛐᚼᚠᛁᛁᛐᛁᛈᚠᛁᛁᚼᚠ
```

---

3   A cultic interpretation of this inscription is emphasised by C.J.S. Marstrander, 'Om innskriftene på Sparlösastenen', *Norsk tidskrift for sprogvidenskap* 17 (1954), 503–16, though for more recent linguistic scholarship, see the survey in Birkmann, pp. 239–55.

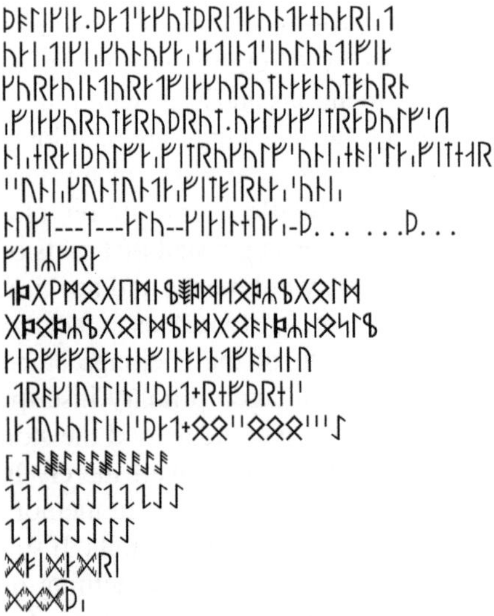

ᚦᚨᚠᛁᚹᛁᚠ·ᛏᚠᛏ�ᚠᚹᚺᛏ�070ᛏᚾᛏᚺᚺᚠᚱᛚᛁᛏ
ᚺᚠᛚᛁᛕᛁᚹᛁᛚᛁᚹᚺᛏᚺᚹᛖᛁᛚᛕᛁᛖᛏᛁᚺᛏᚺᚺᛖᛁᚹᛁᛖ
ᚹᚺᚱᛏᚺᛁᛖᛁᚺᚺᚱᚻᛁᚹᛁᚹᚹᚺᚱᚺᛏᚺᚹᛏᚠᛏᚺᛏᛖᚺᚱᛏ
ᛁᚹᛁᚹᛁᚹᚱᚺᛏᛖᚱᚺᛏᚱᚺᛏ·ᚺᛏᚹᛁᛁᚹᛁᛏᚱᛖᚦᚺᛁᛁᚹᛁᚾ
ᚺᛁᛁᛏᚱᛁᛁᚦᚺᛁᛁᚹᛁᚹᛁᛁᚹᛁᛏᚱᚺᚹᚺᛁᛁᚹᛁᚺᛁᛁᛁᛏᚺᛁ'ᛖᛁᛁᚹᛁᛏᚺᛖᚱᚺᚦ
"ᛁᚺᛁᛁᚹᚺᛁᛏᚺᛁᛖᛏᛁᛁᚹᛁᛏᚹᛁᚱᚺᛁᛁᛁᚺᚠᛚᛁ
ᚺᛁᚹᛏ---ᛏ---ᚠᛚᚺ--ᚹᛁᚺᛁᚺᛏᚹᛁ₁-Þ . . . . . .Þ . . .
ᚹᛁᛁᚺᚹᚱᚺ
ᚤᚦᚷᚹᛗᛟᚷᚦᛁᛚᛁᛊᚤᚻᛁᚺᛟᚺᛚᛊᚷᛟᚱᛁᛗ
ᚷᚦᛟᚺᛚᛊᚷᛟᚱᛖᛁᚻᛁᛗᚷᛟᚠᛁᛁᚺᛁᚺᛟᚤᛁᛊ
ᚠᛁᚱᛁᚠᛁᚱᚱᛖᛁᛁᛁᛖᚹᛁᛁᚠᛖᛁᛁᛗᚹᛁᛖᛁᛁᚾ
ᛁᚤᚱᛁᚹᛁᚾᛁᛁᚠᛁᛁᚺ'Þᛖᚤᛁᛌᚱᛁᛩᚱᚺᚤᛁᚺᛁ'
ᛁᚺᛁᚾᛖᛁᛁᚾᛁᛁᚺᚹᚺᛖᛁᛁᚾᛁ'Þᛖ₁ᛌ᛭ᛩᛩ''ᛩᛩᛩ'''ᛊ
[.]ᛥᛥᛥᛥᛥᛥᛥᛥᛥ
ᛁᛁᛁᛊᛊᛊᛁᛁᛁᛊᛊ
ᛁᛁᛁᛊᛊᛊᛊᛊ
ᚷᚠᛁᚷᚠᚷᚱᛁ
ᚷᚷᚷᚦ₁

Aft Vāmōð standa rūnaʀ þāʀ.
Æn Vārinn faði,   *faðiʀ, aft faigian sunu.*

Sagum mogminni þat,   *hværiaʀ valraufaʀ*
vārin tvāʀ þāʀ,   *svað tvalf sinnum*
vārin numnaʀ at valraufu,   *baðaʀ saman ā ӯmissum mannum.*

Þat sagum annart,   *hvaʀ fur nīu aldum*
ān yrði fiaru   *meðr Hraiðgutum,*
auk dō meðr han umb sakaʀ.

Rēð Þiōðrīkʀ   *hin þurmōði,*
stilliʀ flutna,   *strandu Hraiðmaraʀ.*
Sitiʀ nū garuʀ   *ā guta sīnum,*
skialdi umb fatlaþʀ,   *skati Mœringa.*

Þat sagum tvalfta,   *hvar hæstʀ sē*
Gunnaʀ etu   *vēttvangi ā,*
kunungaʀ tvaiʀ   *tigiʀ svāð ā liggia.*

Þat sagum þrēttāunda,   *hvariʀ tvaiʀ tigiʀ kunungaʀ*
sātin at Sīolundi   *fiagura vintur*
at fiagurum nampnum,   *burniʀ fiagurum brøðrum.*

Valkaʀ fim,   *Hrāðulfs syniʀ,*
Hraiðulfaʀ fim,   *Rugulfs syniʀ,*
Hāislaʀ fim,   *Haruðs syniʀ,*
Gunnmundaʀ fim,   *Bernaʀ syniʀ.*

Nū'k m[inni] m[eðr] allu [sa]gi.
Ainhvaʀʀ. . . [svā]ð. . . [æ]ftiʀ frā.

Sagum mogminni þat,   *hvaʀ Inguldinga vāri guldinn*
at kvānaʀ hūsli.
Sagum mogminni,   *hvaim sē burinn niðʀ drængi.*

Vilinn es þat.   *Knūa knātti iatun.*
Vilinn es þat. . .

[S]agum mogminni.
Þórr.
Sibbi viaværi ōl nīrøðʀ.

'In memory of Vamod stand these runes.
And Varin painted (them),   the father, in memory of his dead son.

I say the folktale,	which the two
war-booties were,	which twelve times
were taken as war-booty,	both together from various men.

I say this second,	who nine generations ago
lost his life	with the Hreid-goths;
and died with them	for his guilt.

Theodoric the bold,	chief of sea-warriors,
ruled over	the shores of the Hreid-sea.
Now he sits	armed on his horse,
his shield strapped,	the prince of the Mærings.

I say this as the twelfth,	where the horse
of Gunn	sees fodder on
the battlefield,	where twenty kings lie.

I say this as the thirteenth,	which twenty kings
sat on Sjolund (Zealand?)	for four winters,
of four names,	born of four brothers:

Five Valkis,	sons of Hradulf,
five Hreidulfs,	sons of Rugulf,
five Haisls,	sons of Hord,
five Gunnmunds,	sons of Bjorn.

Now I say the tales in full.
Someone. . . which. . . from after.

I say the folktale,	which of the line of Ingold
was repaid by a wife's sacrifice.	
I say the folktale,	to whom is born a relative,
to a valiant man.	

It is Vilin. He could crush a giant.
It is Vilin. . .

I say the folktale.
Thor.
Sibbi of the holy guard, nonagenarian, begot (a son).'

Much like the Sparlösa monument, the Rök stone was rescued from a wall in a church (or rather a church outbuilding) and so its original context is unknown. Many different interpretations of what the Rök inscription signified have also emerged, ranging from careful and learned treatises to imaginative and sometimes eccentric offerings – none, however, offering an altogether convincing interpretation of what purpose lay behind the creation of this text, except that it obviously evidences a remarkable, even ostentatious display of runic literacy and poetry. Apart from a typical memorial formula opening the inscription, the later verses include references to Theodoric the Great, the legendary fifth- and sixth-century Ostrogothic king of Italy, as well as what seem to be several other legendary or mythical figures, apparently even including an invocation (in cryptic runes) of Thor. The only god from the pagan pantheon to be named on Viking-age rune-stones, Thor features on several Scandinavian memorials in the invocation 'May Thor bless', which may explain the appearance of the thunder-god's name seemingly without any context here. Several more rune-stone memorials are also decorated with the sign of Thor's hammer, a symbol that may originally have had a consecrating function. In fact these ostensibly pagan symbols even appear on some rune-stones featuring clearly Christian funerary texts. The Rök inscription might be considered a much more elaborate form of these other Thor-invoking memorial texts then.[4]

Given the seemingly supernatural nature of the versified inscription, it is not too surprising that some scholars have sought to find a connection between the references to Theodoric, the twenty kings, Vilin, the man who had a son in his 90s and so on, and pagan Germanic funerary beliefs. One suggestion is that Theodoric had been mythologised in Swedish tradition into a judge of the dead; his architecturally seminal mausoleum in the sometime imperial capital Ravenna, after all, still stands to this day. Another is that Vilin and Vi are local versions of Odin's brothers Vili and Ve, and we are dealing with mythological episodes concerning Odin (who of course also had a funerary aspect) here. It might also be recalled that Odin sired his son Vali at an advanced age in order to avenge his slain son Balder, in a manner perhaps comparable to the aged Sibbi. But surely a simpler interpretation is that the Rök verses constitute several narrative charms recounting famous and presumably unconnected mythical deeds in order to impute some aspect of the events recounted to the memorial stone. Sympathetic magic seems to be at work in the versified and cryptic sections of the Rök text, though the precise type remains debatable. Yet depictions of stories familiar from Norse mythology (such as Thor's snaring of the Midgard serpent, the final battle of Ragnarok or the funeral of the god Balder, among others) are illustrated on several Norse stones of Viking date scattered throughout Scandinavia and the British Isles. Like the narratives on the Rök and Sparlösa stones, these depictions might serve the same function as the Thor's hammers or the 'May Thor bless' inscriptions – they appear to have no specifically funerary function other than to consecrate (if not simply to decorate) the commemorative stones that bear them.

There are also several examples of Scandinavian rune-stone texts that include what are clearly curses, much as two of the rune-stones from Blekinge discussed in chapter 5 have inscriptions on them wishing 'an insidious death to he who breaks this'. It was not only fertility stones, however, that could carry inscriptions of this sort. Many funerary rune-stones also have comparable menacing or magical legends on them. Perhaps the most striking early example is that on a gravestone found at Eggja, Norway, a shaped slab mostly of gneiss and mica with a long message on it that is clearly not simply a funerary dedication.

The 162cm-long and 10cm-thick Eggja stone was found lying flat over what

---

4 For recent linguistic scholarship on the Rök inscription, see the survey in Birkmann, pp. 290–313, though E. Wessén, *Runstenen vid Röks kyrka* (Stockholm 1958) is a more comprehensive treatment. The most recent, though not convincing, work on the stone is O. Grønvik, *Die Rökstein* (Frankfurt a.M. 2003).

appears to have been a man's grave with the rune-inscribed side facing downwards. It was obviously not a text intended for public consumption. In fact its contents are clearly magical – and they clearly represent grave magic. The inscription is probably of seventh-century date and at almost 50 words is the longest of the runic texts inscribed in the older runic alphabet.

Unfortunately, the Eggja inscription is not particularly well preserved. Comprising three parts, a drawing of a horse appears between its two main rows which might be translated as follows:

ᚻᛁᚻᚨᚱᚾᚻᛇᛏᚾᚷᚻᛁᚻᚦᚱᚻᛗᚻᛏᛁᛁᚻᚻᚱᛩᚱᛁᛏᛁᛁᚷ----ᛗᚠᛇᛏᛇᚱᛟᚠᛇᛁᚻᛏᛁᚦᚱᛁᛇᛏᛁᛈᛁᚱᛏᛁᛇᛗᚠᛇᛇᚱ
ᛇᚷᛁᛇ-
ᚻᛁᛏᛈᛇᚱᛒᛇᛇᚻᛗᚾᛟᛗᚠᛇᛗᛇᛝᛗᛈᛇᛁᛗᚱᛇᛁᛒᛇᛁᛒᛩᚱᛗᛩᚦᛇᚻᚾᛏᛁᚻᚾᛈᛇᛇᛩᛒᚱᚠᛗᚻᛇᚱᛁᚻᚠᚾᛁᚱᚠᛏᚷᛩ
ᛏᛇᛇ
ᚠᛁᚻᚱᛇᛩᛇᚠ--ᛇᛇᚾᛁᛗᚻᚾᛈᛁᛗᚠᛗᛗᚠᛩᚱᚠᛁᚠ-ᛇ-----ᚷᛇᛏᚠᛇᛗᛗ
ᛇᚾᚾᛗᛁᚻᚾᚱᛩᛁ

Ni's sólu sótt,
ok ni saxe stæinn skorinn.
Ni l[æggi] ma(nn)ʀ nækðan, is nið rinnʀ,
ni viltiʀ mannʀ læggi a[b].

Hinn varp náséu mannʀ,
máðe þæim kæipa í bormóða húni.
Hvær ob kam hæri(ǫ́)ss á hí á land gotna?
Fiskʀ ór f[ir]navim svimmande,
fogl í f[i]a[nda lið] galande.

Alu. Missurki.

'The stone has not been struck by the sun,
and it has not been scored by a sax.
No man shall lay it bare while the waning moon runs,
neither shall a man lay the stone aside.

This thing a man sprinkled with corpse-sea (i.e. blood),
scraped with it the board in the hole-worn top-rigging.
As what did the army-As (i.e. Odin) come here to the land of the valiant?
As a fish, swimming out of the foul stream,
as a bird, crowing in a fiendish band.

Dedication. For the evil-doer.'

There is some doubt as to the reading of some of the later parts of the Eggja text, although its first two lines seem clear enough. The first section of the first part of the inscription alliterates (*sólu sótt . . . saxe*) and also seems at first to be a riddle. It appears unlikely that the stone was not struck by sunshine when it was being shaped or that its runes were not carved by an edged tool, if that is what the sax stands for here (a sax is literally a 'cutter', but the term usually indicates a dagger or a short sword).

The second section of this line seems to be even more stylised and contains two more negative statements: imprecations against anyone who would open the grave by night (while the moon is waning). This first part of the Eggja inscription seems to be a type of sympathetic 'just as . . . so too . . .' construction (or rather a negative 'not . . . nor . . .' variation of this typical magical style), and it may well be that the stone was especially made at a time or place away from the light of the sun and was also inscribed with wooden chisels rather than a knife. Taken together, these expressions appear to be a spell against thieves breaking into the grave at Eggja, and the first line seemingly recounts a ritual that was carried out as part of the gravestone's protective magic.

The second part of the inscription is more complicated and its interpretation in some parts correspondingly more controversial. The text seems to continue with a further action that was performed as part of a funeral rite. Yet it is couched in such obscure language it is difficult to interpret convincingly. Germanic heroes were often buried in boats. But it is not at all clear what the apparently nautical language signifies.

Then a question follows about the army-As when he came to the land of 'the valiant'. The description 'army-As' is reminiscent of Old Norse bynames of Odin and *gotna* 'of the valiant' features the term which gives us *Goths*, the Swedish tribal name preserved in *Götaland* and *Gotland*, as well as English *guts* and an Old Norse term for a horse (as also appears on the Rök stone). Perhaps this explains the picture of the horse on the Eggja stone, but it is not really certain to whose land Odin was headed. The reason for connecting Odin with a fish is also unclear, though his association with birds is better known. The alliteration of *fiskʀ* with *f[ir]navim*, *fogl* and *f[i]a[nda]* in this line may explain the appearance of the fish, though, whereas the image of the crowing bird more clearly represents Odin's role as the counselling raven god, the one who squawks out magic spells. This section clearly has the suggestion of a mythological narrative charm concerning Odin the master magician, then, one presumably being employed here to render the funerary spell more powerful.

The final part of the Eggja inscription features the charm word *alu* 'dedication' and an imprecation 'to' or 'for the evil-doer'. It may be that this is a descriptive line '*alu* to the evildoer' much like 'baleful prophecy' is at Blekinge, although it seems preferable to accept that *alu* is acting in its usual manner here, i.e. as a generic charm word bolstering the potency of the curse.[5]

The appearance of *alu* at Eggja probably also explains the appearance of the charm word in isolation on the stone excavated from a burial mound at Elgesem, Norway, which was mentioned in the chapter on fertility charms. A clearer example of a text of the five-part amuletic type, however, has been found on a stone actually unearthed in a grave. This 1.05m-long and 75cm-wide monument is of limestone, it was found near Kylver, Gotland, in 1901 and bears the following legend:

ᚠᚢᚦᚨᚱᚲᚷᚹᚺᚾᛁᛃᛈᛇᛉᛊᛏᛒᛖᛗᛚᛝᛞᛟᛡ ᛉᚢᛗᛚᛋ

fuþarkgwhnijpïzstbemlŋdoᛡ sueus.

A text belonging to the early runic period, i.e. not later than the fifth century, the

---

5   Krause with Jankuhn, no. 101. Birkmann, pp. 97–114 and McKinnell and Simek, pp. 163–65 also survey other interpretations, none of which represents an obvious improvement on that given here.

Kylver inscription features a futhark row, a tree-like symbol and a magical word, a palindrome. Like Gnostic palindromes such as *ablanathanalba*, Kylver's *sueus* may originally have been based on some meaningful term, but it is not entirely clear what that may have been.[6] Stones found in early Germanic graves are usually called pillow-stones as they were typically placed under the head of the corpse. If inscribed, though, they normally feature only the name of the deceased, just like a standard gravestone. Yet the example from Kylver appears to have had another purpose. Its amuletic text suggests it may have been a magical protection against thieves, much like the inscription on the Eggja stone. It may equally have had a different magical function, though, as several of the funerary stones inscribed in younger runes bear curses of a quite different type.

A younger inscription comparable to that found at Kylver appears on a rune-stone from Flemløse, Denmark. Less clearly of the five-part amuletic type, it also features a palindrome:

ᚱᚢᚢᛚᚠᛦᛋᛁᛋ

(H)rōulfʀ sis.

A name plus what is usually regarded as a magical word (somewhat reminiscent of Kylver's *sueus*, the Old Saxon word *siso* 'magical incantation', as well, perhaps, as the see-see charms described in chapter 3), this inscription was found along with another inscribed stone that makes its funerary context clearer. The legend on the other Flemløse stone (parts of which are known only from early reproductions) reads:

ᚼᚠᛏᚱᚢᚢᛚᚠᛆᛏᚨᛏᛦ
[ᛋᛏ]ᚼᛁᚿᛋᚼᛆᛁᛁᛆᚢᚼᛆᚿᚢ
ᛦᚿᚠᚢᚦᛁᛆᚿᛏᚢᛆᚢ [ᚿᛁᛦᚿᚠᛏᛁᛦ
ᚠᚢᚼᛁᛦᚠᚿᚿᚦᛁ]

Æft (H)rōulf stændr [st]æin sāsi.
Ēs vas Nøʀa goði.
Sattu sy[niʀ æftiʀ.
Āveʀ fāði].

'In memory of Hroulf stands this stone. He was a priest of the Norer.
The sons erected in (his) memory. Aver painted (this).'

The pagan priest Hroulf (or Rolf) of the Norer is also known from two other Danish funerary rune-stones of a similar date, from the nearby settlements of Avnslev and Helnæs. In both of these cases, however, Hroulf is recorded as having set the stones up in memory of someone else. The name of the deceased is not preserved in the reproductions that we have of the now-lost Avnslev stone, but the example from Helnæs clearly commemorates Hroulf's dead nephew Gudmund.[7]

6 Krause with Jankuhn, no. 1. An interpretation *eus* 'horse' would make the inscription Gothic. The palindrome *siusušuis* on the Kälder pendant (see chapter 4), on the other hand, suggests a more regularly early Nordic *swe-* 'self, kinsman, good' may have been intended here.

7 Moltke, *Runes and their Origin*, pp. 154–56.

Thus the first of the two rune-stones from Flemløse considered here could have been some sort of magical stone connected with Hroulf's death, although, as at Kylver and Elgesem, the inscription does not make clear what its precise purpose was. A different kind of curse to that on the Eggja stone is represented by two more Danish funerary rune-stones, though, which also date from the Viking period and seem to evidence another kind of grave magic, that of confining the deceased to a final place of rest.

Bodies bursting from their graves and causing trouble for the living are a common enough theme in Norse literature. Usually the dead, however, remain contentedly in Valhalla or even linger on closer to home. In the *Eyrbyggja Saga*, for example, it is recounted that a shepherd saw a mountain open in which the dead members of a local leading family dwelt. Other Norse sources similarly talk of the dead living on much as in life in their howes or burial mounds. But it does not seem that the early Norse believed in ghosts as we understand the term today. Medieval sources such as the amulet from Dublin described in chapter 4 speak of *nár* 'corpses' rather than incorporeal shades or phantoms. In Old Norse literature necromancy is referred to as *val galdrar* 'slain incantations' and in tales such as *Grettir's Saga* the living are typically disturbed by walking corpses (*draugar* or *aptrgǫngumenn*) rather than ethereal ghosts. The restless dead of pagan Scandinavia were clearly thought to retain their bodies – in pre-Christian times, haunting in the North was the prerogative of animated corpses or zombies, not disembodied spirits wandering from their graves.[8]

The revenants of Northern experience were not just warded against by amulets like the example from Dublin, though. Some runic inscriptions were apparently meant to ensure that the dead were never able to leave their graves in the first place. An example from early Viking times is the funeral stone from Nørre-Nærå, Denmark. The runes on this 130cm-tall stone clearly read:

ᚦᚢᚱᛈᚢᛏᛅ
ᚿᛁᚠᚢᛏ:ᚴᚢᛒᛚᛋ

Þormundʀ. Niōt kumbls!

'Thormund. Make good use of the monument!'

The final command here at first appears to be similar to a modern 'rest in peace' or the sentiment 'may God rest his/her soul' common on Scandinavian memorials from Christian times. But in fact a grimmer purpose seems to be intended here. 'Make good use of the monument!' is comparable to the command 'make good use of the healing-charm!' on the amulet from Sigtuna discussed in chapter 6. Moreover, another rather more elaborate funerary stone makes the magical aspect of this command more explicit. A further Danish inscription that even shows signs of being written by the same carver (or at least one who employed very similar graphic idiosyncrasies) appears on a rune-stone from Gørlev which reads:

---

8   Norse attitudes to death are the subject of H.R. Ellis, *The Road to Hel* (Oxford 1943). The apparitions in animal form called *fylgjar* also appear in Norse literature, of course, but these guardian spirits tend to appear primarily to warn the living of approaching death.

ᚦᛁᛅᚢᚦᚢᛁ⁝ᚱᛁᛋᚦᛁ⁝ᛋᛏᛁᚾᚦᚬᚾᛋᛁ⁝ᛅᚠᛏᚢᚦᛁᚾᚴᛅᚢᚱ⁝
ᚠᚢᚦᚬᚱᚴᚼᚾᛁᛅᛌᛏᛒᛘᛚᛦ⁝ᚾᛁᚢᛏᚢᛅᛚᚴᚢᛘᛌ⁝
ᚦᛘᚴᛁᛁᛁᛌᛌᛌᛏᛏᛏᛁᛁᛁᛚᛚᛚ:ᛁᛅᚴᛌᛅᛏᛅᚱᚢᚾᛅᚱᛁᛏ
ᚴᚢᚾᛁᛅᚱᛘᚢᛏᛦᚴᚱᚢᛒ. . .

Þiōðvī rēsði stēn þænsi æft Ōðinkōr.
fuþąrkhniastbmlʀ.
Niūt væl kum(bl)s!
þmkiiissstttiiilll.
Iak satta rūnaʀ rētt.
Gunni, Armundʀ grob. . .

'Thjodvi raised this stone in memory of Odinkor.
fuþąrkhniastbmlʀ.
Make very good use of the monument!
Thistle, mistletoe, casket.
I placed the runes rightly.
Gunni, Armund dug . . .'

This 220cm-tall monument features a typical commemorative rune-stone message as well as two clearly magical expressions: a futhark row and a coded example of the 'thistle, mistletoe' formula which was described more fully in the chapter on leechcraft. This is clearly a magical funerary stone, the magic apparently aiming to bind the deceased Odinkor to his grave. It appears to represent a development on the old five-part amuletic formulism with the leechcraft 'thistle, mistletoe' charm performing the bolstering generic, but clearly magical, function of the palindromes at Flemløse and Kylver, or the old runic charm word *alu* on the Elgesem stone. It seems likely, then, given its similar invocation of a name and a magical sequence (*sis*) that the more elliptical text on the Flemløse stone was also a funerary curse of this type, and it may well have been that the five-part amulet-like Kylver and Elgesem inscriptions were meant to represent this kind of curse too.[9]

Perhaps the most impressive of all examples of magical funerary stones, however, was found at Malt, Denmark, in 1987. At 2.5m long, this streaked pink granite slab would have stood just under two metres tall before it was buried. Found at what was probably a former river-crossing, it features a picture of a man's head with a cross on its forehead – a clearly Christian symbol – as well as a runic text, partly running vertically, but mostly horizontally across the stone. The Malt inscription dates approximately to the ninth century, i.e. the very beginning of the Christian period, and its long, complex and in many parts controversial text reads:

ᛋᚢᛅᛅᛁ⁝ᛏᛁᛏᚢᛚᛏᛁᛏᚢᛚ
ᚠᚢᚦᚬᚱᚴᚼᚽᛁᛅᛋᛏᛒᛘᛚᛦ

ᚼᚢᛅᛦᛁᛋᛁ ᛅᛚᛁᛋᛏᚬᛋᛅ:ᚼᚢᛅᛦᛁᛋ
ᚢᛁᚠᚱᚦᚢᛦ:ᚴᛅᚱᚦᛁ:ᛅᚠᚱᛅᚠᛏᛅᛋᛁᚾᛁᚠᛅᚢᚦᚱ
ᚴᚢᛚ:ᚠᛁᚽᛦ:ᚠᛅᛚ-:ᛏᛅᛁᛏᛁᚱᚢᚽᚬᛦ.ᚢ-
ᛅᛁᚢᛁᚽᚱᚢᚽᚬᛦ:ᛋᚢᛚᛁᛅᛚᛏᛅ:ᚼᚢᛅᛦ.ᛯ

9 Moltke, *Runes and their Origin*, pp. 158 and 174–75.

ᚢᛏᚢ⁝ᛏᚢᚢᚢᛏᛒᛁᛚᛁᚴᛅᚴᛦ:ᛏᚢᛦᚱᛅᚴᛁ
ᛏᚢᛚᛁ

Svā æi titul titul.
fuþąrkhniastbmlʀ

HvaR es ī? Ælisti Ąsa hvaR es.
VīfrøðR gærði afr æft asni faður.
KolfinnR fal[h] tæitirūnaR o[k] ævinrūnaR.
Suli alda hvaR. ⇞
utu, tuuut, biligangR, turRægi, doli.

'So has the inscription, inscription.
fuþąrkhniastbmlʀ

Who is within? The eldest As is who.
Vifrød made (this) strong in memory of (his) dear father.
Kolfinn fixes joyful runes and eternal runes.
Everything freezes.
utu, tuuut, denial-of-walking, dire counsel, tarry.'

Some of the phrases in this text are difficult to interpret, but the overall nature of the inscription is clear: the Malt stone is a runic memorial and it is equally as clearly magical. Most of the features typical of the five-part amulet texts are present: names, a magical symbol, a futhark row and two nonsensical palindromes. The repetition *titul titul* 'inscription, inscription', where *titul* appears to be a loanword from Latin (cf. English *title*), even suggests a slightly transformed item description is present here too; cf. the similar doubling on medallion pendants of the runic charm words *tuwa* and *salu*.

The riddle 'Who is within?' could be a reference to the futhark row, as two of the rune-names are those of gods, at least one of whom, Tyr, is clearly one of the Æsir – although the 'eldest As' could equally as well be a reference to Odin. The expressions 'joyful runes' and 'eternal runes' are also reminiscent of phrases from two of the inscriptions on the Blekinge stones as is *turRægi* 'dire counsel' (cf. Björketorp's 'baleful prophecy'), though unlike *ginnorūnōR* 'mighty runes', the Malt expressions 'joyful' and 'eternal runes' are more clearly paralleled in the coupled compounds *æfinrúnar ok aldrrúnar*, 'eternal runes and life runes' mentioned as known to noblemen in the *List of Rig*.

The exact meaning and significance of many of the other expressions in the inscription remain much debated, however, although freezing, tarrying and denial of walking suggest the text is ranged against a walking dead. So given the other magical funerary inscriptions, and given that this stone appears once to have been quite prominently displayed, it seems that the inscription on the Malt stone, too, was intended to stop the dead person commemorated in the inscription from wandering from his grave – or rather, as the inscription suggests, to be denied the ability to walk about and instead be frozen to his burial spot.[10]

10 The best assessment of the difficult Malt stone and its text is K. Samplonius, 'Zum Runenstein von Malt', *Amsterdamer Beiträge zur älteren Germanistik* 36 (1992), 65–91; though cf. Birkmann, pp. 361–72 who summarises other interpretations of the various sections, some elements of which we have incorporated into our translation when they seem to be better

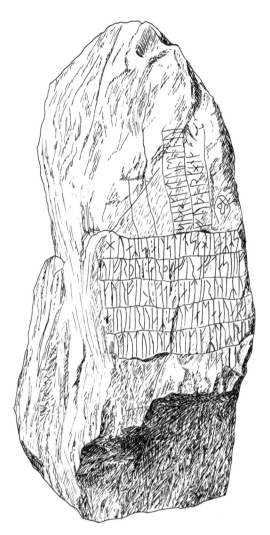

Fig. 16. Malt stone

It is a mixed pagan and early Christian environment that also seems to explain the inscription on the late Viking Age stone from Glavendrup, Denmark. Its long text, carved on three sides of the reddish granite stone, indicates it was raised in memory of what seems to have been an important pagan priest (though his precise description has been questioned by some experts) and clearly includes thoroughly heathen sentiments:

paralleled. For instance *doli* 'tarry' (< **dwelian* 'tarry, lead astray', which would be related to both English *dwell* and *dull*; cf. also German *toll* 'crazy'), presumably referring to the 'wanderer', seems preferable to a meaning 'hide'. And *toʀʀægi* 'dire counsel' seems more salient than *toʀʀæki* 'damage, loss' given Björketorp's *ūþarba spā* 'baleful prophecy' and the use of the verbal root *rag-* 'counsel' in runic expressions like *raginakundo* and *rætta* (see p. 255, n. 12).

ᚱᛆᚴᚾᚼᛁᛚᛏᚱ᛫ᛋᛆ
ᛏᛁ᛫ᛋᛏᛁᚾᚦᛅᛋᛁ᛫ᛅᚿᛒᛏ
ᛅᛚᛆ᛫ᛋᛆᛚᚢᛆᚴᚢᚦᛆ
ᚢᛁᛆᚱᛁᛒᛋᛘᛏᛁᛒᚾᛁᛏᚱᛒᛆᛆᚦᛁᛏ
ᛈᛆ
ᛆᛚᛅ᛫ᛋᚾᛏᛁᛆ᛫ᛒᛆᚱᚦᚢ
ᚹᚾᛒᚱ᛫ᚦᛏᚾᛋᛁ᛫ᛏᛈᛏ᛫ᚹᛆᚦᚾᚱ
ᛋᛁᛏ᛫ᛏᚾᛈ᛫ᚷᛆᛁᛋ᛫ᛈᚾᛏᛏ᛫ᛏᚾᛈᛏ
ᚾᚷᚱ᛫ᛋᛁᛏ᛫ᛁᛏ᛫ᛋᚾᛏᛁ᛫ᚱᛏᛁᛋᛏ᛫ᚱᚾᛏ
ᛏᛆ᛫ᚦᛏᛋᛁ᛫ᛏᛈᛏ᛫ᛏᚱᚾᛏᛁᛏ᛫ᛋᛁᛏ
ᚦᚾᚱ᛫ᚾᛁᛈᛁ᛫ᚦᛏᛋᛁ᛫ᚱᚾᛏᛏᛆ
ᛆᛏ᛫ᚱᛁᛏᛏ᛫ᛋᛆ᛫ᚾᛆᚱᚦᛁ᛫ᛁᛋ᛫ᛋᛏᛁᛁᚦᛏᛏᛋᛁ
ᛆᛁᛚᛏᛁ᛫ᛁᚦᛏ᛫ᛏᛈᛏ᛫ᛆᛋᛋᛆ᛫ᛏᚱᛆᚷᛁ

Ragnhildr satti stēn þænsi æft Alla Solva-goða vēa-liðs hēð-værðan þægn.
Alla syniʀ gærðu kumbl þøsi æft faður sīn, ok hans kona æft vær sīn. Æn Sōti
rēst rūnaʀ þæssi æft drōttin sīn. Þōrr vīgi þæssi rūnaʀ.
At rætta sā værði ǣs stēn þænsi ælti æða æft annan dragi.

'Ragnhild placed this stone in memory of Alli, the priest of the Salver,
honour-worthy thane of the holy-troop (?).
Alli's sons made this monument in memory of their father, and his wife in
memory of her husband. And Soti carved these runes in memory of his lord.
May Thor bless these runes. May whosoever damages this stone or drags it to
stand in memory of another become a warlock.'

The 188cm-tall and rather squat Glavendrup stone is one of two granite Danish
memorials from about the end of the ninth century erected by Ragnhild, both of
which originally stood on mounds at the head of a series of smaller stones
arranged in the shape of a ship – a sure sign that they are pre-Christian burial
memorials. The other stone, from Tryggevælde, which is on the Danish island of
Zealand rather than (like Glavendrup) on Fyn, seems to be earlier and describes
Ragnhild as the 'sister of Ulf' as well as a wife to a certain Gunulf, rather than to
the priest Alla:[11]

ᚱᛆᚴᚾᚼᛁᛚᛏᚱ᛫ᛋᚾᛋᛏᛁᛆ᛫ᚾᛚᚹᛋ᛫ᛋᛆᛏᛁ᛫ᛋᛏᛁᛁᛏ᛫
ᚦᛏᛋᛁ᛫ᛏᚾᛈ᛫ᚹᛆᚱᚦᛁ᛫ᚷᛏᚾᛈ᛫ᚦᛒᛋᛁᛚᛏᚾᛈᛏ
ᛏᚾᛈᛋᛈᛏᛁᚦ᛫ᚦᛏᛋᛁ
ᚹᚾᛏᚾᚿᚹ᛫ᚾᛏᚱᛋᛁᛏ᛫ᚹᛚᛋᛈᚾᚷᛏᛏᛏᛈᛏᛏ
ᛋᚾᛏ᛫ᛏᛏᛁᚱᛒᛁᛋ᛫ᚹᛏᛁᛆ᛫ᚾᛏᚱᛒᛏ᛫ᛏᚾᛈᚾᛏᛁᛆ᛫ᚦᛆᛁᛒᛏᛏᚱᛁ
ᛋᛏᚾᛏᚱᛒᛁ᛫ᛏᛏ᛫ᚱᛁᛏᛏ᛫ᛁᛋᛏᛁᚱᛏᛁᛋᛏᛏᛁᚦᛒᛏᛋᛁ
ᛁᛒᛏᛁᛒᛏᛏᛏᚱᛆᚷᛁ

Ragnhildr, systiʀ Ulfs, satti stēn þænsi ok gærði høg þænsi æft, ok skēð þæssi,
Gunulf, vær sīn, glamulan man, sun Nærfis. Fāiʀ værða nū føddiʀ þēm bætri.
Sā værði at rætta ǣs ælti stēn þænsi æða heðan dragi.

'Ragnhild, Ulf's sister, placed this stone and made this howe in memory – and
this ship-setting – of Gunulf, her husband, a clamorous man, son of Nærfi. Few
will now be born better than him. May whosoever damages this stone or drags it
away from here become a warlock.'

11 Moltke, *Runes and their Origin*, pp. 223–29.

The more elegantly proportioned 325cm-tall Tryggevælde stone, whose letterforms suggest it was also cut by Soti, mentions the accompanying howe or burial-mound as well as the ship-memorial (here called a *skēð*). It also has an epitaph for Gunulf where Glavendrup has the 'Thor bless' formula, and again includes a form of the curse 'may he become a warlock' (a *rætta*). These texts appear to reflect a continuation of the grave-warding type of curse represented by the Eggja inscription, then, and it seems likely that the invocation of Thor in such texts was protective – Thor's hammer amulets were often left dangling on entombed burial carts in Viking times after all, a practice that suggests Thor was seen as a protector of the dead during their journey into the afterlife.[12]

Wishes that any violator of a rune-inscribed memorial become a warlock or something similar are known from several other gravestones of about the same date. An inscription on a memorial stone from Glemminge, southern Sweden, for example, concludes: *Værði at rætta hvas of briuti*, 'May whosoever breaks it become a warlock.' One of the stones from Skern, Northern Jutland, carries a similar formulation: *Siði sā mannr æs þøsi kumbl of briuti*, 'May the man who breaks this monument become a sorcerer.' And similarly, the text on one of the stones from Sønder Vinge, also in North Jutland, concludes: *særði ok sēð-r[æ]tti, saʀ mannr æs øði minni þvī*, 'Fucked (i.e. sodomised) and a wizard, the man who destroys this memorial.' Even stones raised in memory of women sometimes feature comparable wishes, e.g. the slightly damaged stone from Saleby, Sweden has: *Værði at rætta ok at argʀi konu saʀ ēs haggvi [ī] krus. . . of briuti*, 'May whosoever cuts to pieces . . . breaks . . . become a warlock and a misdoing woman.' The description *argʀi* 'misdoing' is related to the term *argʀ* 'perversion' used in the curse on the Blekinge stones as well as *ergi* 'perversion' on a Bergen rune-stick, and seems to indicate that the calling of a misdoer a warlock, wizard or a sorcerer was not a reference to wishing that the victim of the curse gain magical powers, but was an indication that they should be considered unnatural, i.e. social outcasts. The designation 'witch' or 'sorcerer' was already a mark of opprobrium in Roman times; it appears a similar notion, i.e. that users of some kinds of magic were evil perverts, had developed in the North by late Viking times, even before the date of the official Christianisation of the Scandinavian countries.[13]

A runic curse itself is clearly a form of sorcery, however, so it was evidently a particular type of magic that was at issue with these descriptions. The expression *sīði* 'sorcerer' refers to a practiser of *seiðr* (literally 'binding'), the form of magic that is characterised in some Norse sources as somehow less desirable than *galdr* 'chant magic'. Moreover, *seiðr* is also often linked to women (particularly the

---

[12] Zeiten, pp. 49–50. The formal etymology of *rætta* adopted here is from an earlier **rah-t-* or **reh-t-*, a variant form of the 'counsel' word also seen at Malt, Vimose and as the root of *ragina/regin* 'god, adviser etc.' A pejorative magical association of this root is also found in some Baltic and Slavic cognates, e.g. Lithuanian *ragana* 'witch, sorceress' and Old Polish *rezeke* 'bewitch'. Other investigators have mooted a negative sexual meaning for the word, though without proffering a feasible etymology.

[13] Moltke, *Runes and their Origin*, pp. 232–36 and cf. T. Fogg, 'Slaves, Outcasts and Fringe Dwellers' (Unpublished dissertation, Melbourne 2000), pp. 309–26.

goddess Freya), and in fact one of the mother goddesses venerated in the Rhineland in Roman times bears the epithet *Saithamia* 'the binder, the user of *seiðr*'.[14] Hence, presumably, the curse to become both a 'misdoing woman' and a 'warlock' in the Saleby inscription. The other designation, *rǣtta* 'warlock', which is formed from a term for magic whose negative connotation can be seen in the Malt stone's description *tuʀrægi* 'dire-counsel', even seems to be compounded with *seiðr* at Sønder Vinge in the description *sēð-r[ǣ]tti* 'wizard', or literally a '*seiðr*-practising (evil) adviser'. This inscription is much damaged, however, and its interpretation correspondingly somewhat uncertain.

Curses are also encountered on runic amulets, of course, notably those wishing harm upon a lover or banishing spirits of disease. A similarly ominous message, though in this case clearly connected with death, is found on a rune-engraved copper scales-box from Sigtuna, Sweden. Dating from the beginning of the eleventh century, the amulet's inscription appears to contain a versified warning to potential thieves. Thievery is a problem endemic to most societies, of course, and in folklore as well as in learned tradition dating back to ancient Egypt, enchantments were used to force thieves to return stolen goods or to punish them. The runic box has the following runes engraved around its rims:

ᛏᛁᛅᚱᚠᚱ×ᚠᛁᚴᛅᚠ×ᛋᛁᛘᛋᚴᚢᛘ×ᛘᚭᚾᛁ×ᛋᚴᛅᛚᛅᛦ×ᚦᛁᛋ--×ᛁ----------
ᚭᛏᛁ×ᛁᚭᚢᛁᚱᛘᚢᚭᛏᚱ×ᚠᛅᚦᛁ×ᚱᚢᚾᚭᚱ×ᚦᛁᛋᛅᚱ
ᚠᚢᚼᛚ×ᚢᛅᛚᚢᛅ×ᚽᛚᛅᛁᛏ×ᚠᛅᛚᚢᚭᛅ×ᚠᚭᛅᚴᚢᚴ×ᚭᛅᚭᛋᛅᚢ-ᛅ

Diarfʀ fækk af semskum manni skālaʀ þess[aʀ] ī(?). . .*[l]andi. En Værmundr fāði rūnaʀ þessaʀ. Fugl vælva slæit falvan: fann gauk ā nās au[k]a.*

'Djarf got these scales in . . .land from a Samish (or perhaps Semgallian) man. And Vermund carved these runes. The bird ripped apart the pale robber; one saw how the corpse-cuckoo (i.e. raven) swelled.'

Descriptions of birds of prey devouring the bodies of the slain are prevalent in Germanic literature, and the image of the bloated carrion-bird swelling after devouring the robber's corpse seems to be a magical simile warning of the fate awaiting any prospective stealer of the box. Thus the inscription can be grouped with the multitude of charms against robbery familiar from the Germanic countries (including the runic one described in chapter 2), whether they are to protect against theft, to ensure the return of stolen property or to identify a thief etc.[15]

In fact, another somewhat baffling Swedish inscription dated to the eleventh or twelfth centuries also makes reference to ravens and death. Occurring on a slate

14 See p. 10, n. 13. On the other hand, the apparent call on Thor to use *seiðr* on a rune-stone memorial from Jursta/Korpbro, Sweden (in a disputable reading of irregular cryptic runes), presumably, at best, represents an abbreviation of the 'become a pervert/sorcerer' and 'Thor bless' formulas comparable to the isolated 'Thor' at Rök; see MacLeod, *Bind-Runes*, pp. 165–67 and cf. Moltke, *Runes and their Origin*, pp. 243–44.

15 O. von Friesen, 'Runinskriften på en koppardosa, funnen i Sigtuna augusti 1911', *Fornvännen* 7 (1912), 6–19. Alternative appealing but linguistically problematic readings of the amulet identify ᚢᛅᛚᚢᛅ as *vǫlva*, i.e. seeress, rather than robber: Krause, *Runen*, p. 101, for example reads 'the bird-*vǫlva* (the corpse-riding valkyrie) ripped apart the pale one'.

whetstone also found in Sigtuna and resembling a rune-stone in miniature, it clearly reads:

> :ᚦᛅ:ᚼᛂᛁᛁᚱᛁᚱ:ᚦᚢ:ᚼᚱᛅᚠᚾᛅ×
> ᚵᛁᛅᛚᛅ: ᛅᛏ⁝ᛏᛅᚢᚦᚱ:ᛋᛏᚮᚦᛅᚾ
> ᚱᚢᚾᚢᛘ×ᛅᚾᚦ--·ᚱᛁᛋᛏᛁ·ᚴᚢᚦ·ᚼᛁᛅ-. . .
> ᛅᚾᛏ:ᚼᛅᚾ-
>
> *Þā høyriʀ þū hrafna gialla at dauðan(?) Stoðinn rūnum. Ann[a](?) risti. Guð hia[lpi] and han[s].*
>
> 'Then you hear ravens shriek at the deceased. Steadied by runes. Anna (?) carved. May God help his spirit.'

Here, as on the Sigtuna scales-box, we have a reference to a raven appearing at death. In this case, however, the evocative opening line is analogous to the words found in the *Second Lay of Gudrun*: *Þá heyrir þú hrafna gjalla, ørnu gjalla, æzli fegna*, 'Then you hear ravens shriek, eagles shriek, rejoicing in the carrion.' In fact it seems that this whetstone's inscription represents little more than a series of runic and epic quotations – at any rate the call on God to help the deceased's spirit seems incongruous with any sort of malevolent magic. Similarly hard to explain in this context is the phrase 'steadied by runes', a form which appears on a genuine rune-stone memorial from Hällestad in southern Sweden, and is echoed by the similar *bant með rūnum*, 'bound with runes' on a poetic memorial stone from Swedish Nybble (where the term *bant* was clearly chosen for alliterative purposes).[16]

A further charm against theft probably appears on a rune-stick from Bergen containing what has been interpreted as a botched Latin charm (albeit carved in rather elegant runes):

> ᛐᚠᚢᚱᛁᚿᛋ'ᚢᛁᛏᛆᛚᛁ'ᛕᛆᚱᛁᛏᛁᚱ
>
> *Fur insui talis pariter.*

The Latin word *fur* 'thief' can be isolated here and it has been suggested *talis* might refer to the goddess Dalix (Dalis, Dalex, Dallix) who is named as the ruler of thieves in some Scandinavian books of black magic. The term is a regular Latin adjective, however, and the whole inscription can just as readily be interpreted as oddly expressed, but essentially quite normal runic Latin. Translated, it seems to say 'Thief! Equally I have sewn up such', with 'sewing up' probably referring to magical 'binding'.[17]

The warning on the Sigtuna box, like the Viking-era Scandinavian rune-stones cautioning against desecrating or stealing memorial stones, belongs in this preventative category. They also, as we have seen, predict a dire fate for the violator. The Sigtuna curse's foreshadowing of the wrongdoer's fate in verse, however, is reminiscent of the tradition continued to the present time in the jokey

16 H. Gustavson and T. Snædal Brink, 'Runfynd 1983', *Fornvännen* 79 (1984), 250–59.

17 *NIyR* no. 611, although usually read as the three Latin words *furens, vitalis, pariter*, i.e. 'raging, of life, equally'.

written deterrents to thieves which children record in their school-books, such as
'I pity the baker / I pity the cook / I pity the one / Who takes this book' etc. An
identification of owner and scribe, as in the Sigtuna curse, and the inclusion of a
poem to deter any attempt to steal the object, is also found, written in Latin, in the
Anglo-Saxon *Leechbook* of Bald:

> Bald owns this book, which he ordered Cild to write.
> Here I earnestly pray all men, in the name of Christ,
> that no treacherous person take this book from me,
> neither by force, nor by theft, nor by any false talk.
> Why? because the best treasure is not so dear to me
> as my dear books, which the grace of Christ attends.

As at Sigtuna, though, with its image of the gluttonous corpse-cuckoo foreshadowing a grim end, the fate awaiting the robber is often much direr in Old
Germanic tradition. Witness the following Anglo-Saxon charm against a
cattle-thief that wishes the following ill fortune upon him:

> May he quite perish, as fire consumes wood,
> may be as fragile as a thistle,
> he who intends to drive away these cattle,
> or to carry off these goods.[18]

Other narrative charms against theft describe the fates meted out to other wrongdoers, e.g. some Anglo-Saxon charms against theft warn:

> The Jews hanged Christ; they were severely punished for it. They treated him
> in the most evil manner; grievously they paid for it.[19]

The Sigtuna amulet fits into a broader Germanic tradition of preventative curses,
then, one that appears somewhat removed from the curse against theft described
in chapter 2. That curse, instead, with its invocation of Odin, seems closer to the
classical tradition of judicial prayers.

It is not merely the invocation of the divine that is the characteristic mark of an
ancient judicial prayer, however. A judicial curse or prayer is a request that the
powers above (or below) avenge a theft after it has occurred, rather than prevent
one that has not yet happened.[20] A poem on a long Norwegian rune-stick from
Bergen seems to be a curse more in keeping with this kind of magical expression.
The runic text requires some emendation to make sense, but it appears to end with
an appeal for the wrath of God to fall upon a certain Svein, whose misdeed, which
seems to have been refusing to hand over a treasure trove he had found to his king,
is alluded to in the text. The inscription, whose words are arranged mostly in
dróttkvætt metre, reads:

---

18   Storms, no. 15.
19   Ibid., no. 11b, cf. also nos 13 and 14.
20   Versnel, 'Beyond cursing'.

ᛏᛁᚴᛏᛁᚱᛈᛏᛏᛁᚱᛁᚾᛏᛁᚠᛁᛆᛆᛆᛏᛏᛁᛁᚠᚱᛒᛁᚱᚼᛁᛁᛁᚤᛆᚠᛏᚾᛏᚱᚠᛁᛞᛏᛏᛁᛏᛒᚼᛁᚱᚼᛏᚱᚤᛁᛒᚼᛆᚱᚱᛁᚼᛁᛈᚤ
ᛁᚾᚼᛁᛁᛁᚠᛁᛆᚠᚱᛏᛒᛁᚼᛁᚼᛏᚾᚼᛁᚱᚾᛏᚼᛁᛏᛏᛁᛒᚼᛏᛁᛆᚱᛆᚱᛁᚼᛁᛁᛁᛆᚱᚾᚤᛒᛏᚾᛁᛏᛁᛒᛁᚦᛁᚼᛒᚱᛁᛁᛏᛁᛈᛏᚠᚼᛁ
ᛏᛁᚦᚾᚤᚠᚾᚼᚱᛏᛁᚦᛁ
ᛁᛁᚠᚾᚱᚦᚱᛁᛆᚤᚾᚼᛁᛁᛁᛁᛆᚼᛁᛁᚤᛁᚠ

Seint er, þat er Sveinn fann
dynta, silfrberg, í mǫl dverga,
þat segir herr með harra,
heiðmilds í gjǫf reiða.
Hafi sá er laug at logi(s?)
logrýranda dýrum,
þess vítis bið ek þrjóti
þegnleiðum, Guðs reiði.

Sigurðr Amundasonr á mik.

'Very overdue (in being paid) is that which Svein Dynta found,
the silver-mountain of dwarf-pebbles (i.e. treasure trove?)
as a gift to the generous one (i.e. the king)
– so says the army, together with the king.
May he who lied to the dear diminisher (?)
of the sea's flames (i.e. gold, hence the king)
– this punishment I ask for the scoundrel, loathsome to the people –
bear God's wrath.

Sigurd Amundson owns me.'[21]

Other runic poems have also been found that are somewhat reminiscent of this
inscription, although it is not clear with these examples whether their composition
was really inspired by thoughts of vindication or if they are nothing more than
clever metrical texts recorded in runes. A rather oblique message on a rune-stick,
originally pierced with a bronze ring, from Årdal church, Norway, composed in
the skaldic *hrynhent* metre, runs:

ᛚᛁᚠᛏᚱᛁᛒᛏᛏᛚᛁᚠᛁᚱᛈᛏᛁᚤᛏᛁᛆᛆᛁᚠᚠᛁᚱᛒᛏᚦᚾᛁᛆᛁᚱᚼᚱᛒᛁᚾᛁᛁᛁᚱᚼᚾᛁᛆᚾᚤ
ᚦᛁᚱᚤᚾᛁᚾᚤᛁᛁᚠᛆᚱᚤᛏᚱᚼᛏᚱᚠᛏᚾᚠᛁᛁᚤᛁᛁᚾᛁᛁᛁᚠᛏᚱᛁᛁᛏᚼᚱᛁᛏᛏᛁ

Liggr í palli,   *lifir heimskliga*
hinn er beð undir sér   *bleytir stundum.*
Þar munu maðkar   *margir gaufa,*
sem á dúni søfr   *dóttir Atla.*

'He lies on the bench,   lives foolishly;
he who beds underneath him   is sometimes soaked.
There may many   maggots swarm,
as Atli's daughter   sleeps on down.'

This verse, probably from the late twelfth century, is difficult to interpret, and has
generally been taken as a reference to a bed-wetter, or perhaps a masturbator. It
has been regarded as an example of *níð* or ritual shaming, perhaps carved to effect

---

[21] Liestøl, *Runer frå Bryggen*, 25–26, idem, 'Rúnavísur', 47–49, A. Liestøl et al., 'En ny
dróttkvættstrofe fra Bryggen i Bergen', *Maal og Minne* (1964), 93–100 and cf. also Marold,
'Runeninschriften als Quelle', pp. 675–77.

the situation it describes, i.e. the discomfort and death of Atli's daughter, who appears to be contrasted with the fool. The precise meaning as well as the implications of such poems is difficult to fathom – they may well be simply examples of grim poetry rather than genuine curses, as there is nothing about them that gives a clear indication that they were composed as part of magical practice. In fact, there are literary analogies not only to the motif of wetting oneself (in Icelandic *níð*-poetry), but the theme of worms or maggots issuing from a noble woman is also closely paralleled in the Norwegian story of Snæfrid, daughter of Harald Finehair, whose corpse emitted a terrible stench when moved from her bed of down, and from whose body all kinds of vermin emerged.[22]

More obviously malevolent in intent is the following inscription, again in verse, and apparently carved in response to a betrayal:

```
. . .⋈ᛒᚾᛒᚱᛒᚱ.ᚴᚱᛁᚼᛱᚴᛁ.ᚱᛂᛁᛱᛏᚾᛁᛂᚱᛒᚼᛱᚱ.ᛱᛏᚼᚱ.ᛱᚼᚱᛁᚾᛁᚴᛁ.ᛁᚠᛂᚱᛱ.ᛱᚱ⋇.ᚱᛁᛁᚴᛱᚱ.ᛱᛂ⋇ᛁ.ᚴᚱ
ᛏᛁᛱᛁᛂᛏ.ᛱᛂᛂᛂ.ᚴᛱᛂᛂ.
ᚴᛁᛏᚱᛁᛁᛒᛱᚱ.ᛒᛱᛂ.ᛱᛏᛱᚱᛁ.ᛁᚱᛂ.ᚴᛁᛱᛒᚱᛂᛁ⋇ᛒᛱᚾᚴ.ᚴᛂᛱ⋇ᛂᛂ.ᚴᛱᛱᚼᚱ.ᛁᛒᚱ.ᛱᛂᛒ.ᛂᛁᛁᛂᛁ.⋇ᛱᛱᚴᛱᚱ.ᛒ
ᛂᛂᛁᛂ.ᛂᛁᚴᚱ.⋇ᛂᛱᛂᛂ.⋇ᛂ⋇ᛂᛁᚱᛁᛒᛁ.ᛒᛂᚱ. . .
```

. . . *Hallvarðr grenski reist rúnar þessar.*

Sæll er, sá er svíki, fýla,
sorg á reikar torgi;
Grettis sótt at gæti,
geldr eiðar þess aldri.
Er-a feiknbrǫgðum flagða
fallnir niðr með ǫllu
haukar Baldrs, ok halda
hugstríði byr[skíða].

'. . . Hallvard the Greenlander carved these runes.

'Fortunate is he never, the brute who betrays:
Sorrow on the hair-parting's turf (i.e. on his head)
he may expect to get.[23]
(He will) pay for this (broken) oath.
The breeze-blown [skis] (i.e. ships)
of Balder's hawks (i.e. the warriors, hence the sea-warriors)
are not all felled through the treacherous deeds of troll-women,
and (they) hold the memory of battle.'

This *dróttkvætt* inscription, carved into Vinje church in Norway during the popular rebellions of the 1190s, seems to be a form of *níð* rather than an amuletic or spell-like expression.[24] *Níð*, literally 'hostility', 'shame' or 'scorn', was proscribed

---

22 *NIyR* no. 344.
23 Literally 'to get Grettir's sickness' (i.e. the winter), here further identified as a poetic homonym, *vetr* 'winter' for *vættir*, 'he will expect'.
24 *NIyR* no. 171. It seems probable that this message is contemporary or at least related to *NIyR* no. 170, also in Vinje church, which reads 'Sigurd Jarlsson carved these runes on the Saturday after Botolf's Mass, when he fled hither and did not want to reconcile with Sverrir, the murderer of his father and brothers.' M. Olsen in *NIyR* identifies Hallvard the Greenlander as Hallvard bratti who is frequently mentioned together with Earl Sigurd in contemporary sources.

by Icelandic law, but often took a rhetorical form such as offensive verse. It could also appear as a concrete sign, typically a wooden sculpture of two men engaged in sodomy, and was often deliberately feminising and sexual (hence the reference to 'troll-women'?). According to the medieval Danish historian Saxo, though, enemies were easier to overcome if *níð*-verses had been recited against them. The word [*n*]*íð* may also even occur runically on a small wooden handle found at Trondheim and archeologically dated to the late twelfth century. Probably from a spoon or ladle, we can only wonder what may originally have been served in it![25]

Slightly less sinister is a further poetic inscription, which might, however, represent a warning to wrongdoers. It is found carved along the narrow edge of a stone from Hønen, Norway, and apparently reads:

ᚢᛏᚾᚱ·ᚾᛁᚭ·ᚾᚱ·ᚦᚾᚱᚨᚨ·ᚦᛁᚱᚾᚾᚱᛑ'·ᚾᛁᚼ·ᚱᛑᚱᚨᚭ·ᛁ'ᚭ·ᛁᚾᚨᚾᚱᚦᛏᚦᚱᚾᚨᛌᚾᚨᚾᚦᛘᚭᛁᚱᚭ·
ᚾᛁᚱᛏᛀᛏᚾᛁ·ᚨR

Út ok vítt, ok þurfa	*þerru ok áts,*
vindkalda á ísa,	*í óbygð at kómu.*
Auð má illt vega,	*at deyi ár.*
'Abroad and afar and in need	of towels and food,
they came in to the wilderness;	up on the cold, wind-swept ice.
Evil (fate) can take away fortune,	whereby one may die early.'

Carved in an irregular poetic metre resembling *málaháttr*, but with some lines of *fornyrðislag*, this eleventh-century inscription seems to refer to an unlucky expedition which obviously ended tragically for the participants, who were subject, like all of society, to the evils of fate.[26]

Another type of curse well known from the ancient world is that which was commonly left in sepulchres and tombs. Most of these *defixiones* or binding-tablets were clearly deposited in the hope that the spirit of the dead might call on underworldly powers in order to effect a curse. In fact often the tomb was that of an 'untimely' or 'restless' dead – usually someone who had died in a tragic manner or was thought to be otherwise resentful of those still living. Curses of this type were also used by the ancient Celts and some employed formulations like those typical of the early medieval Irish *loricae* – some scholars have even claimed that *loricae* were originally created to be anti-*defixiones*. Yet nothing quite like the ancient tradition of curse-tablets has been found in Germanic tradition.[27]

Many of the rune-inscribed amulets already discussed, of course, were found in graves or burial mounds. Nonetheless most of these were probably buried as a treasured possession of the deceased. Some runic amulets may have been placed in graves secondarily, though, presumably for other purposes. In fact it has been

---

[25] For the tradition of *níð* see F. Ström, *Níð, Ergi and Old Norse Moral Attitudes* (London 1974) and Fogg, pp. 294–308. The wooden handle is *NIyR* no. 852.

[26] *NIyR* no. 102.

[27] J.G. Gager (ed.), *Curse Tablets and Binding Spells from the Ancient World* (Oxford 1992), pp. 18–20; Herren (ed.), pp. 26–31.

argued that some Scandinavian runic amulets were put in graves in order to transfer an illness from someone living to someone dead. Others have been thought, too, like some of the rune-stones more clearly were, to have been deposited in a grave in the hope that the associated corpse remained confined. But on close inspection these amulets remain very problematic.

The first sometimes considered to be of this type, a tiny bronze plate from Ulvsunda, Sweden, hardly larger than a thumbnail, was found in a burial mound and dates to the ninth century. Its tiny inscription, with runes of only 2–3mm in height, is very difficult to read, but is commonly quoted as saying: *Vesat-tū ūrvakʀ ūti, misfylgiʀ! Fangi skaði vā . . .*, 'Do not be over-lively outside (i.e. out of the grave), revenant! May the evil-doer get woe . . .' This reading has to be recognised as speculative in both reading and interpretation, and there are no other examples where a *misfylgiʀ*, apparently an intensified and somewhat irregular form of the *fylgja* or 'fetch' of the sagas, is called upon in runic inscriptions.[28]

The text on the Ulvsunda plate is sometimes compared with an early-tenth-century bronze buckle from Viborg, Denmark. Its runes can be made out fairly easily as ᛚᚢᚲᛁᛋᛚᛁᚾᛏ; the interpretations offered for this text are all contentious, though. There is little to recommend any of the translations, whether as *lok æs læva*, 'ended are misfortunes (hauntings)', *lok æs Liva*, 'buckle (lock?) is Lifa's' or even a more formula-like *Lȳ, gīsli, vā*, 'protection, buckle, woe'.[29]

Neither of these texts is a particularly convincing example of the death or binding magic often believed to dominate the runic amulet inscriptions. Although curses were clearly part of the repertoire of Germanic magic, and there are clear runic examples representing aspects of this tradition, there is nothing from the Germanic world as complex as the curse-tablets whose use was so widespread in the Graeco-Roman world. There is no sense of the 'binding' or 'fixing' in Germanic belief that was essential to classical cursing, a notion often physically represented by nails piercing the tablets bearing the curse or even lead dolls made in the form of their victims. Neither are there clear calls on the powers of the underworld in Germanic curses, references to Hel or malevolent spirits. Runic curses are mostly ranged against thieves or aim to hold the dead to their graves. The sense of haunting by walking corpses also seems to be an idiosyncratically Nordic expression – and the funerary charms that developed in the hope they might prevent the wandering of the dead appear to be an equally unique expression of the magical tradition of the Scandinavian outpost of the pagan Germanic world.

---

28 Nordén, 'Bidrag', pp. 146–54.
29 Cf. Nordén, 'Magiska runinskrifter', pp. 157ff.; Moltke, *Runes and their Origin*, pp. 357–58.

10

Runic Lore and Other Magic

RUNES often feature in magical contexts in Old Norse literature (and to a lesser extent in Old English sources), so it is little wonder that they have often been taken to be essentially magical by those not familiar with the thousands of examples of mundane runic inscriptions. Many instances of runes which are described in literary texts have been referred to already in previous chapters, of course, where they seemed directly relevant to the amuletic and religious inscriptions that have survived. There are passages in old Germanic literature where the appearance of runes is not clearly reflected in actual inscriptions, however, and there has long been a suspicion that most such instances are due to embellishments typical of storytelling. The usually Christian poets and scribes who wrote down these poems and tales might therefore be thought not to have described actual examples of runic practice or genuine beliefs associated with the knowledge of runic writing.

The longest literary texts concerning the old Germanic letters are the runic poems and other similar tracts on the shapes, sounds and names of the runes. We have English, Norse and even a Gothic example of tracts on the rune-names. But these appear to be mostly expressions of the monkish fascination with antiquities or aspects of the lore of learning how to write – it is often suggested that the runic poems are based on a mnemonic similar to a modern-day alphabet jingle, rather than being inventive or descriptive literary creations. In fact the names occasionally seem to constitute semantic pairs, e.g. 'cattle' (runic *f*) and 'aurochs' (runic *u*) or the mythologically opposed duo 'ogre, giant' (runic *þ*) and 'As' (runic *a*). Despite the appearance of letter-pairs in some runic amulet inscriptions, this coupling in runic may never have represented more than a mnemonic device, however – the pairing of the *n*-rune ('need') with the *h*-rune ('hail') on the Roskilde pendant (described in chapter 4) does not seem to have suggested anything more than a generic sense of magic, despite the ominous nature of the letter-names. After all, Germanic poets obviously could not have used alliteration, the typical stylistic device of their poetry, in an alphabet mnemonic. Semantic pairs would be simple to remember – even more so if they were arranged into a poem. Consequently, this type of literary rune lore probably has little to do with magical uses of runes other than as reflected in the practices already discussed in earlier chapters.[1]

---

[1] For a survey of the runic poems see A. Bauer, *Runengedichte* (Vienna 2003), though cf. also Liestøl, 'Det norske runediktet', M. Halsall, *The Old English Rune Poem* (Toronto 1981) and

Contemporary with the practical use of runes for all kinds of transactions in Scandinavian towns like Bergen and Trondheim, however, was the writing down of sagas describing early Viking life in Iceland. The Icelandic sagas are often sprinkled with obscure details of amulets, witchcraft and runic sorcery. Yet fascinating as these literary expressions are, there is every reason to be suspicious of the evidence they present. In fact, they cast disappointingly little light on everyday runic practices and we should be wary of reading too much into the details of runic usage they provide. The incidents described so remarkably in these sources rarely include references to the use of runes for practical purposes which was demonstrably prevalent at the time, focusing instead on improbable and usually otherwise unparalleled forms of runic magic. Thus, rather than the product of authors familiar with runes and accustomed to their everyday use, they seem instead to be the creations of literary minds unacquainted with the mundane reality of runic writing as it was employed on the Scandinavian mainland at the time. The fabulous displays of magic so vividly described in the sagas serve more to embellish the deeds of the protagonists who are associated with them than to cast any light on traditional runic practices. These tales describe the inhabitants of a golden age where some details clearly are often only provided in order to emphasise the greatness of the ancestors. Dramatic and celebrated as the incidents often are, they smack of the overblown and the fantastic. After all, to judge from what remains have come down to us, the runic letters seem not to have been widely used on the remote island of Iceland at this time.

We have already considered some episodes from the sagas, notably the disease-inducing 'secret-staves' deprecated by Egil Skallagrimsson, the protagonist of *Egil's Saga*. The brooding viking Egil (who is not to be confused with Egil the archer of Egil and Olrun fame) is medieval Scandinavia's pagan rune-master without peer, a rather unlikeable but undeniably heroic warrior-poet closely allied to the figure of the god Odin, with whom he shares a sinister duplicity as well as runic powers and military and poetic prowess.

Egil's Saga is a monumental work set in the tenth century, although it was written down in early-thirteenth-century Iceland, centuries later than the events it purports to depict. In the incident already considered in the chapter on leechcraft, where a rune-inscribed piece of whalebone had been placed in a girl's bed in order to try to win her affection, Egil rails against incompetent users of runes. He describes ten secret staves incorrectly carved in the runic charm which had caused the girl to become sick rather than be beguiled:

No man should write runes   unless he well knows how to interpret them.
Many men are led astray   by the dark stave.
I saw on the shaped whalebone   ten secret staves carved
these have caused the linden-tree of the leek (i.e. the maiden)
                                 long and great grief.[2]

Page, 'Icelandic rune-poem'. See also Mees, 'Runo-Gothica', pp. 56–63 for the Gothic letter names and idem, 'The North Etruscan thesis', pp. 70ff. for a consideration of the runes as paired, a characteristic first promoted by E. Brate, 'Runradens ordningsföljd', *Arkiv för nordisk filologi* 36 (1920), 193–207.
2   A runic paraphrase of this verse has been discovered in Trondheim, where a rune-stick (*NIyR* no.

Egil himself is able to cure the girl by burning the bewitched bone and replacing it with a fresh runic message. And though the carved whalebone described in the saga is reminiscent of some runic amulets, the ten secret staves remain fairly obscure.

The most celebrated description of runic sorcery in *Egil's Saga*, however, one which similarly inspires Egil to spontaneously break into verse, occurs with his discovery of poison in a drink intended for him, by carving runes reddened with his own blood on a drinking horn. The saga recounts how Egil cut his hand with his knife, carved runes on the proffered horn, which he smeared with his blood, and then spoke a verse that caused the horn to shatter:

> I carve runes on the horn,   redden the words with blood.
> I choose words for the ear-roots' trees (i.e. horns)
>   of the mad animal.
> I drink ale as I want,   brought by smiling servants.
> Let us see what it does,   the ale that Bard consecrated.

The motif of colouring runes with one's own blood recurs in other early examples of Norse literature, and the Eddic poem the *Second Lay of Gudrun* even mentions a horn with 'reddened' runes which cause the eponymous heroine to forget her grief. Some runic inscriptions also refer to 'red' or 'reddened' runes, though red was a favoured colour for painting inscriptions in classical times, presumably because it made painted letters stand out so well. On the other hand, the motif of messages inscribed in blood is a staple of magical practices everywhere, not least Scandinavia where later spells occasionally describe sigils that were required to be written in human blood. In fact our word *bless*, Old English *blēdsjan*, originally meant 'to cause to bleed' or 'to bloody' as does *blóta*, the Old Norse word for 'to sacrifice'. Whether blood was used in runic magic outside the minds of the writers of the sagas, however, remains questionable.

'Ale-runes' and other magical expressions associated with drinking-horns are also mentioned in the Eddic *Lay of Sigrdrifa*. Yet Egil's carving runes on the horn is suspiciously closer in detail to the miraculous tale of St Benedict found in the *Dialogues* of Pope Gregory the Great rather than any Norse parallel. In the *Dialogues*, St Benedict is offered a bottle of poisoned wine, but makes a sign of the cross over it, whereupon the bottle shatters. Runic symbols and Christian crucifixes, as well as Christian and pagan miracle stories, were often interchangeable in Norse spells and stories. Yet runic inscriptions are found on some few Viking Age drinking horns, only one of which might be described as magic – so rather than representing a genuine Scandinavian tradition, then, it seems likely that Egil's use of runes in this incident was inspired by a continental source, with a pagan's runes substituted for an expression typical of Christian magic.[3]

---

829), dated between 1175 and 1275, reads: *Sá skyli rúnar rísta, er ráða vel kunni; þat verðr mǫrgum manni at es of . . .*, 'He should carve runes, who knows well how to interpret them; many men become . . .' On the Norse runic episodes discussed in this chapter, see also MacLeod, '*Bandrúnir*', F.-X. Dillman, 'Les runes dans la littérature norroise', *Proxima Thule* 2 (1996), 51–89 and cf. Bæksted, *Målruner og troldruner*, pp. 15–117.

3   Cf. McKinnell and Simek, p. 35.

In another celebrated incident from *Egil's Saga*, Egil sets up a hazel pole topped with a horse's head and pronounces a curse, subsequently recorded in runes, on King Erik Blood-axe and his wife Gunnhild. This seems to be a literary instance of *níð* or ritual scorn, but if so, it is atypical in some ways. Two different forms of *níð* are proscribed in Icelandic law, *tunguníð* 'verbal scorn' and *tréníð* 'wooden scorn'. *Níð* was certainly a historical phenomenon, but Egil's erection of a rune-inscribed pole with a hostile message appears, at best, to be a conflation of the two different forms of *níð*. The raising of a rune-inscribed pole with a defamatory message is closely paralleled in a similar scene recounted in the *Saga of the People of Vatnsdæl*, however, while wooden defamation poles of somewhat different kinds, without verse or runes, recur in several other sagas. Egil's actual curse formulation has analogies with others found in Norse literature, including the 'thistle, mistletoe' curse of the *Saga of Bosi* described in chapter 6, and this latter example's motif of a foster-mother threatening an enemy with runes may best be paralleled in *Grettir's Saga*, where Thorbjorn's foster-mother Thurid occasions Grettir's physical incapacity (and indirectly his death) by sending him a piece of wood engraved with enchanted, blood-reddened runes. Although admittedly there is epigraphic evidence that reflects some aspects of the practices recounted in these passages, they are not paralleled by precise counterparts; instead when judged against the evidence of runic finds these episodes seem mostly to represent confused echoes of historical usages, rather than reliable recollections of runic magic.

Grettir's Saga offers a more credible use of runes when it records the act of writing poetry on rune-sticks by the hero Grettir as well as the mysterious figure Hallmund. The latter dictates a poem to his daughter who carves it on a rune-stick, as does Egil, whose daughter Thorgerd similarly records the poem *Lament for My Sons (Sonatorrek)* in order to alleviate Egil's despair at the death of his son Bodvar. Here we seem to have a more realistic depiction of runic usage, quite different from the more outlandish or overblown runic magic episodes typical of the sagas. More prosaic uses of runes, simply as letters or messages, are also found in several literary sources such as *Gisli's Saga*, *Viglund's Saga* and the *Saga of the People of Svarfadardal*. But these usually seem to be less important to the episodes they appear in than do the ones which feature magic. It is hard to be rid of the impression that most magical uses of runes described in the sagas are literary crutches rather than historically reliable expressions, describing magical uses of runes mostly only for effect in often idealised scenes usually first written down several centuries after the miraculous events they purport to describe.

There are other literary sources, however, which are more important to an understanding of amuletic and other magico-religious uses of runes and hence deserve to be treated more comprehensively and systematically than has been possible in earlier chapters. The poems of the *Poetic Edda*, most famously contained in a late-thirteenth-century codex from Iceland, contain material which clearly dates from much earlier, and apart from apparently preserving a considerably more reliable source for evidence of magical usages of runes, represent the main source of our knowledge of Norse mythology. Today, scholars tend to be sceptical of the often-obscure accounts of runic lore and practice suggested in the poems, although perhaps rather needlessly so.

Runes are alluded to or their use is even described at some length in several of the Eddic poems, and the Old Germanic letters are often depicted in these tracts as a desirable form of knowledge. For example in the *List of Rig*, which describes the mythological origins of the different social classes, only the noble descendants of the god Heimdal (called Rig in the poem) are familiar with runes, *æfinrúnar ok aldrrúnar* 'eternal runes and life-runes' (the first of which, as was indicated in the previous chapter, is paralleled epigraphically on the Danish Malt stone). Practical use of runes is also documented, e.g. in the *Greenlandic Poem of Atli (Atlamál in grænlenzku)*, where the heroine Gudrun carves a runic message to warn her brothers Gunnar and Hogni of the planned treachery of her husband; her message is deliberately confused by her husband's messenger Vingi, however, and although Hogni's rune-wise wife Kostbera (stating that 'few are rune-skilled') is able to discern the warning, the brothers nevertheless resolutely set out to meet their doom:

One thing I most wonder	and still do not understand,
what caused the wise one	to write so wildly;
because the underlying meaning	seems to indicate
the death of you both	if you rush off;
the woman has omitted a stave,	or someone else did this![4]

A similarly treacherous manipulation of letters so as to obscure the original message is familiar to literature lovers via Shakespeare's *Hamlet* and is also described by the Danish chronicler Saxo Grammaticus in the earliest recorded version of the Hamlet story. There is no evidence that this is any more than another case of a literary commonplace, though, perhaps underlined by the awareness that an unassuming expression (like *ship's course*) can become a more sinister one (e.g. *ship's curse*) upon the omission of a single letter.

The two longest and most extravagant passages in Norse poetic literature concerning the use of runes, however, are also two of the most suggestive, although at the same time, on first acquaintance, their language and what they describe seems discouragingly obscure. They are often written off by scholars today, then, as imaginative accounts of runic lore and use, much as are many of the instances in *Egil's Saga*. After all, as is often pointed out, not only do these sources date to the late Viking Age or later, but like the sagas they both hail from Iceland, the only part of Scandinavia, apparently, not to have enjoyed a particularly lively runic tradition.

The two substantial passages occur in the *Sayings of the High One* and the *Lay of Sigrdrifa*, both from the *Poetic Edda*. The runic knowledge conveyed in the *Sayings of the High One* comes directly from the mouth of Odin and has been one of the main inspirations for modern magical interpretations of the runes. The runic lore in the *Lay of Sigrdrifa*, on the other hand, is connected less overtly with Odin: it is recounted by a valkyrie, who as one of the choosers of the slain is a

---

4   In fact the term 'rune-wise' is used in several poems and sagas to describe those who clearly are in possession of secret knowledge of some sort, see Bæksted, *Målruner og troldruner*, p. 32.

servant of Odin, the lord of Valhalla, though somewhat perversely, she is one who has just been rescued from one of her master's curses.

The richest literary descriptions of runic sorcery are found in passages known as the *rúnatal* 'rune-lore' and *lioðatal* 'song-lore' stanzas of the *Sayings* and the *Lay*. The first, featuring both a rune and song lore section, comprises over twenty verses of the *Sayings of the High One*, which is substantially a collection of gnomic proverbs and charms attributed to Odin, augmented by fragmentary sections dealing with his many adventures, including his winning of the runes. The wise Odin is undoubtedly the god most closely associated with runes; in the Norse *Saga of the Ynglings* it is told of him that he 'taught all these arts with runes and songs which are called incantations'.

The second of the long runic passages occurs in the latter part of the *Poetic Edda*, the section dealing with the heroes of Norse mythology rather than the gods. In the part prose, part poetic *Lay of Sigrdrifa*, the hero Sigurd awakens a sleeping valkyrie, who rewards him by instructing him in several magical uses of runes. The runic lore revealed by the valkyrie Sigrdrifa, the eponymous 'victory-bringer' of the *Lay*, is mainly concerned with how to use runes in protecting and healing. In fact another Eddic tale, *Gripir's Prophecy* (*Grípisspá*), predicts the meeting of the two protagonists of the *Lay* and the subsequent imparting of healing lore. Sigrdrifa, a semi-divine sleeping beauty, recounts the lore to her beloved hero Sigurd after her awakening in a section of the *Lay* full of magical potions and invocations of healing magic. Moreover, some of the more opaque references in the song and rune lore of the *Sayings* make more sense in light of the information given in the rune lore of the *Lay*, and in turn, the lore of the *Sayings* was evidently the source of two later works that detail runic and magical lore: *The Saga of the Ynglings* and the late Eddic poem *Groa's Incantation* (*Gróugaldr*) which comprises the first part of the *Lay of Svipdag* (*Svipdagsmál*).

The Lay of Sigrdrifa is an alternative form of the tale of Brynhild (Brünhilde) and Sigurd (Siegfrid) that foreshadows the events told of both in Norse sources (e.g. various Eddic poems and the *Saga of the Volsungs*) and in the medieval German *Song of the Nibelungs*. The *Lay* seems to be something of a pastiche though, as if the composer were attempting to bring together several different traditions and sources, and was not completely successful in the effort. In fact the rune-lore stanzas of the *Lay* are no exception: most of them are well crafted and logically consistent, but some, especially the latter stanzas, seem to be clumsy insertions or not entirely relevant carryovers from a previous work.[5]

The fourteen stanzas of runic lore in the *Lay* suggest some aspects of runic practice which are attested in inscriptions and some which are not. The lore generally has the theme of healing and aiding, though some of the secrets do not seem likely to have been of much use to Sigurd. In fact it can be read mostly as a work completely separate from the rest of the *Lay* and interpreted as the kind of advice that a knowledgeable woman might impart to someone other than a warrior like Sigurd.

---

5   The most recent study of the rune-lore of the *Lay of Sigrdrifa* is Markey, 'Studies in runic origins 2'.

The opening stanza of the rune lore is an introduction invoking the idea more fully developed in later verses of scraping runes off whatever they are carved on and brewing the scraps up in a magical draught. The stanza also includes three paired alliterative expressions which together indicate the essential features the runes bring to the magical brew: they are powerful, helpful and delightful. In particular, the *líknstafa* 'healing-staves' may be compared with the healing amulets discussed in chapter 6, while 'pleasure-runes' (*gamanrúnar*) might be compared with the *tæitirúnar* 'joyful-runes' encountered on the Danish Malt stone:

> Sigrdrifa said:
> Beer I bring you,   apple-tree of the byrnie-council (i.e. warrior)
> mixed with the glory   of might and main;
> it is full of songs   and healing-staves,
> of good enchantments   and pleasure-runes.

The next section, as mentioned at the outset of chapter 4, describes the writing of an amulet inscription on a sword, a particularly apt piece of wisdom, it might be thought, to come from the lips of Sigrdrifa the 'victory-bringer':

> Victory-runes you shall know   if you want to have victory,
> and carve them on the sword hilt,
> some on the mid-ridges,   some on the battle-marks,
> and name Tyr twice.

Similar descriptions of runes written on swords for magical purposes are known from other Old Norse and Old English literary sources, though not in what seem to be religious contexts. In fact very few swords from the Middle Ages are engraved with runes, and those that are tend to carry rather prosaic maker's formulas rather than identifiable 'runes of victory'. The call to invoke Tyr here is often thought to have something to do with *t*-runes, rather than Tyr himself, given that this rune shares his name. In view of Tyr's martial role in Norse myth, however, this line seems simply to be a straightforward religious invocation with 'twice' alliterating with 'Tyr'.

The third rune-lore stanza of the *Lay* has provoked more speculation, especially given the interpretation of the charm word *alu* as 'ale' favoured by some experts. The verse begins with a suggestive expression comparable to both the 'victory-runes' of the second and the beer mentioned in the first stanza:

> Ale-runes you should know,   if you want another's wife
> not to deceive you in faith, if you trust (her);
> they should be carved on a horn,   and the back of the hand,
> and Need marked on the nail.

The *Lay* earlier indicates that Sigrdrifa had already given *minnisveig* or 'memory-beer' to Sigurd immediately after she woke. The idea of *ǫlrúnar* 'ale-runes', if not a later re-interpretation of the runic charm word *alu* 'dedication', may be a reflection of the 'drink of forgetfulness' (as may the reference to a drinking horn), such as the mead in a 'rune-reddened' drinking horn that Grimhild gives the heroine to erase her memory in the *Second Lay of Gudrun* and, in the *Saga of the Volsungs*, another version of the tale, also administers to Sigurd, enabling him to forget Sigrdrifa/Brynhild and marry Gudrun instead. 'Memory-ale' (not specifically runic, and apparently causing the opposite effect, i.e. inducing recollection rather than amnesia) also features in the *Song of Hyndla* (*Hyndluljóð*), and of course another connection between runes and drinking, and even a horn, features in *Egil's Saga*, as was discussed above. The function of the ale-runes in the poem is apparently to induce faithfulness in a lover, which is reminiscent of some of the love-charms encountered in chapter 3. The last half-line's reference to 'need', the name of the *n*-rune, on the other hand (which is coupled by alliteration with 'nail'), is paralleled by various runic curses invoking needs, as was considered at length in chapter 6, although what 'need' might represent in this case remains rather unclear.

Runes are not explicitly mentioned in the next stanza. Nonetheless it does further develop the theme of aiding, protecting and drinking:

> A toast you shall dedicate   and guard against danger,
> and cast a leek in the liquid:
> so I know that   you will never get
> malice-blended mead.

The connection between 'leek' and 'liquid' appears to be reflected in the fact that the name of the *l*-rune is given as 'liquid' rather than 'leek' in most Scandinavian and English sources. Like the preceding stanza, then, this verse may describe a protective function of runes, much as in *Egil's Saga*, where runes are used to discover poisonous drink. After all in the Eddic *Death of Sinfiotli (Frá dauði Sinfiǫtla)*, it is recalled that Sigurd's half-brother, Sinfiotli, was killed by a similarly poisoned horn – so we may suppose that knowledge of this kind would have been particularly pertinent to Sigurd.

The *Lay*'s rune lore then proceeds to describe something that does not seem particularly relevant to Sigurd at all, but is very much in keeping with the theme of women and drink, and moreover the connection between leeks, runes and the Reitia cult that was explained in the chapter on fertility charms:

> Help-runes you shall know,   if you want to help,
> and release the child from the woman;
> they shall be written on the palm,   and clasped about the joint,
> and then ask the Disir to help.

The same expression, *bjargrúnar* 'help-runes', is also known from a fourteenth-century rune-stick from Bergen which, as was described in chapter 2, appears to be a charm to compel a woman to love the stick's author. The Bergen valkyrie inscription, however, represents a quite different context to the one here. Nonetheless carved 'help' or 'help-runes' feature in several protective runic inscriptions, presumably indicating that some epigraphic reality lies behind this verse.

The Disir are supernatural figures like valkyries and Norns, guardian spirits probably linked with fertility who attend birth and death and determine destiny. This stanza probably reflects an extension of the use of runic amulets in fertility and healing magic, then, and the reference to the palm used to aid delivery may suggest a literal writing of runes as part of magically aided childbirth. A childbirth charm carved in runes was discussed in the chapter on healing charms and similar spells are known from later sources like the *Galdrabók*. Unlike the previous two stanzas, this charm is obviously an example of active help rather than protection, much as are the 'victory-runes' of the second stanza which are just as clearly reflected in runic amulet inscriptions. Introducing Sigurd to the magical secrets of midwifery seems quite illogical here, although he has a similar dialogue with the dying dragon Fafnir about the role of the Norns in childbirth in the Eddic *Lay of Fafnir (Fáfnismál)*. This may reflect the hodgepodge nature of the composition of the *Lay of Sigrdrifa* and ultimately leads to the suspicion that the *Lay*'s author has lifted this entire section from somewhere else – if not some sort of deliberate foreshadowing of the episode in the *Lay of Fafnir*, the rune-lore stanzas are internally consistent enough to suggest that they were originally taken from another, independently composed exposition of forms of runic magic.

The counsel to Sigurd in the next stanza seems to fit the context of the *Lay* better, however, with the alliterating *brimrúnar* 'brim-runes' following on from the *bjargrúnar*:

Brim-runes you shall carve	if you want to be safe
on the sail-steeds of the sea (i.e. waves);	
they should be carved on the prow	and on the steering-blade
and burnt with fire into the oar;	
though the breakers be high	and the waves so dark,
you will still come safe from the sea.	

The references to 'brim-runes' might at first seem confusing, but English *brim* originally referred to the seashore before being re-used to mean the edge of a vessel containing liquid (or any comparable protrusion, like the rim of a hat). In Old Norse *brim* typically means 'surf', but 'brim-runes' no doubt refer to calm or safe waters as opposed to the dangers of the open sea. This is reminiscent, then, of the Kvinneby amulet with its narrative charm concerning Thor and the Midgard Serpent, and a staff inscribed with runes that was thrown into the surf so as to calm the sea in one of the versions of the Faeroese ballad *King Alvur* (see chapter 2). We are also reminded of the rune-wise Kon in the *List of Rig*, who could 'help (*bjarga*) people, blunt sword-blades and settle the sea'. The application of runes to various parts of the boat is also reminiscent of the employment of victory-runes earlier in the *Lay* to more parts of a weapon than have actually been found to date on any rune-inscribed item – it is presumably a (*lorica*-like) literary device, and is not to be taken literally.[6]

The protective properties of the runes revert to active healing again in the next stanza:

Branch-runes you shall know	if you want to be a healer ('leech')
and know how to see to wounds;	

---

6 McKinnell and Simek, p. 36 discuss some further runic inscriptions which may have a connection with ships and 'sea-runes'.

| they should be written on birch | and on the trees of the wood, |
| those whose branches bend eastwards. | |

The use of runic inscriptions in healing or leechcraft charms was well established in chapter 6. The healing properties of the birch are also well known from Norse folklore, so it is probably no coincidence that the rune for *b* is named after this tree. Branches bent towards the east may be a reference to the effect of prevailing westerly winds, though the connection between such a tree and healing remains obscure. Nonetheless, many Germanic charms prescribe an easterly direction (e.g. the *Field Remedy* described in chapter 6) or the use of leaves or bark taken from the eastern side of trees, i.e. from the side from which they were typically thickest, and facing east to pray (i.e. towards the rising sun) was also common practice throughout the ancient world.

The next stanza of the *Lay* also begins with a compound of 'runes', but seems to indicate a practice somewhat different to those described in the preceding sections:

Speech-runes you shall know	if you want no-one
to repay you harm with hatred;	
wind them about,	weave them about,
and place them all together	
at the assembly,	where people shall
go for full judgement.	

The expression in the first line, *málrúnar*, is conventionally translated as 'speech-runes', and indeed eloquence was highly valued in medieval Norse society. At least three Swedish rune-stones bear inscriptions stating they were raised in honour of men noted for their skill with words, and elsewhere in the *Lay* it is remarked that 'the man who has little to say for himself is known as an absolute simpleton: that is the characteristic of a fool'. The compound *málrúnar*, presumably indicating something like 'the power of speech', also occurs in the *First Lay of Gudrun* (*Guðrúnarkviða in fyrsta*) and it furthermore is found in a runic inscription on a bone from Lund where, given it is followed by a poetic riddle, it could mean something like 'riddling runes'.[7] The same expression in later Icelandic merely meant 'plain runes' (as opposed to secret or cryptic ones), though *málrúnar* possibly originally signified eloquence – especially the type that would have been useful in making legal pleas (i.e. 'runes of counsel') – when it was first used. The word *mál* commonly appears in old Scandinavian legal codes after all, and appears to have originally meant '(speech at a) council'. At any rate the poet seems to be interpreting *málrúnar* here, much as in the text on the Lund bone, as a form of eloquence, spoken magic to be used to influence a court case.[8]

A similar, less literal meaning of magic and runes is probably also to be understood in the next verse, although for the first time the pattern typical of the

---

7 Moltke, *Runes and their Origin*, p. 460.
8 On the etymology and legal usage of *mál* see Markey, 'Studies in runic origins 1'.

rune-lore stanzas begins to break down here, just as the first mention of Odin occurs:

Mind-runes you shall know more strong-minded than any man; Hropt interpreted them, devised them, from the liquid out of Heiddraupnir's skull and out of Hoddrofnir's horn.	if you want to be wrote them, that had leaked

As we saw in chapter 7, Hropt 'Squawker' is a byname of Odin describing him as the god who chants magical spells. It is not clear who Heiddraupnir and Hoddrofnir are, but the liquid is presumably a reference to the Mead of Poesy, a magical drink that conferred poetic inspiration, and so the *hugrúnar* or 'mind-runes' and the strong mind appear to be references to poetic insight, mnemonic faculty or perspicacity. As the knowledge of runes was probably equated with learning, this section seems less inherently magical than those preceding it, although it is rather stronger on mythological references. In fact the following stanzas, which are stylistically quite different to the previous ones, seem to continue the themes of Odin, the Mead of Poesy and runic learning. The verses appear to be little more than a poetic summation of many of the features of the Norse mythological world, though, along with a further mention of some of the themes already encountered in the earlier sections:

On a cliff stood (Odin) he had a helmet on his head; then Mimir's head spoke wisely the first word and spoke true lore.	with Brimir's sword
On the shield he said to write them, on Arvak's ear on the wheel that turned on Sleipnir's teeth	that stands before the shining god, and on Alsvin's hoof, under Rungnir's chariot, and sledge's straps;
on the bear's paw on the wolf's claw on bloodied wings on the palm of deliverance	and on Bragi's tongue, and on eagle's beak, and on the bridge's end, and on the trail of relief;
on glass and on gold in wine and (brewer's) wort on Gungnir's point on nail of Norn	and on people's amulets, and the mind's seat, and on Grani's breast, and on beak of owl.
All were scraped off, and cast into the holy mead and sent on wide ways;	those which were carved there,
they are with the Æsir, some with the wise Vanir, some mortal men have.	they are with the elves,

Here we encounter assorted references to various mythological figures, most of whom are familiar from other Norse poems and tales. Mimir is the wise giant whose head is pickled by Odin and from whom he seeks advice. Arvak and Alsvid (although here called Alsvin) are the horses that draw the sun across the sky in Old Norse myth, and the shield and shining god mentioned just before them also seem to be allusions to the sun. (H)rungnir is a giant slain by Thor and also mentioned are Bragi the god of poetry, Odin's spear Gungnir, his horse Sleipnir and its foal Grani that became Sigurd's mount. Other references are more elusive, however: the 'palm of deliverance' may be an allusion to the help-runes previously written on the palm to aid in childbed. The bear, wolf and eagle are all beasts of prey, with the 'bloodied wings' and 'trail of relief' perhaps signifying death, the opposite of the life brought by the delivering palm. The bridge's end may similarly signify Asgard, the home of the gods, which lies at the end of the rainbow bridge Bifrost. In fact most of this section seems simply to be a description of the knowledge of the whole cosmos that was granted to the elves, gods and some mortals – the universal lore that was represented by the Mead of Poesy. The whole section is then rounded off with a short summary of the magical uses of runes already described and another reference to amulets:

> There are book-runes,   there are help-runes,
> and all the ale-runes,
> and mighty runes of power,
> for those who can use them,   unconfused and intact
> as amulets,
> use them, if you get them,
> until the gods are dispersed (i.e. at Ragnarok).

It is likely that the expression *bócrúnar* 'book-runes' here should be emended to *bótrúnar* 'cure-runes' on the model of the *bótrúnar* and *bjargrúnar* of the Bergen valkyrie stick and the similar use of the expression *būtrūnar* in an amulet text from Skänninge, Sweden, described in chapter 6. The second-last stanza then seems to repeat the main theme of the first, with the powerful, helpful staves and runes of pleasure reappearing here. The *Lay*'s rune lore ends more or less as it begins, then, employing a loose form of framing, a feature that again underlines the impression that it was originally a separate work from the story of Sigurd waking Sigrdrifa/Brynhild.

The descriptions of runic use in the *Lay of Sigrdrifa* do not seem particularly fabulous at all, then, but unlike those mentioned in the Icelandic sagas are often closely paralleled in runic inscriptions or other early traditions connected with actual runic use. The other major source on the magical uses of runes in Norse literature, however, the Eddic *Sayings of the High One*, is rather less explicit.

The *Sayings*, after all, is no less a composite work than the *Lay*. In fact the whole poem seems to comprise several separate elements and is conventionally divided into five parts: a loosely structured collection of gnomic proverbs and counsels, presumably attributed to the High One (Odin); the dalliance of Odin and the giant Billing's daughter, then with another woman Gunnlod; a second collection of counsels, this time specifically addressed to a certain Loddfafnir; a short rune-lore section explaining how Odin discovered the runes; and finally a collection of charms – the poem's song lore.[9]

The first apparent allusion to runes in the *Sayings* appears early in the poem, and contains, remarkably enough, an expression similar to the 'songs and healing-staves' of the *Lay of Sigrdrifa*:

Happy is he	who gets for himself
praise and healing-staves;	
but uneasy is it	when a man wants to own
what lies in another's breast.	

The first explicit mention of runes in the *Sayings* is much further on, however, at the end of a series of counsels to wayfarers and guests. This is the stanza that, as was previously noted, uses phrasing reminiscent of the first line of the votive inscription on the stone from Noleby and the similar section on the Sparlösa monument. The Eddic version reads:

Then it is proved	when you ask about runes,
of gods made known,	
which the great gods made	
and the awesome sage (i.e. Odin) painted,	
that he had best keep silence.	

This stanza also seems intrusive to the main body of the poem, probably reflecting a rather unskilled use of repertoire by the poet. Nor is it at all clear what the reference to silence means.

Two other mentions of runes are also made in the *Sayings* as part of a series of counsels given to Loddfafnir. An unidentified 'I', often thought to be Odin, recounts at the introduction to the Loddfafnir section that he 'heard talk of runes ... at the High One's Hall' in a section that has again been considered an intrusion to the main theme of this section of the *Sayings*. Runes are also mentioned at the end of the Loddfafnir section, where they seem simply to signify protective magic (*við bǫlvi rúnar*, 'runes against misfortune'), much as we might expect from the runic amulets that invoke help and aid. The main part of the *Sayings* that concerns runes follows the series of counsels to Loddfafnir.

The idea of a god inventing writing is common enough in early European tradition, and according to the rune lore of the *Sayings*, Odin learned of the runes in a shamanistic-like rite in which he sacrificed himself to himself on the cosmic World Tree, the ash Yggdrasil. This famous passage introduces the rune-lore section:

I know that I hung	on the wind-blown tree
nine full nights;	
wounded with a spear,	and offered to Odin,
myself to myself,	

---

[9] See O. Grønvik, *Hávamál* (Oslo 1999) and D.A.H. Evans (ed.), *Hávamál* (London 1986), esp. pp. 29–35, for a new commentary and a survey of what has been written by past investigators.

| on the tree | of which no-one knows |
| where its roots run from. | |

No bread was I given	nor drink from a horn;
I peered down;	
I took up the runes,	screaming I took them,
then I fell back from there.	

Nine awesome songs	I learnt from the famed son
of Bolthorn, Bestla's father,	
and I got a drink	of the precious mead,
poured from Odrerir.	

Then I began to thrive	and to become wise,
and to grow and to prosper;	
one word led me on	to another word,
one deed led me on	to another deed.

It seems likely, although it is not stated explicitly, that the 'nine songs' that Odin learnt from Bolthorn, his maternal grandfather, were somehow connected with runic lore. The number nine is of especial importance of course, as not only did it take nine days and nights for Odin to learn the runes, there are nine worlds in the Old Norse cosmology (and several examples of the number nine used in magic were recounted in the chapter on leechcraft). In fact some of the 18 (and notably not nine) songs that the *Sayings* then goes on to recount seem to reflect types of magical runic charms – apparently the *Lay*'s 'songs and healing-staves'.

The two next rune-lore stanzas, which are those that speak most clearly about runes, are in fact very reminiscent of the final part of the rune-lore stanzas of the *Lay of Sigrdrifa* and their reference to Hropt. They are followed by a stanza describing the applications of runes in the metre of *málaháttr*, which may well be an interpolation, but is stylistically reminiscent of some verses that similarly appear to intrude in the metrical Ribe healing charm considered in chapter 6. The succeeding stanza then concludes the section with a mention of Odin as Thund 'the Mighty' (a byname also attested on the Crag-Norns stick from Bergen) and the end of his ordeal:

Runes you shall find	and meaningful staves,
many great staves,	many powerful staves,
which the awesome sage painted,	
and the great gods made,	
and Hropt of the gods carved.	

Odin among the gods,	but for the elves Dain,
and Dvalin for the dwarfs,	
Asvid for the giants,	
I myself carved some.	

Do you know how to carve,	do you know how to read,
do you know how to paint,	do you know how to test,
do you know how to ask,	do you know how to offer,
do you know how to send,	do you know how to sacrifice?

| It is better not to pray | than to offer too much, |
| a gift always demands repayment; | |

it is better not to send   than to sacrifice too much.
Thus Thund (i.e. Odin) carved   before the creation of mankind,
where he rose up,   where he came back.

In all, the rune-lore stanzas seem particularly concerned with Odinic lore. There are hints of the gnomic nature of the first part of the *Sayings*, but like the *málaháttr* stanza they seem mostly concerned with the link between carving runes and sacrificing to the rune-carver *par excellence* – Odin the squawker god who appears to be explicitly venerated in this guise on the Noleby stone.

The *ljóðatal* or 'song lore' begins with the next stanza, a catalogue of 18 magical songs which runs to the end of the poem. Although the songs themselves are not reproduced, each verse describes the application of one of the charms, and though runes are not specifically mentioned, many of the uses of the songs find parallels in epigraphic material discussed in earlier chapters.

Those songs I know   which neither kings' wives
nor the sons of men know:
the first is called help,   and will help you
with troubles and sorrows   and every affliction.

None of the runes has a name that means 'help', however. Rather than refer to a specific practice, then, this introductory verse seems simply to be a general description of a good-luck charm, reminiscent of, without precisely paralleling, the texts of some runic amulets, and using the word *hjalp*, much as on the Ribe cranium, rather than the commoner runic amulet description *bjarg*. The next song, however, though lacking the last three lines, appears to describe a more specific form of healing magic, one appropriate to physicians or leeches. It is somewhat reminiscent of the 'branch-runes' for leeches, or 'leeches' hands' encountered in the *Lay* and on the healing stick from Ribe:

A second I know   which the sons of men need,
those who want to live as leeches . . .

The song that follows is military in nature, but calls for a result opposite to the intended effect of the 'victory-runes' of the *Lay* and also the amuletic inscriptions typically found on military items. Instead the result seems closer in effect to ones found in Norse literary sources. For instance, the wily Odin's battle tricks are elaborated on in the *Saga of the Ynglings*, which states that 'in battle, Odin could make his enemies become blind or deaf or terror-struck and their weapons bite no better than wands'. In the *Lay of Hamdir*, on the other hand, spears 'do not bite' the heroic brothers Hamdir and Sorli, while a dramatic illustration of an inability to fight is found in the *Saga of Hord*, when a *herfjǫturr* 'war-fetter' suddenly descends upon the (otherwise) brave Hord, rendering him unable to defend himself. This song seems to be a curse reminiscent of a classical binding spell:

A third I know   if I am in great need
to put bonds on my enemy:
I blunt the blades   of my opponents
neither their weapons nor their clubs bite.

The theme of binding continues in the fourth song of the *Sayings*, and again, the magic referred to is not paralleled epigraphically. But it does describe essentially the same use of runes that is known from Old Norse and Old English sources referring to spells or runic charms to unloosen chains or bonds. An Old English translation of Bede's *Ecclesiastical History* refers to 'loosening runes' which caused fetters to fall off a prisoner, and this incident was also recorded by the later Anglo-Saxon homilist Ælfric.[10] A charm for unloosening fetters (fastened by the *Idisi*, the German equivalent of the Norse Disir) is also known from the Old German first Merseburg charm and there is a reference to bond-breaking magic in *Groa's Incantation*. This is a series of nine spells chanted by Svipdag's dead mother Groa to protect her son which has many parallels with the songs from the *Sayings*. The fourth song of the *Sayings* reads:

A fourth I know	if men bind me
by the joints of my limbs:	
I chant	so that I can walk,
fetters burst from my feet,	and bonds from my hands.

The next song of the *Sayings* is also martial in nature and seems, again, the opposite of the use of runes that seems to be attested on the arrows found at Nydam. It might be thought appropriate to Odin, however, who was associated with the hurling of spears (as was adumbrated in chapter 2). Ensuing verses also deal with military magic and are somewhat reminiscent of the 'victory-runes' encountered in the *Lay of Sigrdrifa*. Runes of death recur in several Eddic poems: in the *Second Poem of Helgi Hundingsbani* (*Helgakviða Hundingsbana II*), Sigurd describes the battle in *valrúnar* 'slaughter runes' and deadly runes are also referred to in the *Poem of Helgi Hiorvardsson* (*Helgakviða Hjǫrvarðssonar*), where Helgi strikes the troll-woman Hrimgerd with *helstafir* 'fatal runes'.

A fifth I know	if I see a hostile arrow
shot into the war-host;	
it will not fly with such force	that I cannot stop it
if only my eyes sight it.	

The sixth verse of the *Sayings* appears to be a rather oblique reference to a magical rune-stick, carved, like that in *Grettir's Saga*, on a tree root. The use of the roots of trees had a special symbolism in heathen practice and was expressly proscribed in the old laws of Norway:

A sixth I know	if a thane wounds me
with the roots of a young tree,	
and the man	who curses me
then takes the harm rather than me.	

This is followed by two verses describing the use of songs against fire and hatred. They are preventative and are described using expressions derived from the terms *bjarg* 'help' and *bót* 'cure' – two key words in the runic amulet tradition. In fact

---

[10] Page, *Introduction*, pp. 111–12.

the second of the two verses is also somewhat reminiscent of the 'speech-runes' of the *Lay of Sigrdrifa*. Moreover in the *Second Lay of Helgi Hundungsbani*, it is said that Odin alone has the power to place *sakrúnar* or 'hostile runes' between kinsmen. This seems a natural extension, then, of the notion that choice words can cause or allay discord:

A seventh I know around the bench-mates: it does not burn so widely I know the spell to chant.	if I see a high hall burning that I cannot save (*bjargigak*) it;
An eighth I know, useful to learn: wherever hatred grows I can remedy (*bœta*) that quickly.	which for everyone is between warriors' sons,

The next verse of the song lore is more clearly a reference to the 'brim-runes' of the *Lay*, with further parallels in the Kvinneby amulet, sources like the *Galdrabók* and the Faeroese story of King Alvur. There is also a similar section in *Groa's Incantation* where Groa sings a spell to save her son from perishing in a gale at sea. The nautical safety charm of the *Sayings* is then followed by a song in galdralag metre against witches that immediately calls to mind folktales of witches and shape-shifters known from all over Europe. Indeed it seems an especially appropriate charm to be associated with Odin, the shape-shifting master of disguise:

A ninth I know of saving my ship at sea: I calm the wind and soothe the whole sea to rest.	if I am in need upon the waves
A tenth I know sporting in the sky: I arrange it to their own forms, to their own minds.	if I see hedge-riders (i.e. witches) so that they lose their way back

Then comes another invocation of military magic appropriate to Odin, who was renowned for protecting his favourites in war. But again, this verse has no exact parallels in runic inscriptions, except perhaps that on the Thorsberg shield-boss:

An eleventh I know lead my old comrades: under the shields I chant, safe into battle, safe from battle, and they return safely.	if to battle I shall so that they go mightily,

The next verse, then, describes a form of necromancy similar to that practised by Odin at the beginning of the *Seeress's Prophecy* and *Balder's Dreams*. It is also akin to that used by the hero Svipdag who converses with his dead mother in *Groa's Incantation*:

A twelfth I know   if I see up in a tree
a corpse swinging on the gallows:
thus I carve   and paint in runes,
so that the man walks
and talks with me.

Another example of otherwise unparalleled warrior magic then follows, including a reference to pagan baptism, a practice that seems to pre-date the introduction of Christianity in the North.[11] Then come two appeals to the lore of gods and elves, the last featuring Odin (as Hroptatyr, the 'Squawker-god') linked again alliteratively with perspicacity (*hyggio*), much as in the *Lay of Sigrdrifa*:

A thirteenth I know   if I should throw water
upon a young thane:
he will not fall,   though he goes into battle,
that man will not sink before swords.

A fourteenth I know   if in a company of men I must
enumerate the gods:
Æsir and elves,   I can distinguish between them all,
few fools can do this.

A fifteenth I know   that Thjodrerir chanted,
the dwarf, before Delling's (i.e. the dawn's) doors;
strength he sang for the Æsir,   and renown for the elves,
wisdom for Hroptatyr.

The final three songs then concern charms of a type more immediately recognisable from runic inscriptions. These three love charms round off the list of songs, but only after a stanza referring back to the last part of the counsels to Loddfafnir (which is also often thought to be a late interpolation):

A sixteenth I know,   if of a wise woman I want
to have all her affection and pleasure:
the thoughts I turn   of the white-armed woman
and I change her entire mind.

A seventeenth I know   so that slow to shun me
is the youthful girl;
– these songs,   Loddfafnir, you will
long be without,
though it would be good for you if you got them,
useful if you learned them,
helpful if you received them.

An eighteenth I know   which I never will teach
to any maid or man's wife,
– everything is better   which only one knows;
the end of the songs now follows –,
except to the one   whose arms embrace me,
or who is a sister to me.

---

11 See J. Udolph, *Ostern* (Heidelberg 1999).

The *Sayings* then conclude with a reiteration of the value of the lore just imparted, again with echoes of the directive to 'use [amulets], if you get them' of the *Lay*:

Now the speech of the High One has been recited
                                        in the hall of the High One,
very useful to the sons of men,
useless to the sons of giants;
Hail to him who recited!   Hail to him who knows it!
Use it, he who learnt it!
Hail to those who listened!

These two Eddic tracts on runes and magic have many similarities, but at the same time differ in some ways. They share much of the vocabulary of amatory and protective charms, a practice which even leads to the appearance of the same formula-like pairs in each source. There is clearly more magic of a war-like nature in the *Sayings of the High One* than in the *Lay of Sigrdrifa*, though. The songs of the *Sayings* are often quite unlike the magic described by the compounds in 'rune' of the *Lay*, and are clearly spoken charms rather than written runic ones, at least in the strictly alphabetical sense. Instead it seems that runic writing had already begun to take on the attributes sometimes called *wordcunning* or *grammarye* in medieval English by the time these Norse texts were composed, much as would be expected given the two meanings – 'runic character' and 'secret' or 'knowledge' – shared by the designation *rune* at the time. It was not that runes were thought to be inherently magical, but rather that the magical properties associated with runic amulets, the use of *rune* (as 'secret') in terms referring to magic, and the status of runic writing as a learned form of communication led to the association of runes with magical songs or charms in general.

It seems, then, that the references to rune magic in the rune-lore and song-lore stanzas of the *Poetic Edda* are not merely literary embellishments, but are informed by actual belief in the kinds of magical effects that could be achieved by using incantations and runes. They are paralleled, moreover, not just in the general functions both the runic amulet texts and the poetic sources describe, but also, often, in the very vocabulary used. Hence much of the scepticism modern scholars have shown in these descriptions appears to be misplaced. These practices have often been misinterpreted in the past, but they provide an essential corollary to understanding the kinds of magical runic texts that have come down to us.

There is, though, another much later source for runic lore whose interpretation is often even more controversial among runic scholars: the Scandinavian spell books of the early modern period. The longest and earliest of these is the *Galdrabók*, some of the spells of which have been referred to in earlier chapters. The product of at least four authors, three anonymous Icelanders and a Danish copyist writing over the sixteenth and seventeenth centuries, some of the spells of the *Galdrabók* represent a late understanding of runes and magic that has some bearing on a proper appreciation of both runic amulet inscriptions and the practices referred to in medieval literary sources.

Much of the lore of the *Galdrabók* and similar sources, however, seems merely to be a northern expression of southern European traditions of magic that stem back to the ancient Mediterranean tradition of sigils, sympathetic magic and the invocation of supernatural names. Many of the spells compiled in these works also feature Christian prayers, snatches of Latin or Hebrew and Latinate gibberish, and the kind of *voces magicae* typical of continental books of magic which are also found in early Christian prayers like the *Alma chorus Domini* as well as in late runic amulet inscriptions. The first spell in the *Galdrabók* mostly comprises a list of protective holy names including Gnostic and *Alma chorus* favourites such as Sabaoth, Adonai and Athanatos, the names of the twelve apostles, and other descriptions and styles readily recognisable as taken from the Bible or parts of the Christian liturgy.

Several magical sigils also appear in these works (that the *Galdrabók* calls *galdrastafir* 'incantation-staves') which on occasion look rune-like. Many of these, however, are obviously symbols based upon variations of Latin book-hand letterforms, crosses and the like. Some, though, are equally as clearly variations on the late magical symbols such as those (ᚴ, ᛥ) which appear in magical texts like the Bergen eye charm assessed in chapter 6 or the Scandinavian characters known as calendar runes, three symbols (ᛏ, ᚷ, ᚦ) used to record dates in runic inscriptions. These are late expressions, though – the calendar runes for instance are only recorded from the thirteenth to seventeenth centuries and are clearly not alphabetic characters. Some Icelandic magical texts from the early modern period or later also use symbols called *bandrúnir* or 'bind-runes' which look even more rune-like, and there is similar talk of *villurúnir* 'bewildering runes' or *villuletir* 'bewildering letters' that have frequently been thought to include genuine runic characters hidden in complex ligatured forms. These symbols are even often called by names which sound like some of the rune-names known from medieval sources. The calendar runes, after all, were described by expressions derived from rune-names (*árlaug* 'year-liquid', *tvímaðr* 'two-man', *belgþorn* 'bag-thorn'), evidently as they were considered to have been formed as the bind-runes and mirror-runes these names describe in the first place (i.e. ᛁ + ᚱ, ᛦ + ᚼ and a mirrored ᚦ). The names given to the various symbols of the early modern Scandinavian spell books, however, do not seem to have much in common with traditional alphabetical runic forms.[12]

By early modern times, the description 'Thor's hammer' had come to be applied to swastikas ('sun-wheels'), not the hammer symbols seen in medieval runic inscriptions. Similarly, terms once used for other symbols had also come to be associated with new forms, often of unclear origin. The expression *ægishjálmr* 'helm of awe', which is first recorded describing a treasure won by Sigurd from Fafnir in the *Poetic Edda*, is used to refer to several different symbols in this late tradition, most commonly one (❋, ❉) which is apparently in origin a crossed form of the calendar rune *tvímaðr* (ᚷ). The *svefnþorn* or 'sleep-thorn' that Odin used to curse the valkyrie Sigrdrifa also appears in one spell of this type used to describe a decidedly non-rune-like magical sigil. The names of three runes are recalled in an alliterative spell from the *Galdrabók* concerning flatulence (as was mentioned in chapter 2), too, but the sigils which accompany the spell do not look very much like runic letterforms.

---

12 See MacLeod, *Bind-runes*, pp. 282–94, as well as the notes in Flowers' translation of the *Galdrabók*.

Although some spells known from late Scandinavian spell books of this type feature runes being used to write out the words of charms or magical names, this is clearly to be separated from the use of *galdrastafir*. Nonetheless, the mention of *þrijsteipta* 'thrice-dunked' staves, *mollþurs* 'earth-ogre' runes and such in these texts probably represents the result of a terminological development and straying of rune-names to other signs (cf. *tvímaðr* and the name *tvísteyptr maðr* 'twice-dunked man' recorded for the late runic amulet symbol ᚼ). Something similar, of course, is already apparent in medieval literary sources; e.g. the *helstafir* 'fatal-staves' from the *Poem of Helgi Hiorvardsson*, though in this instance the compound employed seems merely to be a reinterpretation of the 'hell-rune' expressions used to indicate a type of sorcery in Gothic, Old English and Old High German. This compound is probably in origin ultimately a calque on *necromancy* which literally means 'cloaked (i.e. hidden) lore pertaining to death'. So, much as *rune* 'runic character' also came to refer to magical charms, the descriptions created from rune-names for signs such as the calendar runes and symbols like ᚼ were later used for magical sigils of local Scandinavian invention developed in a tradition of complex symbols and signs which was substantially originally of continental provenance.

Some of the spells recorded in Scandinavian spell books, however, are very similar to some of the later runic amulet inscriptions as well as comparable charms from other early Germanic literary traditions. They clearly mix foreign with more indigenous magic on occasion. Several call on old Germanic deities such as Odin and Thor (often in the company of Satan or Beelzebub) and otherwise have parallels with some of the later runic legends assessed in chapter 2. In fact one spell in the *Galdrabók* is clearly a *lorica*; others are ranged against troll shot and thieves. These early modern and later sources are interesting taken in comparison to spells known from medieval times. But in many respects their employment of runic terminology often seems to reflect the tradition of the runic 'songs' of medieval literature, rather than that of recorded inscriptions. No doubt these signs actually were used for magical purposes, but they were scarcely 'runes' in the sense of the tradition of the old Germanic letters.

Elements of magical rune lore which are evidenced by inscriptions do seem to have some reflection in literary sources, then. Although seemingly used more as literary devices in the Icelandic sagas, the Eddic material appears more faithful in its descriptions, although somewhat cryptically expressed, of contemporary runic practice. This is not contemporary Icelandic practice, of course, but rather that witnessed in England and mainland Scandinavia at a similar time to the composition of these works, i.e. late in the Viking period and in the early years of the High Middle Ages. Similarly, even some of the lore recorded in the books of black magic of post-medieval date seems to reflect late developments in the epigraphic runic tradition. Of the major spheres discussed in this book, only the use of runes in fertility inscriptions does not appear as well reflected in such sources. Evidently, though, practices that are attested in early runic inscriptions are only reflected in later literary accounts if they continue to be evidenced in epigraphic material of later periods. Nonetheless, the literary rune-lore of medieval and early modern date clearly deepens our understanding of the use of runes in amulets and other expressions of Old Germanic magic.

11

Conclusion

THE creation and employment of amulets bearing runic inscriptions was both an ancient and longstanding tradition. The earliest examples are often the earliest inscriptions in runes that have survived and the most recent are often contemporary with the decline in use of the Old Germanic alphabet in each of the descendent runic traditions. Rune-inscribed amulets are found in England, Frisia, and East and Central Europe, as well as in most of the reaches of the Viking world: from Greenland and Ireland to Denmark and Sweden. It is also evident that the different traditions share a common inheritance in terms of some fundamental aspects of amuletic practice, but notable regional developments clearly occur too. The runic amulet tradition was far from static; instead in some respects it proved rather lively, a feature especially evident in mainland Scandinavia, though this is, of course, the region from where most evidence for the use of runes hails. From the laconic five-part formula to the manuscript-influenced charms of the later Middle Ages, considerable development and variation is a notable feature of talismanic runic texts.

The early amulet legends of the five-part type when taken in the light of votive and otherwise divine aid-invoking runic texts seem to indicate that the first inscribed Germanic amulets developed mostly as an extension of cultic tradition. Comparison of likely models in terms of formulaic types and context suggest a crucial influence from early North Italian and Alpine votive practice is to be recognised in the first Germanic amulet inscriptions. It is only later that evidence of the influence of classical rather than archaic tradition emerges, with the first signs of typical Gnostic and later (fully) Christian traits, first in inscriptions found on the Continent and in England, but eventually also those uncovered in the Scandinavian North. This suggests that the assumption that there is a pronounced Roman influence in early runic epigraphy is not credible at least in terms of magico-religious texts. The lack of runic curse texts comparable to classical *defixiones* or binding spells seems especially to emphasise this independence, even though one of the old terms for Northern magic originally appears to have signified a similar understanding of supernatural 'tying'. Instead, pre-Roman Germanic contacts with the Celtic and Rhaetic-speaking peoples of Central Europe often seem to be a more illuminative connection to pursue, especially in light of how different from the classical tradition early runic epigraphy often seems to be. This finding not only speaks against a Roman origin for the runes themselves, but also the various attempts to show that Imperial Roman (or even provincial) influences are to be recognised in Germanic religion and myth. Archaeology records it was the Celtic and archaic Italian world that had the most significant influence on Germanic Europe in the last centuries BC, and the evidence of the early runic amulet tradition suggests that aspects of this early pre-Roman pedigree remained more influential in Germanic culture than has been recognised in the past.

Some aspects of the early Germanic magico-religious world are surely reflections of directly inherited Indo-European traditions; others appear to represent novel and purely native expressions. The amatory texts of Merovingian provenance seem to be a case in point, though we perhaps cannot rule out some Gnostic or other late classical influence here given the evidence for a few examples of Germanic leading or classical *agôgê*-like texts. The strongly gendered nature of these inscriptions is also reflected by runic legends on items associated with women's work, but few runic amulets seem to reflect the connection between magic and women epitomised in the early modern figure of the witch. Although the pendants are based on Roman prototypes, the legends on the Germanic bracteates also appear to represent aspects of a developing native expression with their invocation of horses, divine powers and leeks, though once again, this does not appear to be a particularly gendered tradition as such objects are found in graves of members of both sexes. Moreover, although the decorations the pendants bear seem fundamentally influenced by classical forms, it is remarkable how unlike comparable Graeco-Roman amulet texts the accompanying runic legends are. The basic formulaic stability and the evident lack of recognisable foreign influence in these texts suggests the Germanic amulet tradition of the five-part type was established so strongly by this date that it remained impervious to Roman influence. This is surely a remarkable development in light of the fundamental social and political transformations often assumed to be transpiring in this demographically so fluid and politically crucial a period in European history.

Nonetheless a significant change in amulet legends does become evident as the Migration Period comes to a close. The laconic texts seem to fall out of favour in Scandinavia as the Viking Age dawns. The terse and often functionally elliptical amulet legends give way to inscriptions that are more explicit in their invocation of protection and aid. The charm words appear to develop into, or be replaced by generic help-invoking, curing and disease-dismissing expressions, i.e. ones more typical of those found in medieval manuscript compilations. The Frisian tradition is the only continental articulation of runic literacy that survives long enough to suggest this development was more than merely a Scandinavian phenomenon, though. Fertility and martial runic amulets stop being produced, replaced by items featuring Christian blessings and a concentration on the curing and exorcism of diseases. Later Scandinavian runic charms become directly influenced by magic of the type preserved in medieval medicinal tracts and even the post-medieval books of spells, and a similar bookishness seems to be evidenced in some late Anglo-Saxon finds. Late runic texts become drawn into the world of medieval leechcraft, Christian mysticism, and finally even the secretive realm of black magic charms. They become more immediately recognisable as influenced by expressions recorded in manuscripts circulating on the Continent as well as the British Isles in this late period. The last amulet inscriptions written in runes seem to share little in common with the earliest texts, except for the enduring connection between divine words or names (especially in threes), religious lore and sympathetic narrative charms. The last outpost of the pagan Germanic world is finally admitted into the orbit of mainland European magico-religious tradition as the Old Germanic divinities take their place among the Christian devils. The main figures that are invoked otherwise on Scandinavian amulets of this date are mostly reflections of pan-European aspects of Christian mysticism, illustrating how strong the cultural and intellectual Latinising of Scandinavia had become by late medieval times.

Bibliography

Aag, Finn-Henrik, 'Slesvig runepinne', *Maal og minne* (1987), 17–23.

Adam of Bremen, *History of the Archbishops of Hamburg-Bremen*, trans. Francis J. Tschan (New York 1959).

Agostiniani, Luciano, *Le "iscrizioni parlanti" dell'Italia antica*, Lingue e iscrizioni dell'Italia antica 3 (Florence 1982).

Antonsen, Elmer H., *A Concise Grammar of the Older Runic Inscriptions*, Sprachstrukturen, Reihe A: Historische Sprachstrukturen 3 (Tübingen 1975).

Árnason, Jón, *Íslenzkar þjóðsögur og æfintýri*, 2 vols (Leipzig 1862–64), 2nd ed., ed. Árni Böðvarsson and Bjarni Vilhjámsson, 4 vols (Reykjavík 1954–58).

———, and Ólafur Davíðsson (eds), *Íslenzkar Gátur, Skemtanir, Vivivakar og Þulur*, 4 vols (Copenhagen 1887–1903).

Axboe, Morten, 'To brakteater', in Wilhelm Heizmann and Astrid van Nahl (eds), *Runica, Germanica, Mediaevalia*, Ergänzungsbände zum Reallexikon der germanischen Altertumskunde 37 (Berlin 2003), pp. 20–27.

Bæksted, Anders, *Islands Runeindskrifter*, Bibliotheca Arnamagnæna 2 (Copenhagen 1942).

———, *Målruner og troldruner: Runemagiske studier*, Nationalmuseets skrifter: Arkæologisk-historisk række 4 (Copenhagen 1952).

Bang, Anton Christian, *Norske hexeformularer og magiske opskrifter*, Videnskabs-selskabets Skrifter, II: Historisk-filos. Klasse (Oslo 1901–1902).

Barnes, Michael, et al., *The Runic Inscriptions of Viking Age Dublin*, National Museum of Ireland, Medieval Dublin excavations 1962–81, ser. B, vol. 5 (Dublin 1997).

Bately, Janet M., and Vera I. Evison, 'The Derby bone piece', *Medieval Archaeology* 5 (1961), 301–5.

Bauer, Alessia, *Runengedichte: Texte, Untersuchungen und Kommentare zur gesamten Überlieferung*, Studia Medievalia Septentrionalia 9 (Vienna 2003).

Birkmann, Thomas, *Von Ågedal bis Malt: Die skandinavischen Runeninschriften vom Ende des 5. bis Ende des 9. Jahrhunderts*, Ergänzungsbände zum Reallexikon der germanischen Altertumskunde 12 (Berlin 1995).

Boase, Roger, and Diane Bornstein, 'Courtly love', in Joseph Strayer et al. (eds), *Dictionary of the Middle Ages*, 13 vols (New York 1982–89), III, pp. 667–74.

Bonser, Winifred, *The Medical Background of Anglo-Saxon England: A study in history, psychology, and folklore* (London 1963).

Brate, Erik, 'Runradens ordningsföljd', *Arkiv för nordisk filologi* 36 (1920), 193–207.

Braune, Wilhelm, *Althochdeutsches Lesebuch*, 14th ed., ed. Ernst A. Ebbinghaus (Tübingen 1962).

Bugge, Sophus, 'Das Runendenkmal von Britsum in Friesland', *Zeitschrift für deutsche Philologie* 40 (1908), 174–184.

———, 'Zur altgermanischen Sprachgeschichte. Germanisch *ug* aus *uw*', *Beiträge zur Geschichte der deutschen Sprache und Literatur* 13 (1888), 504–15.

Cameron, Malcolm Laurence, *Anglo-Saxon Medicine*, Cambridge studies in Anglo-Saxon England 7 (Cambridge 1993).

Capelle, Torsten, 'Ringopfer', in Herbert Jankuhn (ed.), *Vorgeschichtliche Heiligtümer und Opferplätze im Mittel- und Nordeuropas: Bericht über ein Symposium in Reinhausen bei Göttingen in der Zeit vom 14. bis 16. Oktober 1968*, Abhandlungen der Akademie der Wissenschaften in Göttingen, philologisch-historische Klass, III. Folge, Nr 74 (Göttingen 1970), pp. 214–18.

Carmina burana, ed. Alfons Hilka, Otto Schumann and Bernard Bischoff, 3 vols (Heidelberg 1930–70).

Chaucer, Geoffrey, *The Canterbury Tales*, ed. Norman Francis Blake, York Medieval Texts: Second series (London 1980).

Comparetti, Domenico, *Vergil in the Middle Ages*, trans. Edward F.M. Benecke, 2nd ed. (London 1908).

Conway, R. Seymour, et al., *The Prae-Italic Dialects of Italy*, 3 vols (Cambridge, Mass. 1933).

Czarnecki, Jan, *The Goths in Ancient Poland: A study on the historical geography of the Oder-Vistula region during the first two centuries of our era* (Coral Gables 1975).

Daviðsson, Óláfur, 'Isländische Zauberzeichen und Zauberbücher', *Zeitschrift des Vereins für Volkskunde* 13 (1903), 150–67 and 267–79.

Dillman, François-Xavier, 'Les runes dans la littérature norroise. A propos d'une découverte archéologique en Islande', *Proxima Thule* 2 (1996), 51–89.

Dornseiff, Franz, *Das Alphabet in Mystik und Magie*, Stocheia 7, 2nd ed. (Leipzig 1925).

Dreves, Guido M., and Clemens Blume (eds), *Analecta hymnica Medii Aevii*, 55 vols (Leipzig 1886–1922).

Düwel, Klaus, 'Mittelalterliche Amulette aus Holz und Blei mit lateinischen und runischen Inschriften', in Volker Vogel (ed.), *Ausgrabungen in Schleswig*, Berichte und Studien 15. Das archäologische Fundmaterial II (Neumünster 2001), pp. 227–302.

———, 'Pforzen, § 2. Runologisches', in Johannes Hoops, *Reallexikon der germanischen Altertumskunde*, 2nd ed. (Berlin 1976–), XXIII, pp. 116–18.

———, 'Runeninschriften als Quellen der germanischen Religionsgeschichte', in Heinrich Beck et al. (eds), *Germanische Religionsgeschichte: Quellen und Quellenprobleme*, Ergänzungsbände zum Reallexikon der germanischen Altertumskunde 5 (Berlin 1992), pp. 356–59.

———, *Runenkunde*, Sammlung Metzler; Realienbücher für Germanistik, Abt. C: Sprachwissenschaft M72, 3rd ed. (Stuttgart 2001).

———, 'Runen und interpretatio Christiana: Zur religionsgeschichtlichen Stellung der Bügelfibel von Nordendorf I', in Norbert Kamp and Joachim Wollasch (eds), *Tradition als historische Kraft: Interdisziplinäre Forschungen zur Geschichte des früheren Mittelalters* (Berlin 1982), pp. 78–86.

———, 'Runes, weapons and jewellery: A survey of some of the oldest runic inscriptions', *The Mankind Quarterly* 22 (1981), 69–91.

———, 'Runische und lateinische Epigraphik im süddeutschen Raum zur Merowingerzeit', in idem (ed.), *Runische Schriftkultur in kontinental-skandinavischer und -angelsächsischer Wechselbeziehung: Internationales Symposium in der Werner-Reimars-Stiftung vom 24.–27. Juni 1992 in Bad Homburg*, Ergänzungsbände zum Reallexikon der germanischen Altertumskunde 10 (Berlin 1988), pp. 229–308.

Düwel, Klaus, et al., 'Vereint in den Tod – Doppelgrab 166/167 aus Aschheim, Landkreis München, Oberbayern', *Das archäologische Jahr in Bayern* (1999), 83–85.

Dyvik, Helge, 'Addenda runica latina. Recently found runic inscriptions from Bryggen', in Asbjörn Herteig et al. (eds), *The Bryggen Papers, Supplementary Series* 2 (Bergen 1988), pp. 1–9.

Edda: Die Lieder des Codex Regius, ed. Gustav Neckel and Hans Kuhn, 6th ed. (Heidelberg 1993).

Egg, Markus, 'Die "Herrin der Pferde" im Alpengebiet', *Archäologisches Korrespondenzblatt* 16 (1986), 69–78.

Egger, Rudolf, *Römische Antike und frühes Christentum: Ausgewählte Schriften von Rudolf Egger; Zur Vollendung seines 80. Lebensjahres*, ed. Artur Betz and Gotbert Moro, 2 vols (Klagenfurt 1962–63).

Eggers, Hans-Jürgen, et al., *Kelten und Germanen in heidnischer Zeit*, Kunst der Welt (Baden Baden 1964).

Egils saga Skalla-Grímssonar, ed. Sigurður Nordal, Íslenzk fornrit 2 (Reykjavik 1933).

Eichner, Heiner, 'Kurze "indo"-"germanische" Betrachtungen über die atharvavedische Parallele zum Zweiten Merseburger Zauberspruch (mit Neubehandlung von AVS. IV 12)', *Die Sprache* 42 (2000/1), 211–233 [= *Insprinc haptbandun: Referate des Kolloquiums zu den Merseburger Zaubersprüchen auf der XI. Fachtagung der Indogermanischen Gesellschaft in Halle/Saale (17.–23. September 2000)*, ed. Heiner Eichner and Robert Nedoma, pt 2].

Eichner, Heiner, and Robert Nedoma, 'Die Merseburger Zaubersprüche: Philologische und sprachwissenschaftliche Probleme aus heutiger Sicht', *Die Sprache* 42 (2000/1), 1–195 [= *Insprinc haptbandun: Referate des Kolloquiums zu den Merseburger Zaubersprüchen auf der XI. Fachtagung der Indogermanischen Gesellschaft in Halle/Saale (17.–23. September 2000)*, ed. Heiner Eichner and Robert Nedoma, pt 2].

Elliott, Ralph W.V., *Runes: An introduction*, 2nd ed. (Manchester 1989).

Ellis, Hilda R., *The Road to Hel* (Oxford 1943).

Enright, Michael J., *Lady with a Mead Cup* (Dublin 1996).

Eriksson, Manne, and Delmar Olof Zetterholm, 'En amulet från Sigtuna. Ett tolkningsförsök', *Fornvännen* 28 (1933), 129–156.

Euler, Wolfgang, *Dōnum dō-: Eine figura etymologica der Sprachen Altitaliens*, Innsbrucker Beiträge zur Sprachwissenschaft: Vorträge und Kleinere Schriften 29 (Innsbruck 1982).

Evans, David A.H. (ed.), *Hávamál* (London 1986).

Faraone, Christopher A., 'Taking the 'Nestor's cup inscription' seriously: Erotic magic and conditional curses in the earliest inscribed hexameters', *Classical Antiquity* 15 (1996), 77–112.

Faraone, Christopher A., and Dirk Obbink (eds), *Magika Hiera: Ancient Greek magic and religion* (New York 1991).

Favreux, Robert, *Les inscriptions médiévales*, Typologie des sources du moyen âge occidental 35 (Tournhout 1979).

Fell, Christine E., 'Runes and semantics', in Alfred Bammesberger (ed.), *Old English Runes and their Continental Background*, Anglistische Forschungen 217 (Heidelberg 1991), pp. 195–229.

Fingerlin, Gerhard, et al., 'Eine Runeninschrift aus Bad Krozingen (Kreis Breisgau-Hochschwarzwald)', in Hans-Peter Naumann (ed.), *Alemannien und der Norden: Internationales Symposium vom 18.–20. Oktober 2001 in Zürich*, Ergänzungsbände zum Reallexikon der germanischen Altertumskunde 43 (Berlin 2003), pp. 224–65.

Fischer, Svante, 'Merovingertida runfynd i Ardennerna, Frankrike', *Nytt om runer* 14 (1999), 12–13.

Fischer, Svante, and Jean-Pierre Lémant, 'Epigraphic evidence of Frankish exogamy', in Ernst Taayke et al. (eds), *Essays on the Early Franks*, Groningen Archaeological Studies 1 (Groningen 2003), pp. 241–66.

Fletcher, Richard A., *The Conversion of Europe: From paganism to Christianity, 371–1386 AD* (London 1997).

Flint, Valerie I.J., *The Rise of Magic in Early Medieval Europe* (Princeton 1991).

Flowers, Stephen E., *Runes and Magic: Magical formulaic elements in the older runic tradition*, American University Studies, Series I: Germanic Languages and Literature 53 (Frankfurt a.M. 1986).

Fogg, Trevor, 'Slaves, Outcasts and Fringe Dwellers' (Unpublished dissertation, Melbourne 2000).

Friesen, Otto von, 'Runinskriften på en koppardosa, funnen i Sigtuna augusti 1911', *Fornvännen* 7 (1912), 6–19.

Fulk, Robert D., and Christopher M. Cain, *A History of Old English Literature* (London 2003).

Gager, John G. (ed.), *Curse Tablets and Binding Spells from the Ancient World* (Oxford 1992).

Galdrabók, ed. Natan Lindqvist as *En isländsk svartkonstbok från 1500-talet* (Uppsala 1921).

The Galdrabók: An Icelandic grimoire, trans. Stephen E. Flowers (York Beach, Maine 1989).

Galsterer, Birgitte and Helmut, *Die römischen Steininschriften aus Köln*, Wissenschaftliche Kataloge des Römisch-Germanischen Museums Köln 2 (Cologne 1975).

Gjerlow, Lilli, '*Deus pater piissime* og blykorsene fra Stavanger Bispedømme', *Stavanger Museums Årbok* 64 (1954), 85–109.

Gosling, Kevin, 'Runic finds from London', *Nytt om runer* 4 (1989), 12–13.

———, 'The runic material from Tønsberg', *Universitetets Oldsaksamling Årbok* (1986–1988), 175–87.

Grattan, John Henry Grafton, and Charles Singer, *Anglo-Saxon Magic and Medicine: Illustrated specially from the semi-pagan text 'Lacnunga'* (London 1952).

Grimm, Jacob, *Teutonic Mythology*, trans. James Steven Stallybrass, 4 vols (London 1880–88).

Grønvik, Ottar, *Hávamál: Studier over verkets formelle oppbygning og dets religiøse innhold*, Skrifter (Det Norske videnskaps-akademi. II–Hist.-filos. klasse), Ny serie 21 (Oslo 1999).

———, 'En hedensk bønn. Runeinnskriften på en liten kobberplate fra Kvinneby på Öland', in Finn Hødnebø et al. (eds), *Eyvindarbók. Festskrift til Eyvind Fjeld Halvorsen 4. mai 1992* (Oslo 1992), pp. 71–85.

———, *Die Rökstein: Über die religiöse Bestimmung und das weltliche Schicksal eines Helden aus der frühen Wikingerzeit*, Osloer Beiträge zur Germanistik 33 (Frankfurt a.M. 2003).

———, 'Runeinnskriften fra Ribe', *Arkiv för nordisk filologi* 114 (1999), 103–127.

———, 'Runeinnskriften på gullhornet fra Gallehus', *Maal og Minne* 1 (1999), 1–18.

Guðmundsson, Helgi, 'Rúnaristan frá Narssaq', *Gripla* 1 (1975), 188–94.

Gustavson, Helmer, 'Christus regnat, Christus vincit, Christus imperat. Runblecket från Boge och några paralleller', in Lennart Karlsson et al. (eds), *Den ljusa medeltiden: Studier tillägnade Aron Andersson*, Statens Historiska Museum, Studies 4 (Stockholm 1984), pp. 61–76.

———, 'Verksamheten vid Runverket, Stockholm', *Nytt om runer* 9 (1994), 25–28.

———, 'Verksamheten vid Runverket i Stockholm', *Nytt om runer* 12 (1997), 24–31.

———, 'Verksamheten vid Runverket i Stockholm', *Nytt om runer* 13 (1998), 19–28.

———, 'Verksamheten vid Runverket i Stockholm', *Nytt om runer* 14 (1999), 19–25.

———, 'Verksamheten vid Runverket i Stockholm', *Nytt om runer* 16 (2001), 19–34.

Gustavson, Helmer, and Thorgunn Snædal Brink, 'Runfynd 1978', *Fornvännen* 74 (1979), 228–50.

———, 'Runfynd 1980', *Fornvännen* 76 (1981), 186–202.

———, 'Runfynd 1983', *Fornvännen* 79 (1983), 250–59.

Gustavson, Helmer, et al., 'Runfynd 1982', *Fornvännen* 78 (1983), 224–43.

———, 'Runfynd 1988', *Fornvännen* 85 (1990), 23–42.

———, 'Runfynd 1989 & 1990', *Fornvännen* 87 (1992), 153–74.

Hall, Alaric, 'The meanings of *elf* and elves in medieval England' (Dissertation, Glasgow 2004); available at http: //www. alarichall.org.uk

Halsall, Maureen, *The Old English Rune Poem: A critical edition*, McMaster Old English studies and texts 2 (Toronto 1981).

Hammarberg, Inger, and Gert Rispling, 'Graffiter på vikingatida mynt', *Hikuin* 11 (1985), 63–78.

Hammerich, Louis L., 'Der Zauberstab aus Ripen', in Hans Kuhn and Kurt Schier (eds), *Märchen, Mythos, Dichtung: Festschrift zum 90. Geburtstag Friedrich von der Leyens am 19. August 1963* (Munich 1963), pp. 147–67.

Hauck, Karl, 'Brakteatenikonologie', in Johannes Hoops, *Reallexikon der germanischen Altertumskunde*, 2nd ed. (Berlin 1976–), III, pp. 361–401.

———, 'Die runenkundlichen Erfinder von den Bildchiffren der Goldbrakteaten (Zur Ikonologie der Goldbrakteaten, LVII)', *Frühmittelalterliche Studien* 32 (1998), 28–56.

———, 'Völkerwanderungszeitliche Bilddarstellungen des zweiten Merseburger Spruche als Zugang zu Heiligtum und Opfer', in Herbert Jankuhn (ed.), *Vorgeschichtliche Heiligtümer und Opferplätze im Mittel- und Nordeuropas: Bericht über ein Symposium in Reinhausen bei Göttingen in der Zeit vom 14. bis 16. Oktober 1968*, Abhandlungen der Akademie der Wissenschaften in Göttingen, philologisch-historische Klass, III. Folge, Nr 74 (Göttingen 1970), pp. 297–319.

Hauck, Karl, and Wilhelm Heizmann, 'Der Neufund des Runen-Brakteaten IK 585 Sankt Ibs Vej-C Roskilde (Zur Ikonologie der Goldbrakteaten, LXII)', in Wilhelm Heizmann and Astrid van Nahl (eds), *Runica, Germanica, Mediaevalia,* Ergänzungsbände zum Reallexikon der germanischen Altertumskunde 37 (Berlin 2003), pp. 243–64.

Haynes, Sibylla, *Etruscan Bronzes* (New York 1985).

Heizmann, Wilhelm, 'Der Fluch mit der Distel. Zu For Scírnis', *Amsterdamer Beiträge zur älteren Germanistik* (1996), 91–104.

———, 'Lein(en) und Lauch in der Inschrift von Fløksand und im Vǫlsa þáttr', in Heinrich Beck (ed.), *Germanische Religionsgeschichte: Quellen und Quellenprobleme,* Ergänzungsbände zum Reallexikon der germanischen Altertumskunde 5 (Berlin 1992), pp. 365–95.

Herren, Michael W. (ed.), *The Hisperica Famina, II. Related poems: A critical edition with English translation and philogical commentary,* Studies and texts 85 (Toronto 1987).

Hoffmann-Krayer, Eduard, 'Zum Eingang des Weingartner Reisesegens', *Schweizerisches Archiv für Volkskunde* 8 (1912), p. 65.

Hofmann, Heinz, 'Satorquadrat', in Georg Wissowa et al. (eds), *Paulys Real-Encyclopädie der Altertumswissenschaft*, 2nd ed., 59 vols (Stuttgart etc. 1894–1980), 15th supplement volume, pp. 477–565.

Holtsmark, Anne, 'Kjærlighetsdiktning', in Johannes Brøndsted et al. (eds), *Kulturhistorisk leksikon for nordisk middelalder*, 22 vols (Copenhagen 1956–78), VIII, pp. 438–43.

———, 'Kjærlighetsmagi', in Johannes Brøndsted et al. (eds), *Kulturhistorisk leksikon for nordisk middelalder*, 22 vols (Copenhagen 1956–78), VIII, pp. 444–47.

Homolle, Théophile, 'Donarium', in Charles Daremberg and Edmond Saglio (eds), *Dictionaire des antiquités grecques et romaines, d'apres les textes et les monuments*, 5 vols (Paris 1877–1917), II.1, pp. 363–82.

Hopfner, Theodor, 'Mageia', in Georg Wissowa et al. (eds), *Paulys Real-Encyclopädie der Altertumswissenschaft*, 2nd ed., 59 vols (Stuttgart etc. 1894–1980), XIV, 1 (27. Halbband), pp. 301–93.

Horodezky, Samuel Aba, 'Agla', in Jakob Klatzkin (ed.), *Encyclopaedia Judaica: Das Judentum in Geschichte und Gegenwart*, 10 vols (Berlin 1928–34), I, pp. 1042–43.

Jansson, Sven B.F., *Runes in Sweden*, trans. Peter G. Foote (Stockholm 1987).

Jónsson, Finnur, 'Interpretation of the Runic Inscriptions from Herjolfsnes', *Meddelelser om Grønland* 67 (1924), 273–90.

Jungandreas, Wolfgang, 'God fura dih, Deofile', *Zeitschrift für deutsches Altertum und deutsche Literatur* 101 (1972), 84–85.

Jungner, Hugo, 'Högstena-galdern: En västgötsk runbesvärjelse mot gengångare', *Fornvännen* 31 (1936), 278–304.

Kabell, Aage, 'Die Inschrift auf dem Schädelfragment aus Ribe', *Arkiv för nordisk filologi* 93 (1978), 38–47.

Kantorowicz, Ernst R., *Laudes Regiae: A study in liturgical acclamations and medieval ruler worship*, University of California publications in history 33 (Berkeley 1958).

Kapteyn, Jan M.N., 'Eine altalemannische Runeninschrift', *Anzeiger für schweizerische Altertumskunde* NF 37 (1935), 210–12.

Kieckhefer, Richard, *Magic in the Middle Ages*, Cambridge Medieval Textbooks (Cambridge 1989).

Kloos, Rudolf M., *Einführung in die Epigraphik des Mittelalters und der frühen Neuzeit* (Darmstadt 1980).

Knirk, James E., 'Arbeidet ved Runearkivet, Oslo', *Nytt om runer* 6 (1991), 13–16.

———, 'Arbeidet ved Runearkivet, Oslo', *Nytt om runer* 13 (1998), 18–19.

———, 'Learning to write with runes in medieval Norway', in Inger Lindell (ed.), *Medeltida skrift- och språkkultur: Nio föreläsningar från ett symposium i Stockholm våren 1992*. Runica et Mediævalia 2 (Stockholm 1994), pp. 169–212.

———, 'Runic inscriptions containing Latin in Norway', in Klaus Düwel (ed.), *Runeninschriften als Quellen interdisziplinäre Forschungen: Abhandlung des Vierten Internationalen Symposiums über Runen und Runeninschriften in Göttingen vom 4.–9. August 1995*, Ergänzungsbände zum Reallexikon der germanischen Altertumskunde 15 (Berlin 1998), pp. 476–507.

———, 'Tor og Odin i runer på Bryggen i Bergen', *Arkeo* 1 (1995), 27–30.

Knudsen, Anne M., and Helge J.J. Dyvik, 'Et runekors fra Sogn og Fjordane', *Maal og Minne* (1980), 1–12.

Koch, Robert, 'Waffenförmige Anhänger aus merowingerzeitlichen Frauengräber', *Jahrbuch des Römisch-Germanischen Zentralmuseums Mainz* 17 (1970), 285–93.

Kotansky, Roy, 'Incantations and prayers for salvation on inscribed Greek amulets', in Christopher A. Farone and Dirk Obbink (eds), *Magika Hiera: Ancient Greek magic and religion* (New York 1991), pp. 107–37.

Krause, Wolfgang, *Runen*, Sammlung Göschen 1244/1244a (Berlin 1970).

———, with Herbert Jankuhn, *Die Runeninschriften im älteren Futhark*, Abhandlungen der Akademie der Wissenschaften in Göttingen, phil.-hist. Klasse, III. Reihe, Nr. 65, 2 vols, 2nd ed. (Göttingen 1966).

Lambert, Pierre-Yves, *La langue gauloise: Description linguistique, commentaire d'inscriptions choisies* (Paris 1991).

Larsen, Henning (ed.), *An Old Icelandic Medical Miscellany: MS Royal Irish Academy 23 D 43* (Oslo 1931).

Lewis, C.S., *The Allegory of Love: A study in medieval tradition* (Oxford 1936).

Liestøl, Aslak, 'Det norske runediktet', *Maal og minne* (1948), 65–71.

———, *Runer frå Bryggen*, Særtrykk av *Viking* 1963 (Bergen 1964).

———, 'Rúnavísur frá Björgvin', *Skírnir* 139 (1965), 27–51.

———, 'Runefunn under golvet i Lom kyrkje', *Foreningen til norske minnesmerkers bevaring* 132 (1978), 177–90.

————, 'Runeinnskriftene frå "Mindets tomt" ', in Helge I. Høeg et al., *De arkeologiske utgravninger i Gamlebyen, Oslo* 1 (Oslo 1978), pp. 214–24.

————, ' "Will you marry me?" under a church-floor', *Mediaeval Scandinavia* 10 (1977), 35–40.

Liestøl, Aslak, et al., 'Dróttkvætt-vers fra Bryggen i Bergen', *Maal og mine* (1962), 98–108.

————, 'En ny dróttkvættstrofe fra Bryggen i Bergen', *Maal og minne* (1964), 93–100.

Linderholm, Emanuel, 'Signelser och besvärjelser från medeltid och nytid', *Svenska landsmål och svenskt folkliv* 41 (1917–40), 1–479.

Lindquist, Ivar, *Religiösa runtexter 3: Kvinneby-amuletten. Det vikingatida kvädet på en kopparplåt från Södra Kvinneby i Stenåsa socken, Öland; Ett tydningsförslag*, ed. Gösta Holm, Skrifter utgivna av Vetenskaps-Societeten i Lund 79 (Lund 1987).

Lönnroth, Lars, '*Iǫrð fannz æva né upphiminn*. A formula analysis', in Ursula Dronke et al. (eds), *Speculum Norroenum: Norse studies in memory of Gabriel Turville-Petre* (Odense 1981), pp. 310–27.

Looijenga, Tineke, *Texts and Contexts of the Oldest Runic Inscriptions*, The Northern World 4 (Leiden 2003).

Louis-Jensen, Jonna, ' "Halt illu frān Būfa!" – Til tolkningen af Kvinneby-amuletten fra Öland', in Séamus Ó Catháin et al. (eds), *Northern Lights: Following Folklore in North Western Europe. Essays in honor of Bo Almqvist* (Dublin 2001), pp. 111–26.

————, 'Norrøne navnegåder', *Nordica Bergensia* 4 (1994), 35–52.

————, 'To halvstrofer fra Bryggen i Bergen', in Jan Ragnar Hagland et al. (eds), *Festskrift til Alfred Jakobsen* (Trondheim 1987), pp. 106–9.

Lozzi Gallo, Lorenzo, 'On the interpretation of **ialuns** in the Norwegian runic text B257', *Arkiv för nordisk filologi* 116 (2001), 135–51.

MacLeod, Mindy, 'Bandrúnir in Icelandic sagas', *Scripta Islandica* 52 (2001), 35–51.

————, *Bind-runes: An investigation of ligatures in runic epigraphy*, Runrön 15 (Uppsala 2002).

————, 'Ligatures in early runic and Roman inscriptions', in Gillian Fellows-Jensen et al. (eds), *Jelling Runes: Fifth Symposium on Runes and Runic Inscriptions, Jelling 16th–20th August 2000* (Copenhagen 2006).

MacLeod, Mindy, and Bernard Mees, 'On the **t**-like symbols, rune-rows and other amuletic features of the early runic inscriptions', *Interdisciplinary Journal for Germanic Linguistics and Semiotic Analysis* 9 (2004), 249–99.

————, 'The triple binds of Kragehul and Undley', *NOWELE* 38 (2001), 17–35.

Macrae, George W., 'Gnosticism', in Bernard L. Marthaler et al. (eds), *The New Catholic Encyclopedia*, 15 vols, 2nd ed. (Detroit 2002–2003), VI, pp. 255–61.

Makaev, Ènver Akhmedovich, *The Language of the Oldest Runic Inscriptions: A linguistic and historical-philological analysis*, trans. John Meredig, Kungl. vitterhets historie och antikvitets akademiens handlingar, Filologisk-filosofiska serien 21 (Stockholm 1996).

Mancini, Alberto, 'Iscrizioni retiche', *Studi etruschi* 43 (1975), 249–306.

Marcellus, *De Medicamentis*, ed. Maximillian Niedermann, 2nd ed., ed. Eduard Liechtenhan, 2 vols, Corpus medicorum Latinarum 5 (Berlin 1968).

Markey, Thomas L., 'The dedicatory formula and runic *tawide*', forthcoming.

————, 'Early Celticity at Rhaetic Magrè (Schio)', forthcoming.

————, *Frisian* (The Hague 1981).

————, 'Icelandic *sími* and soul contracting', *Scripta Islandica* 51 (2000), 133–39.

————, ' "Ingveonic" **ster(i)r-* "star" and astral priests', *NOWELE* 39 (2001), 85–113.

————, 'An *interpretatio Italica* among the Casalini (Sanzeno) votives and another Helbig hoax', forthcoming.

————, 'Studies in runic origins 1: Germanic *maþl-/*mahl-* and Etruscan **meθlum**', *American Journal of Germanic Linguistics and Literatures* 10 (1998), 153–200.

————, 'Studies in runic origins 2: From gods to men', *American Journal of Germanic Linguistics and Literatures* 11 (1999), 131–203.

————, 'A tale of two helmets: The Negau A and B inscriptions', *Journal of Indo-European Studies* 29 (2001), 69–172.

Marold, Edith, 'Die drei Götter auf dem Schädelfragment von Ribe', in Wilhelm Heizmann and Astrid van Nahl (eds), *Runica, Germanica, Mediaevalia*, Ergänzungsbände zum Reallexikon der germanischen Altertumskunde 37 (Berlin 2003), pp. 403–17.

————, 'Egill und Ǫlrún – ein vergessenes Paar der Heldendichtung', *Skandinavistik* 29 (1996), 1–19.

————, 'Runeninschriften als Quelle zur Geschichte der Skaldendichtung', in Klaus Düwel (ed.), *Runeninschriften als Quellen interdisziplinäre Forschungen: Abhandlung des Vierten Internationalen Symposiums über Runen und Runeninschriften in Göttingen vom 4.–9. August 1995*, Ergänzungsbände zum Reallexikon der germanischen Altertumskunde 15 (Berlin 1998), pp. 667–93.

Marstrander, Carl J.S., 'Om innskriftene på Sparlösastenen', *Norsk tidskrift for sprogvidenskap* 17 (1954), 503–16.

————, review of Helmut Arntz and Hans Zeiss, *Die einheimische Runendenkmäler des Festlandes* (Leipzig 1939), *Norsk tidskrift for sprogvidenskap* 11 (1939), 280–329.

Mastrocinque, Attilio, *Santuari e divinità dei Paleoveneti* (Padua 1987).

McKinnell, John, 'A runic fragment from Lincoln', *Nytt om runer* 10 (1995), 10–11.

McKinnell, John, and Rudolf Simek, with Klaus Düwel, *Runes, Magic and Religion: A sourcebook,* Studia Medievalia Septentrionalia 10 (Vienna 2004).

Meaney, Audrey L., *Anglo-Saxon Amulets and Curing Stones*, BAR British Series 96 (Oxford 1981).

Mees, Bernard, 'Early Rhineland Germanic', *NOWELE* forthcoming, 2006.

————, 'The gods of the Rhaetii', forthcoming.

————, 'A new interpretation of the Meldorf fibula inscription', *Zeitschrift für deutsches Altertum and deutsche Literatur* 126 (1997), 131–39.

————, 'The North Etruscan thesis of the origin of the runes', *Arkiv för nordisk filologi* 115 (2000), 33–82.

————, 'Runes in the first century', in Gillian Fellows-Jensen et al. (eds), *Jelling Runes: Fifth Symposium on Runes and Runic Inscriptions, Jelling 16th–20th August 2000* (Copenhagen 2006).

————, 'Runic **erilaʀ**', *NOWELE* 42 (2003), 41–68.

————, 'Runo-Gothica: The runes and the origin of Wulfila's script', *Die Sprache* 43 (2002/3), 55–79.

Megenberg, Konrad von, *Das Buch der Natur*, ed. Franz Pfeiffer (Stuttgart 1861).

Meid, Wolfgang, *Heilpflanzen und Heilsprüche: Zeugnisse gallischer Sprache bei Marcellus von Bordeaux*, Innsbrucker Beiträge zur Sprachwissenschaft, Vorträge und kleinere Schriften 63 (Innsbruck 1996).

Mercier, Claude, and Monique Mercier-Rolland, *Le cimetière burgonde de Monnet-la-Ville* (Paris 1974).

Meroney, Howard, 'Irish in the Old English charms', *Speculum* 20 (1945), 172–82.

Mitchell, Stephen A., 'Anaphrodisiac charms', *Norveg* 38 (1998), 19–42.

Moltke, Erik, 'Greenland runic inscriptions IV', *Meddelelser om Grønland* 88 (1936), 223–32.

————, 'En grønlandsk runeindskrift fra Eirik den rødes tid. Narssaq-pinden', *Tidsskriftet Grønland* (1961), 401–10.

————, 'Mediaeval rune-amulets in Denmark', *Acta Ethnologica* (1938), 116–47.

————, 'Runepindene fra Ribe', *Fra Nationalmuseets Arbejdsmark* 1960, pp. 122–36.

————, *Runes and their Origin, Denmark and Elsewhere*, trans. Peter G. Foote (Copenhagen 1985).

Morandi, Alessandro, *Il cippo di Castelciès nell'epigrafia retica*, Studia archaeologica 103 (Rome 1999).

————, *Nuovi lineamenti di lingua etrusca,* Scoperta e avventura 5 (Rome 1991).

Morris, Richard L., 'Northwest-Germanic *rūn-* ›rune‹. A case of homonymy with Go. *rūna* ›mystery‹', *Beiträge zur Geschichte der deutschen Sprache und Literatur* 107 (1985), 344–58.

————, *Runic and Mediterranean Epigraphy*, NOWELE supplement 4 (Odense 1988).

Mørup, Poul Erik, 'Lægelig runemagi i 700-tallets Ribe', *Fra Ribe Amt* 24 (1989), 408–14.

Much, Rudolf, 'Germanische Matronennamen', *Zeitschrift für deutsches Altertum und deutsche Litteratur* 35 (1891), 321–23.

Muir, Bernard J. (ed.), *The Exeter Anthology of Old English Poetry*, 2 vols, 2nd ed. (Exeter 2000).

Musset, Lucien, *Introduction à la runologie, en partie d'aprés les notes de Fernand Mossé*, Bibliothèque de philologie germanique 20 (Paris 1965).

Nagy, Gregory, 'Perkúnas and Perenū', in Manfred Mayrhofer et al. (eds), *Antiquitates Indogermanicae: Studien zur indogermanische Altertumskunde und zur Sprach- und Kulturgeschichte der indogermanischen Völker; Gedenkenschrift für Hermann Güntert zur 25. Wiederkehr seines Todes am 23. April 1973*, Innsbrucker Beiträge zur Sprachwissenschaft 12 (Innsbruck 1974), pp. 113–31.

Nedoma, Robert, 'Die Runeninschrift auf dem Stein von Rubring. Mit einem Anhang: Zu den Felsritzungen im Kleinen Schulerloch', in Wilhelm Heizmann and Astrid van Nahl (eds), *Runica, Germanica, Mediaevalia,* Ergänzungsbände zum Reallexikon der germanischen Altertumskunde 37 (Berlin 2003), pp. 489–92.

Nielsen, Hans Frede, *The Early Runic Language of Scandinavia: Studies in Germanic Dialect Geography*, Indogermanische Bibliothek: I. Reihe (Heidelberg 2001).

Nielsen, Michael Lerche, et al., 'Neue Runenfunde aus Schleswig und Starigard/ Oldenburg', in Karl Düwel et al. (eds), *Von Thorsberg nach Schleswig. Sprache und Schriftlichkeit eines Grenzgebietes im Wandel eines Jahrtausends: Internationales Kolloquium im Wikinger Museum Haithabu vom 29. September – 3. Oktober 1994*, Ergänzungsbände zum Realexikon der germanischen Altertumskunde 25 (Berlin 2001), pp. 201–80.

Nielsen, Niels Åge, *Danske runeindskrifter: Et udvalg med kommentarer* (Copenhagen 1983).

Nordby, K. Jonas, 'Arbeidet ved Runearkivet, Oslo', *Nytt om runer* 16 (2001), 13–18.

Nordén, Arthur, 'Bidrag till svensk runforskning', *Antikvariska studier* 1 (1943), 143–231 [= Kungl. Vitterhets Historie och Antikvitets Akademiens handlingar 55].

————, 'Magiska runinskrifter', *Arkiv för nordisk filologi* 53 (1937), 147–87.

Noreen, Adolf, *Altisländische und altnorwegische Grammatik (Laut und Flexionslehre) unter Berücksichtigung des Urnordischen*, Sammlung kurzer Grammatiken germanischer Dialekte 4: Altnordische Grammatik 1, 4th ed. (Halle a.S. 1923).

Nowak, Sean, 'Schrift auf den Goldbrakteaten der Völkerwanderungszeit: Untersuchungen zu den Formen der Schriftzeichen und zu formalen und inhaltlichen Aspekten der Inschriften' (Dissertation, Göttingen 2003), http://webdoc.sub.gwdg.de/ diss/2003/nowak/nowak.pdf

Odenstedt, Bengt, *On the Origin and Early History of the Runic Script: Typology and graphic variation in the older futhark*, Acta Academiae Regiae Gustavi Adolphi 59 (Uppsala 1990).

Ohrt, Ferdinand, *Danmarks Tryllefomler*, 2 vols (Copenhagen 1917–22).

The Old English Herbarium and Medicina de quadrupedibus, ed. Hubert Jan de Vriend, Early English Texts Society old series 286 (London 1984).

Olsen, Magnus, 'Om troldruner', *Edda* 5 (1916), 225–45 [= *Om troldruner*, Fordomtima 2 (Uppsala 1917)].

Olsen, Magnus, and Haakon Schetelig, *Runekammen fra Setre*, Bergens Museums Årbog 1933, no. 2 (Bergen 1933).

Page, Raymond I., 'The Icelandic rune poem', *Nottingham Medieval Studies* 42 (1998), 1–37.

———, *An Introduction to English Runes*, 2nd ed. (Woodbridge 1999).

———, *Runes*, Reading the Past (London 1987).

Parsons, David, *Recasting the Runes: The reform of the Anglo-Saxon futhorc*, Runrön 14 (Uppsala 1999).

Pellegrini, Giovan Battista, and Aldo L. Prosdocimi, *La lingua venetica*, 2 vols (Padua 1967).

Philippson, Ernst Alfred, *Germanisches Heidentum bei den Angelsachsen*, Kölner Anglistische Arbeiten 4 (Leipzig 1929).

Pierce, Marc, 'Zur Etymologie von Germ. *runa*', *Amsterdamer Beiträge zur älteren Germanistik* 58 (2003), 29–37.

Quak, Arend, 'Nachtrag zu Bernsterburen', *Amsterdamer Beiträge zur älteren Germanistik* 36 (1992), 63–64.

Rosenström, Per Henrik, 'Nya medeltidsundersökningar i gamla Lödöse', *Västergötlands fornminnesförenings tidskrift* (1963), 259–85.

Rouse, William Henry Denham, *Greek Votive Offerings: An essay in the history of Greek religion* (Cambridge 1902).

Russell, James C., *The Germanization of Early Medieval Christianity: A sociohistorical approach to religious transformation* (New York 1994).

Samplonius, Kees, 'Zum Runenstein von Malt', *Amsterdamer Beiträge zur älteren Germanistik* 36 (1992), 65–91.

Sanness Johnsen, Ingrid, *Stuttruner i vikingtidens innskrifter* (Oslo 1968).

Santesson, Lillemor, 'En blekingsk blotinskrift. En nytolkning av inledningsraderna på Stentoftenstenen', *Fornvännen* 84 (1989), 221–29 [= *Frühmittelalterliche Studien* 27 (1992), 241–52].

Sawyer, Birgit, *The Viking-Age Rune-Stones: Custom and commemoration in early medieval Scandinavia* (Oxford 2000).

Schulte, Michael, 'Early Nordic language history and modern runology, with particular reference to reduction and prefix loss', in Barry Blake and Kate Burridge (eds), *Historical Linguistics 2001: Selected papers from the 15th International Conference on Historical Linguistics, Melbourne, 13–17 August 2001*, Amsterdam Studies in the Theory and History of Linguistic Science, Series IV: Current Issues in Linguistic Theory 237 (Amsterdam 2003), pp. 391–402.

———, 'Nordischer Sprachkontakt in älterer Zeit: Zu einer Kontaktphonologie', *NOWELE* 38 (2001), 49–64.

Schwab, Ute, 'Runen der Merowingerzeit als Quelle für das Weiterleben der spätantiken christlichen und nichtchristlichen Schriftmagie?', in Klaus Düwel (ed.), *Runische Schriftkultur in kontinental-skandinavischer und -angelsächsischer Wechselbeziehung: Internationales Symposium in der Werner-Reimars-Stiftung vom 24.–27. Juni 1992 in Bad Homburg*, Ergänzungsbände zum Reallexikon der germanischen Altertumskunde 10 (Berlin 1988), pp. 376–433.

See, Klaus von, et al., *Kommentar zu den Liedern der Edda, II: Götterlieder (Skírnismál, Hárbardsliód, Hymiskvida, Lokasenna, Þrymskvida)* (Heidelberg 1997).

Seebold, Elmar, 'Die Inschrift B von Westeremden und die friesischen Runen', *Amsterdamer Beiträge zur älteren Germanistik* 31/32 (1990), 408–27.

―――, 'Die sprachliche Deutung und Einordnung der archaischen Runeninschriften', in Klaus Düwel (ed.), *Runische Schriftkultur in kontinental-skandinavischer und -angelsächsischer Wechselbeziehung: Internationales Symposium in der Werner-Reimars-Stiftung vom 24.–27. Juni 1992 in Bad Homburg*, Ergänzungsbände zum Reallexikon der germanischen Altertumskunde 10 (Berlin 1994), pp. 56–94.

Seim, Karin Fjellhammer, 'Grafematisk analyse av en del runeinnskrifter fra Bryggen i Bergen' (Unpublished thesis, Bergen 1982).

―――, 'Runes and Latin script: Runic syllables', in Klaus Düwel (ed.), *Runeninschriften als Quellen interdisziplinäre Forschungen: Abhandlung des Vierten Internationalen Symposiums über Runen und Runeninschriften in Göttingen vom 4.–9. August 1995*, Ergänzungsbände zum Reallexikon der germanischen Altertumskunde 15 (Berlin 1998), pp. 508–512.

―――, 'Runic inscriptions in Latin. A summary of Aslak Liestøl's fascicle (vol. VI, 1) of *Norges Innskrifter med de yngre Runer*', in Asbjörn Herteig et al. (eds), *The Bryggen Papers, Supplementary Series 2* (Bergen 1988), pp. 24–65.

―――, *De vestnordiske futhark-innskriftene fra vikingtid og middelalder – form og funksjon* (Trondheim 1998).

Snædal Brink, Thorgunn, and Jan Paul Strid, 'Runfynd 1981', *Fornvännen* 77 (1982), 233–51.

Snorri Sturluson, *Heimskringla*, ed. Bjarni Aðalbjarnarson, Íslenzk fornrit 26–28, 3 vols (Reykjavík 1941–1951).

Söderberg, Barbro, 'En runstrof från Bryggen', in *Ingemar Olsson 25 augusti 1988, Meddelandan från Institutionen för nordiska språk vid Stockholms universitet 28* (Stockholm 1988), pp. 361–367.

―――, 'Till tolkningen av några dunkla passager i Lokasenna', *Scripta Islandica* 35 (1984), 43–86.

Sørensen, Preben Meulengracht, *The Unmanly Man: Concepts of sexual defamation in early Northern society*, trans. Joan Turville-Petre (Odense 1983).

Spurkland, Terje, 'En fonografematisk analyse av runematerialet fra Bryggen i Bergen' (Unpublished dissertation, Oslo 1991).

―――, *Norwegian Runes and Runic Inscriptions*, trans. Betsy van der Hoek (Woodbridge 2005).

Stoklund, Marie, 'Arbejdet ved Runologisk Laboratorium, København', *Nytt om runer* 12 (1997), 4–10.

―――, 'Bornholmske Runeamuletter', in Wilhelm Heizmann and Astrid van Nahl (eds), *Runica, Germanica, Mediaevalia*, Ergänzungsbände zum Reallexikon der germanischen Altertumskunde 37 (Berlin 2003), pp. 854–70.

―――, 'Neue Runeninschriften um etwa 200 n. Chr. aus Dänemark: Sprachliche Gliederung und archäologische Provenienz', in Edith Marold and Christiane Zimmermann (eds), *Nordwestgermanisch*, Ergänzungsbände zum Reallexikon der germanischen Altertumskunde 13 (Berlin 1995), pp. 205–222.

―――, 'Objects with runic inscriptions from Ø 17a', *Meddelelser om Grønland* 18 (1993), 47–52.

―――, 'The Ribe cranium inscription and the Scandinavian transition to the younger reduced futhark', *Amsterdamer Beiträge zur älteren Germanistik* 45 (1996), 199–209 [= *Frisian Runes and Neighbouring Traditions. Proceedings of the First International*

Symposium on Frisian Runes at the Fries Museum, Leeuwarden 26–29 January 1994, ed. Tinneke Looijenga and Arendt Quak].

——, 'Runefund', *Aarbøger for nordisk Oldkyndighed og Historie* (1986), 189–211.

——, 'Runer', *Arkæologiske udgravninger i Danmark* (2001), 252–60.

——, 'Runer 1995', *Arkæologiske udgravninger i Danmark* (1995), 275–294.

——, and Klaus Düwel, 'Die Runeninschriften aus Schleswiger Grabungen', in Volker Vogel (ed.), *Ausgrabungen in Schleswig*, Berichte und Studien 15. Das archäologische Fundmaterial II (Neumünster 2001), pp. 141–168.

Storms, Godfrid, *Anglo-Saxon Magic* (The Hague 1948).

Strid, Jan P., and Marit Åhlén, 'Runfynd 1985', *Fornvännen* 81 (1986), 217–23.

Ström, Folke, *Níð, Ergi and Old Norse Moral Attitudes: The Dorothea Coke Memorial Lecture in Northern Studies delivered at University College, London, 10 May 1973* (London 1974).

——, *Nordisk hedendom*, 3rd ed. (Gothenburg 1985).

Strömbäck, Dag, 'Sejd', in Johannes Brønsted et al. (eds), *Kulturhistorisk leksikon for nordisk middelalder*, 22 vols (Copenhagen 1956–78), XV, pp. 76–79.

Svärdström, Elisabeth, *Nyköpingsstaven och de medeltida kalenderrunorna*, Antikvariskt arkiv 29 (Uppsala 1966).

——, *Runfynden i Gamla Lödöse*, Lödöse – västsvensk medeltidsstad IV: 5 (Stockholm 1982).

——, and Helmer Gustavson, 'Runfynd 1972', *Fornvännen* 68 (1973), 185–203.

Tacitus, Cornelius, *De origine et situ Germanorum*, ed. John George Clark Anderson (Oxford 1938).

Thomas, Keith, *Religion and the Decline of Magic: Studies in popular beliefs in sixteenth and seventeenth century England* (London 1971).

Thompson, Claiborne, 'The Runes in Bósa saga ok Herrauðs', *Scandinavian Studies* 50 (1978), 50–56.

Todd, Malcolm, *The Early Germans*, The Peoples of Europe (London 1992).

Tubeuf, Karl von, *Monographie der Mistel* (Munich 1923).

Udolph, Jürgen, *Ostern: Geschichte eines Wortes*, Indogermanische Bibliothek, 3. Reihe: Untersuchungen 20 (Heidelberg 1999).

Versnel, Hendrik S., 'Beyond cursing: The appeal to justice in judicial prayers', in Christopher A. Faraone and Dirk Obbink (eds), *Magika Hiera: Ancient Greek magic and religion* (New York 1991), pp. 60–106.

——, 'Magic', in Simon Hornblower and Anthony Spawforth (eds), *The Oxford Classical Dictionary*, 3rd ed. (Oxford 1999), pp. 908–10.

Watkins, Calvert, *How to Kill a Dragon: Aspects of Indo-European poetics* (New York 1995).

Waurick, Götz, et al. (eds), *Gallien in der Spätantike: Von Kaiser Constantin zu Frankenkönig Childerich* (Mainz 1980).

Wessén, Elias, *Runstenen vid Röks kyrka* (Stockholm 1958).

Westergaard, Kai-Erik, *Skrifttegn og symboler: Noen studier over tegnformer i det eldre runealfabet*, Osloer Beiträge zur Germanistik 6 (Oslo 1981).

Westlund, Börje, 'Kvinneby – en runinskrift med hittills okända gudanamn?', *Studia anthroponymica Scandinavica* 7 (1989), 25–52.

Wilson, David M., 'A group of Anglo-Saxon amulet rings', in Peter Clemoes (ed.), *The Anglo-Saxons: Studies in some aspects of their history and culture presented to Bruce Dickins* (London 1959), pp. 159–170.

Winckler, John J., *The Constraints of Desire: The anthropology of sex and gender in ancient Greece*. The new ancient world (New York 1990).

————, 'The constraints of Eros', in Christopher A. Faraone and Dirk Obbink (eds), *Magika Hiera: Ancient Greek magic and religion* (New York 1991), pp. 214–43.

Wood, Juliette, 'Virgil and Taliesin: The concept of the magician in medieval folklore', *Folklore* 94 (1983), 91–104.

Zeiten, Miriam Koktvedgaard, 'Amulets and amulet use in Viking Age Denmark', *Acta Archaeologica* 68 (1997), 1–74.

Zemmer-Plank, Liselotte (ed.), *Culti nella preistoria delle Alpi: Le offerte – i santuari – i riti* (Bolzano 1999).

Index